Transsexualism and its Discontents

Sheila Mengert

Transsexualism and its Discontents
First Edition, published 2023

By Sheila Mengert

Copyright © 2023, Sheila Mengert

ISBN-13: 978-1-942661-06-1

Published by Finn Hill Publishing

Praise for Transsexualism and its Discontents

"I must first of all quote Sheila in her own description of the book as she states," The journey of gender variance is a perilous one."

When I first met Sheila and engaged in conversation with her, I found myself continually asking her to " Help me understand......."

Out of those queries came her encouragement to read her book.

As I dove deeply into uncharted territory and superbly articulated revelations of transsexual life, I was deeply moved. Sheila's writing style encompasses the extremes of laughter and the dark " Midnights of the Soul" in such a way as to hold your attention. Upon reading the final written words of this book, I awoke to a greater admiration of her life and the continuing expression of herself as she continues to evolve in her understanding of who she is. Yes, I was brought to tears of empathy as well as tears of laughter t her well-described life experiences. My soul, as well as my life has been enriched beyond our first meeting by reading this honest, no-holds-barred writing of her first-hand experiences of being Transsexual from a bold and courageous woman."

—Mike Ferry

Contents

Incantation

Who is Sheila would you know?
Scarlet Trollop? Virgin Snow?
Mighty Diva or much less?
Hear me now as I confess...

I'm a phantom of the night
Ivy, bay, and fairy sprite
By the shadows of the moon
Shades of solstice coming soon

Mistletoe and doleful rue
Cauldron, broom, and witch's brew
These I fashion, dark and fair
Long-nailed hands and waving hair

In the clearing work my charms
Wand and Grimoire: Do no harms!
Cast the runes and keep it low
Make the crops to seed and grow.

Harvest maidens, wan and sere
Leave your homes and meet me here.
Form the circle round the fire
Dance the dreams of heart's desire.

Fear my eye foreswear my touch!
Love me but not overmuch.
Work my magic force my will
Seize the moment hold me still.

Over meadow sage and thorn
From the place where I was born
Mountain spring or barren land
Pause you must and understand

Who I am and where I've been
Dancing in the spiral spin.
Words from siren mouth a kiss
Tells you this and only this:

Guess you must just what will be
Who I am by night's dark sea
Where I vanish or appear
Dwells my spirit far or near.

Weave by moonlight in the glen
Patterns intricate and then
All around me finds its voice
Summons all to make their choice.

Form behind me in a line
(Is your wish the same as mine?)
Share my pain and dry my tears
Through my long sequestered years.

I am Sheila listen all
Velvet midnight lifts her pall
Sing my desolation blues
Read my discontented views.

Diamond, emerald, sapphire light
Ride the winds this winter's night!
Works my magic book and bell
Candle Sisters, Sheila's spell.

Epigraph

Being an Extract upon the Discontents
Attendant on the Human Condition
Drawn from
The Anatomy of Melancholy
Written in the 17th century
by Robert Burton
{Compared to him I am an Optimist}

*A general cause, a continuate cause, an inseparable accident, to all men
[and women], is discontent, care, misery; were there no other particular
affliction (which who is free from?) to molest a man in this life, the very
cogitation of that common misery were enough to macerate, and make
him weary of his life; to think that he can never be secure, but still in
danger, sorrow, grief, and persecution.*

*For to begin at the hour of his birth, as Pliny doth elegantly describe it,
he is born naked, and falls a whining at the very first: he is swaddled,
and bound up like a prisoner, cannot help himself, and so he continues
to his life's end. Cujusque ferae pabulum, saith Seneca, impatient of heat
and cold, impatient of labour, impatient of idleness, exposed to fortune's
contumelies. To a naked mariner Lucretius compares him, cast on shore by
shipwreck, cold and comfortless in an unknown land: no estate, age, sex,
can secure himself from this common misery.*

*A man that is born of a woman is of short continuance, and full of trouble,
Job xiv. 1, 22. And while his flesh is upon him he shall be sorrowful, and
while his soul is in him it shall mourn. All his days are sorrow and his
travels griefs: his heart also taketh not rest in the night. Eccles. ii. 23, and
ii. 11. All that is in it is sorrow and vexation of spirit. Ingress, progress,
regress, egress, much alike: blindness seizeth on us in the beginning, labour
in the middle, grief in the end, error in all.*

*What day ariseth to us without some grief, care, or anguish? Or what so
secure and pleasing a morning have we seen, that hath not been overcast
before the evening? One is miserable, another ridiculous, a third odious.
One complains of this grievance, another of that. He is rich, but base born;*

he is noble, but poor; a third hath means, but he wants health peradventure, or wit to manage his estate; children vex one, wife a second, &c. *Nemo facile cum conditione sua concordat*, no man is pleased with his fortune, a pound of sorrow is familiarly mixed with a dram of content, little or no joy, little comfort, but everywhere danger, contention, anxiety, in all places: go where thou wilt, and thou shalt find discontents, cares, woes, complaints, sickness, diseases, encumbrances, exclamations.

If thou look into the market, there (saith *Chrysostom*) is brawling and contention; if to the court, there knavery and flattery, &c.; if to a private man's house, there's cark and care, heaviness, &c. As he said of old, No creature so miserable as man, so generally molested, in miseries of body, in miseries of mind, miseries of heart, in miseries asleep, in miseries awake, in miseries wheresoever he turns, as *Bernard* found, a mere temptation is our life.

Who can endure the miseries of it? In prosperity we are insolent and intolerable, dejected in adversity, in all fortunes foolish and miserable. In adversity I wish for prosperity, and in prosperity I am afraid of adversity. What mediocrity may be found? Where is no temptation? What condition of life is free? Wisdom hath labour annexed to it, glory, envy; riches and cares, children and encumbrances, pleasure and diseases, rest and beggary, go together: as if a man were therefore born (as the *Platonists* hold) to be punished in this life for some precedent sins. Or that, as *Pliny* complains, Nature may be rather accounted a stepmother, than a mother unto us, all things considered: no creature's life so brittle, so full of fear, so mad, so furious; only man is plagued with envy, discontent, griefs, covetousness, ambition, superstition.

Our whole life is an Irish sea, wherein there is nought to be expected but tempestuous storms and troublesome waves, and those infinite, no halcyonian times, wherein a man can hold himself secure, or agree with his present estate; but as *Boethius* infers, there is something in every one of us which before trial we seek, and having tried abhor: we earnestly wish, and eagerly covet, and are eftsoons weary of it.

Thus between hope and fear, suspicions, angers, betwixt falling in, falling out, &c., we bangle away our best days, befool out our times, we lead a contentious, discontent, tumultuous, melancholy, miserable life; insomuch, that if we could foretell what was to come, and it put to our choice, we should rather refuse than accept of this painful life. In a word, the world itself is a maze, a labyrinth of errors, a desert, a wilderness, a den of thieves, cheaters, &c., full of filthy puddles, horrid rocks, precipitiums, an ocean of adversity, an heavy yoke, wherein infirmities and calamities overtake, and follow one another, as the sea waves; and if we scape Scylla, we fall foul on Charybdis, and so in perpetual fear, labour, anguish, we run from one plague, one mischief, one burden to another, and you may as soon separate weight from lead, heat from fire, moistness from water, brightness from the sun, as misery, discontent, care, calamity, danger, from a man.

Our towns and cities are but so many dwellings of human misery. In which grief and sorrow as he right well observes out of Solon innumerable troubles, labours of mortal men, and all manner of vices, are included, as in so many pens. Our villages are like molehills, and men as so many emmets, busy, busy still, going to and fro, in and out, and crossing one another's projects, as the lines of several sea-cards cut each other in a globe or map. Now light and merry, but as one follows it by-and-by sorrowful and heavy; now hoping, then distrusting; now patient, tomorrow crying out; now pale, then red; running, sitting, sweating, trembling, halting, &c. Some few amongst the rest, or perhaps one of a thousand, may be Pullus Jovis, in the world's esteem, an happy and fortunate man, because rich, fair, well allied, in honour and office; yet peradventure ask himself, and he will say, that of all others he is most miserable and unhappy.

A fair shoe, but thou knowest not where it pincheth. It is not another man's opinion can make me happy: but as Seneca well hath it, He is a miserable wretch that doth not account himself happy, though he be sovereign lord of a world: he is not happy, if he think himself not to be so; for what availeth it what thine estate is, or seem to others, if thou thyself dislike it? A common humour it is of all men to think well of other men's fortunes, and dislike their own: how comes it to pass, what's the cause of it?

Many men are of such a perverse nature, they are well pleased with nothing, saith Theodoret, neither with riches nor poverty, they complain when they are well and when they are sick, grumble at all fortunes, prosperity and adversity; they are troubled in a cheap year, in a barren, plenty or not plenty, nothing pleaseth them, war nor peace, with children, nor without.

This for the most part is the humour of us all, to be discontent, miserable, and most unhappy, as we think at least; and show me him that is not so, *or that ever was otherwise. There is no content in this life, but as he said, All is vanity and vexation of spirit; lame and imperfect.*

Hadst thou Sampson's hair, Milo's strength, Scanderbeg's arm, Solomon's wisdom, Absalom's beauty, Croesus' wealth, Pasetis obulum, Caesar's valour, Alexander's spirit, Tully's or Demosthenes' eloquence, Gyges' ring, Perseus' Pegasus, and Gorgon's head, Nestor's years to come, all this would not make thee absolute; give thee content, and true happiness in this life, or so continue it.

Even in the midst of all our mirth, jollity, and laughter, is sorrow and grief, or if there be true happiness amongst us, 'tis but for a time. A handsome woman with a fish's tail, a fair morning turns to a lowering afternoon. Brutus and Cassius, once renowned, both eminently happy, yet you shall scarce find two whom fortune sooner forsook. Hannibal, a conqueror all his life, met with his match, and was subdued at last, One is brought in triumph, as Caesar into Rome, Alcibiades into Athens, crowned, honoured, admired; by-and-by his statues demolished, he hissed out, massacred, &c. Magnus Gonsalva, that famous Spaniard, was of the prince and people at first honoured, approved; forthwith confined and banished.

Grievous enmities, and bitter calumnies, commonly follow renowned actions. One is born rich, dies a beggar; sound today, sick tomorrow; now in most flourishing estate, fortunate and happy, by-and-by deprived of his goods by foreign enemies, robbed by thieves, spoiled, captivated, impoverished, as they of Rabbah put under iron saws, and under iron harrows, and under axes of iron, and cast into the tile kiln. He that erst marched like Xerxes with innumerable armies, as rich as Croesus, now shifts for himself in a poor cock-boat, is bound in iron chains, with Bajazet the Turk, and a footstool with Aurelian, for a tyrannising conqueror to trample on. So many casualties there are, that as Seneca said of a city consumed with fire, One day betwixt a great city and none: so many grievances from outward accidents, and from ourselves, our own indiscretion, inordinate appetite, one day betwixt a man and no man.

And which is worse, as if discontents and miseries would not come fast enough upon us: we maul, persecute, and study how to sting, gall, and vex one another with mutual hatred, abuses, injuries; preying upon and devouring as so many, ravenous birds; and as jugglers, panders, bawds, cozening one another; or raging as wolves, tigers, and devils, we take a delight to torment one another; men are evil, wicked, malicious, treacherous, and naught, not loving one another, or loving themselves, not hospitable, charitable, nor sociable as they ought to be, but counterfeit, dissemblers, ambidexters, all for their own ends, hard-hearted, merciless, pitiless, and to benefit themselves, they care not what mischief they procure to others.

Praxinoe and Gorgo in the poet, when they had got in to see those costly sights, they then cried bene est, and would thrust out all the rest: when they are rich themselves, in honour, preferred, full, and have even that they would, they debar others of those pleasures which youth requires, and they formerly have enjoyed.

He sits at table in a soft chair at ease, but he doth remember in the mean time that a tired waiter stands behind him, an hungry fellow ministers to him full, he is athirst that gives him drink (saith Epictetus) and is silent whilst he speaks his pleasure: pensive, sad, when he laughs. He feasts, revels, and profusely spends, hath variety of robes, sweet music, ease, and all the pleasure the world can afford, whilst many an hunger-starved poor creature pines in the street, wants clothes to cover him, labours hard all day long, runs, rides for a trifle, fights peradventure from sun to sun, sick and ill, weary, full of pain and grief, is in great distress and sorrow of heart. He loathes and scorns his inferior, hates or emulates his equal, envies his superior, insults over all such as are under him, as if he were of another species, a demigod, not subject to any fall, or human infirmities.

Generally they love not, are not beloved again: they tire out others' bodies with continual labour, they themselves living at ease, caring for none else, and are so far many times from putting to their helping hand, that they seek all means to depress, even most worthy and well deserving, better than themselves, those whom they are by the laws of nature bound to relieve and help, as much as in them lies, they will let them caterwaul, starve, beg, and hang, before they will any ways (though it be in their power) assist or ease: so unnatural are they for the most part, so unre-gardful; so hard-hearted, so churlish, proud, insolent, so dogged, of so bad a disposition.

And being so brutish, so devilishly bent one towards another, how is it possible but that we should be discontent of all sides, full of cares, woes, and miseries? If this be not a sufficient proof of their discontent and mis-ery, examine every condition and calling apart.

Kings, princes, monarchs, and magistrates seem to be most happy, but look into their estate, you shall find them to be most encumbered with cares, in perpetual fear, agony, suspicion, jealousy: that, as he said of a crown, if they knew but the discontents that accompany it, they would not stoop to take it up. What king canst thou show me, not full of cares? Look not on his crown, but consider his afflictions; attend not his number of servants, but multitude of crosses. Sovereignty is a tempest of the soul: Sylla like they have brave titles, but terrible fits: which made Demosthenes vow, if to be a judge, or to be condemned, were put to his choice, he would be condemned.

Rich men are in the same predicament; what their pains are, they feel, fools perceive not, as I shall prove elsewhere, and their wealth is brittle, like children's rattles: they come and go, there is no certainty in them: those whom they elevate, they do as suddenly depress, and leave in a vale of misery. The middle sort of men are as so many asses to bear burdens; or if they be free, and live at ease, they spend themselves, and consume their bodies and fortunes with luxury and riot, contention, emulation, &c. The poor I reserve for another place and their discontents.

For particular professions, I hold as of the rest, there's no content or security in any; on what course will you pitch, how resolve? to be a divine, 'tis contemptible in the world's esteem; to be a lawyer, 'tis to be a wrangler; to be a physician, 'tis loathed; a philosopher, a madman; an alchemist, a beggar; a poet, an hungry jack; a musician, a player; a schoolmaster, a drudge; a merchant, his gains are uncertain; a serving-man, a slave; a soldier, a butcher; a smith, or a metalman, the pot's never from his nose; a courtier a parasite, as he could find no tree in the wood to hang himself.

I can show no state of life to give content.

The like you may say of all ages; children live in a perpetual slavery, still under that tyrannical government of masters; young men, and of riper years, subject to labour, and a thousand cares of the world, to treachery, falsehood, and cozenage, you incautious tread on fires, with faithless ashes overhead.

The old are full of aches in their bones, cramps and convulsions, silicernia, dull of hearing, weak sighted, hoary, wrinkled, harsh, so much altered as that they cannot know their own face in a glass, a burthen to themselves and others, after 70 years, all is sorrow (as David hath it), they do not live but linger.

If they be sound, they fear diseases; if sick, weary of their lives: One complains of want, a second of servitude, another of a secret or incurable disease; of some deformity of body, of some loss, danger, death of friends, shipwreck, persecution, imprisonment, disgrace, repulse, contumely, calumny, abuse, injury, contempt, ingratitude, unkindness, scoffs, flouts, unfortunate marriage, single life, too many children, no children, false servants, unhappy children, barrenness, banishment, oppression, frustrate hopes and ill-success, &c.

Thus much I may say of them:

That generally [these discontents] crucify the soul of man, attenuate our bodies, dry them, wither them, shrivel them up like old apples, make them as so many anatomies they cause tempus foedum et squalidum, cumbersome days, ingrataque tempora, slow, dull, and heavy times: make us howl, roar, and tear our hairs, as sorrow did in Cebes' table, and groan for the very anguish of our souls. Our hearts fail us as David's did, Psal. xl. 12, for innumerable troubles that compassed him; and we are ready to confess with Hezekiah, Isaiah lviii. 17, behold, for felicity I had bitter grief; to weep with Heraclitus, to curse the day of our birth with Jeremy, xx. 14, and our stars with Job: to hold that axiom of Silenus, better never to have been born, and the best next of all, to die quickly. Or if we must live, to abandon the world, as Timon did; creep into caves and holes, as our anchorites; cast all into the sea, as precipitate ourselves to be rid of these miseries.

Introduction

The literature on transsexualism consists primarily of two types, studies by psychologists and first person accounts in the form of autobiographies of transsexuals. The first are clinical and formal and approach the subject as a unique and puzzling mental disorder, the second are informal and personal and generally follow a path from confusion to successful adaptation and happiness achieved in the new gender role. There is also a minority literature that I call the literature of abuse written by various people with a preexisting axe to grind. In the literature of abuse transsexuals are portrayed as strange subversive figures with an alien agenda. That agenda may be to fracture (the already broken) family structure or to reinstate and reinforce patriarchy by infiltrating or worse penetrating "female space" by taking on the female body (even if it is one's own body). The religious diatribes see transsexuals as cultural revenants, symbols that have assumed dreadful form and embodiment, literally constructed examples of the deconstruction of sex, and the enemies of a natural order that in the fashion of Leibniz is directly willed by God as though God was some sort of gatekeeper pointing to either the male or the female side of the human stadium one with a pink door and one with a blue. Even at times in the male gay community transsexuals were disparaged as retrograde sexual essentialists in denial of their homosexuality and seeking to legitimate it by sporting a female anatomy. The one thing common in many of these discourses has been that transsexuals are mistrusted, despised, or seen as a threat to some established group. When transsexuals are not feared they are merely ridiculed. If the transsexual did not pass she was grotesque, a circus freak. If she passed perfectly she was a sex icon to be used at will as in the she-male and trannie-porn industries. What all of these attitudes share is that they take a group of people whose very sense of self has been a source of personal and constant anguish from their earliest memories, who have often been bashed, exiled, and/or isolated in their families, at school, and in their churches and making them a handy target and minimizing their lives through diminished employment prospects and social exclusion. In the worst cases transsexuals are simply killed or commit suicide out of despair.

This book will address the issues raised by the other types of literature dealing with transsexuals or gender confusion or conflict. When I speak of Transsexualism and its discontents I am echoing Sigmund Freud's book, "Civilization and its Discontents." What this book will attempt is to blend informal essays drawn from my own life as a transsexual person with more formal essays designed to create a "unified-field theory" of Transsexualism. I use the word "Transsexualism" rather than "Transsexuality" designedly. Transsexuality appears on its face to mirror homosexuality implying that what is involved is a sexual activity rather than a status and that the activity in question is precisely the act of transition from one sexual and gender status to another. This very idea tends to imply that what is viewed as self-realization and completion by the transsexual is seen from the outside as an abandonment of the old and the establishment of a new gender by an act of will and hormonal and surgical intervention. A corollary of this approach is that without intervention and technology, transsexuals as transsexuals would not exist. Transsexualism on the other hand acknowledges the validity of a complex set of feelings and behaviors that predate and provide the basis for any sort of therapeutic or medical intervention to make the life of the transsexual more balanced, productive, and free from unnecessary pain.

What then are the discontents that will be discussed in this book? Are those discontents co-extensive with the term "Gender Dysphoria" which is often used as the primary symptom or indicator of a transgender identity? My answer is no. By discontents I mean to trace the sources of primary opposition to the validity of being transsexual as well as the pain that is caused for transsexual persons by those assumptions and institutions that call into question the very existence of being transsexual as a validly ontological form of human reality.

I begin with the idea that gender serves a function analogous to a passport. The function of a passport is to allow entry to those who may be identified by the passport if their visa is valid. Together a passport and a visa allow one to pass a defined border. The difference arises in the assumption that a mere possessor of a passport will eventually return to his home country whereas in gender transition it is assumed that one desires to emigrate between the sexes. The turmoil arises because it is assumed by many people and institutions that an impenetrable wall exists between the sexes. That this assertion of mutual exclusivity between the sexes is not true is shown by both the ubiquity and universality of transsexual phenomena in all times and places. When a border is under assault without a valid passport, various modes of violence and oppression are used to shore-up the border and to prevent entry, exit, or free migration. It is this that is the primary external cause of discontent in transsexuals. But there are interior causes for discontent as well. Transsexuals do not exist apart from their cultural and social contexts. Is it any wonder then that many transsexuals both pre and post operatively feel profound inner conflict as they attempt to address the issues presented by their conflicted gender feelings? By exploring these topics in the case of my own reflections and autobiography I hope that I may fill in gaps that currently exist in the literature on Transsexualism.

Whereas in most other areas of life the data of experience are used to resolve questions of nature, in the case of Transsexualism this has not been the case. Instead moralists assume that there is always a personal congruity between body, mind, identity, sexual preference, and presentation. To put this crudely, God gave Eve a lipstick shortly after creating her and Cain and Abel were signed up for little league. It isn't that transsexuals hold nature in contempt so that they choose to violate the natural law by "changing" their sex, it is precisely the other way round, social and current moral norms demand that the transsexual person deny everything that they spontaneously feel to be integral to who they are so that they can be tailored to a role, feelings, and behaviors that violate the transsexual's deepest and most primordial sense of self, of who she is. The "trans" part of transsexual is therefore inaccurate and by the way so is the "sexual" since one could remain virginal for life and still be a transsexual. Maybe we need a new term for ourselves like "integral people resisting indoctrination by hostile opposing viewpoints and ideologies."

One of the most determined of these adversaries at the present time happens to be the Roman Catholic Church which is currently engaged in facing the challenge posed to its historical assumptions about sexuality by shoring up its defenses in a sort of theological Maginot Line. I say assumptions rather than teachings because I believe that the Church has yet to be in the position to make a definitive statement on the nature of human sexuality. It is rather in the position that it once occupied when dealing with the question of the existence of witchcraft or the validity of the celestial mechanics of Copernicus. The Church is not protected from error when its teachings are merely cultural as opposed to dealing with its infallible teaching on faith and morals. Cultural assumptions and historicity affect all human institutions and the Roman Catholic Church is no exception to this. It often takes time to separate what are mere assumptions from what must be definitively and clearly taught as within the deposit of faith.

This is not to dismiss all theological concerns by assuming that the human body is like plastic and therefore can assume any form on demand. It is not easy to accept the interventions and expense of the current treatments meted out to transsexuals. This alone should indicate how much is at stake for transsexual people when they enter upon transition. Religious organizations should learn the borders of their competence before taking embarrassing positions that will be shown by history to have been incorrect and even abusive and thus to violate the mandate of charity. Transsexual identity will never be a mere pragmatic choice; there will always be something within us that demands embodiment of some type of inner essence as regards gender. I am not arguing then for gender relativism or implying that there is no underlying gender reality. Fluidity manifests various degrees of viscosity and to act like an alternating current constantly reversing itself would be alien to the experience of most transsexuals.

I cannot speak for all transsexuals though even when I adopt universal language. What you are reading is my perspective but it has been based upon careful observation and reflection over many years. The reader need not always agree with me or even approve of me in order to receive some profit from reading this book. If the reader is led to reach his or her own synthesis and to realize the many and heavy discontents that often fill the lives of transsexuals by reading this book, it will have served its purpose.

It is strangely difficult for me to talk about my own life even to myself. Perhaps this is because it seems to be assembled out of fragments and to lack that single cohesive narrative sweep that I always intended that my life should have. There is no wife and children or normal career trajectory followed by a mellow retirement and a much lamented death. Instead my story is more like a gypsy life of pursuit and vagabondage, always looking for that magic place, that perfect love, and that elusive sexual identity that matches my inner sense of self. I have desired nothing more than to be "normal" (though all my heroes and heroines were those who held society in contempt and sought that deeper wisdom pursued by the outcasts).

So it is that I have emerged into the swift cataract of age out of the whitewater of a life that seems alternately boring, trivial, and disappointing only hoping that death will keep in abeyance for a time and allow me to construct some semblance of what I feel a life must be in order to be complete. I would hope for reincarnation if it were not for the fact that things might be even worse the second time around and I would hate to have to learn again to diagram sentences and learn to factor quadratic equations. For people such as I am, one incarnation is quite enough even if it was spent for the most part in the wrong sex role. In any case, like all of us, it is the only life that I am ever likely to have and it's not over yet.

Upon re-reading the above essays many of which were written with the long-suppressed anger and resentment that often comes with a Catholic upbringing in the dark days of the 19th century Catholicism that prevailed before Vatican II, I know that I have been unfair here at times. I have not refrained from various cheap-shots. Yet I love the Church. My present parish, a stoutly Roman Catholic one, has found room for transsexual me. Many supposedly liberal friends on the other hand have requested at various times through the years that I appear as a male when they might face exposure that they have a transsexual as a friend. My parish has never asked that of me. May this testimony show how very deep is the charity and kindness of many Catholic priests and parishioners to members of the GLBT community. If I have been hard on the Catholic Bishops in this book, I do not envy them their tasks and mission. Our present Pope Francis gives many people confidence or at least hope that GLBT people will be seen as not persons living in moral eclipse but as persons who have been handed a very difficult task in managing their one life on this earth. I trust that I will not weary my non-Catholic audience if I at times wax theological, but it must be remembered that over a billion persons in this world are Catholic and that as an organization the Catholic Church has manifested a historical record of success and an impact upon civilization greater than any other organization that has ever existed. It is still the base for all ensuing versions of Christianity, Therefore to establish peace with the Catholic Church as a transsexual may be a first step to universal moral understanding and is certainly adequate to endow Catholic transsexuals a with badly needed peace of mind and soul. Understanding may help to do battle upon any residual prejudice that is not within the authentic teaching of the Magisterium of the Church. It is time to purify and correct what may be a residuum of error bred from a too early presumption that all that has been known of human sexuality is complete and adequate for all times. Even having said this however I am personally willing to suspend my own convictions and to question my own experience if need be because it is far more likely that I am in error than that such a balanced and venerable institution as the Catholic Church has failed to choose and to chart the better course for each individual human life even if that course entails suffering.

Transsexual orientation as a human condition is still a mystery and may remain so. As a cautionary note I must say that for those who imagine that gender reassignment will always answer all of their ills and that a degree of "gender euphoria" lies at the end of the technology of gender reassignment I would suggest that each sex experiences unique burdens drawn from the common human condition – to change sexes does not remove one from the universal pain of human loneliness and incompleteness.

It is only when suffering is simply pointless that it should be rejected as such. Modern life it seems to me is so permeated by technology that we are no longer living under a strict regime of natural law. Human ills that would in former ages have led to a swift death are now set aside so that years of useful life are restored when formerly the body would have long since been surrendered to the soil's embrace. Destiny and the givens of nature are frustrated each day by our human ingenuity so that to assume that gender alone is indicative of the unalterable will of God and as such must never be altered or changed so as to give persons who are transsexual some relief from gender pain seems the opposite of charitable. The testimonies of transsexuals report their life-long gender pain as the reason for their conviction or desire that sex-change measures should be devised and facilitated for them. To deny such relief as is now available is to ask that transsexuals alone shall walk while others fly. It seems to me to be an obtuse reverence for biology that adopts mere genes and chromosomes to call into question what is a transsexual's deepest sense her selfhood and thus to condemn her to remain as she is when something may be done to remedy her situation.

But I also question whether the current proposed remedies are adequate to bestow a new history upon the transitioning individual and sufficient to graft the individual into the separate communities of men and women that every culture on earth has kept separate and alien from each other by various strictures and by various means enshrined in custom. I would therefore advise transsexuals against undertaking an Odyssey that only the most enduring may sustain each day in an insensitive and ill-informed world that may call into question what the transsexual person (even post-operatively) says she really is, a woman. A happy ending is by no means guaranteed for all and I for one do not wish to bear any share in the responsibility for another transsexual person's discouragement or despair.

For this reason I have emphasized the discontents of being transsexual in this book. The journey of gender variance is a perilous one and this book bears witness to parts of my own experience on the frontlines of the emergent transgender community. I do not claim that my experience is typical because these unsettled times have favored some and crushed others. The transgender journey is one that can reinforce any initial isolation in one's spirit and for this reason nurturance and support must be sought out rather than merely awaited. The transsexual person must forge her life in the smithy of her own soul to echo the words of James Joyce at the end of his <u>Portrait of the Artist as a Young Man</u>. After a lifetime in one gender it is difficult to edit out the prior training and ideals that were imprinted upon us. Many transsexuals live in a state of perpetual adolescence never finding the safe port of maturity and the support of the general community. To be transsexual is to be part of a tiny minority but one that is much larger than was initially supposed when Christine Jorgensen first returned from Denmark to the gawking notice of a world that was stunned that a man could ever become a woman.

The human parade goes on around me every day and on occasion I feel myself fully a part of it rather than a boulder in midstream with a wave of backwash betraying my presence. At such times I am allowed to forget for a time that I am a transsexual person, one who is and has been gender-conflicted to the point that I have felt myself to be an ultimate outsider for most of my life. The tone of these "occasional essays" varies from the quite serious to the deliberately frivolous just as my own inner dispositions have varied. Persons like me cover a wide sexual and gender canvass within their inner experience and sense of themselves. Many people have urged me through the years to write a book specifically addressing these issues. I am surprised, as many other transgender people as well are, that our cross-gendered experience, one that is so intimate but ordinary to us as transsexuals, is not prosaic to others but a source of wonder and confusion. After all of the talk shows, the celebrity transsexual autobiographies, and the crime dramas or hospital shows with the requisite transsexual character, one would think that there was nothing new to say about being a transsexual. However, I have my own slant on things and I thought it was time that someone with my particular background and unique history explored the full gamut of the transsexual experience from a more jaundiced and disillusioned point of view than is commonly encountered in books by transsexual authors.

For this reason and to sound a cautionary note to the purely clinical or unjustifiably sanguine portrayal of gender transition I have determined to discharge my mind without resolving the questions presented for others as it is neither my role nor within my ability to do. I am responsible for my own decisions and that is quite enough. As a Catholic I know all too well the centrality of the sacraments and it is no small part of the exile of gay, lesbian, and transgender people that many find themselves at least in practice outside of the full sacramental life of the Church. I have never formally left the Church and I never will but I do respect the need and the duty of the teaching office of the Church to regulate the sacraments. I hope that this central concern will be further addressed by competent ecclesial authority considering the sheer numbers of GLBT people who are being lost to the Church and to what it is its business to promote and to foster, the life of God within us through Divine Grace.

It may be a sad truth but lives are broken up and ruined by the pursuit of a transgender identity and by the questing behaviors undertaken by transsexuals in pursuit of their inner gender peace. Marriages and families break up, transsexuals are assaulted and killed, and lives are wasted through misplaced hatred and discrimination in our regard. So it is that I have spoken here of the manifold discontents that go with being transsexual. The entire book is impressionistic and lacking in the cohesive and comfortable summation that real life almost always makes impossible. But if some inner understanding and compassion has been gained and at least a few mysteries made clearer by reading this book, then this book has served its modest purpose.

I would like to believe that my life has been more than just a simple experiment on the fringes of human experience or that I am part of what was only a bizarre exercise in human hubris toying with our sexual nature. I believe that transgender persons represent a small but integral sub-set of humanity and that our pain is not a calling to merely demonstrate endurance but that we may with careful professional guidance and much soul-searching find a path to a happier life in the sex to which we feel that we actually belong. We are moving rapidly into a new era when these issues are being faced early rather than as was the past practice of the times in which I have lived, in middle-age.

I was an early transsexual a pioneer, one who was all too often walking on high-heels over an abyss. I begin this book with a chapter called "Loomings" in imitation of Herman Melville. I will now close this introduction by echoing the end of his great saga of the pursuit of the mysterious and elusive White Whale Moby Dick: I was an early transsexual in the great period of early gender change and I among a few others of that era who have recorded their stories have escaped alone to tell thee.

A Brief Note on Method

A book begins with its cover art. The cover of this book is meant to be somewhat seductive and iconic as its subject is as well. By being edgy and visually inviting I hope to imply that the subject of transsexualism will be treated here as one where dream and disillusion may meet, where promise and betrayal cross each other at an ill-defined border. I believe that the prospect of dread is a part of most invitations and that the degree of promises made often measures the magnitude of disillusion whenever we encounter the dilemmas posed by human life. Comedy in literature often portrays undeserved reprieve more often than the arrival at our just desserts while tragedy records how even our efforts to arrive at nobility may only advance the time and extent of the hero's tragic fall.

We live in an ironic age, one of air-brushing and of deconstructed meanings. Who can say where appearance ends and reality begins? Much is uncertain as our technical power and control exceeds all former expectations for human lives. We are skating on thin ice. The very ground seems to move beneath us. It is one thing to live on borrowed time but we now live on borrowed money as well. This book is being written during the declining days of the American Empire. It is about one of the last groups seeking protection as a class under our fragile constitution in our radically divided nation. It is a time that is reminiscent of the 14th century when war and schism were in the air. It is also a time in my own life when disillusion and discontent have caused me to question many of my past aspirations and conclusions. What you have before you is a self-portrait in oils that are as likely to run together as to afford a final perspective at last.

The sense of the temporary and vacillating nature of promises, the tension between appearance and reality, and the edginess of our search for perfection is not to be found in the cover alone but in the text as well. As regards the body of the text I have sought an impressionistic technique through short essays on diverse topics. I am a fan of single artist soundtracks and I have always marveled at the ability of a single song to encompass both an idea and a mood in a single short interval of performance. I have wondered if the short essay on a single topic might capture some of the intensity of song though lacking the added elements of musical accompaniment and vocal style. I believe that a life can better be captured through a presentation of short integral incidents or limited essays than through a continuous discourse that must of its nature bore the reader with the many parts of life that were boring enough to live through without recapitulating them for innocent readers.

It is also advisable for the reader of this book to recall that it is being written by an attorney and not by a psychologist or by a theologian. It is a profoundly personal book and as such partakes of the habits of mind and biases of the author. In one sense it was written, as all works of art finally are, to please the author and to embody an aesthetic whole. Not all statements, assertions, or expressions are up-to-date or cited for their factual accuracy or for their institutional, linguistic, or political correctness. Think of an impressionistic collage rather than a dissertation and you the reader will be closer to the spirit and the nature of this book.

In our modern society it is often forgotten that texts are not to be univocally interpreted but should rather be seen as partial articulations rather than the last word on any subject. As an attorney it is natural to me to ask whether any authority or citation is on-point and binding or whether it represents only persuasive authority. Even when a case is on "all fours" as we say, there is always a question whether what the judge has said in a case is the holding of the case or merely dictum and as such not essential to resolve the dispute between the parties but a mere hint by the judge of the further manifestations that may flow from the holding or a guide to its future interpretation. It is in this manner that I would have the reader approach what is written here: as partial, preliminary, and subject to refutation by better evidence or more accurate and complete reasoning. I would also ask the reader to recall that attorneys, at least in our common law system, believe in a circuitous and indirect path to truth by way of the adversary process. This process is one of conflict between mutually exclusive positions each of which is allowed to press its advantage by stringent advocacy while always maintaining an ability to see the other side of any question so as to be able to address a contrary opinion in an effective manner. This way of looking at things is not the same as that of a philosopher, a mathematician, or a scientist. Above all else it differs from the approach asked of the believer under the discipline of faith. As it was written so it should be read. All too often disclaimers like this one are not issued and the result is that all data is received and arguments accepted as though no bias or error can be ascribed to one who has managed to get his words within the cover of a book. I welcome the critical spirit but still deplore the mind that closes all too swiftly about its own contrary convictions. To enlighten need not be to persuade, least of all when many uncertainties remain in the author herself.

I would also like to add a further note regarding sensitivities as to the terminology used in this book. I have lived most of my TS life in the generation that inherited the camp tradition of gay-male culture. Camp sensibility includes the ability to laugh at ourselves and to do what is called "throwing shade." None of this is meant to disparage or diminish the pain of being transgender or a member of any racial or other minority. Rather, it is meant to diffuse tension with humor and willful exaggeration. If I sound flippant at times I ask the reader to recall that I am writing out of a historical nexus in which to be transsexual meant simultaneously to exist on the margins of the demi monde where ironic humor, biting comments, pseudo-insults, and innuendo provided ways to manage the involuntary stigma that came with living on the edges of straight society and in various urban ghetto cultures that overlapped and provided a rich milieu for the expression of various counter-cultures and minority groups whose only common denominator was being outside of the straight, white, and conservative mainstream experience of most of post-war American suburbia. Finally no person living or dead is meant to be identifiably described in this narrative with the exception of myself.

These disclaimers having been made I think we may venture forth and lift the curtain...

The Transsexual Experience

(Adagio con Appassionato)

Prelude: Loomings

David Copperfield begins his account of his life by saying words such as these: Whether I shall be the hero of my own history or whether that place shall be reserved for another I cannot say. To an extent every transsexual is a hero of his or her own story for the simple reason that the function of the hero in literature is to encounter a set of challenges which lead to either insight and to victory or to downfall and defeat.

To write a book like this one is to emerge out of silence and to let other people enter the private zones of my life. But that is not why I hesitate in letting this book go out into the world. My hesitations are due to my fear that, for all of my diva pretentions, I do not really want to take on the fearful responsibility of shifting the constellation of the opinions of others in what may prove to be the wrong direction. I would much prefer that my mistakes be confined within the shallow perimeters of my own life. It isn't easy to be transsexual. I feel at times like the character of Ali in my favorite movie, "Lawrence of Arabia" pointing out across the great Nefud Desert, which the small band of Arab revolutionaries hope to be able to cross in order to attack the Turkish held port of Aqaba from the landward side. Lawrence asks how much of the desert there is and Ali says that only God knows but that after a certain number of days the camels will start to die and when they do the men will begin to perish as well. It is a stern moment in the film; there is still time to turn back and to devise another plan. But Lawrence answers by saying that if time is so pressing then there is no time to waste and the tiny party sets off into the desert. Lawrence may have been impetuous or foolish but there is always something majestic in displaying so much will on a quixotic quest. Lawrence insists that nothing is written but what is written inside our own heads. Transsexuals think the same way.

The function of any transsexual autobiography is to attempt to answer the question of why people ever encounter the dilemma posed by the transsexual condition. From whence comes this driving urge to adopt, portray, inhabit, or exhibit cross-gender behavior and identification? Because this question poses issues of freedom and of individuality, and because it affects the entire course of an unfolding life, as well as because it may never receive one final and complete answer, these stories fascinate anyone who wishes data from the field of human experience regarding the differences between the sexes and whether they may be bridged in a single human body.

I have often thought that the great unanswered question for transsexuals is how we may hope to traverse so great a distance and whether we do not eliminate in attempting to do so the anguish that leads us to cling to the otherness of the other which is the very strength of the bond between the sexes in marriage. Is not the very word transsexual then problematic? Can one exist always in transit between two poles? Do we ever arrive and in doing so may we not then look back from the standpoint of the other pole of gender only to find it as frosty and forbidding as that pole which we have left behind? I have reviewed many autobiographies of other transsexual people only to find that in spite of common features the central mystery still remains. Why do some people feel so uncomfortable within the confines of the gender roles that usually accompany the genitals and inner anatomy on the basis of which they were assigned a gender at birth that they feel that they must now reclaim the other sex? It is precisely the answer to this question that may serve to communicate to non-gender-conflicted people the uniquely painful life experience of transgender individuals. I will attempt to answer that question within this book.

Perhaps the most puzzling aspect of transgender identification is the extraordinary significance and centrality that all forms of gender symbolism play in the lives and inner experience of the transgendered. It is as though the entire sense of self is sometimes reduced to that single parameter of human experience. This can leave readers of the autobiographies of transsexuals wondering if the people involved are ever freed of their obsession with gender long enough to assemble a life upon some other basis. Or is it true that one's gender identification is so determinative of all else that all human happiness and all aspects of life must first be referred to gender solidarity and social recognition? If so then the entire transsexual life-course is often reduced to attempting to repair and to reconstitute an alternate life course which might have emerged had one been identified as the opposite gender at birth and raised within its social parameters. The transsexual experience then is one of inner pain coupled first by every effort to comply with the social parameters of their assigned gender (some would say their actual sex) and later by an equally strong desire and series of actions designed to resolve the issue by creating various degrees of physical change and behavior alteration so that the transsexual may assume the role expected of the opposite sex with varying degrees of consistency and success.

That this task of adaptation is arduous and often met with misunderstanding is obvious. The fact that transsexuals have been made the butt of jokes and exploitation is also obvious but insufficiently condemned. It is time for empathy and understanding and if I must use the telling of my own life story to achieve some measure of comprehension and justice, then I am resolved to do so. I cannot but regret though that I am of the generation of transsexuals that has met with such a large measure of plain stupidity and lack of awareness and imagination by persons who have had no trouble whatsoever in admitting the reality of other puzzling and life-limiting human conditions. We have left the days of leper colonies behind us. We understand many aspects of schizophrenia. Dyslexic children are now taught to read. AIDS which was once referred to by complacent evangelicals as the "gay plague" is now seen as an unfortunate disease that may afflict anyone. But transsexuals were once line-item excluded from coverage by the Americans with Disabilities Act thanks to the peculiar hatred and scorn that is often shown for their life experience and their courageous and desperate efforts to find a solution.

The phenomenon that religions that mandate compassion and love have been used to veil ignorance and malice is a source of shame. That even families have opted for hostile exile and

3

non-recognition of the very people that they should have loved is a tragedy. If it is true that sexuality and its embodiment is so absolute that a person may be treated as a stranger for under-going sexual-reassignment surgery, then it is equally true that it is this very fact which should show why a truly cross-gender identified person could not hope to exist and find happiness and integration in what is perceived by her as a sex role that is alien at every level of her being. In other words Gender Dysphoria is real. It is not a whim, a lifestyle choice, or a symbolic expression of rebellion or contempt for a spouse or parent. Its cause is only relevant insofar as it might prevent costly medical procedures since some people may find an adaptation point short of final gender reassignment. But if they do so it does not lessen the anguish of their condition or the very real sacrifices that may be entailed in whatever actions they choose to take or refrain from taking for economic or other reasons. My story is only one story among many and perhaps not even the most typical. I would like to think that I found my own way. I am also aware that I belong to the Paleolithic Era of transsexuals and that fact alone will be evident in the story that I have to tell. I do not think that fact to be irrelevant for we are all part of the times in which we have lived and transsexual history has much to tell us about where we are today and where we are headed tomorrow.

I believe that the best way to tell my story is not through the use of strict chronology. To do so might bore even me and my own life is the subject after all. Besides, I do not believe that we live our lives chronologically. The stream of life is a wandering one and often doubles back upon itself. Nor should a life story take the shape of mere narrative for there lies within each life those moments of insight and epiphany which perhaps alone are wor-thy to be recounted. I have always believed that form determines substance. So it is that I shall adopt in these pages a preference for the fragmentary and the suggestive, even the contradictory, as often as I will resort to affirmations. Those who know me and understand me well will recognize how truly this method corre-sponds to a life lived in fragments of an unassembled whole. The truth of our lives is lived not in continuity but in those dramatic moments that we remember out of the welter of our days. There are so many possible versions of our lives that we might write but all involve to an extent a reading from a present disposition and perspective to universalize our experience as always having been true. But only the discreet moment as remembered may preserve life as it was actually lived. The three sections of this book (with the appended tempo designations, meant to be humorous) may be thought of as comprising a sort of verbal concerto for violins and bassoon. This book presents a series of discrete and often discordant reflections on the process of becoming my composite yet unified self. So without further preamble we set out across the desert, one with few guideposts and even most of them contradictory...

A Brief Philosophical Disquisition

We are living today in a philosophical climate where it has become customary to speak of virtually any assertion as amenable to deconstruction into its constituent elements. So common is this mode of thinking that the idea of categorical distinction is seen as an unjustified and arbitrary effort to impose static definitions on a changeable world. It is important to realize at the outset that this particular way of seeing things is historically conditioned by the predominant technological way in which many people approach problems today. There appears to be what might be called a "technological imperative" in operation here that says that if something may be done then the advance of knowledge requires that we should do it. The post-modern mind revolts at any a priori restrictions. So it was perhaps inevitable that the issue of transsexualism would arise even independent of individuals who due to intense Gender Dysphoria request a physical and social change of sex status, the so-called sex change.

In past eras this type of question was less likely to arise because sex was seen as one of nature's great binaries. Male and female were seen as mutually exclusive conditions rather than as points along a continuum. Long before the discovery of the supposedly dispositive agents of sex, the X and Y chromosomes, the ancients believed in the substantial difference in mind and matter between the sexes. In fact the very word "substance" implies an underlying reality or substratum out of which characteristics

5

emerge. To be assigned a sex was then absolutely determinative of one's essence. Each sex was assigned a certain unchanging set of innate characteristics and it was up to the individual to embody, with various degrees of success or failure in his or her own life, those characteristics that were deemed appropriate to the sex to which nature had assigned him. A common human soul differed as it was assigned by God to one or the other type of body. To differ or dissent from this assignment, which by its very nature was seen as fundamental and unchangeable, was then necessarily impious and blasphemous. The very idea of possessing androgynous characteristics was to blur fundamental essences and to do so was monstrous because at variance with nature's assumed perfection as emanating from God. Yet such divergences did exist as manifested in homosexual activities and certain inter-sex physical conditions. These could not be denied but their occurrence was seen as, at the very least, a physical evil and those who manifested them were regarded as something less than fully human so that rather than change the mutual exclusivity of the discrete substantial categories it was elected to allow the individuals so visited by personal divergence to bear the cost in social exclusion or even by putting them to death as monsters and not human beings at all.

It shall be the effort of this book to abjure both philosophical positions – that sex is discrete and mutually exclusive but also the facile deconstructionist ethic that everything is relative and that sex change should occur on demand as though it were as unimportant as one's choice of salad dressing. Instead I will argue that gender is a massively determinative human category in that it affects almost every area of personal and social functioning while at the same time admitting that certain individuals are to various degrees and with varying amounts of prior justification unable to live complete and fulfilling lives in the sex that nature has apparently assigned them. For this group of people what is currently called a sex change is the most prudent and even necessary course to follow if we as a society are not to condemn them to lives of vastly diminished quality.

The essays that follow will explore the implications of this point of view by showing in brief vignettes the life experience that has

6

led me to assert this position, and to make various appeals to the religion that I continue to profess which is still in the process of conceiving a proper Christian response to the questions posed by transsexualism. I would like to think of this book as by its very nature controversial in that there will be elements that may irritate all sides of the debate. I find myself often admiring history's great iconoclasts such as Voltaire and assuming that truth is best served by resisting easy summation or a too ready assent to any position at least on issues of importance.

So Just Why Is It That
You Are So Discontented?

It may seem ungrateful for one who has been allowed to at least taste something of her dreams in this marvelous era of enablement, raised in America during its period of greatest global influence and "affluenza" to complain. Our "Weekly Readers" told us what to expect and it was all marvelous. After all we had just won the war. Our future was atomic.

But perhaps among the number of my discontents are those that primarily stem from myself, or at least reside there. The assignment of blame is usually a futile pursuit though and I will not enter upon that infernal quest at this time. It was customary to tell the boys of my generation and to an extent the girls as well that we could become whatever we wished. Oh, but not a girl ... some things are just impossible ... or at least ill-advised.

Life's discontents of course are all relative. A fender-bender is upsetting until you hear about someone who has died in a head-on collision. Most people who are not transsexual take this tone when dealing with those of us who are. The temptation to just tell us that we should simply let go of our delusional wish or conviction that our identity does not match our bodies can be overwhelming. Transsexuals are made to feel shame because our gender pain just doesn't seem real. "Just be glad that you're a man and don't have to menstruate. You have all the privileges anyway. Be glad that you were dealt a winning hand in the poker game of life."

Of course this comparison game can be played with anything as long as the pain isn't yours. This book will explain some of the discontents that are particular to transsexuals, at least those that stem from my own experience. There is no one life though that can set a paradigm for an entire class of people. Some of us have it worse than others. The question is not how much worse can it be, but whether human pain can be lessened without imposing overwhelming costs elsewhere. The human race is improved when anyone advances and can find a better mode of living. From this perspective it is a human tragedy when:

- ✓ More transsexuals make wages below $15,000 per year than almost any other group that might be chosen;
- ✓ When each year we lose people who are murdered specifically because of their transgender status;
- ✓ When transgender children are forced to act out gender roles that are not in congruence with their inner sense of self;
- ✓ When transsexuals are shamelessly and unapologetically used for cheap laughs in various forms of media exploitation;
- ✓ When transgender people are denied proper health-care because their condition is deemed to be cosmetic and not indicated by medical necessity;
- ✓ When transgender experience is simply denied rather than given credence, consideration, and respect;
- ✓ When transgender people are denied the full and equal use of public facilities;
- ✓ When transsexuals are systemically condemned by the misapplication of various forms of moral opprobrium to their condition per se;
- ✓ When transsexuals are reduced to our commercial function in sex work or to enhance various career building activities for "professional" persons who claim to possess an expertise about us but are not qualified by being transsexual themselves.

These issues and many more as this book will explore and explain are the reasons why transsexuals may work to improve our position in life rather than being content to be marginalized and walled in or walled out by the indifference and contempt that are often shown towards us.

So Why Isn't Just Everyone Transsexual?

If this seems a fatuous and cutesy question then give it a second look because it captures the anguish of the transsexual condition better than any argument that I could initially make. The tendency to universalize our most intimate experiences and sense of self is so natural that we cannot imagine how deeply rooted is the instinctual base of body awareness unless we share it. This explains the division of the sexes and the problems of communicating across that divide. Transsexuals do not simply envy the bodies and experience of the other sex as some sort of dreamy adventure in arcane speculation; no, they feel that they have been robbed and condemned to a gender role and a bodily experience at complete variance from their inner sense of rightness.

This means that transsexuals begin life with the necessity of adopting a constant supervision of their own feelings and behaviors. They are co-opted by some inscrutable cause into a systematic duplicity even with their families in order to be who and what they are expected to be by virtue of their assigned sex. That assignment appears just as arbitrary and at times almost as offensive as for Gregor Samsa, in Kafka's short story "The Metamorphosis," to wake up one morning as a bug. Unless in fact that we assume that transsexuals are lying about their pain and sense of "wrongness" we should imagine ourselves in a mandatory cross-gendered alternative universe and ask how we would feel. What if being transsexual was the norm?

The fact is that most people do not experience gender conflict within themselves let alone life-long gender pain. The very rarity and initially perplexing quality of Gender Dysphoria is the guarantee of its reality and validity as a normal human variation. We should respect transsexuals then precisely because their feelings seem alien and crazy to those people who are not transgendered; they "just like us" know who and what they really are – transsexuals, just as in a similar fashion we non-transsexuals know that we are not.

We should not assume that transsexuals desire to be like a sexual traffic circle by serially assuming the attributes of each sex so that no partner is desired of either sex. Most transsexuals would be quite happy to engage in sexual relations with another person but only on condition of feeling right within themselves first. The often reported hatred for their present genitalia is better understood as reluctance to employ bodily structures that act as a constant reminder of their cross-gendered status prior to surgical reconfiguration of their genitals and breasts or other markers of mature human sexual development. All too often transsexuals have been made victims simply because others do not share the same feelings which if you think of it is like denying that another person has a cold because you don't happen to be sneezing.

That most people will never manifest this particular condition does not deny that others do and when they do they must be accommodated if human ingenuity can devise a solution. Once transsexuals are admitted to their full civil rights and to general visibility their condition becomes simply one other of the countless variations within the human condition. It is the artificiality of our current assumptions about gender that has mandated that transsexuals remain out-of-sight and invisible. When gender variation becomes as open and acknowledged as variations in skin color, age, and other human traits, transsexuals will cease to be treated as aliens and subjects of ridicule and rejection.

Why Would ... A Man
Want to Become ... A Woman

I have heard more than once through the years that being born as a woman is bad enough but for one who was born with the innate immunity to womanhood that goes with possessing a Y-chromosome to not only risk contagion but to court the affliction was little short of madness. Who would envy menstruation, labor pains, the ever proximate danger of sexual assault, carrying about breasts everywhere that interfere with jogging and that are ogled, grabbed at, and must be mammogrammed, squished, compressed, and finally end up by being sagging relics, a daily reminder of what one was in youth? Who would want big hips and a protruding butt subject to more ogling? Who would take on willingly cellulite, corseting, dieting, girdling, and pantyhosing? Who wants eyeliner, lipstick, long nails, and the endless upkeep that all of the above entail? Who wants skirts that ride up and hose that rides down? Who wants to stand in endless lines every time they have to pee and wonder what havoc has been wrought to the toilet seat by the woman just in front of them? Who wants to be in a meeting and speak up knowing that everyone is just waiting for you to finish so that the men can continue the real business of the meeting now that you have been politely heard? Who would want to have to always consider the time of day, the conditions of traffic, and the lighting conditions just in case you have to call for help and what if nobody comes to your aid? After considering the plight of single moms, the risks, the expenses, the constraints, and the treatment of women around the world who would want to become a woman?

But now suppose that in addition, just to get there, you had to be head-shrunk and had to run around getting signatures and approvals from gender professionals and had to go through the famous "full-time-woman-test" with no gender-training course to prepare you, with no insurance aid, and sometimes with no job or spouse to lend moral support? What if years of facing the scalpel lay ahead to carve you up from head to foot with silicone breasts, vagina construction, a plastic vaginal dilator three times a day, electrolysis which feels like a hundred little bee-stings, hair implants, wigs, forehead and eyelid lifts, cheekbone implants, lip-plumper's, estrogen pills, spironolactone, etc.? Who wants to live such a medicalized existence? Look at the people who are already women…are they so happy? What about sex and the debate as to whether a woman has had an orgasm or not? If you aren't sure it may have been a technical orgasm, but who cares. So what if an occasional woman has multiple orgasms when most men get bored just waiting around for the first one so that they can finish and go to sleep?

Who wants to carry a purse that can be snatched, a purse filled with tampons, Kleenex, lipstick, compacts, cuticle scissors, and books on self-esteem? Who wants an apartment with a walk-in closet that is bigger than the bedroom and who cares anyway when only other women seem to notice what you are wearing? The only thing worse than being hooted at is being ignored. Besides you never really know what's in his head…so ask him…and he gets so tired by these questions that never seem to change… of course you look pretty tonight…you're a woman. Who would sign on for all of this? But if you listen to the hysteria of some members of Congress or certain family fascist organizations you would think that in their minds at least this is all so appealing that it will catch on like the hula-hoop. Give transsexuals insurance coverage for sex-change and everyone will be signing up for the big chop, even Republicans.

The real point of course is that transsexuals do not choose to be female as though they occupy some sort of sexless original position where such a choice is possible. It is simply not like this. Transsexuals find their gender identity to be as natural, as innate, as given, and as permanent as other people do. The difference is that transsexuals are put in the horrible and untenable position of being forced to adapt to what they perceive at the deepest level of their being to be wrong and completely against the spontaneous inner current of their desires, images, and sense of themselves. It is this enforced "gender appropriate" indoctrination that leaves them feeling not just stress but depression and a horrible life-long mourning for their lost life before finally embracing transition.

There can be no greater prison than enforced self-betrayal at an age when most children are being aided and helped to navigate the normal maturational gender steps. Transsexual kids are stuck in neutral and cannot move. Instead they learn to adapt to various outer imperatives that violate their own inner sense of being simply to avoid ridicule, misunderstanding, and violence. The success of these efforts is usually less than perfect. Others read through the charade of normality by pretence. The result is a childhood spent in functional exile in which fantasy alone provides some occasional relief.

If their childhoods are maimed, adulthood for transsexuals is often a further disaster of assumed marriages with efforts to mask their true desires by assuming ever more stringent and extreme gender activities within the sex assigned to them at birth. Others seek early gender reassignment and may pay for their surgical procedures by entering the sex-industry as "she-males." Even those who succeed in adapting their bodies to their inner selves have so much to do in order to catch up with the maturational level of their peers that many remain trapped in various states of emotional dysfunction. These dysfunctions are then used by anti-transsexual theorists to bolster the case that transsexual identities do not really exist but that cross-gender feelings are merely indicative of some other mental illness such as schizophrenia or borderline personality disorder. These confuse the effect for the cause. It is my personal opinion that transsexuals who have been forced by their life circumstances to live out their lives in an enforced cross-sexed role suffer from a form of post-traumatic stress disorder.

Until transsexuals are diagnosed and treated at an earlier stage of life with the appropriate sex hormones and/or surgery, these unnecessary and tragic life-outcomes will continue. I hope that this book may be of some use to clarify for transsexuals and others the issues involved in producing the profound discontents that come with being a transsexual person at least in the era that coincided with my one and only life. I am constantly amazed that supposedly educated persons refer to some completely extraneous need to preserve a univocal image of human life as though it is only in this one area that the physical norm breaks down and then holds its victims morally accountable for one of nature's less usual but still very real manifestations. Transsexualism is real. It is not an ideology or a subversive program. It is high time for study, general recognition, and treatment for individuals who experience this intense gender discomfort and for a mature and compassionate response at all levels to this all-too-human condition.

A Basic Taxonomy of the Genus Woman from a Transsexual Perspective

Women as a rule, far from being inscrutable, unfathomable, and illogical are the expressive sex. Nature appears to have decided that the species is best preserved by clear signals from its nurturers and caregivers. A woman's face can convey a larger range of emotions than that of a male by virtue of her eyes alone. Human males in contrast to women look out at the world from under the beetling frontal brow bone, lowered eyebrows, and thinner lips. The general aspect of the male face conveys a certain degree of truculence simply by being male. Compare this to the way that a woman's countenance seems to be specially prepared to smile or to look interested or surprised by whatever should come before her. There is a sense of primacy in the female sex as though nature had her in mind when fundamental design options were being considered. She is contoured whereas the male is angular; she is built upwards from a solid base whereas males seem somewhat top-heavy and unbalanced. The male seems designed to face the physical demands of acute necessity while the female is designed for endurance and for the needs of daily life. Males appear to be in a perennial and silent dialogue with an unpleasant fate whereas women carry about within their very selves a center of gravity around which their primary relationships turn. The face to face dialogue of women is something to behold. Humor, sympathy, and understanding radiate from the energy exchanged.

To become aware of women is to notice their omnipresence. Much of modern American life caters exclusively to a woman's needs and desires. The average department store is filled with foundations, shoes, and various types of women's wear from formal to casual to contemporary chic whereas the men may choose from a few lines of dun-colored sweaters, t-shirts, and jeans or appear in the even more uniform fashion of the all-purpose business suit. So it is that for an M to F transsexual to adopt the dress of the preferred gender is to find herself not simply delivered from gender pain but to discover, often for the first time in her life, a basic human identity that is not strained through a filter of absurd male pretense and a dull pragmatism. It has often been remarked that women tend to notice and to relate to each other whereas men are suspected of being gay if they should even approach another male and instigate a conversation except when business or some exterior task provides a context for meeting and for cooperation between them. This lack of what the British call "mates" may explain much American male isolation. A man is expected to maintain a certain oblique angle to the world so as not to threaten other males or to suggest sexual aggression to a strange woman. The attitude he assumes seems always to say, "Well, what do you want?" whereas from a woman the same overture would be perceived as a request for aid or for a simple friendly connection to another woman.

There is a price to be paid for the instant authority and credibility that males are given, particularly men of wealth and power, that price is loneliness and a constant fear that one's basic status as a male may be lost through inadvertently behaving like a woman. She is allowed a degree of latitude in emotional expression and intimacy that males simply are not. At the same time she is not expected to threaten males by a too unyielding insistence upon a point and she is expected to yield ground if need be to maintain the peace of all parties. What the more accomplished woman may need to bear may be made less burdensome to her by the generally easier social realm that she inhabits as a female which at least does not demand that she be more than human and as such without excuse if she fails in any way. If she is at times reduced to a mere function of her body, she is at least allowed to have one. She is not expected to conform first to a stringent exterior code and only secondarily to the changing feelings of the moment. She is allowed a basic authenticity in direct proportion to her supposed denigration as a member of "the second sex." For this reason to come out as transsexual is often a double gift: to find oneself, and to find the true core humanity that we entrust to women while saving men for other uses, uses that are often tangential to simply being a human being: alive, sexed, and occasionally fearful in the face of what often appears to be a cold and non-sentient universe.

Having said this though, I must admit the difficulty of embracing an identity as female when one has been raised to be a male, a sex that finds little to borrow in the supposedly innate traits of the female sex. Which young males are commended for their emotional response or nurturing qualities? Are these traits, even when they arise spontaneously not instead punished and shamed? How much more then will social ostracism necessarily follow one who desires the very bodily structures and form of the female body so as to be indistinguishable as far as possible from genetic females. Thus transsexuals are, in a very real sense, victims of a culture that is left over from more primitive eras. Just as modern humans must learn to reject war and to curb the wholesale waste of natural resources they must approach a less confrontation-structured existence and listen to all people. When they do so it will be easier to be a male-to-female transsexual because the gender divide will be less absolute and the female standard will be less disparaged.

So what do you do if you're
a Jewish American Princess?
(Locked in the body of a Catholic Boy)

One of the silly phrases once used to describe the transsexual experience and its sense of alienation was to describe us as prisoners in our own bodies. The problem of course is that most people cannot imagine that degree of inner alienation. This meant that our experience was often perceived as delusional or as a hysterical exaggeration and a plea for sympathy. Transsexuals were desperate though; make no mistake about that. The only relief in the early days often entailed a visit to Tijuana or to Morocco for a sex-change. Results were variable. So it was that many of us learned early on to adapt ourselves to the psychological jargon or categories that would make us acceptable candidates for surgery or at least for hormones. We learned also that certain magic words or phrases would confirm mental health and other professionals in their own self-images and appeal to their curiosity about our anomalous feelings.

Part of living when survival skills become a necessity is learning to adapt, often on a moment's notice, to environmental cues. Transsexuals learn when to diffuse immanent attacks with humor or self-deprecation. Most people leave "street culture" behind early on and are protected by their education or professional status from the practices of overt name-calling and physical violence. I learned while transitioning during law school while living in what most people would have thought was a "nice part of town" that when you are transgender anything can happen from rock throwing to, on one memorable occasion, a bullet through the window of a restaurant where I was eating and reading my law books. I concentrate better surrounded by white noise and the smell of pizza (go figure). I can still recall the speed of the bullet which ricocheted three times. Can I ever be absolutely certain that I was the intended target of what may have been a random act? I only know that I and other transsexuals are often selected as the target of a rage that is somewhat akin to that unreasoning fear displayed by horses who taking fright from some obscure cause engage in a headlong flight.

Is gender so essential a category that to violate expectations is to set in motion a cascade of associations in others? What is the nature of an indoctrination that implants such gender absolutes within us and why is it that these rules are so mandatory and universally enforced? If they are natural, then why are they enforced so stringently? Or is it rather that they are unnatural, that so called normative gender expression and roles are in varying degrees constraints that are really arbitrary and designed to sustain unequal power relations between the sexes so that gender differentiation is perceived to be a rebellion in the ranks that must be swiftly and decisively opposed by verbal and physical abuse, by shame, and by disassociating oneself from these contaminated ones, these aliens in our midst, these transsexuals.

Far from being spoiled princesses I am astonished, when I review my own life's experiences and compare them with the immunity that returns with a strategic retreat back into the closet of denial, that I have managed to survive. The result of sustained abuse is that many transsexuals get caught in a revolving door between authenticity to their feelings and the demands imposed at all levels of their relations to the world. Progress is always defined by denial and repression imposed by the dominant culture. Transsexuals live in an inverted world where duplicity is rewarded and all attempts to seek alliances and affirmation are punished, often severely, from early childhood and often until late in adulthood. The result of this pressure and the relentless threats of often very real consequences for open avocation of one's feelings and the need to live as a member of the other gender is the phenomenon of the late-in-life transition, one made in the twilight of successful professional careers. Only then do many transsexuals ask themselves questions that have been expressed like shadow slides by various symptoms of stress that they have experienced throughout their lives. What they have been spared in the early struggles for GLBT rights and acceptance has been paid for in other ways, denial, depression, and self-loathing.

I tended to identify more with the street queens of Stonewall and their sisters, but I have compromised when necessary in order to survive. If even law students and attorneys can be treated as I have been treated during the course of my rather extended transition then it has come as no surprise to me when trans-sexuals end up filling the victim files of police rosters. I believe that when confronted by overt violence that the gentle paradigm of counseling breaks down and all too often we can only look to ourselves for aid. Rebellion may seem to invite reprisals, but without overt protest the GLBT movement would not have arrived at the more discreet and comfortable stage for all parties that is now going on. The desire for a belated welcome is natural, but for our more visible representatives it may still be necessary to overcompensate by what some might see as provocative acts. These may be more of an expression of a cultural private language that creates affinity groups when other human support systems and alliances are out of reach. What is usually called, "flaunting it" may simply mean daring to be visible. It is not always easy to separate and define what a just accommodation is between competing interests. My own preference is for unapologetic assertion. I have a bias towards those who have been called "flame queens" even if their function as torch-bearers may someday be as antiquated as revolutions always are after they have succeeded. It is not that I scorn those who have escaped some of what I have seen but I tend to see no movement as complete until it takes care of its trailing sector. Solidarity means taking care of those least able to bear up under battle. It means not dismantling our defenses too early through imagining that what has been so long opposed has not left smoldering piles of resentment in those who for whatever reason fear and despise what they seem either unable or unwilling to ever understand.

Is Changing Sex a Luxury

Is changing your sex like a taking a shopping spree, just another example of "bling?" Do transsexuals say, "I was watching an episode of Real Beverly Hills Housewives one night and I suddenly thought: 'Why don't I just be one? I'll just trot down to the local sex-change doctor and by next month I'll be buying thousand dollar handbags.'" Well darlings it just doesn't happen that way. Transsexuals report a history of life-long gender pain from their earliest memories. Things just don't line up from day one. The costs of transsexual surgeries and the pain involved tends to weed-out anyone who might like to just take a short little walk on the wild side or someone who would like to bargain away his gender just to win a rich and well-endowed man. Even entertainers who make flawless women in appearance are usually men when they are off-stage. Transsexual surgery may be expensive, but it is certainly not a luxury to try and reclaim a life from constant pain and alienation. Simply because a medically remediable condition entails high costs does not mean that the ailment to be treated is imaginary or frivolous or that those procedures are unjustified.

The real problem is that absent a handy, "Are you a transsexual test?" with a little pink tab showing, "Your test was positive. Congratulations, you're a girl," the diagnosis of transsexualism is to a large extent subjective. People are diagnosed as transsexuals because they keep coming back for more. There is just no getting rid of real transsexuals. We are a demanding crowd. We keep on keeping on. We want hormones, electrolysis, various implants in various places, and many of us can't really rest until snip, snip, snip… If that's a luxury baby don't expect most males to trade in their cars and break open their cash accounts just to see how the other half lives.

But what if this is merely a crazy obsession based on a misinformed over-estimation of the joys of being a woman? I have often asked myself this question since I never wanted to join the ladies at K-Mart buying ugly cotton tops, wearing no make-up, and whirling around a shopping cart filled with one or maybe three crying children. Maybe the aversion therapists should set would-be transsexual candidates down while a parade of embittered and disappointed 50-somethings tells them about what being a woman is really like. Summon up images of waiting for a bus in the rain while carrying wet shopping bags and with your panty-hose slipping down to your knees and your foundation running…

Or maybe just have them read "Transsexualism and its Discontents" by Sheila Mengert, a transsexual who always insists on asking all the hard questions of everybody. This is all just part of my generalized cross-examination of the world while trying to get at the truth. Perhaps the truth of any phenomenon, particularly one as complex and deep-rooted as cross-gender identification can only be approached by using a variety of metaphors and points of view, some of which it is the intention of this book to provide.

Experience over time is the best indicator of what human beings are when we speak of identity issues; everything else is mere theory imposed after the fact by others who are seeking to understand and as such it is one step removed from the thing itself. Of course in asserting this I am speaking strictly from the point of view of social science which leaves unanswered the deeper question of whether human behavior should be the source of our moral imperatives. What if human nature itself is viewed as incomplete and fallen from its original destiny? These questions are addressed in Part Two of this book. Social science can never be normative because its province is to study what is not what should be, for this we need philosophy or religion.

Generations

I am a dinosaur as a transsexual, but not one of the earliest of these. There were others before me. My generation is the one that got to see our dreams fulfilled and even to see the beginnings of transsexual acceptance in the law and in other critical areas. We are the ones who remember the first ones, those primeval gender-amphibians who first crawled up onto the land out of the sea. We are the ones who sought out the few books that told of our condition when so few cared about what we felt inside. We remember names like Finnocchios and the Jewel Box Review, although we were too young to go to these places where "people-like-us" so often ended up. They remained for us though a witness that there were men who liked to dress up as women. Some of us had even heard of hormones and we asked our parents if it was true that a man could become a woman and we were told, "Of course not," and that it was just impossible. It made us very sad to hear that. We had hoped for just a moment that there were other means than make-up and secret dresses stashed away in the backs of closets ahead for us to make our heart's desire come true.

We were the television kids who watched matinee science fiction and monster movies with our baby-sitters and wished that we would grow up like them with black skirts and saddle-shoes and could wear red lipstick. We wanted to be rescued from the Creature from the Black Lagoon and have our breasts pointing up at the sky and our long legs dripping water. Some of us (like Candy Darling) got to live their dreams in that unsavory period when transsexuals first dared to hit the streets and claim an actual life. But Candy died early and most of us didn't hear about her again for a long time if we ever knew of her at all.

We were the ones who called up plastic surgeons asking for help only to be told that "the doctor doesn't see those people." We would move down the list until we had called every plastic surgeon in town with the same results. We would give up then and drink or whatever else we had to do to forget. We were dead inside. Some of us found our way to gender clinics which were very big for a time at college medical centers. You could hardly be a big university medical research center if you didn't have a small gender clinic for the really desperate cases. The early surgeries weren't much to speak of. Nobody was worrying much about your feelings. You didn't get a clitoris but you ended up with a canal of sorts and at least "that thing" was gone. The early gender clinic craze didn't last long and after Johns Hopkins closed its doors so did many others. After all there had been a study of post-ops and many said they were still unhappy after the surgery. No one could understand why unless transsexualism wasn't real or we were just impossible to please. (Like poverty and rejection were so mysterious?) Nobody thought to ask if it was because we couldn't find jobs in the new sex role and when we told our spouses about our pasts they divorced us and people threatened to kill us. Some of us couldn't pass as women and we disappeared into strange gothic hovels or retreats where we lived lives of structured anonymity. As time went on the surgery got better and people went to Trinidad, Colorado or to Montreal or to Belgium instead of to Morocco or Tijuana. There were fewer deaths from people in strange off-shore locations who claimed that they could make you a woman although many of us were still injecting industrial silicone and dying as a result. The rest of us who didn't die or make it to Trinidad just got older. Some of us married and had children and tried to be straight. Later when the kids were raised our wives divorced us when we finally told them the truth about ourselves.

I for one never married. I just watched and waited for surgery; along the way though I did manage to live as a woman. I was able to join what I call "the ice-breaking transsexuals" the one's heading bow first into the great ice-field of America's hatred for gender ambivalent people. I was one of those who were spit on by teenagers in parking lots while trying to get to my car, one of those that people threw rocks at while yelling "faggot." I was one of those listed by the KKK in my hometown for trying to get an early civil rights ordinance passed. I was pictured in the newspaper in my hometown. I was looking into a mirror with one hand pulling a strand of hair away from my forehead and a long-nailed index finger on my hand was pointing upwards at the sky, prophetic or provocative...

The ordinance was voted down of course because the people felt that giving "special rights" to people like us meant acceptance of our deviant and "freely-chosen life-style." But I was fresh out of law school then and I thought that I was like Evita and I would liberate my people. At that same time another transsexual sent my writings to each member of Congress when they were voting on the Americans with Disabilities Act which in an appendix said that transsexuals are not to be covered by this otherwise forward legislation. "Why?" Because we choose to be transsexuals and even if we would seem to qualify and were listed as having a mental illness at the time, ours could be cured by simply using will-power. Besides, unlike most mentally ill people our mental illness made us evil and worthy of social scorn.

The law cases didn't bring us much relief either. One judge put it this way, "Whatever is produced by these surgeries, I cannot say, but it is certainly not a woman." When you are a judge your private judgments equal the law. So there wasn't much help for dinosaurs like me. When the vegetation got sparse we just died out. Some of us made it past the days when the only way we could qualify for surgery was to sound just desperate enough

23

to kill ourselves if we didn't get the operation but not desperate enough to sound overtly psychotic. If we could walk that bridge some of us became women, but just in time to find genetic women questioning what it was to be a woman after all.

Some of us tried to be feminists then only to be told that we were really gender spies trying to invade and colonize space reserved for "womyn-born-womyn." Others of us found a guy who didn't care what we had been and found love but no children. Others, like me, always kept a foothold in the old male camp because we had learned to be gender guerillas. We had learned to be what the circumstances demanded of us at various times. We could not locate whatever it was to have an inner self because we had played too many roles over our lives to commit to anything. It was enough for us that we were still alive and not statistics, as so many of us were. We had seen much of human hatred but also of kindness. But people that were Christians were still walking up to us and telling us that we would burn in "the lake of fire" for our wicked ways. We would turn to them and say, "Well Honey, St. Paul also says that revilers will not enter the kingdom of heaven. Now maybe he meant those who make fun of religion but maybe he meant anyone who holds another person in hatred and contempt. So maybe you and I will be in the same changing room putting on our bikinis for our first dip in that lake of fire." Being a dinosaur can make you a real bitch.

Anyway, I am a transsexual dinosaur who came before the internet tranny-porn, the thrifty sex-change craze in Thailand, and before facial-feminization surgery. We played the cards as they were dealt to us and left the great gender casino with whatever we could scrape together at the end of an evening. Some of us did better than others. Maybe I am happier than my own introspective nature would lead you to believe. At least I am here to write about how it was. In any case I am still becoming me, whatever that means....

Invidious Comparisons

The presence of competition within each of the genders is one of the most characteristic elements of human sexuality. It has often been remarked that women dress for other women. The male of the species is only marginally impressed by subtle variances in color or pattern in a dress and may miss the fine gradations of meaning in various shoe styles. Beyond a rough but instantaneous assessment of the general pulchritude of a passing female, which considers and calculates certain breast and hip measurements and angles and compares them with an inner template that determines the decision to pursue or not to pursue, the average male is immune to the fine points of fashion and accessories. In fact the single most persuasive point from the purely procreative perspective is the prospective female's relative youth and child-bearing capacity. It takes a gay male to note the difference between off-the-rack and couture. Why then do women spend such ungodly amounts of money on staging an extravaganza when a more modest spectacle of jeans and a t-shirt could get the job done? Why pay weekly for the delicate half-moons of a French Manicure instead of a quick application of a bargain nail polish at a lunch break? Why do women carry about with them expensive handbags that may be noticed by potential thieves?

The answer of course is that they do so for other women; the whole thing is a variation on the territorial displays of other species. "Look out honey Miss Rodeo Drive is coming through!" Well transsexuals are not immune to these same pressures to engage in invidious comparisons though they may take other forms. Whereas a drag queen goes for color, big hair, and red-carpet bling, many transsexuals go in for just how many surgical procedures they have had and how much they have spent in the ever elusive pursuit of "realness." The transsexual professionals may have taken an unconscious advantage of this drive by keeping surgical costs high. Nobody wants to brag about their sex-change in a Bosnian clinic anymore than they want to admit to once having owned a Yugo. For the really sophisticated gender-enhancement consumer the vaginal lips may be tightened post-surgically for a more "realistic appearance" (as though the average male evaluates more than the mere presence and availability of a wet tunnel-like opening that is not fenced in by some prohibition or reluctance to engage in intercourse before forging manfully ahead with intromission). It takes another transsexual to understand and be impressed by the numbers of spironolactone pills ingested on a daily basis, the cubic centimeters of silicone jogging along with every bounce in their Lane Bryant bras, and the many steps towards genital perfection that she has undergone.

Some transsexuals who are now clearly female (because everything indicating male has been systemically removed) will embark upon further cranial-facial procedures in order to fine-tune a female visage and if she is older will seek to re-attain the open-eyed innocence of female youth by various eyelid lifts, cheek fillers, and lip enhancers so that they can look surprised enough and pouty enough and plump enough in the right places. The standard of perfection (or even adequacy) is always rising so that she can finally say with all confidence, "I am woman," without fear of being contradicted.

My question here is a simple one: What is the reason that more than half of the human race must be forever in pursuit of femininity, while the other half wants to possess it by proxy through sexual-intercourse? Is mere sex worth an industrial empire of fashion magazines, hair stylists, nail technicians, and all manner of other appearance professionals and advocates? And if luck has bestowed a partial immunity to this tyranny of fashion by endowing a person with that critical Y-chromosome, then why jump into the piranha tank and spend a lifetime pursuing sex-change? If women were as rare as the Sumatra Rhinoceros it might make some sense, but there seem to be quite a few women around so why join the stampede to the lingerie sale?

But perhaps it is that being a man is really so terrible that no one would really want to be one of these either. The one thing that can be generally said about penises is that from about the age of fourteen until about the age of fifty they tend to behave in an out of control manner. Carrying one about in adolescence is like using Big Ben as a wristwatch and various camouflage techniques often need to be employed to hide the almost barometric readings that are registered with every passing female. It doesn't get much easier with time until one reaches the age of the dreaded "male erectile dysfunction." To some this return of genital sanity may prove to be a relief. Whenever I hear one of those ED commercials I picture some poor wizened individual walking about his lonely apartment frantically calling numbers from his superannuated little black book hoping that someone will be able to commute over before his allotted four hours is up. After that he will have to go to the emergency room and explain to a startled nurse at the reception desk what his problem is and wonder whether his insurance will cover the required deflation.

All in all sex and sexual identity are problematic to all of us no matter how one looks at it. Whether one is beset by vaginal itch, irregular periods, or a drying up of the perennial spring of the satyrs is irrelevant. What is always present from youth to old age is one long series of potential problems and discontents and of no group is this truer than for those of us who are currently called transsexuals. But let us continue and consider some of the likely common experiences that go along with Gender Dysphoria as examined in this book.

The transsexual solution is a rare one, but it does follow its own inherent logic. If this is the only book that you ever read on the transsexual experience, I hope that it will help you to find common ground with people whose life-experience has forced them to confront at the most basic level who they in fact are.

Silent Movies

Transsexuals spend their lives watching other people but particularly women. In that act of watching there is often a silent monologue going on, "Am I one of these people or am I one of those people?" Notice that the question, though tinged by doubt, also manifests a conviction that the question is a reasonable one. A principle of verifiability is defined as a means or action that can definitively resolve doubts. But for Transsexualism there is no single definitive test beyond the mere fact of questioning itself. It is irrelevant what one's chromosomes say or what set of genitalia one may already possess. The question is one of a most absolute subjectivity, one that exists at that critical point where self-definition and identity reside, which is to say that a conviction that one is transsexual is both deeply rooted and pervasive. The questioning is both lasting and impervious to change with maturation, changes of circumstances, intimate relationships, career changes, and other temporal events. All of this is merely another way of saying that the condition or disposition to question one's apparent sex seems to be as permanent and fundamental as any character-trait or self-image may ever be. Transsexuals are said though by some to be mere caricatures of women and are scorned precisely to the degree that they manifest what are called extreme traits or mannerisms, the use of elaborate make-up, or that we display exaggerated role behaviors. But should transsexuals seek to occupy a more middle ground we are scorned as well, but this time for failing to "pass as women." This failure is caused by the body changes wrought by testosterone at male puberty and is not our fault.

Even when transsexuals are extremely lovely (some have even have been beauty pageant contestants) they are still viewed as curious objects of inappropriate desires rather than as authentic women. It is then that the subject of vaginas and uteruses come up as dispositive evidence of authenticity as female. Transsexuals are sterile, at least after genital reassignment, so the argument goes they cannot be "real women." Fertility suddenly becomes of great and indeed decisive importance to a culture that takes pride in frustrating fertility at every juncture among its genetic females. Is it any wonder then that some transsexuals, finally weary of the process of denial and denigration by others that meets their every effort at transition, finally decide to question the categories of gender in a more radical way by calling gender itself into question as a valid category of human experience? If anything needs to be deconstructed it would appear to be gender because it breeds so much human unhappiness by its supposed naturalness and appropriateness as one's life-calling or vocation. So it is that genders are multiplying in the recent theoretical literature (much to the alarm of what might be called the "gender fundamentalists)." I once thought of carrying a sign that would say: "Silicone for Everyone – Proud Transsexual forming a better world - one cup at a time." A transsexual re-make of Mutiny on the Bounty might involve a scene where Captain Bligh gives the order, "Mr. Christian, give that man a hundred lashes...and some mascara as well." But then I have always agreed with the Norma Desmond philosophy that in the golden era, "We had faces!"

If there is such a thing as transsexual over-kill where we totter too close to the line where being a drag-queen begins I have never feared crossing that line or advocating that other transsexuals might learn from the more colorful gender-rebels among us. Just as the silent movie stars conveyed what might be termed excess emotion in their gestures and mannerisms, just so it seems to me that the drag-queens, sparkled with stardust-glitter and lipstick, with cleavage and sequins, with six-inch heels and an attitude to match, are glorious creatures. If acceptance on conventional terms is so difficult for us to achieve and if conventional standards are applied so as to deny transsexual people social acceptance as their authentic selves, then let transsexuals raise an eyebrow or two if we must. Let the judgmental ones among us echo Dorothy's suspicion that we are not in Kansas anymore.

But before we leave the silent movie era let us talk about age as well. I refuse to self-censor as I age by adopting "old-lady drag" in preference to what may capture the lens of a member of the paparazzi from Milan. Of what use is it to be an apologetic transsexual, one who is simply seeking three square feet on which to erect the base of a statue to celebrate gender rectitude? I prefer an impressionistic canvass to mere statuary. I rely for my identity on no certification to say that I am real, one that is derived from some practiced surgeon who can testify that my labia are tailored down to the centimeter. I am real because I say that I am and that should be sufficient to all of this world's self-appointed gender police. Who looks first at chromosomes anyway? I walk out into the same world each day that other people do, and like Norma Desmond in "Sunset Boulevard" I am always ready for my close-up.

A Sense of Dread

Soren Kierkegaard, who is perhaps the earliest existential philosopher, explained in his book, "The Concept of Dread," that the primal problem in life is the development of a sense of self. The experience of alienation, of being a stranger in one's own body with a total lack of affirmation from the surrounding society, is the first and most basic experience of every transsexual. It forces us as children to live in an atmosphere of studied bewilderment and duplicity regarding our own desires and sense of being. Transsexual children are forced inward to seek solace and confirmation from a sense of self that is still in the process of formation. They are asked to draw upon resources that they often do not yet possess. They are further asked to make this journey alone and without emotional support from parents, teachers, or the media.

The result of this abuse by neglect is that transsexuals often develop early in life an intense fantasy life with role-playing and symbolic representation of their cross-gender identity. These techniques of self-soothing and nurturance to the degree that they are present make it possible for the young transsexual to mentally survive in an alien world. But to say that they survive is to ignore the incredible stresses that such subterranean adaptation demands of them. Those stress lines may create depression and periods of intense anxiety in them and result in a lack of social skills. Various acting-out behaviors may be present and later on substance-abuse or suicidal tendencies may be present. These stresses may on the other hand create a person who becomes compliant to other people's expectations or to larger authority structures in a desperate attempt to conform to outer expectations so as to win approval, not for what they really are, but for what they are trying so hard to be. Meanwhile the basic maturational processes of taking risks, accepting correction, and learning must go underground. The compliant child nurses a deep inner resentment, rage, and fear of exposure. Children with their innate sensitivity soon sense this desperate struggle going on within transsexual children and see in the young transgender person a ready scapegoat for their own incomprehension and insecurity. This only adds to the alienation and sense of loneliness and rejection of the transgender child. In the end the world is perceived by them as an alien and rejecting place.

Fortunately I was raised in a world of books and television which allowed me to find all manner of comfort in assuming in imagination a gender role that I dared not manifest in real life. The memories of certain places and even the very texture of life was different for me because of being my being transgender. Experiences would tend to reverberate with a different meaning and depth for me, much as a still-life by Cezanne embodies the fruit or as a mirror facing another mirror contains an inner infinity of reflected ripples from a single image. The result was that I, along with many sexually conflicted young people, can well understand the search within the past for time lost. Transsexuals of my era often exist in a state of mourning for a life that was lived in archipelagoes of delight when they found for an instant a possibility to leave the surrounding cold and to find the inner fire of comfort and congruence and to feel for a moment whole and complete. If there is a certain compulsiveness and lack of maturity that comes with addressing gender issues later in life it is due to the regression effect of finding again that lost child within whose emotional maturity has never been integrated with the functional personality that managed to adapt to the demands of the outer world in a purely mechanistic way but without weaving its outward skills and roles into the center of the emotional life, a life which still exists in its original archaic state. If there is one thing more difficult than being a woman in a man's body, it is finding an adolescent in a middle-aged body. The more that the avenues of maturity were foreclosed through repression and resistance it is often the case that this very resistance has locked the primal self in an earlier age of psychological and sexual immaturity. The transition process is then for many transsexuals one involving a re-acquaintance with the self, which perhaps for the first time may see itself as a union of impulse and rational adaptation to a more nurturing outer world than the one that the young transsexual encountered at home and at school in their years of childhood and early adulthood.

To understand what it means to be cross-gendered it is essential to understand the transsexual life course as a narrative. As more and more people find this avenue to integration of their lives, one provided by gender change, the question must arise whether gender change is an example of homecoming to the "real self" or is gender change a quest for an idealized persona, a sort of living work of art designed to answer the manifold pain and lack of self-acceptance of transgender people. If the latter is a better description of the transgender condition, then the process of transition becomes the creation of a coherent life narrative, a transsexual story written upon our very flesh.

Every narrative contemplates a reader. For transsexuals that ideal reader is first of all our own self. We read our fate in the mirror of social roles and often in a set of idealized expectations of what we imagine the other sex to feel. We look to externals to fill a sense of inner void in the assigned role to us at birth. As our new body emerges transsexuals hope to bond at last with the gender dictates and rituals of what has heretofore been the envied "other." What has been symbol now becomes the given of every day's experience. Even after a successful transition it is still possible to feel that one's own body has become a theater staging successive dramas for a hostile or indifferent audience so that in looking into a mirror one asks, "Was this what it was all for?" Only in that moment does one know by one's answer if one has made the right choice after all.

I often think that the real problems encountered by transsexuals as they enter transition are caused by people who with varying degrees of success have accepted the idea that our lives are written before us by another hand, that our lives are not original works at all but rather simply new editions of prior books with familiar themes. The real problem then is that transsexuals dare to question a limitation that seems to be most given and natural, a role that is perhaps more determinative of every aspect of life than any other, our sexual and gender role expectations. Transsexuals are often confronted by a unified protest because if change is possible in sexual identity, then what source of ultimate stability, what primal coordinates on the axis of life remain? To assume that transsexuals are immune from this dread and are in a sense visiting upon others some mere whim or fantastic and elaborate hoax made out of some desire to injure others is a common response, though a moment's thought should be sufficient to show how unjustified this response is.

Not only are transsexuals out of step with the gender norms and requirements in a physical sense but they are years behind in socialization to the gender to which they feel that they actually belong. In order to survive at all transsexuals have learned to adopt masking behaviors to hide their feelings from others and a vast reservoir in many cases of shame and self-condemnation. If to these injuries and disabilities is added actual physical or sexual abuse it may be imagined how great a task is involved to simply address these issues, yet alone to bring them to some amelioration by a mid-life gender change.

But we are still not done. Now imagine that transsexuals are submitted to the further indignity and insult of being castigated by our very laws and religious mandates. The law which should be among the more enlightened of institutions has often manifested a degree of hardness and inflexibility, an imperviousness to the data of medicine, and even a vindictiveness that has made the transgender journey more difficult and has called into question the new relationships formed by transsexuals in their new lives. One need only think of the actual words of one judge who summed it all up by saying, "Whatever it is that result from these surgical interventions it is most certainly not a woman." Or one may recall the famous Corbett v Corbett case in English law when the exquisitely beautiful transsexual model, April Ashley, suffered the indignity of having her marriage denied although no one could deny her most utter and complete femininity and completeness. But perhaps the most scandalous case of all is that in which transsexuals were denied any accommodation or recognition under the provisions of the Americans with Disabilities Act because one ignorant and hateful Senator offered an amendment that transsexuals were to be lumped into a vague category of unrelated mental conditions, with pyromaniacs and kleptomaniacs, categories of mental illness clearly he clearly grabbed at random, and assumed to be united by only a factor of being (in the eyes of the Senator) examples of self-inflicted or improvised conditions the sole purpose of which was to injure others.

Is it any wonder then that the first and primary characteristic of being transsexual is often to feel within oneself at the deepest level a sense of inner betrayal and conflict, the depth of which can hardly be imagined by one who does not feel compromised in her very being by a gender assignment to which she feels that she does not belong? Under these conditions can any transsexual autobiography be other than one of a history of pain only bright-

33

ened now and again by the unique and often wonderful ways through which transgender children have kept some part of their inner souls alive while acting out a part for a world that they have neither chosen nor ever mastered? Instead these children have been forced to meet the expectations put upon them so that the illusion of gender-normative expectations and universality in the complacent adults that surrounded them might prevail.

Transgender children live an experience of inner duality the demands of which far exceed their maturity level and coping mechanisms. The stresses that these children face result in a sense of incredible loneliness and alienation, but these children also develop an inner self-reliance that allows them to sustain a parallel universe of dreams and aspirations even while they attempt to meet the expectations of others that they will conform to the gender norms of the sex assigned to them at birth. To rebel in this one area of their lives, that which is most basic, often gives them the courage to sustain their own convictions when faced with other demands, ones that are equally arbitrary and unfair which more nurtured, and hence compliant children, will tolerate without protest.

My own childhood was a mix of just these characteristics. The habit of seeking the reason and rationale for any decision or social policy finally led me to embrace the two most contentious of human professions: that of being a philosopher and an attorney. Even in these areas of study I found my place in the most extreme and willfully contentious schools of thought. In philosophy I embraced the existentialists with their emphasis upon personal authenticity and the ability of the sovereign individual to structure his or her world by action. This existential ethic arose out of the chaos and ruins of the post-war world. The bleak description of all of human life in existential philosophy as that of being thrown into a world and abandoned without any means of finding a stable ordering principle, a world that was not dissimilar to my own experience of childhood and youth of being placed in successive situations, each of which appeared sudden and arbitrary, to which I was forced to adapt without any real understanding or concern being expressed for my own fears or bewilderment. Existentialists tend to believe that in the last analysis community is impossible and that each of us confronts the human dilemma alone. To perceive all things as mere changing aspects drawn from an inscrutable and unknowable base that lies beyond and behind us clothed in shadow seemed to me the best definition of truth.

I do not believe now that the existentialists were right. To grow older is to begin to dream again of a synthesis based upon a transcendent and absolute basis of all things and to hunger for the certitude of the Medieval Scholastics Philosophers and the Christian Realists like Jacques Maritain. To reject the strictures of a dull-witted bourgeoisie need not mean that no basis for social reality can ever exist.

I also turned to the study of law. In Jurisprudence I found myself drawn to Critical Legal Theory which holds that laws are in the last analysis indeterminate and that the entire legal enterprise may fail because, for all of its occasional wisdom, law is essentially the exercise of power. There are no meta-concepts that can provide for law what a physical world does for physics. The elaborate distinctions of legal opinions are in fact post-hoc justifications meant to weave the arbitrary decision of the day into the great web of the pre-existing legal opinions of cases that have already been decided with as little damage inflicted upon the order and symmetry of the latter as possible. Between the twin poles of legal formalism and the wisdom of a case-by-case judgment applying the wisdom of a Solomon there is a great ocean of legal opinion and analysis the margins and extent of which grow with every year. To plunge into this vast sea of controversies and to expect to unite them into a vast synthesis is pointless. Attorneys might just as well cast yarrow sticks and turn to the I-Ching as to expect anything other than a momentary and subjective reading when consulting the great barometer of the law. The law is most stable where it is least used. In areas of contention the well-worn channels are only regularities of process, not of substance. The greatest truth of going to law is that it is an endurance contest in which the one left standing after the long process grinds to a halt is the winner. Is it any wonder then that from my transgender experience it was but a small leap to understanding and finding a strange inverse reflection of my inner dislocation when I perceived and studied the ambiguity and

35

cruelty of the world in which I found myself living as an adult? I have called this total life experience of my life as a transsexual the experience of dread. It has been all too often an experience that time and again has brought me to the edge of the abyss where like so many of my brother and sister transsexuals who have, out of the inner violence done to them, come all too close to joining those who are no longer with us because they took their lives into their own hands by suicide. Who can hope to count the loss to the world of so many of our talented and sensitive youth, transsexual and non-transsexual alike who succumb to this tragic and avoidable decision? One of the most promising musicians and singers that I ever knew, one so talented that even her early work was so finished and polished that not one note of interpretation failed to achieve its aim of perfection, died in precisely this way. Her distraught mother, unable to bear the loss, soon followed her. The membrane that divides any future life that we can aspire to embrace is not to be punctured at will. For all we know more will be exacted from us to repair this loss on the other side than if we had stayed to fight it out here as best we may. Time's seasons seem most insupportable when relief may be only hours or days away. It takes a fundamental will to survive that must be strengthened daily by renewed commitment to weather the storms of life. Healthy habits of thought must be reinforced as a bulwark against despair. It is often the most refined and sensitive who perish and it is an indictment upon us all that we do not guard them and attempt to mediate between their sorrows and the accidents and defaults of our changing and contingent world.

As for me, I endured because I felt compelled to seek a reason for all things. My curiosity has been my saving feature and my anger and umbrage have been my sword and shield. My own life has made me sympathetic to all rebels. Often the only comfort that the rebel ever knows is simply to know herself as a rebel and quite often this is enough.

Compensations

Most transsexuals report periods of what might be called reactive depression throughout their lives as they attempt to compensate and adjust to the imposed requirement that they manifest the interests, appearance, mannerisms, and sexuality of the sex to which they were assigned at birth. Perhaps no more silly phrase has ever been uttered than, "Oh well, he'll eventually grow out of it." Transsexual children know that something feels desperately wrong, that they simply are not boys (or in the case of female to male transsexuals, girls). It is not just being deprived of their real sex's appropriate maturation and socialization that is troublesome but that they are further asked to imitate and to convincingly embody the roles appropriate to the other sex, the one assigned to them. It is like being forced to be the ultimate undercover agent behind enemy lines. But in this case the enforcers are the very people who are expected to listen, love, and support children as they develop their parents and teachers. While most children are allowed to declare who they are and to express their wants and needs transsexuals are told to be quiet about their real desires. Transsexual children are simply asked to accept that the world is arbitrary, demanding, and punitive from day one. This inevitably produces what used to be called "nervous or disturbed children." Many of us as we grew up were sent to various counselors and therapists to deal with our nervous habits, unexplained outbursts of anger, frustration tolerance issues, or other manifestations of the intense inner agony that we were not allowed to talk about because, of course, "we will just grow out of it." Of course our peers knew differently. They knew that we were in some strange way faking who we were. Children knew that we were what used to be called sissies or tomboys. Today such children are often openly called fags or dykes in school.

Now this would be bad enough if with adulthood we could finally escape this lifelong legacy of oppression, the one to which we have been subjected by various bullies, but by the time we are finally able (and in fact expected) to manifest our adult independence most of us have learned to always look outside of ourselves for validation and guidance and are ill-prepared to pursue our own authenticity. Spontaneity is often impossible for us; we are simply too alienated from our feelings. We are like prisoners who have at last adapted to the attitude towards us of our guards and have assumed it towards ourselves. We have never been allowed to express what was always closest to us. The result is that when the doors are opened and freedom beckons we are simply afraid to leave our cells. We don't know what we want anymore. So we sit in the corner and shiver like a dog that has always been beaten.

Some of us just look around at 18 or 21 and do what everybody else is doing we marry and start having children. Others of us try to embody a form of intense masculinity by what psychologists call the defense of reaction formation. We double down on what was already a bad bet. In my own case it meant adopting a life that would permanently deny me any sexual expression at all; I planned to take religious vows of chastity and obedience in the Jesuit Order and become a priest. Others of us go into the military or take up professions that entail danger or physical discomfort and risk in order to prove that they are not sissies after all. For us adjustment and compensation has always meant over-compensation; we just never learned anything else. We are used to living according to the expectations of others. We sometimes marry controlling or abusive wives, many of whom have their own gender issues or lesbian desires and are as deeply in denial of these issues as we are. They in turn are desperately trying to follow their assigned female life-script by marrying a "man" whom they must intuit at some level is really a woman.

The pain just doesn't go away. We grow from being confused, angry, and depressed children into being bitter, angry, and depressed adults. Worst of all many of us walk along the edge of self-destruction by alcohol, drugs, or suicidal ideation and behaviors. We do this because we feel powerful and defiant when we self-destruct. We play with death or extreme situations as a form of substitute gratification. Respect and nurturing are alien to what we have always known so we do not know how to give these things to ourselves. Our health-care often suffers. Some of us develop weight issues or eating disorders as children or other obsessive or compulsive tendencies. When we attend family gatherings it is said of us, "Well, I'm not surprised. He (or she) was always difficult growing up; we did everything for him that we could," [Except perhaps to listen to us and to believe us].

The least "adaptive" of us punish ourselves by dying or getting thrown into jails where we are raped and beaten or farmed out by guards to other prisoners. Others of us do the same thing outside and end up as transsexual murder victims. All of which is to say that we are an "at risk population." There are exceptions of course but these children grew up to find a place in the less condemning confines of being "only gay." Only recently has it become possible to identity transgender children early by exploring their gender issues with them and giving them a childhood that allows them to explore who they are without punitive sanctions being imposed upon them by school or society for being transgendered. It is still far from being a rose garden though and it may still be advisable for even these favored children to develop some of the old defiance and strength that allowed us early ones to come through (those of us who did). I make it a habit to read the comments that appear under transgender-themed news articles that appear on the Internet. One recent tragic news entry had responses like these that provide an informal survey of the world that transsexuals must encounter every day:

- ✓ Good riddance.
- ✓ Natural selection at work.
- ✓ They will all burn in the Lake of Fire.
- ✓ Perverts have no rights.
- ✓ There are only two sexes; go back to biology 101.
- ✓ Go ahead then and have it hacked off.
- ✓ When will we ever escape the gay agenda and give rights to ordinary decent people as opposed to these deviants?
- ✓ Stay out of my bathroom as long as I have a gun.

Coming out in a world with people like this who are defined as "normal" is it any wonder that transsexuals like me learned early to shut up and keep quiet about how we identified?

I was blessed with a good family (one that has never abandoned me). I was also blessed with a very stubborn temperament and with a fertile imagination. I used my imagination to design a better world than the one in which I lived. I used my stubbornness to just keep on going and to insist in my twenties and early thirties that it was okay to be an "out" transsexual. I felt that the more successful a person was at passing or alternatively at being defiant and colorful the more imperative it was to stay within the TS community and to encourage others by providing an example of resistance. I liked what Harvey Milk, the first openly gay city counselor in San Francisco, always said about giving them hope and what Larry Kramer, the founder of the AIDS health-options advocacy group Act-Up, said about silence equaling death. Besides I wanted to enjoy being free at last. What had it all been for if I could not spread my wings and fly? I have been visible for a long time and although I still feel inside like a very private person, I know that I have affected lives. I take pride in being in my own way a sign of contradiction. My sympathy is always with the rebels. Maybe this is because I have observed at close hand the face of conformity when it is distorted with hatred or with a smug attitude of complaisance. No people talks more about freedom than Americans do while being more afraid of actually seeing people who exercise it. When people ask me how I walk so well in heels I tell them it is due to two things:

1. I started walking in heels at six and;

2. By chasing bigots who yelled "faggot" at me across various parking lots while demanding, "What did you just call me?"

It takes lots of attitude to be transsexual even today. I like people who have that little extra edge. So although I do not advise transsexuals to chase guys across parking lots or to get beat up as I have been for calmly writing down the car-license numbers of people who use derogatory language towards us, I do advise that when compensation means taking it out on ourselves that my sister and brother trans-women and trans-men recall that there are friends out there to support us and to demand justice and human dignity for us at last. My generation is passing the torch – be sure and carry it high and proud even when that is very difficult to do. Oh and one other thing, know that strategic retreat does not mean defeat; it means taking time to regroup one's forces for a new assault on the citadels of ignorance and oppression. History moves slowly but it does move. Be sure that when the gates finally yield that you are there to enjoy the victory.

So why is Bitchy Ever Sexy?

Most transsexual autobiographies portray a journey from discontent and misery to a well-adjusted identity in the gender of identification once the body and the mind are finally brought into congruence. This is the standard story of the well-adjusted and pre-operative transitioned patient. For many years transsexuals may have felt that they owed it to the world to be happy because if they weren't they were either considered to be terminally maladjusted people who had conned the professionals into believing in the whole syndrome of transsexualism as an entity in the first place or they were ungrateful to the creative surgeons who had worked out the artistry to re-design their genitalia. Then there was always the reluctance of giving people the last laugh so they could claim, "We told you so."

In fact to be an unhappy post-op transsexual often calls into question the validity of one's initial diagnosis. To be transsexual then was to require one and only one thing for happiness: genital reassignment. "What more do these ungrateful people want who keep insisting that everybody else change their comfortable and common-sense definitions to accommodate their peculiar beliefs and their particular needs?" From this point of view, sex change is a luxury for the terminally bored and those who simply like to try everything. From this viewpoint again gender identity support groups should serve caviar and champagne and meet in malls instead of in old buildings in low-rent districts as we have often been forced to do because it was all that we could afford. So in order to correct this bright and cheery mandate I thought it might serve as a valuable corrective to portray the sadder but wiser girls here for a change because, as the rich never cease reminding us, what is the point of having money if you can't still be miserable. Toothy smiles may get you a crown at beauty pageants but on music album covers smiling only makes people think that you are lacking in intelligence.

Being sexy often demands a face that embodies anger, boredom, or if possible, both as one's customary disposition. Every facial muscle should say, "I dare you to bring me to climax. I don't like you. Therefore you should buy my album." It may not be logical but it works and the cash registers ring to the mournful melodies of discontented but beautiful chanteuses every day of the week. Why then should a transgender woman be happy? It will immediately testify to the degree of her cross-sex identification as a transsexual it seems to me for her to walk out of the surgical clinic with her plastic dilators and her pain pills, not with a daffy smile on her face, but instead sticking her tongue out, pounding on piano keys, and assuring everyone that she is born only to die. There is something primal about girl-anger and guys will do almost anything to avoid it. They pant for the lady with the razor-edge cleavage and a tongue to match. They may not marry girls like this, but who marries anyway today unless they are gays, lesbians, or debutantes. Marriage is passé for everyone except gay people; heterosexuals either live together or change partners at intervals. Our society seems to find happiness and geniality to be affectations. We scorn the kindly and the grateful, the open and the honest, so it may be wise advice to court dissatisfaction and discontent because to simply say thank you and to go on with life is to invite scorn and rejection.

When transsexuals cease to be mysterious and daring and become just like people with dyslexia or autism and are seen as normal human variants, then beware! The tide of retribution and revenge can restore those dark-age mentalities that merely slumber during periods of social advancement. Someone will suggest that transsexuals have not yet suffered enough and new hoops will appear overnight to the attainment of gender congruity and acceptance for them. It may be a good idea therefore to learn from the old professionals, the drag queens, to strike an attitude. Whoever saw a happy drag queen? Their motto is always: to be a diva first, last, and always (and don't steal my music)!

Enforcing Gender Conformity

Gender norms are enforced around the world and in every society because they involve primal power relations. The differences between the sexes are the basic biological currency for the most fundamental human transactions such as sex and the various forms of marital covenants the terms of which vary according to the various religions and cultures around the world. It is because so many laws and customs are based upon gender distinctions and because many of these relations play a role in economics and trade, let alone our vision of the sacred, that they are enforced with shame and even with violence.

Even the youngest of children will set upon the sissy or the tomboy in school to bring them into conformity with American cultural norms. Sexual segregation at an early age indoctrinates children into the mental alienation that builds a mental wall between characteristics and traits of the "opposite" sex." These culturally induced differences when supplemented by nature's role in molding and differentiating the sexes at puberty creates between the sexes the possibility of exchange which is a prerequisite for any market. That sexual currency allows exchanges to develop is strictly controlled because with trade comes power. One need only think of the institution of the payment of a dowry, which is demanded of the bride in so many countries before a marriage can be contracted, to see exchange in action. Part of that dowry may even involve the expectation that should her husband predecease her that her own life is at an end and she should immolate herself by fire upon her husband's death as is the case in parts of India. But we need not go so far afield to see that societies guard with vigor the signs and privileges of membership in a gender class. It is for this reason that families who might have forgiven every other type of offense even if criminal will turn their teenage gay, lesbian, or transgender children into the street rather than accept their gender non-conforming behavior.

That there are still Americans who would gladly enforce the full rigor of Leviticus upon sexually active gay men and who trot out Deuteronomy to castigate transsexuals while not insisting that their wives and daughters are unclean because of menstruation and must spend time outside our suburban neighborhoods that are the modern version of the camps of the Israelites shows how we use religion to make GLBT lives miserable and to use GLBT people as sacrificial victims to enforce our particular gender norms. What, to this way of thinking, are a few gay, lesbian, or transgender suicides or homicides as long as gender and sexual norms are thereby reinforced? As one who has been on the receiving end of anti-GLBT sentiments and violence I can testify to their reality. Shall I share a few instances?

I was attacked in broad daylight by three men while I was dressed in male attire. One of the assailants had seen me at Church which I usually attended as a woman. He and his three friends started shouting faggot at me and attacked me after I calmly walked to the rear of their car and began calmly writing down their license plate number. I told them that if they really believed that their verbal harassment of me was correct they should not be afraid to defend it in a court of law. Unfortunately, their subsequent physical attack was witnessed by an off-duty highway patrol officer and other generous citizens who rushed forward to me with their numbers and said they would be happy to help later if they were needed as witnesses. I had fought the three off as best I could. When they pled guilty several months later to a gross misdemeanor offered as a plea bargain in order to avoid felony charges and resulting jail-time I was in the courtroom. I remember how weary of it all I was by then. I was allowed to make a statement to them at their sentencing and I said,

"In the past months you have each paid a retainer for private counsel of perhaps $5,000. You must now each do 240 hours of social service and you now have a criminal record and all for what? You insulted and then physically assaulted someone who was essentially a stranger to you when you might have despised and ridiculed me at will privately with no consequences to yourselves at all; but now you are bound to that incident and at what cost to yourselves, let alone to me. I have today only one question for you: was it worth it?"

But by then the tide was changing somewhat. The law was beginning to protect GLBT people. I was able to escape the days when the police would throw a drag queen into the male holding-pen and ignore her cries as she was raped or beaten up. It should be noted though that:

✓ It was still perfectly legal at the time to evict cross-dressed people from mall shopping centers because the stores and even the walkways of malls are private property or to refuse them service in restaurants or to evict them from their apartments for being gay, lesbian, or transgender. During those years I lived in constant fear that a manager might interrupt me as I sat quietly reading and ask me to leave because my very presence offended some people. When I pointed out, as I always did, that I was a customer too and that I had my own cross-complaint to make about officious bigots complaining about the transsexual reading in the corner with her cola glass and her book and highlighting pen, I was summarily shown the door with an "or do we have to call security." I have often thought since that they need not have worried since they were quite secure in whatever consensus the society at the time must have had to act as they did. Not even the presence of my legal textbooks spread out in front of me deterred them (I was a law student at the time).

✓ I recall then going to the guide in our law library that lists law review articles to see what had been published regarding protections for transsexuals. I read all about the former pilot who was successfully dismissed from her job because a transsexual must of necessity be too mentally unstable to fly a plane. I read about the April Ashley case and why a transsexual could not marry and how U.S. courts had followed Britain's lead in non-recognition of a post-operative transsexual's right to marry. I kept reading backward until the few transsexual entries ended. I now read: transsexual see homosexuality. There followed year by year a list of articles on homosexuality until these grew fewer also. At last I came to this entry: homosexuality see sex crimes.

✓ Of course the response at the time was always that GLBT people have a choice. All they need to do was to deny what they were inside and try and conform (as if every GLBT person that I have ever known had not tried to be straight appearing in order to escape the relentless bullying and name-calling during their school years). One of the privileges of adulthood was or should have been that age alone would confer immunity from the abuses of the playground. Never during all those years when I was subject to attack in my early transition period did any0ne ever stand up, protest, or interfere in any way when teenage males would shout faggot at me. Neither did the management ever ask *them* to leave. I remember realizing that the young are often the Hitler Youth of anti-GLBT feelings. They are the storm-troopers of gender role conformity and they know it.

✓ I recall debating on television one of the main spokesmen of the group of religious zealots opposing GLBT protections in our city and thinking that I could appear on television and at least be granted the status of going head to head with a man who claimed that it was a *"special right"* to not be denied service in restaurants or evicted or fired for being gay or transsexual. "Why was this special?" I asked myself. Wasn't it because it was precisely those who like me insisted on being what we in fact were that we met these actions from a straight society? Did we ever think then to suggest that it was straight people who had the most "special rights" of all by possessing the right simply to be while we did not? That was it after all, this whole matter of being! I came to realize that Hitler's demand that GLBT people wear the pink triangle badge and be killed at Dachau was alive and well in America in its essential philosophy which was that GLBT people should simply disappear. I write these things today because I realize that many of my brothers and sisters in the GLBT movement are not here to bear witness to what it was like in those days, which were not so long ago and they are not yet over by any means.

✓ I think of the man leading a Christian group who once stood in my face at the State Capitol where I had gone to support a gay rights ordinance. He called me "a freak of nature." I asked him if the mandate of universal love in his religion also applied to "freaks of nature." Some of his flock seemed to get the message as the man started and then turned and walked away.

✓ But these people are essentially strangers. We learn to expect rejection, hatred, and contempt from people who do not know us personally. The people who hurt transsexuals the most are the friends who cease calling after they hear that we are starting transition or the family members who explain that it would be awkward to have us appear at family gatherings. Even when we promise to appear in the guise of our former sex there is still that pregnant hesitation. It is like some gender Gestapo exists in the neighborhood to ferret out any behind-the-lines transsexual who has climbed down the stairs of some secret annex and infiltrated a gathering of "normal people."

✓ Or is it that gender confusion is a sort of latent virus, some bird-flu that we carry with us and that might infect wives with lesbianism, husbands with homosexual impulses, and children with a wild desire to emulate us in our life-long rejection and pain? If any of that was so, there would be more transsexuals than there are. No, being

46

transsexual is not contagious. What I do suspect though is that the shared stigma attached to cross-gender behavior is so intense that it constitutes a sort of reservoir of hatred for us, a reservoir backed up behind a dam of denial and repression. The fear is that there is enough hatred to spill-over to taint anyone who claims an alliance with us. We just aren't good people to know. All of this has left me with very little respect for what are termed "good decent people." I expect that they were the very ones who requested that Pilate crucify Christ.

✓ In those days the gatekeepers were very strict. Even those who claimed to want to help us seemed anxious that no one cross the barrier between the sexes unless they were "true transsexuals." These gatekeepers devised means to keep us out. The biggest criterion was whether we could make "convincing women," which translated meant: 1. that we should be attracted to men, 2. that men would be attracted to us as women, 3. and that we adopt a properly submissive attitude to the doctors who held our lives in their hands. The more pliable the clay the easier it is to mold. Oh, and we had to hate our penises which meant denying that we had ever managed to adapt form to function and settle for what we could get with what we had. Just to be sure they would dole out hormones like they were gold and see how plastic our bodies were which also meant that it helped if we were young. The doctors would have to rule out any self-rejecting homosexuals who thought that by being women they could justify being gay. They would also have to be sure that our delusion that we were "women trapped in men's bodies" was our sole delusion so that post surgically we would not say, "Oh by the way Doctor, I never told you this before but I'm not only transsexual; I'm actually Marie Antoinette!" That would never do. It was also not a good idea to claim to hear voices, to have pronounced anxiety disorders or depression, or to think that people were out to get us (even if they were). Nope, you had to appear to be in a normal image of whatever the doctor thought a woman was if you wanted to qualify. If you were brash, demanding, or aggressive you were probably a person with anti-social personality or in any case an angry gay male and as such a poor "candidate for surgery." If you got desperate and said, "Uh, Doctor, I'm not a candidate. I'm not running for public office, I just want a vagina, your chart might read something like this: "Patient manifests periods of extreme hostility and resistance to authority, surgery is contraindicated until the unresolved anger issues are resolved and patient learns to tolerate frustration better." So years of costly therapy might lie ahead for you as you got older and more desperate all the time. Of course the gender clinics kept your scrounged together money that paid for your initial evaluation. Transsexuals were in other words a hidden market for those willing to risk the ridicule of their peers and treat us. Since we were not political types and didn't consider ourselves gay and since we were isolated and apparently few in number we had no political clout even well into the eighties and nineties. It took the internet to finally set us free.

I could continue these reminiscences but since each one brings me great pain and since all share a common cause in the hatred and contempt for GLBT people, I will not linger over these instances. I do wish to say here though that each one of these experiences alone and even more when they are considered as a whole showed me how frail are the protections of law and the supposed common humanity of our democracy that should unite us when issues of gender or sexuality are at stake. The Stonewall Riots of 1969 are not so distant after all because these anecdotes took place in the decades of the 1980's and 1990's and in places throughout America they take place every day even now. At this writing in 2014 I have just finished reading the comments on the web after President Obama has (temporarily at least) given protection among Federal contractors to sexual and gender orientation. This created a storm of internet outrage. What will happen if a Republican President is returned to office?

Phrases Used to Hammer Us

People who love silly sound-bites rely on phrases as a substitute for thought. The problem with this is that the use of these phrases is often taken seriously, but phrases can break our hearts. An example was the great Nazi lie, "Arbeit Macht Frei" which was engraved at the gates of Auschwitz in order to imply that with sufficient labor it would be possible for the inmates to be set free. What it meant in actuality was that the inmates of the camp had been reduced to one essential function, to labor on behalf of the Third Reich until their deaths. There simply was no residual humanity within them to entitle them to pursue their own ends of freedom and of happiness. Similarly people use phrases to beat up gay, lesbian, bi-sexual, transsexual, and other gender non-conforming people every day. Let's look at a few of these dumb phrases:

✓ "God didn't make Adam and Steve; He made Adam and Eve." This simply can't be true I have wanted to point out to people who like to use this phrase to me. I would then continue, "If there was no Adam and Steve who would have catered the wedding of Adam and Eve and done the interior design of their house in the style of 'Early Eden'?" Oh and did Adam and Eve have belly-buttons?

✓ "God doesn't make mistakes." The idea hiding behind this phrase is that God fine-tunes eggs and sperm so that the body always matches preexisting boy or girl souls so that what we experience in ourselves with regard to gender identity was divinely ordained rather than a natural outgrowth that we first experience within ourselves and then declare to the world. This means that transsexuals are either misreading their own experience of their inner gender reality and discontent with their assigned gender or that their feelings are an act of rebellion against God rather than opposing the recalcitrant facticity of the body. But we do that all the time! Each time you take a laxative you are toying with some bodily limitation and let's not even talk about conjoined twins. Does God will all of the genetic aberrations and human ills and ailments from which we suffer? Think about it!

✓ "The body and the soul are so inextricably linked that the body's sex defines the soul." This implies that the body is like a passport or license that must govern all of the complex thoughts and feelings that we possess, some of which are clearly labeled male and others female. Trying to make sense of this is like trying to figure which nouns in German are masculine, feminine, or neuter by some preexisting formula.

✓ "Your behavior is simply confusing to everybody." To this phrase transsexuals could answer that the behavior of people demanding that they just *be what you are supposed to be* is very confusing to them. Transsexual children simply cannot understand why everybody keeps insisting that they are a boy or girl when they know that the opposite is true.

✓ "You'll make an ugly woman!" My recommended answer to this goes something like this, "Well one more won't make much of a difference."

✓ "No one will ever love you." The best answer to this one is, "Why don't you just speak for yourself?" The idea here is that gender nonconformity deserves rejection, ridicule, hatred, or (worse than all) just being discounted as being a human person at all. Where does all of this negativity come from? Is the other sex so hateful in itself? No? Then what is really being condemned is the transition from one sex to the other. But why? Why aren't people more explicit in probing the source of their own gender and sexual anxieties which are the real source for the feelings that they project outward onto

49

transsexuals?

✓ "No one will hire you." This one is more a statement about society than it is about the transsexual. "We don't want to hire people who make our customers uncomfortable; we would lose business (money)." But what if it was the other way round and businesses were praised for showing moral courage and hiring minorities? I keep waiting for the day that some business owner comes up to me and invites me to sit at his lunch-counter because he wants to prove that his business is "trans-friendly."

✓ "We can't let the children know." This idea that children are so vulnerable is not honored in most areas of life. Part of being a child is being open to a world of different skin colors and the radically divergent shape and age of human bodies. Would you tell a person of age that you are raising your child to assume that all faces are smooth and unwrinkled? What would you say if while grocery shopping your child said, "Mommy, ooh look, at that wrinkled old mummy over there; she looks just like Boris Karloff!" Would you hush the child up and merely remind her that there are old people in the world? What then would your response be if the child said, "Mommy, ooh look, that person looks like a man who is dressing like a lady?" Would it be so hard to say, "Yes honey, some people are very unhappy with their bodies and feel better dressing differently." Of course if the transsexual is really pretty and the child says, "Ooh Mommy, look at that pretty lady; why don't you look like her?" Mommy can say, "Shut up kid and forget about getting that sugar-packed cereal that you like. You are going to eat that dry old bran and flax meal that grandma eats for her constipation and like it!"

Twenty Really Dumb Things to Say to Transsexual People…

The following is a list of things that people say to transsexuals all the time and how I wish we could answer them. Bear with me if I am occasionally sarcastic or even bitter. When you get to the end of the list I think you will understand why. It is not that I am surprised that people are curious. I don't even mind answering some of these questions or comments now and again. But it is the sum total and the constant lack of imagination and comprehension of others that over a life-time can make even transsexuals with patience and goodwill grow weary.

Here are the questions or comments:

1. "I can tell you're a man or [like a friend of mine said recently] "Oh yeah you blend." Answer: Really? Well then I guess the jig is up. Fooling you was always my intention from the first. It was in anticipation of your arrival someday that I was teased or bullied at school, tried reading every book available to get some insight into my feelings, purged wardrobe after wardrobe in order to seek a cure, sought out professionals at last, went through the expense of hormones and/or surgical procedures, found myself economically marginalized, and sexually in-between during my whole life. The whole thing was just one big elaborate hoax to fool you. Now that I am "read," "clocked," "spotted," "identified," or whatever you choose to call it, what should I do now, just disappear?
2. "Why do you wear so much make-up, it makes you look just like a drag queen?" Answer: Thank you. I think drag queens are beautiful.
3. "If you want to be transsexual why don't you live in San Francisco?" Answer: Right. I guess what you are trying to tell me is that although transsexuals have always existed in every society and culture and can be statistically found in every neighborhood with above 10,000 persons in America what we should all do is go running off to a few "Mecca spots for deviants" where we can have freedom-day parades every other day rather than simply staying where we are and just living our lives as best we can.
4. "What does your family think about all of this?" Answer: (sarcastically) oh they were delighted of course. The transsexual experience is such a source of joy that every loving family can think of nothing better for their children than to wish that they were all transsexual.
5. "Have you had your penis cut off yet?" Answer: No, although I have haunted back alley's and butcher shops to try and find the perfect surgeon to do to me what you think that Board Certified and Licensed Plastic Surgeons do at gender clinics all around the world on a regular basis.
6. "Are your breasts real?" Answer: What do you care, since the chances of your getting even the slightest touch or glimpse of them is about as remote as the chance that your I.Q. will ever be tested over 80?
7. "If God had wanted you to be a female, he would have made you that way." Answer: Right and God decrees every other genetic, anatomical, and physiological human variance by a direct act of will so that who are we to attempt to alleviate human pain, misery, or maladjustment? Or is gender the one area where no variance occurs in nature. Sorry, but perhaps you should read up a little on inter-sexed conditions such as Androgen Insensitivity Syndrome, Turner's Syndrome, Klinefelter's Syndrome, and many other cases of genital ambiguity. In the light of all of this, can you be sure that the brain alone is exempt from variations of structure or function that may

51

determine our transsexual feelings that are life-long? Is it only here that we must stay our hand for fear of upsetting some primal order when we find disorder in all other aspects of our physical being? Is it only in this peculiar type of suffering that we will decide that the will of God is operating to fix our gender in stone?

8. "What you are doing must be terrible for your children." Answer: We transsexuals were children once too. Where was the concern about the condition of transgender children when we were growing up? For that matter where is it today when transgender kids are trained to simply shut-up and behave according to gender norms that are inapplicable in their case? How many transsexuals have adapted to these intolerable demands and the stress that they entail by lives of addiction, depression, or even suicide?

9. "I could never find a transsexual attractive; you all look like big men in dresses." Answer: Yeah, right, some transsexuals so far meet or exceed the primal archetype of female beauty that they are fashion models let alone the many other categories where attractiveness may aid one in finding employment. The question is not then whether *you* might find them attractive but whether *they* would find anything attractive in you, Mr. Bonehead.

10. "You can never be a real woman because you can't bear children." Answer: Neither can most women after age 45 or 50 at which point women still have about 35 years of life ahead of them. Does sterility or age rob them of the right to be called a woman?

11. "I admire your courage." Answer: Don't admire me for simply being who I am. Between the choice of unending inner alienation and mental pain and simply walking out the door and living my life like anybody else, even if that brings misunderstanding and discrimination, there was never ever any real choice for me.

12. "Okay, but you'll never find anyone who will hire you so you may end up as a prostitute." Answer: Is that the transsexual's fault? If we are marginalized and exploited doesn't that say more about the sickness of non-transsexuals that makes a fetish object of "she-males?" First give us some alternatives and reduce the cost of gender reassignment and cover it by insurance like any other handicap or life-threatening condition, before you condemn young and uneducated persons from finding money though illicit and dysfunctional means to pursue their goals and to survive.

13. "Which restroom do you use?" Answer: That's always the big one isn't it? One would think that the sacred restroom was the center of some sort of cult with incense and sacrifice rather than merely a convenience for elimination. Both sexes eliminate waste products from their body; there is no secret about that. Women's rooms have the luxury of stalls and privacy in any case.

52

14. "My husband thinks he's gay and he wants to sleep with you in order to find out." Answer: Of course. As a transsexual I realize that I am some sort of public convenience, available on notice to resolve sexual conflicts for others. Or maybe you think that we are all so desperate that we require access to your dysfunctional marriage in order to find any partner at all, Miss Brainless!

15. "Can you have an orgasm with your new vagina?" Answer: You'll never find out.

16. "Didn't I see you on a talk-show?" Answer: No, because I have more self-respect than to buy a trip to the big city at the price of being hooted at by every idiot and yahoo who can afford a ticket price to add to the cheap celebrity of most talk show hosts.

17. "Why do you want to take men from real women?" Answer: I am a real woman Honey; get used to it.

18. "You don't know what its like to menstruate, so you can't be real." Answer: If you could avoid it would you? In any case is that all you ever do bleed all day?

19. "Some of you transsexuals look so real, I couldn't tell that they were really men!" Answer: Oh thank you! I guess I fooled you didn't I? But in any case my less attractive transgender sisters are just as real as I am and just as entitled to respect, understanding, and a full and meaningful life.

20. "Why would you ever want to be a woman; men have all the advantages!" Answer: I didn't do a cost-benefit analysis to decide to be transsexual. It was never anything other than my deepest sense of who I was; my identity and sexual self-image were at stake. In any case, we could dispute all day about which sex is most favored by fate. If the many options of personal appearance and expression, if emotional freedom to express the entire range of human emotions, and the ability to nurture life within your own body as a woman is burdensome to you, then you may be transsexual also, female to male.

The Request

Perhaps the dumbest single thing that people ever say to transsexuals runs something like this:

"You know how much I respect you for being out about your feelings that you have always felt like a female (or in the case of female-to-male transsexuals, like a male) inside and of course you know that I don't have any of the usual religious hang-ups where transsexuals are concerned but, and I just hate to ask this of you, but I wonder if you would come to [name the event] in male attire because unfortunately some of the people who

will be attending are not as liberal and informed as I am and they might be made uncomfortable."

Of course there is really only one answer to this request:

"What part of 'I am a female' did you not get? Did you really think that I have endured life-long anguish surrounding gender issues and am currently spending a small fortune to surgically and hormonally alter my body just to assume my former shackles every time someone would like to pretend that transsexualism doesn't exist? Why don't you just throw a tablecloth over me and tell everyone that I am a rare old Chippendale that you picked up in an antique store? Or do you intend to condemn me to running a slalom course for the rest of my life around people who don't want to tell themselves (or their children for that matter) that all kinds of people exist in this world?"

The answer is usually a defensive,

"But they just won't [or can't] understand!"

To which the answer is:

"And they never will as long as the great lie is maintained that gay, lesbian, and transsexual people either don't exist or that they exist but only in some far off Never-land that has nothing to do with everyday life."

The even more defensive response then is usually:

"But some people will be offended because to even deal with you as a human being violates their value system by implying that it is okay to do what you are doing to yourself."

And the answer to this by the out and proud transsexual is:

"If you still think that this is just another option among many then you haven't been listening to me at all. This decision is a fundamental one and as such beyond a mere weighing of options. As for approving of what procedures I have been able to afford or to contemplate and unless I am running around with a voting petition seeking signatures their mere dealing with me no more commits them to support my 'agenda' than does any other occasion when people deal with other human beings in daily life."

The person then usually looks crestfallen or indignant and says something like…

"Well just please do it for me then. After all, I'm your friend!"

And what is the answer to this?

Do you know what it is?

"Well there are always certain contingencies that test relationships and I guess this is one of them. I don't like it and I'm sorry to have to put it this way to you, but really there is only one me. It may not have been the me that you thought I was when our relationship commenced, but it is the truth and I am paying a higher price to tell you this truth than most people ever have to pay. If I lie about this, then you will never be sure that I won't lie to you on all of the minor occasions of life when it is advantageous for me to do so, whenever it is easier to either you or to me or to the relationship. So I am standing right here right now and telling you that I am betting the rest of my life that I have read my dispositions and feelings correctly. I am transsexual and I am willing to take what comes, however painful that may be."

Marriages, friendships, and filial loyalties break up on the reef of what I am calling here "the request." I hate broken relationships and I do not think it advisable to take offense at every conceivable sleight or dumb oversight of other human beings, but somewhere, sometime in the lives of most transsexuals the only proper and proportionate response is *to stand by yourself* and to just walk away.

Transsexual Anger

Those persons who still take time to read the strange poetic diatribes of Baudelaire in "The Flowers of Evil," the "Hymns to the Night" of Novalis, or "The Song of Maldoror" by Lautreamont will know the dark fruit that alienation can bring to sensitive souls. After lifetimes of being bullied at school and being mentally maimed by being forced into silence regarding every impulse toward our true identity that we could not deny within ourselves, and deprived of even the comfort that our suffering was unjustified and unjust, we transsexuals are angry. Angry because our impulses were condemned out of a perverse refusal to simply accept our testimony that our birth-assigned sex-role was wrong. We were told to just make the best of it. There are societies that recognize this anger and its legitimacy and as a result these cultures fear transsexual anger. It is beyond mere bad luck to offend a transgender person because such persons are seen as possessing certain special powers to bless or to curse those who awaken their ire. These societies do not see transsexuals as contrary to nature but rather as representing within their own bodies both of the primal energies of the sexes. Their double nature makes them able to understand many of the mysteries of life and death. They have ventured into the underworld and obtained the fire that burns within the unconscious mind.

In my own life I have been both amused and secretly convinced that I possess some of these powers. I often tease my friends that they had better watch their step lest they run afoul of what I call, "the trannie curse." Some people have suggested that it is a violation of the Wiccan three-fold law of return to curse anybody and I agree with this position. As a good attorney though I realize that a favored position may be argued from many angles so I immediately point out that the trannie curse is in reality a self-executing clause of the social contract. It is not that I place it upon anybody; it is simply that having gone out of their way to be obnoxious to me they have already brought upon themselves the dreaded "trannie curse." This reflection further allows me to feel a certain pity for my tormentors. In the days of old, which still exist in various jurisdictions all over America, when it was perfectly legal to refuse to serve transsexuals and I was asked to pack up my law books, leave my barely tasted cola, and quit the premises, because "we are a family friendly establishment," I would cast off the dust of that place from my feet and within a year I would drive by to find that they were out of business. If this happened only once, I might have concluded that it was coincidence but I have noticed the same phenomenon to be operative time and again. Its mechanism of course is not hard to fathom without resorting to various numinous powers. It is simply that the same people who discriminate against transgender people are also those who treat their employees poorly and engage in other practices that invite that retribution that some call karma or nemesis and that I, desiring at least some partial personal vindication, call "the trannie curse."

Of course if there is a "trannie curse" there is also a "trannie blessing." I like to remind my friends that if they shop where I want to shop or go to explore the beach access road that I have just pointed out, bouncing up and down on the car seat (of course as a sacred trannie I expect to be chauffeured about) that all will turn out well. Naturally whatever I choose will result of necessity in the greatest good for the greatest number and add on a "trannie blessing" besides. Much of this of course is the repressed child in me finally demanding her way. Some may be simply my own imagined sense of female prerogative and events may turn out this way simply because I am of course right. In any case, things do seem to work out after all and I am tempted to say, "See, I told you so," but the natural discretion of a Goddess makes me modest and reticent.

I am then like one of those sibyls of old, who in their sacred temples or circles of Diana that met in groves, would await consultation from the great and powerful. I possess a massive library, one that is entirely out of proportion to the reading abilities of any single human being, but I know that within those books culled from many fields there exists the answer that may be mine at any moment. In this I take comfort so that their mere existence and my knowledge of where to look for them is sufficient to give me endless wisdom. I have the comfortable illusion that my years of powerlessness and humiliation at being a boy who wished he was a girl have been met in my later years by a corresponding influx of shamanic powers.

On a Halloween two years ago I expressed this power by dressing as Mother Nature in a green velvet dress with long sleeves and a plunging neckline. My desire was to show a good portion of the bounties of nature in symbolic form. Everywhere I went I spread grace and fructifying ebullience and joy (for what Mother Nature would be stingy with the poor benighted and starving denizens of earth). There is nothing that makes one feel more generous than a plunging neckline! It is the gift that keeps on giving. We may have been a starved generation, for both men and women seem starved for a generous bosom. Indeed were the sands of all the seas turned overnight to silicone, I would be one of the first to stake a substantial claim upon that vast resource.

I realize, of course, that this is what psychologists call compensatory behavior. But even if it be recompense, is that so hard to understand when one considers the time lost to needless alienation in my transsexual youth? As the second part of this book will show I have tried to hang on to my Catholic faith through it all, though not without experiencing difficulties at times. The appeal of a thoroughly naturalized religion of symbol and imagery has been appealing to me at times – a woman religion like Wicca or a sort of benign surrender to Gaia. But beneath the romanticism of Oak and Elder trees or dancing naked beneath the moon at Beltane I see a form of late-stage hippy as the crone. So I have stuck with the religion of my childhood and pressed on. Evil is a two-edged sword and when we harbor vengeful thoughts, the harm that we may wish to another or rejoicing in their misfortune will certainly embrace us as well. Still it seems to me that cautionary words are in order for those who wish to harm, transsexuals. Even now I encounter people who are willing to face varying degrees of "the trannie curse." They are not all evil of course. I do not know their souls nor they mine and I am sorry that we all may not be friends on this sad and lonely journey though life; but so it is.

There was the case for instance of the man at Church who objected that even with about three average butt widths between us I had scooted over too near to him and his wife during the Sunday Mass. He was an interesting looking fellow, a dead ringer for Somoza of El Salvador. His wrath was worthy of that man in his outrage that a depraved trannie dared to sit next to him in church rather than being properly ejected at the door. He was as angry as though I were leading some peasant rebellion against his regime, so perhaps there is a "dictator curse" that I should fear. If so, I have no doubt that he wished it upon me that day. As it is though he walked out of Church mad (always a bad sign) since it is in parting after anger is expressed that we would hope for some sign of reconciliation and the universal benevolence that is mandated by the Christian faith. His attitude would no doubt remain with him perhaps for some time and it is that attitude, the same attitude that motivates the wanton slaughter of transsexuals by outraged Johns and by irate and insecure teens with baseball bats, that I call "the trannie curse." I call it this because it destroys its possessor.

The woman who I met during that same week was a lesser case of rejection but more detailed in her maledictions about my way of life. The woman made it a point of telling me that Jesus loved me, to which I responded, "I know and Jesus loves you too." She proceeded to explain how St. Paul made it quite clear in her view that I was sinning by simply being transsexual. She also said that my make-up drew attention to me. I pointed out that my make-up in both color and quantity was exceeded by most of the women televangelists that I have seen, so that I was in good company. She pointed out that I am not on television. I was tempted to say, "But Darling, I am still in entertainment. The world is my stage."

I did not though. I did what I have always done. I accepted the judgment on my life from those who have never lived it and tried to bear in mind that life is not easy for any of us. As a passing note the man mentioned above surprised me one day by a changed attitude of toleration and courtesy and extended his hand to me at Mass. He is no longer under "the trannie curse" as a result. I bear general grudges to institutions but try to forgive specific instances of offense. I have managed after all to survive worse insults. Besides, I always have "the trannie curse" at my side to guard me from the malice felt towards transsexuals and other outcasts just like me. Bitterness of soul breeds not only a literature of sorrow and of resentment but it can poison the individual heart and blind us to the surprising acts of kindness that I meet far more often these days. Anger may awaken us to remedy injustices, but when it becomes a mode of being it does far more damage to the victim of abuse than to the abuser.

Deconstructing the Body

I am currently living at a time when various traditional linguistic and meaning structures are undergoing a process called deconstruction. For transsexuals it is as though we are all made up of elementary and independent parts that can be reassembled into various configurations without destroying in the process the integral unity that is a person. Whereas early transsexuals considered their quest to be one of personal authenticity, the new gender theorists see gender constraints as artificial and arbitrary mandates derived from various outer referents and power structures. This means that any initial position is subject to questioning and refutation, even if that initial position is rooted in recalcitrant human flesh.

But just how malleable is an organic system that is as complex and integrated as the human body? Whereas texts are human creations our bodies are complex adaptive systems designed to carry on life processes rather than to embody symbolic meanings. For this reason there will always be something inherently suspect in altering the bodily gender balance and surgically modifying structures that form the basis for sexual response and human relationships at the most intimate levels of our being. Transsexuals exist therefore at a unique polar outpost surrounded by icy storms of anxiety and contempt from others with various agendas of their own and at times we manifest a numinous quality that makes us almost mythical creatures. Even if we experience ourselves as prosaic and normal in most aspects our lives are subject to appropriation by media and by image. We are often scapegoats for generalized cultural anxieties for "having gone too far" in our unique pursuit of happiness and well-being. What many of us view as the ordinary process of established gender-transition is portrayed or experienced by non-transsexuals as a state of being possessed by some alien spirit of primal rebellion against a legitimately imposed fate or status and we are advised or rather commanded to remain as we are no matter how unnatural it feels to us or how unhappy we may be.

As gender change becomes more a matter of routine it is not impossible, indeed it is highly probable, that some persons will adapt various hybrid arrangements in which body parts will show a mixed set of formerly discreet gender traits. This causes panic and condemnation of the entire transsexual enterprise as one of wrongheadedness or even of blasphemy. Is the transsexual body a new Tower of Babel to scatter and to dislocate sexual signifiers? Will the story of our lives be lacking in the unities and as such make of our lives a series of displaced dramatic fragments rather than an orderly process of birth, maturation, reproduction, and death as nature decrees?

Since the purpose of this book is more to raise issues than it is to give definitive answers I will not attempt to resolve these tensions. They must be resolved in some way though by individuals and by various institutional embodiments of our social and religious notions and norms. If I thought that the responsibility to resolve these questions was mine I would be even more reluctant to release this book than I already am. I do not wish to unduly strengthen any camp in the ongoing debate when such key relationships are at stake. What I do desire is to throw enough illumination upon the stage from various strategically placed sources of illumination that the drama posed by transsexualism may be seen by a curious audience many of whom will never understand how anyone could be so alienated from such a fundamental starting point for all future articulation of the human personality and social reality as transsexuals state that they in fact are.

So let me state here emphatically that I am writing from out of a region of tempest and storm from the waters of which I would advise all prudent mariners to stay clear. The charts are simply inadequate to predict what reefs may exist or what strange currents may cause vessels to drift further than they have imagined since their last sextant reading. Even when I sound most persuaded and convincing I advise my readers to beware; impressions are not systemic conclusions. I do not know that my own views are not tainted and biased. In fact I assume that they are.

Words and sentences lend themselves to deconstruction and radical inquiry in ways that our poor flesh does not. I am not a cunning screensaver on a computer screen taking on various forms. I am a person who has wandered or pursued the will-of-the-wisp of the feminine body and the sexual identity of my own body while always retaining a tenuous toe-hold to the narrow ledge of all that was expected of me when the doctor said at my birth, "You have a boy."

It should be morally possible, it seems to me, to responsibly and creatively articulate areas of concern here and to freely explore problematic concepts involving transsexualism without advancing when retreat is more advisable or deterring surgical intervention when that seems the more prudent choice. But to steer a middle course in such a controversial area, one so polarized and plagued by competing nomenclatures as this topic is, cannot be an easy task. Yet silence has its own penalties to impose, particularly when there may be an affirmative duty to speak out. It is in this conflicted spirit that this book is being written and published. I cannot choose my readers or prevent the misuse of fragments of what I have dared to express and to have set down here. As an attorney I know the dangers of selective citation to authority. The only authority here of course is drawn from my own fragmentary and limited existence. I am not a paradigm nor am I the sound of one hand clapping. I am … well that is the question is it not?

Easy Rider

Transsexuals are sometimes accused by cis-gendered women of being the gender equivalent of "easy riders." We don't menstruate, our behind-the-muscle silicone implants don't sag. We will never know labor pains. Instead we have tight and newly-constructed vaginas, enhanced bust-lines, and our waist-hip ratio may resemble those of the tall and willowy model-types. Some feminists consider us to be male-constructed and engineered fantasies of what men wish that "real women" could be. The unanswered question of course is what normal heterosexual male would sacrifice his own prized genitalia in order to conduct a covert reconnaissance mission into the realm of female experience. It is just when they are faced with that prospect that most potential "recruits" will quickly take one step back.

We transsexuals try to look as good as we can manage and some enjoy the power that goes with the Circe song of intense and stereotyped femininity, but surely these are compensations and are desires that many genetic women also share. We are not the only ones who seek out surgical enhancement and our reasons are more valid than those of many women who have already been dealt a winning hand by the beneficent chance of possessing two X chromosomes. So don't hate us because we are beautiful; we have paid for it, often dearly.

Toys

For me it started early. The fifties and sixties in America were a very gender conscious age in which to be raised. There has always been a difference between boy toys and girl toys. In part these differences depended upon what was assumed to be the natural gender-based preferences said to exist between boys and girls. Boys were assumed to be rehearsing in their play the competitive spirit of sports which would in turn prepare them to play an aggressive role later in the world, so boy's toys were designed to prepare them for their vocational goals later on in life. Boys would have for instance toy trucks to prepare them for work in construction or for transporting goods. They would have erector sets to prepare them to be engineers or chemistry sets to prepare them to be scientists. They would have active toys like play guns, soldier sets, or wood-burning sets for those boys who were more artistically inclined. Girls toys on the other hand stressed three major themes, baby or child nurture, which were taught by gifts like dolls or stuffed animals, sociability skill builders such as tea sets or jump-ropes, and items that would enhance homemaking skills or homemaking images such as doll-houses, toy ovens, or pretend house furnishings.

As childhood progressed girls were also encouraged to think about their grooming and attractiveness with mirrors, vanity sets, and pretend lipsticks. To desire cross-gender toys was to meet immediate disapproval by adults, not because toys were in any sense overtly sexual, but because they were the means by which society indoctrinates its young into gender solidarity and the resulting social coherence. Boys in particular would incur ridicule if they wanted a magic wand for Christmas or a Barbie Doll. Fantasy play and image modeling seemed innately feminine and not sufficiently grounded in hard reality. It would have been pointless for a boy of my era to say in response that his future plans for adulthood were to start his own line of haut couture or to spend his days in Milan with beautiful models, perhaps to drive a Lamborghini, and to have a lovely home on the French Rivera where he might work on his designs when he needed a rest from meeting with the buyers in New York. His strange preferences and sophistication would still be looked upon with suspicion. It would be far better that he grabbed his toy dump truck and explained that his plans were to join a union, drive a dump truck to the local gravel pit, and spend his evenings bowling or drinking with the boys at the local tavern while plotting how he could seduce the plump and succulent bar-maid; "Nothing to worry about with this kid."

Meanwhile the girls were being groomed "to land a man," keep him from straying by having a delightful and supportive personality like Samantha Stevens had on "Bewitched," and to start raising a brood of their own. The days of Mary Tyler Moore as Mary Richards and of Marlo Thomas as "That Girl" were far in the future. The main tasks for girls, even in high-school, were to be watchers of male activities or cheerleaders or drill team members in order to keep male confidence at the max and to assure them that whatever victory they won on the basketball court or playing field would redound to the everlasting glory and honor of their team and community while the losers would have to slink away in shame. [With such primitive and primeval training is it any wonder that Americans enlist in the military so that they are given a license to kill people in their foreign lands, in Iraq, Afghanistan, or anywhere else where American power and the right to exercise imperial rule may be questioned?] The terror of long-hair on boys at the time of the war in Viet Nam was that it indicated a threatening descent into femininity that might somehow compromise our martial spirit.

Where did young transsexuals fit into this American "bi-polar universe?" We were raised in an emotional desert. Girls were taught to bond with their toys, to give them personality. What would we think of a little girl who wrenched the limbs off of her dolls so that she could rehearse being an orthopedic surgeon? What would we think of a little boy that gave his trucks names and cuddled them? It would in those days have been time to be referred to the school guidance counselor who would later meet with the parents of the unfortunate child to point out that though there was no cause for immediate concern or alarm, the child was definitely manifesting an adjustment problem but one which might be remedied with appropriate bonding with the same-sex parent. The boy then would be whisked off for a day at base-ball games eating hot dogs and a masculine girl would be taken to the beauty parlor for a day with mom. All of this was done in the name of nature. No one ever thought to question that if gender was so natural, then why was it that an entire society was mobilized as though fighting a war with a hostile fascist power in World War II to reinforce these "natural gender norms." Gender blurring was as forbidden then as if the communists were planning to subvert America from within by turning the boys into pansies and the girls into baby-dykes. "How insidious can those commies get?"

[What red blooded American boy would refuse to napalm a village in Viet Nam and watch the little brown people scurrying about far below? What American girl who would not support our brave boys bringing American ideals of wanton consumerism to a benighted peasant culture?]

Every boy over eighteen during the Viet Nam years needed to carry his draft card with him at all times so if he was stopped and searched he could prove that he was not a long-haired hippy or an un-patriotic homo too impatient to wait for Nixon to achieve "peace with honor" by turning more of Viet Nam into a defoliated moonscape by the use of bombing raids and defoliants. Our illustrious nation would never, our Presidents told us, be accused of being an impotent giant or what was called later a nation of pathetic girly-men. Even now the biggest item of our national budget has little to do with homes, food, education, community development, or health-care. These are all rather feminine concerns after all and as such "girl toys." No, we spend our money on defense spending and good, honest, death-dealing weapons, boy toys all. After all it's the American way to assume that the defense of home and hearth and the women who tend them is the highest function of masculinity rather than building, preserving, and sharing in order to build a better world for all of the peoples of the earth.

Secret Societies

The result of all our gender training is that there are two secret societies among us, each one based upon gender distinctions. If a set of transcripts could be made based on the conversations that take place in gender exclusive areas it might be possible for each gender to understand the other one at last. The reason of course that no one has done so is that mystification and secrecy are requirements for the current dance of the sexes to continue. Each sex must retain a somewhat idealized notion of the other in order to continue to find its members attractive.

Fear, envy, and mistrust may exist within each gender when confronted with the other, but if each knew what the other secretly suffers it might be possible to end sexism and cross-gender cruelties at last. Each sex has the power not only to answer the deepest psychic incompleteness of the other but to use that very dependency to manipulate and to degrade the other sex as well. Often that mutual distrust and even hatred is voiced by using directly disparaging names or comments about the genitalia particular to each sex. This process of deliberately cheapening the other is designed to deny the abject fascination and lack of complete fulfillment and possession that often makes marriage the scene of a struggle for dominance between husband and wife.

If one were completely cynical one might define marriage as an extended truce between potential foes. Men and women tend to seek their own society once the minimum for maintaining a household is met. In spite of a desire for quality time and romance most women can think of nothing worse then having a man about the house all day. When would she call her girlfriends on the phone for some real talk? Similarly men tend to flee to sports-bars or golf courses with a lightened spirit as soon as their chores at home are done on a weekend.

To be transsexual then is to have a foot in each camp. Male-to-female transsexuals may never really understand male feelings since they were overlaid with what they were trained to consider as their sex-inappropriate interests. Transsexuals, at least for most of our lives, were in effect prisoners behind enemy lines in male locker rooms, athletic teams, and even in military service since we were always female in our identifications. It is naturally difficult then for many male-to-female transsexuals to turn about after transition and to regard men as attractive. The memories are still too recent of male lavatories and the bluff physicality of male bodily functions.

I cannot speak of this directly, but it seems to me that female-to-male transsexuals might find it as awkward to initially approach a woman acting out of a male identity when he remembers the cutting comments and laughter of those long post-mortems where women inevitably discuss the blatant tactics to embody their femininity and major fashion mistakes of their date for the evening later with their girlfriends. A female-to-male transsexual may also need to adapt to the fact that except for the occasional "good buddy" or when they are very intoxicated, most men do not live in the same verbal and confessional universe that women do. Except for anger, most men keep their feelings to themselves and carefully hide their vulnerabilities from each other so as to maintain the subtle pecking order of male society. A man's interests have very little to do with his body for instance with his aches, pains, or other health concerns. Sex may be discussed, but not in detail. No man is comfortable hearing details of another man's sexual performance although there might be a passing fascination in imaging what the women did or felt. Men tend to channel their emotions through the medium of women just as women may channel their own aggression through men.

The best way for a man to drive a woman crazy is simply to ignore her. The best way for a woman to drive a man crazy is to ask him what he is feeling when he doesn't even know himself. Each sex would like from the other sex what it can never provide on a continual basis from its own ambiance and asks for what, if each sex could receive it, would rob the opposite sex forever of its own piquant challenge and charm. We need to believe in the carefully wrought mythos of the opposite sex. Human beings are born in a state of primal severance and it is not impossible, though it is simplistic to say, that the transsexual condition of alienation is less distinct than we presume it is.

Transsexuals are not alone in seeking for some primal unity within their own persons by embodying something of the other sex. Perhaps some degree of domestic production may lessen the need for continual psychic imports from abroad. One may wish for some degree of sexual "energy independence." It is not only oil that is a scarce commodity in the modern world requiring more domestic production. This is not to say that every husband is engaged in looking longingly at his wife's negligee (although some do). It is to say though that men would like at times to be able to speak the entire truth of their hopes and fears to at least themselves if not to their close male friends and business associates. Women similarly might enjoy being freed at times from their constant reminders of the burdens of female sexuality, to dance with the maenads in midnight revels, and to escape above all else from the expectation that as a woman she must always act like a lady.

Transsexuals, as professional transgressors of our most sacred norms, come at last to see society as massively artificial and to wonder whether the game is worth the candle, as the saying goes. If there is such a thing as "transsexual-power," in our often sad and lonely lives, it is that to varying degrees we have come to understand this mutually exclusive secrecy maintained between the sexes by virtue of our experience of involuntary reconnoitering of foreign ground. That secrecy, though it may be necessary, bears with it a terrible price. We transsexuals by being forced to know the confines of each prison house come to understand that inner dynamic that feeds desire and fear between the sexes and is also the source of our deepest delight in each other when on occasion we meet as equals.

Of Cross-dressers

The cross-gender literature speaks of primary and secondary transsexuals. The main differentiating factor between the two appears to be the age at which gender change wishes occur. Primary transsexuals usually cross-gender identify from their earliest years and seek at least some form of cross-living in their teens or twenties whereas secondary transsexuals often marry and have children in a heterosexual union and only seek transition in their forties or fifties. Secondary transsexuals often start out by identifying first as what were once called transvestites and are now called cross-dressers and only later on decide that their cross-gender feelings are not relieved by clothing alone.

68

To transsexuals the constant talk about clothes by cross-dressers is as boring as the talk of hormones and surgery by primary transsexuals is to the male cross-dressers in support groups. (While to those who are not gender-conflicted both groups may appear to be making much ado about nothing). In fact post-operative transsexuals are often so tired of the whole rigmarole of transition that the entire subject of gender change can become as boring as talking about last year's ulcer. I will go further still and say that the experience of transition makes sexual differences boring. The entire phantasmagoria of sex with its various body-parts around which society has elaborated various fetishes, becomes silly and comic after awhile. This is why pornography is so absurd, because it tries to retain the fascination of the hidden when it is spread all over a page like so much stale deep-dish pizza in a cardboard box. Cross-dressers may make every effort to retain an aura of magic in the process of sexual transformation but the process finally becomes as repetitive and pointless as watching a child's electric train making endless circles on its limited expanse of track. The increasing acceptance of gender divergent behavior may eventually kill the frisson of cross-dressing just as all ritual becomes empty when it is no longer surrounded by a sense of awe and fear.

Cross-dressing seems to transsexuals who risk taking their act out on the road everyday before an often hostile public to be too tainted with middle-class conventionality to deserve respect. Real women do not enjoy lounging about in fluffy dressing gowns unless they are movie stars of the Norma Desmond vintage. If the drag queens are the runway models of the cross-gender world and the transsexuals the average women, the heterosexual cross-dressers usually resemble a collection of plump and awkward women from a political fund-raising event. Many cross-dressers in the various pride parades that take place in June appear in their paisley blouses and navy blue skirts looking like they just came from a PTA meeting. No threat is posed but people still seem frightened of such a mundane and harmless activity.

I cannot tell you how often I have heard transsexuals insist that they are glad that they are conservative and can pass as real women (read boring) not like those (said with scorn) drag queens. These will preen and brag for hours that their wives even went shopping with them and they were accepted as real women. Uh maybe that was because they were flashing credit cards, the fruit of living a masculine life while their drag-queen sisters were working as hair-dressers or florists and being beaten up on the streets fighting for gay rights. If I sound indignant it is because I believe in solidarity with the street queens and resent comfortable middle-class insularity. I also can't understand why anyone who comes from the GLBT community can ever even think of voting Republican.

Many transsexual autobiographies wear everybody out with tales of the reluctant and disapproving spouse who finds in middle-age that she has hitched her star, not as she hoped to a broad-shouldered hero, but to a man who secretly wants to wear her pantyhose. What if a husband abandoned her because she just wasn't feminine enough? A little competition along the gender spectrum need not be a game changer. He may on occasion look like a younger version of her but is that the end of the world? Many kind and loving cross-dressers end up getting thrown out of their houses and are denied custody of their children while their butch-looking wives walk away with generous divorce settlements from sympathetic judges. If there is anything dumber than persecuting people for wearing girl drag in a society where men and women appear daily in camouflage fatigues in our new unisex armed-services I cannot image it. A more harmless if perhaps confusing predisposition than to cross-dress has never existed. Yet human lives are broken in pieces over the issue of that secret stash of lady-garb in the closet. Ridiculous! What a waste of decent human lives!

I am sorry to be less than sympathetic with wives who feel that they have been brought down in the world because their mate no longer sits with the pot-bellied, masculine, beer-chugging boys salivating over the occasional shots of the cheerleaders on the side-lines of football on television but instead may have been caught by their wives watching a women-oriented cable channel while wearing a dress. Of course if she is transsexual she may watch almost nothing but these stations. Why worry? [Unless he also starts dancing in the bathroom to Abba CD's and has more than five albums by Cher or Barbra Streisand...psssst, he just might be gay and not transsexual at all!]

Tragic Trannies

The term "tragic trannies" is the transsexual equivalent of the old drag-queen term "booger drag." Of course the term is relative because to anyone who is younger or prettier anyone might be called a tragic trannie. The term has its use though because it acknowledges the simple truth that there are transsexuals who do not even begin to approximate a sufficient number of the gender clues of their destined gender to pass as members of that sex. But their pain is no less real than those who are gifted with beauty and grace. The significance of "tragic trannies" is that they both testify to the reality of their condition by the abuse and ridicule to which they are often subjected and the jarring nature of a non-conforming gender presentation in public. The standards of appearance that we impose upon women are such that when even genetic females fail to meet them, they are objects of humor, embarrassment, and even aversion. For this reason surgery is anything but "cosmetic" in the case of transsexuals and should be covered by insurance. No greater disability exists than to be a focus of ill-intent and misunderstanding whenever one appears out in public.

At many a Freedom Day Parade I have observed the brave march of the various cross-dressing groups, which usually contain a substantial contingent of "tragic trannies." What is noticeable is that their expressions share the same enjoyment of a day when they can be supported by the larger GLBT community and affirmed for the courage and dignity of simply being who they are. No one who has not experienced it can imagine the freedom of being out in the open air without fear of rejection, ridicule, or (in the old dark days) arrest for appearing in one's inner gender as best one may. To that degree there are no "tragic trannies!" For such as these there is now facial feminization surgery as a remedial option to enhance the quality of their lives. But even as they are they are beautiful and valuable people and we in the GLBT community treasure and are proud of them.

Why do People Kill Transsexuals?

Of course the ultimate tragic fate of transsexuals is to be a murder victim. It has always been my opinion that the transsexual life course is a set-up for contradictory imperatives, exclusion, and victimization. Even the requirement of full-time living in the preferred gender role irrespective of readability sets transsexuals up for acts of violence. What sort of doctor would advise a man with angina to shovel heavy loads of snow, but the medical transsexual service industry mandates full-time cross-living before consideration for the very surgeries which might guarantee a successful transition experience. Many transsexuals spend years paying high priced medical professionals and therapists off by pursuing lives of prostitution and may acquire AIDS and physical abuse for their efforts. By assuming the very victim roles that genetic females are trying to shake off they double the tragedy of our genetic sisters.

There are all too many assassins out there. How many rich talkshow hosts have profited by using the tragedy of transsexual lives and confusion to boost their ratings? Transsexuals appear to generate primal anxiety in certain types of people, particularly bigots and egotists who imagine that transsexuals have adopted deliberately transgressive behaviors in order to infiltrate or compromise fundamental categories of gender or sexual experience. This implies that transsexuals are the sexual equivalent of illegal immigrants and should be hunted-down, revealed for what they are, and expelled. Of course the ultimate expulsion is to be ejected from life itself through violence.

Transsexual behavior is seen by such as these self-appointed gender police to be deliberately and arbitrarily subversive rather than as manifesting the true expression of the transsexual's inner sense of herself. It is precisely the type of man who defines himself as above all else not-female and who refers to women as bitches who is likely to resort to violence when he encounters a transsexual who he might find attractive. The sexual insecurity that makes him denigrate women makes him hold in utter contempt and horror any male-to-female transgender person who has penetrated his outer perimeter, which denies any conceivable homo-erotic attraction possibility. Violence may also be acted out towards female-to-male transsexuals or lesbians, not because of any attraction towards them, but because they represent a threat to his presumed sexual territory, to his imaginary right to possess any female at will without any competition from what he views as an illegitimate quarter.

It is this feeling of justification and entitlement that explains why transsexuals are so often killed. Who are these "things" that they deserve to live, to love, and to be treated as human beings? It is only a matter of degree between prejudice and lethal violence because both deny the dignity of the other person. Once transsexuals are denied the full measure of consideration due to all people because their experience and self-definition is seen as alien, it becomes possible to kill them with impunity and all too often with immunity.

The same pattern of exile that greets transsexuals in employment, public accommodations, and insurance coverage are the gender equivalent of the Nazi Nuremberg Laws and they tend towards the same final solution. The path to Mauthausen and the Pink Triangle is paved by negative and exclusionary attitudes. The people who laugh at or ridicule transgender people are for me little better than closet fascists. The heartbreak that this can cause still rankles within me. The shame and tears are often born by a vulnerable part of the self that resembles a child and this makes these assaults even crueler. It must stop. Any society that overlooks anti-gay or anti-trans slurs is ignorant and barbaric and when done in the name of religion they are simply inexcusable. People of good-will should confront this type of behavior with the same condemnation and outrage that apply to racist comments or vulgarity, strip away the anonymity of abuse and the implied assumption that it is okay to abuse us. It is not!

Trannie-Fests

What happens to transgender people of various stripes and colors who for whatever reason cannot afford to transition? Are they cured? No, what they do then is to live in various states of denial and various degrees of frustration and anguish. Many find symbolic ways to act out their gender role and by doing so find some measure of comfort. Some may find solace in a certain type of sustained mourning or a low-grade depression, a depression grown familiar from their lonely and secretive childhoods. Others may simply put their heads down like a bull and rush headlong into the various challenges of life and keep busy and distracted and so forget their cross-gender urges. Some may finally enter transition at the stage of life when others are grandparents (as they themselves may be) and start wearing mini-skirts rather than the long dresses and discrete pantsuits of their gender congruent age-mates. Finally there are those who save it all up for a big gender blow-out at one of the many trannie-fests that occur around the country.

What I call a trannie fest is a week of workshops and various activities that allow the cross-gendered to live for a time in a supportive atmosphere the lives that they wish they could live all the year long. There are workshops on make-up, hair or wig styling, feminine deportment, dealing with family issues or religious concerns, and all manner of evening activities from shopping with trans-friendly (or trans-greedy) merchants, to fashion shows, talent exhibitions, and usually a formal dinner and dance. For one week the order of the universe is reversed and the secretive becomes open and behaviors that are usually met with ridicule or even violence are replaced by praise and an atmosphere of security and general acceptance and encouragement.

Trannie-fests bear little resemblance to the drag-balls and vogueing of the big cities. You will not see lean and skinny drag-artistes, painted to within an inch of their lives, all big hair, attitude, and a prissy sense of the adulation that is their due as royalty. No models or lovely young things that may look like plucked squabs out of drag, where they work in fast food establishments or flower shops by day, are seen at a trannie-fest. No, some of these ladies have substantial jobs and live in comfortable houses. They may have wives, children, and grandchildren at home. No one shouts faggot at them outside seedy bars in the old part of town. They are called sir wherever they go in daily life. They know what it means to have male privilege and respect. But something is still missing, so they board a plane, train, or car

74

and come to out-of-the-way places for a Women's Woodstock, a trannie-fest.

There they will pack up their bras and girdles, their mail-order pumps in sizes 10 to 13. They will look forward to greeting old friends, all the Sandy's, Yvonne's, Carla's, and Heathers who will be tottering around all week between frenzied workshops and changes in their hotel room. They will sit on chairs stiffly and smile coyly through beaded lashes at their peers and know for once that they are not alone. They will look admiringly at the few among them who have been able to afford to go all the way. Some will even have had their faces reconstructed and wired or stitched together once again to form a more feminine version of themselves.

Some of the guests at a trannie-fest are even beautiful, perhaps not as pretty as the fragile drag queens many of whom could never have passed as men if they tried, but they are still pretty. There may not be the easy flow of line and contour that nature provides, but there is still something that says woman and only woman about them. They have crossed over the great desert of transsexual being to arrive at Mecca at last. Others will need to be satisfied that they may not be pretty, but still they are post-ops genitally and as such are women at last. Our society focuses on genitalia as the definitive signifier of sex. But the dry legal mind will always see a penis-bearer as a male even if she is feted in Milan after walking the catwalk to display the latest creations of haut couture. The point is that being yourself to the best that you can be should not be reserved only to the beauties among us or to those who have the wherewithal and courage or desperation to "go all the way."

Trannie-fests are democratic. The title of Miss is bestowed upon all comers and everyone has the right to be what is called en femme. It would be easy to laugh or poke fun at the occasional musk-ox or water-buffalo that goes sashaying past until one remembers that many respectable and well-connected and fully genetic dowagers do not look much different.

Many trannie-fests cater to the senior set. As transgender life has become more widely accepted and as laws protecting us have passed, it has become possible to go out for a night on the town without being arrested as in the barbaric days of old, when reading your name in the newspaper the next day was not uncommon as you explained to your weeping wife who planned to start divorce proceedings (unless that is you promised to "never, never, do that again.)" If this all seems to be much ado about nothing, we must remember that the domestic laws of America were until recently enforced by strictures that, if they were merely to reinforce doing what is "natural," need never have existed at all. We may forget how revolutionary was Dr. Frankenfurter's admonition to Brad and Janet that they not get strung out by the way he looked. But then to recall those days of major oppression we would all now have to do the time-warp again.

Not that the oppression is over by any means. If you keep your ears open at a trannie-fest you will hear of some people who do not know what will await them when they return home after a week among "those freaks." How many wives see a trannie-fest as a week of sexual orgy among scantily clad bacchantes? These events are really more like a cross between a little girl's tea party and a convention or a meeting of sorority sisters with everyone showing off pictures of themselves in their best outfits. No, there is nothing to fear at a trannie-fest, just a little love, empathy, and support, perhaps the first that they have ever received from their fellow males who are for this week friends and sisters.

As is true for so much in the transgender world a time may come when trannie-fests are passé. They may someday be the gender equivalent of suffragette conventions. Will gender categories grow more fluid in time or will a new essentialism make the barrier between the sexes grow more impermeable and sexual identity more determinative of the course of our whole lives and the governors of our behavior? Is the whole LGBT thing a phase of human rights long overdue the advocacy of which is soon to be forgotten or will a winter of new oppression soon pass over us? Only the future can tell if the current Taliban-like fulminations of the advocates of religious freedom to oppress others will triumph.

In the meantime the question is whether we will be willing to understand that such cross-gender events spent away from their home communities, even if they result in actual sex-change for some, may serve a real and essential purpose to find clarification for individuals who are trying to deal with such a personal issue and to finally be comfortable with themselves in their gender.

A Day at the Make-up Counter

The cis-gender equivalent of what I have called a trannie-fest is a visit to the mall. A day at the mall wouldn't be complete without visiting department stores. Front and center as you enter are the make-up and fragrance counters that sell items worn by one half of the population to please and hopefully attract the other half of the population. The ladies behind the various counters look like the magazine covers while the ladies in the various chairs look like the women that you meet everyday at the grocery store. Each woman leaves though looking a little bit more colorful and dramatic and with a smile on her face. Most men traverse this gauntlet of women with perfect brows and scarlet smiles quickly so as to gain entrance into the more gender neutral areas of the store. Getting past the area of make-up counters though is as difficult as getting past a big-busted woman in an airplane isle without looking. High-chairs or stools are set out before mirrors and busy women with various color palettes and brushes are working industriously away to create that high-cheek-boned and contoured illusion of perpetual youth and loveliness as best they can on what they have to work with.

While not as threatening to heterosexuality as the foundations department where no man feels comfortable unless he is accompanied by his wife and even then he looks alternately bored or fascinated at all the voluptuous forms of the displays bulging with lacy cups. However, the area with the various heavy-duty foundations for stout Wagnerian women made of spandex that could resist a tsunami can so traumatize a man that only repeated trips to Victoria's Secret can make the female form attractive again and erase the ghastly image of grandma's unmentionables hanging in the guest bathroom at home when he was a child. But let us not think of foundations here. Faces are so much more pleasant and less threatening while fragrances at least are pleasant to all sexes.

One of the primary bonding stations in the life of a female is a visit to the make-up counter. Women love fussing over each other's faces and talking while they do so and often finding in the process that they share common ground.

"Everything on my body is about four inches lower than it used to be. My butt is now my upper thighs and I have to stand on my head each morning to put on my bra!"

"My daughter asks me not to wear my favorite black dress and I ask her who made her the chief of the clothing police."

The young "twenty-somethings" sit among their elder sisters. These young things are possessors (for a time) of one of those perfect faces that require no contouring to achieve, one of those fortunate feline faces that are so fine-tuned that makeup is completely superfluous on them, like using a nail file on a diamond. But one of the problems with perfection is that it cannot be improved. The slightest variation is already a step away from the ideal so that whereas most women improve with make-up those with perfect faces tend only to recall past glories as they age. Makeup can never restore "the glory that was Greece or the grandeur that was Rome." Too much perfection can be a disadvantage. Drag queens and transsexuals often look as good as we do because bigger faces allow for a greater margin of error when painting. Contouring and color can create form just as a landscape or seascape on a large white canvas can contain anything that you want to paint there whereas an ivory cameo allows little space for error and the etching must be perfectly chiseled into form.

The importance of a visit to the makeup department though is simply being in this accepting and friendly environment and seeing how generous and caring women can be with each other. How they talk one another through crises and make the day a little brighter with colors, powders, and pigments. Maybe their men at home will notice, maybe not, but the woman feels better and her peers have told her how nice she looks and she is smiling when she leaves and that is more than enough.

Of Early Sex Change Clinics

If it seems ungrateful to refer to sex change clinics as predators let me ask you this question:

What would you call it if a group of people who in the comparative leisure and esteem granted by their professional knowledge and the social acceptance of their role as psychologists, surgeons, and their appending clerical types of nurses or assistants were allowed to make what amounts to life and death decisions about the lives of transsexuals and all the while knowing well that society has (unjustifiably in my opinion) made them the gatekeepers of gender reassignment, these "candidates" only hope, that it was them or nothing? Who gets that sort of power over others?

The raison d'être of sex change clinics is the assumption that these clinics and their personnel know what they are talking about and can decide just who is to be a likely "candidate for sex reassignment surgery." How would you feel if a group of people, no matter how bright and educated, could sit around a table and discuss whether you deserved to retain your current gender assignment or should be re-categorized, in other words that your sexual citizenship could be revoked at will by their power?

What if you are gender non-conforming? Should you fear that a group of people could send you forth into a lifetime of gender-exile simply because you do not meet *their criteria* and be denied a clitoris or a penis as the case might be? I for one have learned to detest petty bureaucrats in public office, but I despise even more the bureaucrats of supposedly complete and official areas of human knowledge that are really still inchoate and uncertain. To use socially assigned power thus presumptuously is for me the very essence of predation.

No one has ever calculated the suffering and death among early transsexuals who were denied some means to alleviate their profound unhappiness in the last three decades of the 20th century and instead were simply dismissed as a "poor candidate for surgery." Fine, but were they a candidate for something at least? How about just survival? Or were the un-pretty, unpopular, abrasive street queens and T-girls unworthy of a chance at life and happiness. Even a tragic trannie deserves some happiness and care.

But those were the days when medical supply and demand and the rarity of aid made it possible to pick and choose the cherries and to reaffirm sexual stereotyping by choosing candidates who could pass most easily as genetic females. "Strut your stuff pretty baby and make your doctor proud." But, for good measure consider the real costs of "the real life test" that mandated a year of complete cross-gender life before surgery (which many transsexuals undertook prematurely only to fail). Who was there to help the brutalized transsexuals pick up the pieces of their shattered lives? What social insurance can restore broken relationships?

The whole thing was profoundly self-serving though for the gender clinic personnel desiring to avoid future liability and damage to their professional reputations for any bad outcomes. The more honest thing would have been to simply admit openly that they were engaged in a premature social experiment and that the rest of society was not willing to follow them. The legal right to exist must precede the medical! Even today many "pre-op and post-op" transsexuals who are indistinguishable from genetic females for most purposes are denied designation as female and the same for male-to-female transsexuals.

I can still recall bringing up this issue in transgender support groups and making everyone uncomfortable. What if you step off of the elevator and there is just no floor there? Well during most of my life spent as a transsexual person that has been the reality, one denied by both transsexuals, gender clinics, and society at large, that no matter how "passable" a transsexual is she is still considered as transsexual and as such not "really real." Transsexuals are like social ghosts haunting our callous society and just waiting to be reported or found-out. This is why I have argued from day-one that until transsexual status is out and open, proud and free, that we have not arrived, that we do not really exist as full human beings.

So forget the "real-life test!" Transsexuals are guerilla fighters on the gender frontier where to fail is economic marginalization, ridicule, ostracism, and death. To leave transsexuals alone to bear these costs indicts the entire society and makes those who practice this distancing predators – that some of these predators claimed to be trying to help us makes no difference because they at least should have known better. Until transsexuals are treated with the imagination and sensitivity appropriate to such a profound dislocation in their lives as that caused by transsexualism all merely ameliorative efforts will be inadequate. Transsexuals are what might be called "designated victims" or "test cases" for social experimentation as the society decides the political and social significance of sex and gender roles and in street lingo, "That just ain't fun honey!"

I for one don't feel grateful that just to exist as gender congruent can cost upwards of $50,000 in America for what is still called cosmetic surgery. What are the insurance companies afraid of, that if they open their coffers to cover surgery that just everyone will want a sex change? If there were that many transsexuals out there we could form our own co-op! The beginning of human dignity is the right to be ungrateful for small favors when what you are asking for is a human right to just be who you are.

Of Power and Powerlessness

If power is the means of getting what you want, then the big question is what do you want? Transsexuals if they are male-to-female may seem to be giving-up their power because we assume that men are the powerful sex. We think that men take the active roles from business to sex, but even as a child I knew that although it may seem to be the bee who is the more powerful, always buzzing about, it is the flower that has the power with its deep inviting funnel and nectar. Oh and those buzzing bees are females so my analogy breaks down here but they are the active principle so that's what I'm emphasizing here. In Wicca to be a woman is to draw down power into oneself from the Goddess. No bonds hold tighter than those made of silk. The thorns of the rose are always below the blossom. They are designed to ward off those that would cut the flower before its mission is complete. No flower wants to end up in a bowl sucking water instead of the rich nutrients of the soil. So woman is actually the primary sex.

It is said that woman is from the earth and man from the heavens in the I-Ching and in many other conceptions of the primordial principles of life. To be a woman is to be reconciled to femininity. Women learn finally to make peace with the biological in themselves. A woman learns that her life pulses with the tides and the seasons. Her body is less responsive to acts of pure will. She can fight this but if she turns and swims with the tides, her body will be born up by the great ocean of the universe. She will find in the end that she is bigger than her own ego. She is part of the life-force that flows all about her and within her. What we term female artifice is actually as natural to her as it is for the fields to bring forth flowers after the rain. Her entire being represents contradiction and stress, the hunger of the earth for the lightening of male desire. The force of a women's sexuality lies in its power to excite, to arouse, and to fulfill. Hers is the great polar magnetic field that orients all things to itself. Everywhere she enters there is a subtle change in the atmosphere of the place. Women note that another woman has entered the room and men check her out. She is why fashion exists, why beauty pageants exist, and why it is the bride who walks down the aisle and not the groom.

So I wonder which sex is the active principle after all and who really has the power? It just may be that male-to-female transsexuals have always known this, so that genital surgery is not castration, with its aura of decimation and emptying out and loss of power, but is rather an "envagination," an acquiring of power. Suddenly there is a rose between the thighs, something to dilate. She possesses at last something that is waiting to be filled. Suddenly she knows the power of invitation. She can feel what it is to be possessed by a force that mirrors her own. Her power is so great that it can be fulfilled even on those occasions where her own climax is not achieved because she can see the effect that her mere bodily being has on the male now clasped and encased within her. She can see in his eyes and feel in his pulsing body the force of life itself flowing through her and in her and about her.

She can feel life within herself as well, so that every menstrual period is a loss, a something that might have been and wasn't. If her life is filled with mourning for every little death, she is also the source of life, the very ocean of being. This makes her somewhat fearful and dangerous and that is why men (and women too) have always feared sorceresses and witches. Life and death are closely allied and to be able to give one is simultaneously to be able to bring the other. Death follows all life. We bless woman and curse her, revere and despise her, because she is reality itself. Woman resists the force of will. She will be what she is in spite of all efforts to contain her and to make her over into a predictable pattern. Life is filled with asymmetry after all. Power is never equal because if it was the flow of events would cease. One side or the other must always yield for when it does there is an explosion of joy and life is renewed.

To want power then on all occasions is as absurd as to be always powerless. The current of life is an alternating one. The same man who seems to conquer you may lie like a child at last, weeping at your bosom, grateful that you are there and will be there tomorrow when his strength returns and he comes seeking you again in your unfathomable darkness. Woman as goddess is something that every woman seems to know.

Culture Victims

Do I make too much of womanhood by speaking of women as Goddesses? So you want to a woman huh? No, not really; I want to be a star, yes a star, or maybe a debutante walking out on a dance floor with some young man from Yale or Princeton who smokes a pipe and discusses Camus and Sartre and even then I don't want to start aging and have him leave me one day for some new hottie on the corporate payroll. I have wondered if I were a transsexual in an African village would I walk around with fifty pounds balanced on the top of my head. If I was a Chinese trannie in the 19th century would I want to have little tiny feet and be carried about because I couldn't walk? Well then, why do I want all of those little symbolic ways that we signify gender in America? Why did I always scan the models and actresses for role models growing up and read gothic romances with pictures of helpless heroines in flimsy silk frocks with their hair blowing in the wind on the grounds of the ancestral mansion? I loved these novels where the young governess had come at twenty-two only to be sheltered by some rich but sinister distant cousin who might suffer from the ancestral curse of madness? Maybe transsexuals are simply culture victims like their genetically female siblings. Woman as signifier, it call comes down to semiotics in the end.

That's fine of course but when does real life begin? I used to ask that at gender support group meetings? I used to say, "So after the hormones and the silicone breasts and the operation, what then?" I used to get silence at that, because not a lot of transsexuals were political then. I used to get tired of hearing of the marginal triumphs of passing as "real girls." It all seemed so sad and pathetic … but it was my life too.

I think most women reach a point where they look around them and ask, "Was this what it was all for? The hair-color, the nails, the fills, the dieting, the avidly scanned magazines, and later the silicone, the Botox, the lifts and tucks, all so some guy will look at us and manage to wrestle a little blood into his middle-aged penis and ask us if we are ready? Even if you go the lesbian way, a day comes when you look across at a mirror image of yourself and when you start to complain she says, "Don't tell me honey, I'm a woman too you know."

So basically, who needs it? What's the point in being a woman or a man either because they don't have it any better than us? They may not have to pad their bras but they have to carry around a bit of equipment that leads them around like a bull with a ring in its nose for most of their adult lives only to end up with broadening hips, a big gut, a bald head, and an "old buddy" who just lays around all day while the girls seem to get younger and more distant every day and their daughters tell them, "Daaad, I wish you wouldn't stare at my friends."

Transsexuals age just like everybody else. The difference is that most of us have to compress vast arenas of unlived life into the years remaining to us in our identified gender after transition. But for those of us who have become worn down through dealing with the strain of meeting the expectations of others throughout our lives as transsexuals, sex and gender may have become a tiresome topic for us.

This is what Robert Burton had to say about sexual desires in old age in his 17th century treatise, "The Anatomy of Melancholy:"

Some dote then more than ever they did in their youth. How many decrepit, hoary, harsh, writhen, bursten-bellied, crooked, toothless, bald, blear-eyed, impotent, rotten, old men shall you see flickering still in every place? One gets him a young wife, another a courtesan, and when he can scarce lift his leg over a sill, and hath one foot already in Charon's boat, when he hath the trembling in his joints, the gout in his feet, a perpetual rheum in his head, a continuate cough, his sight fails him, thick of hearing, his breath stinks, all his moisture is dried up and gone, may not spit from him, a very child again, that cannot dress himself, or cut his own meat, yet he will be dreaming of, and honing after wenches, what can be more unseemly?

Worse it is in women than in men, when she is aetate declivis, diu vidua, mater olim, parum decore matrimonium sequi videtur, an old widow, a mother so long since (in Pliny's opinion), she doth very unseemly seek to marry, yet whilst she is so old a crone, a beldam, she can neither see, nor hear, go nor stand, a mere carcass, a witch, and scarce feel; she caterwauls, and must have a stallion, a champion, she must and will marry again, and betroth herself to some young man, that hates to look on, but for her goods; abhors the sight of her, to the prejudice of her good name, her own undoing, grief of friends, and ruin of her children.

So there it is, the human condition, so who needs it? Is it possible to resist culture and biology as well and just be well, a post-sexual? Why should I have any gender at all if it is such a joke? Why not just feel sorry for everybody, rich and poor, gay and straight, young or old? Why not just sit like a Buddha beneath a tree and throw away that charge card, purge the wardrobe of all those running and knotted nylons that in a few years will go creeping down your skinny legs while you wait to cash your social security check at the bank? Why not stop gathering your bosom together and packaging it in an uplift bra and wonder at church if the people standing in the row behind you are looking at your butt in those baggy knit pants? Why confront an aging stranger in the mirror while wishing sometimes that we could wear what Muslim women wear when we go out every day, not because it is required, but just to hide. Do women in Afghanistan call each other up and say, "Oh Darling, you should see the cute little tent I bought at this little shop just down from the Madrassa. You can't even see my eyes. As I walked home a young guy said to me, 'Great grill, baby.'"

Well, are our own fashions any less dumb? Who needs these cultural absolutes if gender is merely a construct and not a destiny? So I say that we are all culture victims and maybe transsexuals more than most, because we pay all our lives, not to reach the heights of the gender Himalayas (although some do), but just to reach that chilly first base-camp above the plain of androgyny. So the question that every transsexual must ask is like the one that the guy in a Dirty Harry movie had to ask, "Do I feel lucky?" I say this because it takes a lot of luck to be culturally happy in a society that keeps happiness just two steps ahead of us all the time.

New Generations

I just thought I'd see what was new in TS support groups since my memories of early support groups are of crowded rooms of heavyset middle-aged ladies, often with a larger contingent of cross-dressers than of transsexuals. What I observed recently was interesting primarily because of the age differential and a corresponding change in acceptable gender vocabulary. My use of the casual abbreviation "trannie," which in my day was cute, is highly disfavored today as not only retro but disrespectful and tinged by the "sex-for-hire" exploitation of transgender people. The new terms are more political and fluid.

The other thing that stood out was that many of the participants seemed already to occupy a sort of undifferentiated body-space only awaiting the final assignment of hormone therapy to move them out of what appeared a common midpoint existing between the genders. The young participants seemed more savvy and confident than those from my class of transsexuals. I represented the legacy of high-drag in a setting that was street-chic

86

or casual. There was an overriding sense of the present and little in the way of long-term goals or visions in their lives. Gender change appeared to be viewed as simply one normal course or option among many that they might pursue.

Meanwhile I was always looking for that desire to reintegrate at some point with straight norms which was a common attitude among transsexuals of my generation and a principle motivator for our genital surgery. The goal of sex-change for us was always the prospective reacquisition of a status of legitimacy that was latent somewhere "out there" and to be conferred upon us by others. These young people seemed content to simply declare a status to be justified in claiming it and I found that admirable but surprising. They seemed content to be permanently different whereas my own generation saw transition as a path back into the normative structures and life courses of the majority of people who were not gender conflicted. I still saw some of the usual pain and alienation and the unease that these produce. But above all else I wondered how they saw me.

Perhaps I was seen as a legacy of the past, a high-camp dinosaur transported from the fabled midnight double-feature picture show. Be that as it may I was all too aware of the long decades that now stretched between us and I feared for them because I knew that they too would have to weather much to be like the "trannie" relic that sat with them in their circle that evening. I came from the era of primitive and experimental sex-changes, the clanking Franken-chicks fresh from the gothic slab, grateful for whatever we got, and often it wasn't more than an unfeeling four-inch canal between our legs.

Mutual Deception

Part of the mystique that keeps the sexes bonded is the pretence that the other sex is somehow preserved from some of the unsavory aspects of possessing a human body that must use metabolism to sustain its existence. Entire industries exist to sustain these illusions so perhaps some of the anxiety that surrounds our sex-segregated bathroom facilities is the fear that the truth may come out at last, all about sanitary napkin dispensers and women who follow the "hover-craft" policy to save time.

Maybe it is feared by some that male-to-female transsexuals might report back to the men, "All that stuff about velvet-lined chairs and couches, perfumed fountains, and Houris serving iced-tea and sushi is just nonsense. There are just a whole long line of private stalls and one long mirror with about twenty women wiping the corners of their mouths with tissue and reapplying lipstick and talking about their relationships. Oh, and it took forever. I couldn't get out of there quick enough."

Transsexual Voices

When we hear someone speak either in actual conversation or in print we look for the male or the female "voice." So deeply rooted is our gender-identified world that we learn to discern and to discriminate between the finest gradations of tone, pitch, manner, and even vocabulary and to assign the speaker to one gender or the other. What I call "voice" is so primary that even when other gender insignia indicate that a female person stands before us we will often say sir or madam based on how we perceive the voice of the interlocutor. The voice even more than the eyes is the true mirror of the soul.

So it is that when I read transsexual autobiographies I find myself listening for the "voice of the writer" for what has sometimes been called "the core gender identity." Are transsexuals really women trapped in male bodies or are we disillusioned males who have chosen the female gender as a sort of fall-back position? Since there has traditionally never been a box marked "neither" or a box called "all of the above" in human life, it appears imperative to definitively sound either male or female. This means that it is essential to learn and develop a voice that is appropriate to the gender that one seeks to embody or portray in the many transactions of daily life.

We are all seeking for the soul of the speaker and since we assume that even the soul is gendered and manifests the sacred inner essence of the other, we always listen in order to make that primal discrimination between the sexes. To do this seems to be innate in human beings as though mating decisions were constantly being made (and perhaps they were and are). It is not impossible that healthy humans at the hunter-gatherer stage of hominid existence spent all their time, in the absence of the internet and video games, exploring one another and engaging in sex play. Our preoccupation with voices then stems from our primal origins.

There is all the difference in the world between a conversation between men in a bar and that of a woman and the woman manicuring her nails at a nail salon. Women tend to speak more freely about all of the various aspects of their lives and relationships. This is traditional among women. It was the women who laid out the corpse and keened at Irish wakes while the men drank stoically in a corner and amidst well-timed toasts spoke of the virtues of "himself that is now gone nivermore to return, God rest his soul." We portion out our verbal styles. We expect a woman to allow her voice to rise slightly at the end of declarative sentences as though any assertions made are subject to correction by any better informed person present, especially if that person is male. We do not expect from men the same finely honed emotional distinctions about their bodies, health, or their feelings and relationships as we do from women. Even the time spent in personal grooming is allotted according to sex and we would assume a man to be very vain or fey who spent much time in the men's room scrutinizing his face or general appearance and if he stood for a moment sideways to the mirror to check out his profile he might cause a general stampede of men away from his immediate vicinity in anti-gay panic.

Women relate to each other in intense face-to-face encounters and can discuss almost anything, whereas men feel extremely uncomfortable when one of them is in a confessional mode or frame of mind (unless both are very drunk in which case they can bridge the usual body-gap that must be maintained at all times between straight men). In contrast we allow all manner of intimacy between women, although a prolonged kiss may raise eyebrows. Whereas two men kissing even at a gay wedding, no matter how perfunctory, is seen as scandalous (and yucky besides).

So it is that when transsexuals come to write their autobiographies it becomes natural to insert various gender insignia: cutesy comments or lush and gushy outbursts to stress and to say to readers, "I am woman." I am no exception to this rule. But what do you hear in my voice? Can you tell that I am a tall and willowy blond who drives a jaguar and never ventures outside the house unless I have matching shoes and handbag? Or am I a small and narrow-shouldered brunette, a blue-stocking with thick glasses who likes to hang out in a New England internet café? Or am I a butch Montana cowgirl type? Once conjure up an image of my body and the voice changes to accommodate the image. Or maybe I am an arch and satirical drag-queen? If so the image changes once again. Maybe I am a dry professional woman in a severely cut business suit and carrying a brief case who drinks very dry martinis each day after her workday spent in a high-rise office complex. Or do I betray my origins and does some faint whiff of testosterone pervade even these sexless sentences? Who can say? But you are listening aren't you for some clue to my "real gender." It is the natural thing to do after all.

Autogynephilia

One of the theories of transsexuality is that the transsexual simply wishes to assume the sexual function of a woman, not because we are women inside, but because we want to imagine what a woman feels, a sort of vicarious life. Not only does this theory, which bases itself on the sex drive, fail to consider the early pre-pubertal onset of transsexual feelings and Gender Dysphoria, but it also fails to consider the pervasive extent of cross-gender interests in transsexual persons. Transsexuals resent the implication that what they are looking for is a mere sexual thrill by "masquerading as the opposite sex."

Like the song says, "But that's not the way it feels." I will go so far as to say that transsexuals feel something equivalent to the absent-limb syndrome. Gender Dysphoria is more than merely mourning for what never was. There is a real sense that one is wired for different sexual organs. It is like the track has been laid on the path to womanhood (for male to female transsexuals) from our earliest memories. Our entire childhoods and often even more of our lives are spent swimming against the inner current of our being so as to be accepted and to fit in. When we finally turn around and swim with the current we want everything that we have been denied for so long. We are like a homely girl in grade school who suddenly realizes at eighteen that she can be pretty. This can lead during transition to a certain degree of vanity and pre-occupation with looks. It can also lead to what might be called feminine over-compensation, what is termed "flaunting it," or in street lingo from the sixties being a "flame queen." This is simply caused by the desire to secure our tenuous foothold in the female camp by some definitive action or the acquisition of sufficient bodily integrity that we will never again be mistaken for men. This is not exhibitionism but an inner struggle to build a moat or firewall around our long-sought gender identity and expression. We are also seeking some recompense for the lost days of preening with hair ribbons and lace as little girls. Some observers have said that transsexuals do not represent the women of the current age but the women of their mother's generation. We are sexual dinosaurs fresh out of some fifties beauty parlor or some sixties flower-power commune or whatever age matched our adolescent dreams of being women.

In my own case I was raised in a house where Vogue Magazine covers provided my early images of what I wished I was. I am a face-trannie. I simply love faces. I have been looking all my life for the perfect contours of cheek-bone, upturned nose, and eyes, eyes, eyes that would shout to the world: I'm a girl. I have a certain preference for the aesthetic distance that leaves actual sex in abeyance.

For other transsexuals it is all about vaginas. They are haunted by that "thing between my legs." For them their desire is always centered on getting rid of "the thing." For others, and I am in this camp also, it is all about cleavage. I don't want a mere lady-like PTA meeting bust line. I want to join the camp of those girls whose sweaters beckon the male gaze and leave a little trail of erections behind me wherever I go. Some of this may be revenge. Some of it may be generosity. In any case I was born to have a silhouette and I am willing to bounce when I run and put up with a little neuralgia of the spine to add a cup size or two to my bra. I don't want to look like a cow of course, but I like what I've got and still want that extra inch or two of projection. I want my advance guardians to let the world know I am coming. I want perky trumpets to blow reveille at dawn and at nightfall to feel them nestled together snuggly as a sigh off to sleep. I want them to feel free to move around when I move and to carry the rhythm of my step for a millisecond after I come to a full stop. I'm not looking to play lots of tennis. Sports bras have little appeal for me. At the same time I don't want to fight sixty year old nurses and grandmas for the last ugly bra on the shelf in triple D. I think what we need is a Victoria's Secret for the girl who couldn't keep her secrets if she tried. Finally, I want just enough left over so that the cup overflows on top without achieving that effect by side-to-side pressure that makes me spend the day wishing that I was not wearing a bra at all. I want the face of an angel and the body of, well not an angel. I think Jessica Rabbit had the right idea: "It's not that I'm bad, I'm just that I'm drawn that way."

Can we talk booty now? Many women would love the slimness of boy hips and would be willing to regain the behinds that they had in early adolescence. I think that I am of this camp. I don't want a behind that makes me think that someone is following me beneath my skirt. I don't want hips that make me wedge into airplane seats. But I do want curves laterally and just enough behind to sway gracefully in a long evening gown.

Since I can't get pregnant I don't need pelvis width. It is from bone that most posterior curves take their source. Above all else I don't want a flat behind or worse a side-dimpled guy butt. This means that I take my hormones like vitamins every day and keep just enough extra fat on my body that I don't see my butt melting away like an ice-crème cone in the sun. I could use foam rubber of course to build me up "back there," but it pleases me that everything on my body is flesh and blood or behind-the-muscle silicone and hence forgotten. I don't want to feel that if I am peeled that the luscious fruit within will peel away as well. I would like to stand there all perky and powdered with each curve beckoning potential lovers to some final valley of desire and fulfillment. Is this Autogynephilia...or is it...me?

Of Indeterminacy

When trying to explain these essays to a friend he suggested that I try to work them over or at least think them through to avoid misinterpretations or disagreement by the reader. I in turn argued that it was the very process of thinking a thing through that distorts primary experience. I tried to explain to him that what I call evocative writing as opposed to expository writing calls for an entirely different approach to the writing task and makes different demands upon the reader.

Expository writing attempts to reach a conclusion that can be evaluated for credibility while evocative writing simply is. If evocative writing has a purpose at all it is to evoke a reader response rather than to persuade or to convince by being formal, finished, or comprehensive. The goal is simply that the reader should enter into the experience of the writer even if that experience is temporary or even contradictory and invalid when viewed from some outside standard. Evocative writing is not true or untrue but rather is incomplete, unfinished, bristling with burrs like cut but unfinished steel. This type of writing seems highly appropriate for as problematic a subject as transsexualism is.

Transsexualism is by its very nature unfinished and incomplete. Any transition between two conditions that are presumed to be mutually exclusive must by its very nature be impossible to traverse because there is no common ground, no bridge, and no isthmus to connect the two. The problem that my friend was having then in desiring to hold the writing of this book to a higher or more serious standard was, to my way of thinking, that he was asking that it be other than what it is. I am writing about transsexualism, which is all about being what you are by not being what you were. What is this process but one of profound indeterminacy?

My friend then suggested that I try to use a little more right brain, or was it left brain, as though I am aware when one shades into the other or can control that slide anymore than I can keep the masculinity out of my femininity or vice versa. He ended up by telling me that he has the same problem with his wife's writing. He pointed out that my high-flown and elaborate explanations of my intentions indicated that I am in fact a female. I don't doubt for a moment that his intentions were that I write the best book of which I am capable whereas I merely desire that the book be written any way that I can get it out because it is painful to write about these things for me. It does occur to me though that it is just these sorts of disagreements that may be indicative of a fundamental difference between the sexes with men preferring either/or and women preferring a both/and approach to life.

Of Oedipal and Other Nasty Complexes

It is a point that may never be settled, which came first the transsexual or the fathers who may create transsexualism in their sons in order to avoid competition from them or prevent the necessity of bonding with them. It would be a tragedy if a transsexual's identity was really a split-off portion of an insecure man who could not tolerate competition in his own house from another male. How many fathers who tried in every way to eclipse their sons with their own ego needs while those sons were growing up blame their sons for not measuring up to a manliness that was systematically crushed within them at an early age? Is this why some fathers loath their transsexual sons, because they hate looking upon their own handiwork? By the same token, many transsexuals never emerge out of the shadow of the only parent left for them to emulate with some prospect of success, their mothers. It would be an interesting study to attempt to answer these questions.

Many fathers either hold women as idols or hold them in contempt and often both at the same time. Insecure with the feminine in themselves they punish it in their transsexual sons. By the same token many transsexual sons are nauseated by masculinity in general in order to hide a secret desire for revenge on the one who was the first male model of their lives. It would be the ultimate tragedy would it not if a life in search of the paraphernalia of feminine seduction was simply a desire to find love from a man who had proved again and again that he could never accept a close relationship with his own son because of his own insecure masculine ego.

Such fathers use other family members as slaves. Their wife and children are all too often treated as property and as mere reflections of themselves. The problem with their transsexual sons then may be that the reflected image is all too true. It reflects the actual man and not the ideal image that the father would like to believe about himself. Woe to all truth-tellers to the king! What these fathers hate in themselves they also loathe in their sons. The sons in turn seek to awaken desire in men only to deny its fulfillment. This dynamic may be true in those transsexuals who are asexual or who wish to control by seduction and also in those transsexuals who are acting-out and promiscuous. It is all the same game after all. In castration is safety - no more wounds are possible to those who embrace the wound as a state of being – the vagina as display of an eternally open wound that ends the transsexual's pain by making her pain manifest to all.

Similarly it is just possible that female-to-male transsexuals come from homes where the father, perhaps fearing the desperate love and desire of his transsexual daughter for his love only pushes her away. She then unconsciously opts for identification with the male in order to be a pal or accepted by him since he appears to denigrate the feminine and only to revere the masculine.

But these psychodynamic theories however great or small of a role they may play in the development of transsexualism are probably superseded by an inner biological causation factor. How we become what we are will always be a mystery. Our personalities emerge out of an impenetrable bank of fog and indeterminacy. It is often asserted by conservative religionists that every child deserves to be brought up in a home with parents of different genders so that these diverse-sexed parents may serve as role and relationship models for their children, but I suggest that the nuclear family is in many cases a war-zone of hidden conflicts, jealousies, inhibitions, and suppressed incestuous desires. Love within the family must always be tempered lest it overstep boundaries or suppress the budding identity of the child. Competition for the sometimes scarce emotional validation and limited emotional supplies may arouse resentment for the parent of the same sex, or in the case of those children who are moving towards a homosexual identity, resentment of the opposite-sexed parent.

Other theorists blame homosexual and transsexual identity formation on an excessively close identification with the parent of the opposite sex so that the child's own natural identity or heterosexual development is impeded. However, I suggest that the two-parent-two gender households in which most gay, lesbian, and transsexual children were raised somehow produced these divergent offspring, so it may not be too much to say that being raised in a so-called normal home may be more psychologically challenging than is commonly believed. To negotiate the minefield of disappointments and sheer economic dependency that holds many families together and to create any sort or degree of personal self-worth and emotional stability is all that many children can manage to achieve.

It is the family then that is the breeding ground for social ills as often as it is the refuge from the cold, cruel world. For transsexual children, who make up a sizeable group of America's "street kids," it was precisely the vehement insistence upon "normality" that caused their expulsion from the family unit as exiles. They were not "cured" by the environment of rejection and suppression that they encountered in the pious family crucible.

I have also heard many stories of the sense of betrayal and infidelity that many wives express when their husbands, who have long suppressed their transsexual identity, finally crumble into a late acceptance of it and become women in later life. Transsexuals often enter their new lives with a tsunami of recriminations and rejection following them as the price of their decision to finally try and forge a stable identity in the gender opposite to that which was assumed and assigned to them at birth. These pressures are no small measure of the discontents from which transsexual persons suffer even after negotiating a successful and complete gender reassignment. Add to this the effort to unlearn the old gender patterns and body language and the often severe social reprisals to which they are subject, the discrimination they often face, the costs of counseling and surgical procedures, the loss of jobs and friends, and the difficulty of forging new primary relationships and you have the reason why books such as this one are being written.

Begging for Permission:
The Plight of the Lesbian Transsexual

One of the great commonplaces of transsexualism is the case of the late in life transsexual. Many transsexuals marry women and raise families only to discover that what they chose to regard as merely a haunting fantasy of another life becomes a sex-change imperative in their forties or fifties as their testosterone ebbs. The pattern of their life-long depressive episodes becomes clear and much to the surprise and chagrin of their mates and children they announce that they have always been female inside. What often follows is a typical transgender tragedy. If these latter-day transsexuals are spared the street life of those who have declared themselves earlier on that often follows telling their parents that they wish they were girls, the tragedy of the late identifying transsexual can be even worse as she watches the esteem and achievements of a lifetime melt away as she begins her transition. Lost wives and children, lost homes and jobs, all are often the outcome faced by those who are trying to live as women after a lifetime of bending all of their efforts toward presenting themselves as heterosexual and as male. Sometimes a modus vivendi has been concluded with wives that has allowed a certain amount of secret cross-dressing during the marriage, but the announcement of a final transition has been a different story for many an aging transsexual. The permissive attitude that she has hitherto maintained is replaced by chagrin and hostility.

It is to prevent the human damage of this scenario that today's young transsexuals are being protected in their identity from early youth and prescribed hormone-blockers to delay the onset of puberty. The male body morphology that comes then with the wave of testosterone can only be reversed later by costly and painful surgeries and with varying degrees of success. Delaying puberty can avoid most of this damage and give the male-to-female transsexual a chance to lead a more normal life. Hopefully this new generation of transsexuals will see the last of the dinosaur transsexuals, the heavy-set and brow-bossed women with the frightened smiles who are attempting to make their debut at mid-life into the world of femininity. The very heroicness of their efforts though should be seen as the proof-positive authenticity of their feelings, but instead it is precisely these people who are seen as manifesting a horrific delusion and desire to embarrass those who are near and dear to them by entering so late in life upon the sex-transition process.

As someone who came-out early in life and paid the price for grabbing the ring early, mine is a case of the primary transsexuals who adapted guerrilla tactics in order to survive. I am a remnant still living from those pre-Stonewall days. I am still HIV negative, alive, and almost as pure as the driven snow although I have walked on the wild side and witnessed what I did not dare to do. From the safety zone provided for me by Catholic prohibitions I have walked past many a tiger pit unscathed. If any wine and roses still exist for me it will require from me a little body-shop work and polish at this stage to knock back the decades by one or two notches. I won't get my teens or twenties back with their delightful opportunities to commit folly in the pretences of love with all and sundry; instead I have opted for serial heartbreaks with women as my sexual lifestyle. This has allowed me to safely traverse the sexual minefield of AIDS and the other consequences of reckless living during the times I have lived through.

I have neither wife nor children. I didn't get an early sex-change operation paid for by a willing male sponsor seeking a lover as many transsexuals of my age and time did. Instead I took whatever paths opened for me and compromised when I needed to do so. I survived inside as best I could. Still I received more of the goodies of being a girl by being young and open. Daring brought me early the freedoms that are only now being assumed as obvious human rights in schools and wherever transsexuals are beginning to be protected.

The function of age is to survive to get to the better times. I now expect to join the rapidly thickening genetic females who are morphing towards the male as the floodtide of their estrogen wanes. I am less stooped by osteoporosis than they are. My residual testosterone has kept me from simply drying up and blowing away like a wisp of straw as so many women do at my age. Nature appears to cancel swiftly the Goddess gifts of youth to women. As a former model once said, "When you're out of eggs, you're out of business." But I never had any eggs in the first place and silicone has a long shelf-life so I am looking better than my years would indicate. I like playing age-roulette and being taken for a decade or two younger than I am, but the clock is still running for me and I know it. Sadly, I still carry an ingénue inside of me. I would have liked to be a heartbreaker and to have spread ecstasy abroad with a mere smile or the wave of a manicured hand. Instead, I may be beset soon by suitors with string ties and gray hair only to tell them that I have always loved women, but desired what only a man could ever give me (go figure). I suppose in the end I will be just another literary mother figure with tales to tell, a good cook, and one who wonders and regrets that her life turned out the way that it did. But I'm alive and as I said above I could easily have gone the way of many. Now there is only me and others like me to tell how it once was, what we went through, of the great vacuum that existed then of information and of hope, and the pain of carrying another soul about in what always felt to me like an alien sex-role.

Of Silver-back Males

I would like to say here a few words about how physical maleness appears to people like me who share an idealized concept of what being a woman would mean. Male characteristics appear to male-to-female transsexuals as a personal deformity. Even those male-to-female transsexuals who desire a male partner are not looking usually for what I call "a silver-back male." The boardrooms of corporations are filled with them. Pot-bellied and with scraggly hair growing over their backs they resemble nothing more appealing than their wives who often appear to be slightly feminized versions of their husbands.

I have often thought that transsexuals who have experienced in their youth the assaults of social ostracism and who by whatever means have finally somehow attained their goals take a certain cruel pleasure in reflecting back upon society the very norms that social expectations once dictated that they must embody in order to be accepted as female. So it is that there is a subtle hunger within some transsexuals to not pass as genetic females. After all, as one approaches the goal of womanhood many transsexuals begin to appreciate for the first time how little value our commercial order places upon women except as consumers of products and services that cater to a female market. One need only think of the costs of hair-care, nail salons, and clothing boutiques, let alone the costs of day-care for single moms or home schooling costs. These burdens are often in the minds of straight women who turn with amazement to male-to-female transsexuals when they ask, "Why would you ever want to be a woman?" The answer of course is to avoid the alternative which is to turn over time into a silver-back male.

Yuck!! The entire male body, at least to the male-to-female transsexual, is a horrifying throw-back to the Neanderthals. What is the use of their male heavy brow-bossing unless they plan on getting hit in the head by a club? Do males really need heavy jaws and great jowly cheeks? Is there something innately appealing in their bald heads and their great whisky-barrel torsos? Is it really necessary to look as cross and forbidding as men so often do? Was this characteristic evolved so as to frighten off marauding foes? The male face is an exercise in asymmetry. If male faces are attractive at all it is because they signal some primordial source of power or protection as well as a certain humor or kindness at times, but when regarded simply as an aesthetic object they only appeal to someone who loves angles and leans toward the paintings of Picasso.

Still to be fair it must be said that even female faces may be improved at times by a slightly wider mandible, a more piercing eye, or a slightly firmer chin. But if this is so, then are not men more handsome when they leave the male behind? Would a woman rather wake up next to someone who looked like Ernest Borgnine or to someone who looked like Tyrone Power in the morning? As one who must navigate alone through the world each day, I enjoy the prospect of seeing as few silver-backs as possible. I prefer to reserve them for a trip to the Congo (if I ever go there). Above all else I do not want to see one staring back at me from the mirror!

Trannie-Chasers

There are men though who prefer transsexual women as their sexual partners. For such men transsexuals are women without the problems that come with possessing uteruses. Since transsexual women work so hard to develop and manifest the extreme end of femininity and are often grateful and thrilled by any intense male desire directed towards them as women, it would appear that the contract between transsexual and trannie-chaser or trannie-wolves as they are also called would be the ideal match from the point of view of the fulfillment of mutual desires. The problem of course is that, as is true for most compulsive sexual behaviors, the end result is usually heartbreak for the transsexual woman when the man goes on to a new embodiment for his "ideal woman." It appears that part of being a woman is all too often the experience of eventual abandonment. The trannie-wolf may never cease reminding her of her former status by putting her down as not a "real woman."

On the other hand there are transsexuals who will frankly exploit willing male benefactors to finance their surgeries only to leave them afterwards. All this may be saying no more than that the sexual arena is usually menaced by selfishness and subtle cruelty on both sides. There is a subtle form of sadism in being desired, in knowing that a man is firmly on the hook. I have often thought that the entire industry of stripper-clubs exists so that each sex may show its resentment and contempt for the other. The entire industry is based on the illusion of control. The patrons think that they control the dancers by getting them to perform for money while the dancers know that the patrons will always come back to the lure of their bodies. What looks like a free exchange is actually motivated by mutual fear and hatred and no one is really better off in the exchange because they are all cheated of real intimacy. This same dynamic often operates in phone-sex, on the internet, and in she-male clubs. People settle for control rather than the uncertainty and terror of real relationships. After a few years transsexual women learn what hookers learn, to always get the money up front.

Brooding over the entire scene is also the specter of time. Transsexual women soon learn what women in general learn, that time is not their friend and as the model Lauren Hutton once said, "When you're out of eggs, you're out of business." The last half of a woman's life is the part where she has to learn to survive with diminishing powers that were derived from her mere sexuality and her ability to offer or withhold sexual favors. Even if women are daughters of Diana and of the moon, the period of waning far exceeds that of their waxing powers. Partly, this is true because women as a group will likely outlive their lovers and husbands only to mourn in solitude with the other widows who soon grow to outnumber the available men.

Women learn at last that the real reason that nature was once so abundant in the favors granted to them was to ensure the survival of the species. In four short years from twelve to sixteen she grows from girl to goddess. Nature appears to flower in her with the very suddenness of spring. The whole world turns in wonder at the generosity that she may assume will always be expended on her to deck her out with an abundance of fullness and charm. But what nature gives is as swiftly taken away and the years soon bring a new set of faces to the covers of Vogue and Cosmopolitan. That is why the new baby-boom is currently occurring: women are remembering again the virtues of their fertility as women. The old days of sterile careerism and contraception appear to be over at last. It is currently "in" to be pregnant.

Since young transsexual women with their slim hips and silicone busts cannot bear children, many are beginning to suspect that they may have to settle for trannie-wolves because the straight men that they desire may actually want babies after all. Transsexual women may be in the process of losing their one big advantage over the genetic females of the era of the seventies through the nineties, that period which represented the high point of the feminist tide, the advantage of their sterility. There was always something remarkably clean and neat to trannie-wolves about vaginas that never bled and that didn't have a uterus waiting like a beast of prey behind the cervix to entrap them into the responsibilities and permanence of fatherhood. Only the most extreme forms of Gender Dysphoria may also include a desire to be able to conceive and to lactate. Transsexual women may soon find that the center of their own needs includes more than simply instilling a state of desire in a man. We may want to fulfill that desire and to manifest those very biological factors that a generation of feminists told women they did not need in order to have a full life.

Can a body though ever really be female that is not a conduit for new life? Was there a reason after all that little girls loved their dolls? If women are rediscovering their post-political selves, where does that leave transsexuals? Will we all end up in smart disco-bars dancing before businessmen from Japan in Bangkok who need a weekend's entertainment? Or will they come to the states looking for investment opportunities in our newly exploitable nation? Maybe the fate of transsexual women is best read by that of the Kathoey of Thailand; we are fun girls. We are the new breed of geishas scientifically constructed to fulfill male desires. This raises the question of the body not as an essential mode of being human but rather as signifier, as a thing and an exploitable one at that. Is our authenticity as women only evident to ourselves and others when we are as easily exploited as our genetic sisters?

Fighting Words

One of the reasons that I have personally drawn the line where I have by not accepting sexual attention from any male is that it is incomprehensible to me. I have spent my life seeing males as the enemy and their domain as the embattled zone that I was trying to infiltrate, not for sex but just to avoid trouble growing up by appearing as one of them. I tend to reduce most males to their lowest common denominator. Of course gay males are more approachable, but as is the case with many transsexuals to be affirmed by the sexual interest of a gay male would be like being dragged back into masculinity. If I wanted to be buff I would hope to attract women not men. Besides, I still carry within me all of the instincts of male mistrust and territoriality. I love a verbal struggle and will argue all night about almost anything. I am too invested in my face to value exchanging blows but my own past has been peppered with getting into various people's faces.

As an example, one night in a local bar/steakhouse in my early years of transition, I ran into an instance of the usual name calling that most people cease having to deal with in grammar school. I didn't like the downtown gay bar scene then because I hated the whole idea of being forced to assume a ghetto existence just to survive. Besides I liked the fact that this particular place was warm and cozy in winter and with an elegant outside terrace in summer. It had a gas fireplace and clean walnut tables. I could bring my books and read quietly and look up now and again and see a familiar face to greet.

On this particular night the bar was more than usually crowded. Suddenly over the din I heard the familiar chant, "F---ing faggot!" shouted by a male voice as loud as he could. I scanned the room but met no eyes directed at me so I eventually returned to my book. About five minutes later the incident occurred again. Again I did nothing, but my concentration was broken and I was angry, very angry. I felt that electric tickling sensation of shame and irritation that is physiological in origin. The crowd had shown no particular interest or herd behavior at the periodic outbursts and the bar-tenders were too busy to protest. Besides, it was almost impossible for bystanders to locate the voice. It was not an everyday event though, except on one other occasion when a regular had gratuitously offered to punch me in the face apropos of nothing, since then I had not been forced to deal with any "situations." I had never had real trouble there before and I was fairly well known as a regular patron. On that prior occasion I had reminded the would-be assailant that as an attorney I would see to it that any assault upon my person would result in a lawsuit of such dimensions that he would be answering interrogatories and saving to pay attorney fees rather than bar-tabs for the rest of his life. He decided to reconsider at the critical moment and return his hands to his sides.

I think what I hate most about anonymous name-calling is the sheer effrontery of uttering insulting words addressed to a complete stranger. Besides, yelling "faggot" conveys very little information, even when accompanied by the adverb "f---ing." Why not tell me something that I don't already know? Also, as a transsexual I always wanted to suggest that the speaker might be a little more specific in his assignment of my person to a specific group. For instance how about trying this one for a change, "You damn Gender Dysphoric individual. Why don't you go back for more electrolysis, your beard is showing?" I mean try and vary your program once and awhile so you don't sound so boring. But it was always the same phrase whether shouted from a passing car or like it was that night at the restaurant.

In any case I figured that this particular evening was functionally over anyway, at least for me. So I got up and pushed back my chair and while walking out I stopped at a table to say hello to some people I knew there. I asked them what they had thought of the shouted comment. They explained that they were so sorry but the speaker had been sitting at their table earlier and was now circulating through the bar to get another drink. I told them it wasn't their fault but thanked them for taking some of the mystery away. I was almost out of the restaurant before it hit me. Why was it I who was leaving? I thought for a minute, weighing consequences. I was dressed pretty sharp that night and was feeling my oats so I pivoted on a heel and walked right back and re-entered the bar.

I saw that the guy in question was now back at the table and busy crowing and taking credit for having driven "the faggot" away. He had a big stupid smile on his face which faded to amazement and then a weird deer-caught-in-the-headlights look as I approached the table. I bent down to about two feet from his face and said in the most flirty, sassy, feminine, homosexual-from-hell voice that I could find, "Hi Honey, I thought I'd just come back so you could get a real good close look at a genuine, lavender wearing, butt-wiggling, real-to-life honest f---ing faggot." A look of horror came over his face. He was frozen in place and could only gasp over and over like a catfish on the edge of a pond and mutter his famous and original phrase again and again. His friends laughed and he never got up. I was laughing too. I turned my back on him then and made a little swishy exit with my head held high in a classic DQ style exit, an exit like one of the ladies on Dynasty would execute.

That kind of thing was a recurrent theme in the years of my early transition. It has not happened to me since for many years. One day it all just stopped. I'll never know why. Maybe society has changed. Maybe I am living in a safer place. Maybe I'm older now and not as sexually threatening to males as I was in my thirties. In any case I'm glad not to need to prove anything anymore, but old habits die hard and something of the old guard attitude is always there still (just to be sure that no one yelling "faggot" has buddies close by with baseball bats). Anti-GLBT violence is a group phenomenon in most cases. So like the sergeant on a television show from that same era always used to say as the police officers left the briefing room for their shifts on the streets, "Hey, hey, hey ... be careful out there!"

Sex

Most transsexuals have needed to spend so much of their lives just attaining gender congruity that sex takes on a secondary place. It is very alienating to say the least making love with organs that you feel belong to the other sex. This produces an inner shame and revulsion that is incompatible with intense sexual feelings. Something just feels wrong. Even after gender reassignment surgery many transsexuals as opposed to the group of professional sex workers sometimes called she-males are not particularly sexually active. Surgical results vary as to depth and ease of penetration and orgasmic potential can be problematic for some. In any case we often tend to desire romance more than sex as such. This may be the reason why transsexual autobiographies are surprisingly reticent in precisely that area where the non-transgender public may be most curious about our lives. Transsexuals are in the unique position to testify as to how it feels to have experienced sex from both sides. Not completely of course because we do not have uteruses. This means that a post-op transsexual's orgasm can only be explained to other transsexuals and even they may not report identical feelings. It may therefore be impossible to really convey feelings as such about sex but attitudes and desires are another matter.

We can say what we want from a sexual relationship and we can explain how we would like to be treated. Even here transsexual autobiographies have been on the whole surprisingly reticent. No Nancy Friday has shown up yet to poll us as to our inner imagery of sex, our secret gardens of desire and fulfillment. So until one shows up, this account will have to do. The sample is only one so is not statistically significant, but perhaps some genetic women may act as the control group for this little exercise in gender science.

Is it possible to talk about sex openly and still remain a lady? Men do so but usually in the most general terms. It is not that they fear that if they explain things that their friends will not think that they are gentlemen, it is that men imagine that male sexuality is so powerful and simple that all men will understand what they are talking about without going into detail. It is women then who have been left to explore the intricacies of the maze of actual sexual feelings. The path to the female orgasm is not a simple one. It has many winding curves and may be upset at any moment by failing to adhere to the chessboard of female imagery, feelings, and fantasy. I will leave it to the experts to explain every gambit on the board. This short essay may only hint at the path to checkmate by exploring a few of the major pieces and how they move.

The first principle of course is to understand that to checkmate me it is imperative that all players understand that there is only one queen on the board, me. The task of the male then is to play his humble pawns as best he can in order to fence me in. He should keep his knights in reserve to render me some signal service when I require it, such as rescuing me from dragons, climbing towers where I am imprisoned, or leaving his friends to rescue me because my car is stuck somewhere and I'm not a member of AAA. His bishops should never preach at me. Their sole function is to bless and approve of my position in any quarrel that I may have with anybody. They should listen, nodding their heads and clucking with sympathy during my confession which may be of some length. They should never grow impatient or ask me to cut to the chase.

As for castles, there should always be two: one is of course my dream home most of which is decorated according to my tastes although he may reserve a small and squalid den for himself. He may also have the garage where he stores his tools, toys, and weightlifting equipment as well as anything that I have grown tired of like his clothes and any other weird item to which he has grown attached through sheer longevity.

The other castle is our second home or retreat. This is where he can be allowed to shine. It should be a quaint mountain chalet, a beach house, or a lake cabin. It is there that he takes me so we can be alone all weekend doing things that are forbidden in suburbia. It can have a big couch and a substantial hearthrug with lots of pillows. The rug should be soft and not itchy to my naked back or put runs in my stockings. There should be a big stone fireplace where he builds me roaring fires in case what we are doing on the rug or the couch isn't enough to heat the cabin unaided. We should take long walks in the snow and I should be wearing a designer sheepskin coat with a fur collar and maybe a cute hood out of which I peer and purr with softly parted lips and laugh occasionally at his witty jokes and conversation as we walk with his arm about my waist. If he makes an occasional effort to grab anything I remind him that the hearth rug awaits us when we get home at which point he urges me to walk faster.

If it is summer I spend the day on the softly lapping shore in a bikini with a novel and wave to him with a long-nailed and perfectly manicured hand as he makes an effort to bring us in trout for dinner. If he is a hunter I will allow him to bring in pheasants or ducks but no deer. When we return to the city our nanny explains that our two darling adopted Rumanian children Hansel and Gretel have been as good as gold and wish to see their darling Mamushka before drifting off to untroubled dreams of remote castles in their far-off land. They are so excited about being sent off to summer camp so that we can be alone in the city. It is then that our devoted British nanny takes her vacation to Brighton so that we can be alone and really get down to business.

My husband is a much sought-after designer or architect or engineer or something (I have never been quite sure). He makes just gobs of money by making obscure marks on paper set out on some drafting board in a spare room. I knock on the door now and again and bring him snacks before walking out of the room with swaying hips, giving him one over-the-shoulder cat-like look and catching his gallant blown to me kiss before I gently and reluctantly shut the door. He usually only requires three or four industrious mornings per week to generate our three figure income. The rest of the time is more or less his, which means that it is mine.

I don't want him underfoot all the time though. When would I take my long bubble baths, comb my long blond hair, talk to friends, or go shopping with my five credit cards. I just love it when he looks at the statements at the end of the month and raises an eyebrow. I just tell him to wait a moment while I go to the bedroom and slip on a perfectly ravishing cocktail dress which I can wear to the local neighborhood party where I will spend the evening getting jealous looks from my friends and clandestine admiring glances from every man in the room. He agrees that the dress may join its mates in my giant walk-in closet and mutters something about how he might be able to write it off as a charitable contribution. After all it does beautify the neighborhood.

I don't want you to think that I am not socially conscious or spoiled. No, I do lots of things for him too. You need only look in the drawers of my vanity to find the latest in non-surgical beauty technology. I am still keeping the plastic surgeons at bay for my later years. For the present I rely on the many creams, powders, liners, and moisturizers (all of them state of the art) that I use to create the bewitching image smiling back at me from the glass. He on the other hand only needs to shower once a day, not rub me raw with beard stubble and not smell like a moose in heat when he takes me which he does at least twice everyday.

I wake in the morning and lift one pale and lily-stem like arm over my head to blot out the blinding sun shining through the windows of our home in the hills above Santa Barbara. I reach over with the other hand and pull up my spaghetti strap which has carelessly revealed one silken breast usually contained with some overflow in my DD bra. He has already gotten up to shave (so thoughtful of him) and to put on some lime after-shave. I just love it when he smells like a margarita. It would have been neat if he had gone down to the garage and brought out his arm definition by a few quick curls and lifts to give him that small touch of the ravening Cossack but he is trim and in good shape always and my nails can find all manner of ridges and declivities to explore to suit my fancy. He understands from long practice that I require at least an hour to make love. I like to consider that my vocal abilities contain a perfect symphony of sighs and moans with which to communicate and I expect him to listen in rapture to my every vocalization. Should I grow ardent and bassoon-like, I would expect that even this unaccustomed playing of lower notes may only serve to remind him that I desire him as much as he desires me. Men like to feel that you want them.

All of that is for later though, definitely fourth movement stuff. At the beginning I would wish him to treat me with all of the delicacy of a melody by Edvard Grieg. I do not want to be pounced on like a cat on a mouse. I want to be unwrapped until I lie there like Venus fresh from her clam shell. I need lots of eye contact and softly murmured praise as though he is just seeing me for the first time. No whipped cream and kitchen tables, I am not kinky, just a big bed with the covers forming a frame for our artistry. He lies next to me and kisses me until I feel his lips like some ardent young creature begging admittance to my mouth. I like to see him nestled against my breasts like Odysseus home from a long voyage. My breasts are really never mine until I feel them cupped in his hands. I like to reach down and feel him as he grows large and to feel his scrotum tight against his lean thighs. That is when we pause and he moves down to my legs and I feel him exploring the inside of my thighs. It is usually about then that my woodwind section, my oboes and clarinets begin a slow largo. I like love to be a little melancholy as though he was to soon be leaving on a long journey in a Viking boat at sunset and I would then be waving to him across a chill fiord with a scented handkerchief. I like him to remember that although further delights may await him I do not like being lapped like a dog slurping water at a dish. I have read something about hygiene. This means that I reserve my sweet pink orchid for only penile exploration. I am not like some fricassee!

An hour is alas all too short. Besides, something must remain for the evening since the hours of nine until eleven are reserved for adoration at my shrine. So it is that I communicate to him that the moment has arrived. He like Cortes may step-ashore in armor upon the continent of me. I expect him to take me like a rising tide creeping ever deeper into the bay of my being. At a certain point I want to forget about either of us and feel that we are part of some primal pattern of earth and sea. I want to hear the sound of waves crashing against rocks and see them grow thin and crystal green just before they break. I want to see sunlight dancing through the spray and I want all of the energy within him like some great wave to come over me so that I lie there drowning for an instant in all the bubbles that make my skin all cold and shivery so that my nipples are ready for the re-ceding tide of his grateful passion.

Afterwards, I want us to lie there like two bathers in a shallow tidal pool that is been warmed by the sun all of a long tropical af-ternoon so that when he leaves me and I lie there with the sweet salt tang of him still upon me I can fall asleep again and barely hear the close of the door later when he leaves the house to enter that bigger world that I don't have to understand because he is there doing battle for me...

[Oh, by the way, I've never really made love to a man, but if things had been different for me the above scenario would have been nice. This is what it feels like to be transsexual: to dream of what might have been].

Of Sterility

One of the problems of what I call a mediated existence, and by that I mean coming to inhabit a body that has been hormonally and surgically altered, is that the ordinary flow of events as dic-tated by nature has been deflected in some way. Of course we do this all of the time in this new medicalized world that we now inhabit. We prescribe insulin for diabetics, blood thinners for those liable to have strokes, antibiotics for formerly lethal infec-tions, etc. We implant new hearts, livers, and kidneys. We install stents in blocked arteries. All of these measures are adopted to preserve or to enhance human life. A similar rationale may be applied to those procedures which alter sex when this is mandated for mental peace and the complete human functioning for transsexual persons in the world. However there is one major issue remaining in regard to changing sex and that issue is its effect on one's intimate life, that of sexuality and the family.

I will leave the sexuality component for part two of this book while dealing with only one key aspect of sexuality here. One of the costs imposed by sex change is sterility in the sense of producing children by ordinary means. Transsexuals are not mere inanimate clay to be molded at will for purely aesthetic reasons. We are living persons and part of being a person is normally the ability to pass on one's genetic legacy. Before surrendering that fundamental aspect of being alive at all much thought should be required. Procreation is not something that all people do in all circumstances, but it is something that constitutes a source of unparalleled wonder and from it comes much of what human beings value in life. To forego this ability to share the gift of life after hormonal or surgical alteration is a great sacrifice when it is seen against the background of an entire life rather than simply from the point of view of present feelings of Gender Dysphoria. These feelings can admittedly at times assume such alarming proportions that self-destruction for some individuals may seem immanent. But still I advise caution before surrendering too early what may later be regretted. There is a very real sense in which our bodies are vehicles for linkages to other human beings and those links are usually forged within the family. It is precisely in family relations that many transsexuals suffer the most intense pain through rejection, divorce, or the loss of custody of their children. The validity of sex change procedures must at least weigh what may be lost forever before embarking on such an irremediable course of action. Being transsexual often entails great loneliness and a sense of being an outcast. To add to that burden a physical incompleteness and disability in such a fundamental area, particularly for young people, may lead to later regrets that may be hard to anticipate. For male-to-female transsexuals the inability to bear and to nurse children may actually be part of the gender pain that we endure.

On the other hand, parenthood may entail too much for those persons who are not even at peace in their own bodies. Children pick up on parental sadness and often blame themselves for it. Then there is the entire question of adoption and the adequacy of homes where the spouses manifest a sexual orientation or a gender orientation that is not that of monogamous heterosexuality. I am sure that most transsexuals would agree that life would have been easier and more complete had they been born in the sex that they now aspire to fully embody. Transsexuals often adopt a conservative outlook on sexual issues that seems to belie their own radical position as transsexuals. I am no exception to this rule. I often envy the happy families that I see at church and feel that I have missed much in not having married and not having had children of my own. These feelings are only becoming more intense as age begins to hint that the door of my own existence is softly closing. The torch of life has not been passed from my hands to others whose youth and promise might have been some solace for the pain that has been such a big part of my own days and nights. I do not have an answer for what other transsexuals should do with feelings such as these, but the issues remain and must be addressed and the consequences weighed before taking the path of measures that, however aesthetically pleasing they may be, cannot restore the lost functionality of one's prior gender attributes.

Looking for the Cure

Most transsexuals that I have known have done their best to avoid the ultimate solution of sexual reassignment. Some have joined the military, many have married and fathered children, and others have sought the ideal mate imagining that sex with a beautiful woman would cure them. But apparently the human spirit is not a sponge that can soak up masculinity from outside behaviors in order to implant a masculine core if it isn't already there.

For me "the cure" has always been symbolized by the phrases "breaking out" or "finding the dream." These mean, in the inner language of my being, those moments when I hoped that I could achieve a tenuous beachhead on the island of independence and power that I felt come with possessing a secure and unquestioned male identity. But I wanted even more than that. I wanted to achieve a state above gender, one superior to all desire, a state perhaps even above the human where I would be made one with my sense of power and pain and stand like a granite cliff rising above the sea on a summer day. I desired nothing less than that thrill of infinite possibility that comes upon us only in our youth, the hunger that my favorite writer Thomas Wolfe described so well in his great novels. I wanted the sense of power that usually only listening to music can evoke in me, not because I wanted the power for myself or to exercise some absurd political tyranny over others you understand, but so that I could feel it flowing through me so that I could be vicariously a part of it. It would be clean and pure, yet tinged with the salty tang of pain, but above all else this feeling would be fresh and untainted with the sodden human malady of sex. In this state I could perhaps forget myself and lose desire by being whole within myself and serenely independent so that I would never need to ask for anything and feel so dreadfully needy.

Even describing this set of feelings I can see how lurking behind its description there was always a sexual component remaining after all. Ideas and images seem to flow from those darker sources pulsing within the brain-stem. These echo along the spinal chord and take shape within us as images. Perhaps transsexuals are hard-wired for female sexual responses so that even when we think that we are feeling a sense of male power and climax what we are really feeling is that sympathetic passion, that desire to feel what the other is feeling, that opens a woman to embrace the onrushing life that fills her in sexual intercourse.

What is that strange fusion of separate natures that is called sex? What does it mean to live within a body? If that body seems to be the body of an alien sex then where do we look for the body that matches our inner sense of who we are? Yet even when we finally attain it and look down at our new vaginas and feel the weight of our breasts have we only exchanged one type of hunger for another so that now we go in search of an organ that will fill our new emptiness and hands to hold our long desired breasts, someone to tell us that we are at last beautiful?

Where did our former maleness go, the maleness that once saw female beauty as eternally outside of us and now must be found within ourselves while we seek out what, in outward form at least, was once the form of our own bodies? Where does this new hunger for the male within us come from? Is it new or was it there all the time but only awaiting release by the estrogens that our boy-bodies could not independently produce? Now more than ever we want to be women and to feel that the fire's feeble flame that we so long nurtured within us has called forth a male response and the fire is now burning fiercely between our legs and inside of us at last, the way it was always meant to be.

Who but we transsexuals alone can speak of such experiences from both sides of the human equation? This is why people find transsexuals alternately fascinating or fearsome, because we are driven by this strange cross-gender need to embark upon mythic journeys in our search to be whole and complete at last.

The Body as Signifier

The science of semiotics views language as conveying meaning through sign values. Is it possible I have often wondered that what transsexuals are really seeking is in the last analysis to be sexually bi-lingual? If so then transsexual surgical interventions are like many signs accumulated so as to produce not only a sense of inner congruity of thought, feeling, and self-image but also to allow the transsexual person entry into a social world that operates according to what might be called the syntax of the sexes.

If transsexuals are caught up in a world of signifiers than the question becomes what if anything lies behind the signs? Is it meaningful to speak of a transsexual essence and if it exists is it identical to the essence of a "real man" or a "real woman?" What does it mean to be real? May one exist alternatively or even simultaneously as both "real" and "unreal?" What is it that pushes us over the edge from pretense into reality? Or is it possible that the transsexual condition is not a thing at all but a drama, a work of art and hence a product of artifice?

Some theories have suggested that transsexuals are simply acting out one of the many games or transpersonal scripts that are ways of seeking meaning in a society and a culture that is obsessed with image and projection. If this is true then the definition of transsexual identities may not be univocal at all but should rather be approached by making the script conscious so that variations are possible and so that free-will may again assert itself. If transsexuals are living out a life script, then who is the author? Are transsexuals the victims of ambiguous or confused power relationships in the nuclear family? Are they the product of medical hubris, first to deconstruct (literally) the gender assigned or assumed at birth so as to reconstruct it later through technical means? Perhaps transsexuals are merely a natural variant and as such either a third-sex or even a neutral sex positioned between extreme versions of gender phenotypes and as such open to human decision and choice. Or are transsexuals simply another version of the old Frankenstein motif? Are we all versions of Myra Breckenridge? Should the artifice of our lives be evaluated and judged according to the degree of approximation to some ideal model of femininity or masculinity (what is called "passing)?" Or should the category of male/female be entirely fluid or subjective?

Should it be enough if the post-operative transsexual simply reports that she now feels a sense of inner peace, less conflict, greater social acceptance, or a better occupational adjustment? Are the people correct when they look at what is now apparently a beautiful young woman (or at least a plastic replica of one) and still insist that the order of the cosmos has been diminished by just that much, that it would be better to restore the skinny male kid with the big eyes and soft mouth that always drew abuse from his young male peers; at least then the "objective categories" could be preserved? What if she *is* miserable, maladjusted and condemned to living in her assigned gender as a man, as long as the planets orbit with less distortion and nature (that is in so many respects red in tooth and claw) is preserved unsullied?

Are we transsexuals not really persons at all but rather creatures of late industrial urban ghettos so that we are never more "real" than when we are seen shimmying and gyrating under disco lights to the sound of a synthesizer? Or do the "real" transsexuals put on an aprons somewhere in a small mid-western town and kiss their husbands goodbye before returning to the kitchen to do the breakfast dishes and set off for their own jobs at the local coffee-shop?

What about the trannie "death script" that includes a brutal death by strangulation at the hands of some incensed client while she is working as a prostitute to save up money for her surgery? May her murder be reduced to its sign value as the ultimate social reinforcement of the commonly accepted gender normative roles by killing the transgressor?

I have often wondered whether if Gender Dysphoria did not exist whether a multi-option society would not still have invented transforming surgeries simply to meet the market demand for sexually ambiguous or mixed signifiers? Have the bodies of all people today become no more than models of efficient or outmoded body-types? When technology mass-produces holograms and virtual-reality technology becomes perfected will it be possible to simply buy some software program and plug in our senses to translated images of what we would like to purvey to a willing consumer as our identities? Maybe a few museums will keep stuffed replicas of early transsexuals, those who actually used our original flesh and blood to be who we were. A dusty curator will show display cases stuffed with the soft pillows of our silicon breasts, left behind us like fossils when we die. A learned mathematician will explain the theories of sex-differentiated proportionality in facial features. Each season will show a perfected and interchangeable image of the ideal transsexual. Or are we artificial at all? Maybe the semiotics approach is wrong. Maybe we who are called transsexuals are really persons imprisoned as alien personalities in bodies that we always felt as resistance, not in their totality as physical, but only insofar as they condemned us to role expectations that we could never accept as our own.

To find an answer to these questions it becomes essential to listen to us. It requires an effort of imagination. Beyond all else it demands empathy and acceptance of our essential humanity, that we are not mere flesh upon a slab, that we are after all real. What if we aren't constructs, mere sociological data, or case studies after all? What if we have been demonized and used by various politicians to get votes or television to boost ratings? What if our sign value has eclipsed our value simply as human beings?

The Body as Artifact

In the beginning the very concept of being transsexual was one calling for desperate measures for desperate cases. The belief was that the transsexual condition represented such an extreme form of mind/body mismatch that only heroic and creative measures could save the patient (for patients we were) from a lifetime of mental suffering and in some cases from suicide. The task then for the prospective candidate for surgery was to convince the doctors that without being actually psychotic he or she was still sufficiently desperate so as to require these extreme measures of intervention. It was enough for the early transsexuals to be allowed any measure of gender congruity even if it entailed the loss of the ability for sexual climax. The transsexual candidate for surgery in other words was willing to sacrifice everything in order to gain integrity and congruity. The decision was motivated from deep within the personality and the result of that decision was to grant us at surgical hands the legitimacy of a re-integration with the social norms of a binary society in which heterosexual identity and not sexual preference dictated everyone's life-course.

With the current acceptance of gay, lesbian, and bi-sexual orientations the transsexual experience might at first glance seem to be unnecessary. Sex might now be consummated from any given body type in multiple directions. But such is not the case because a transsexual is in pursuit of a social role and a body-goal and not a sexual goal alone. It is for this reason that the treatments were first devised for us, from hormone therapy to surgery. What was not foreseen at the time though was that continual refinements might make the transsexual goal not merely gender-congruity but gender perfection. As techniques have been refined a cottage industry has emerged as a part of the new global economy that promises us beauty as well as utility.

The focus has moved from the genital reassignment surgery to various other procedures that may enhance and sculpt the body as though it were so much clay in order to reach as closely as possible the status of a constructed Aphrodite. This in turn has created a new sexual preference among the non-gender-conflicted public, a desire among some for transsexuals, precisely because we are transsexual, particularly those of us who opt to forego final genital surgical change. This new market in turn has created a desire in many transsexuals to see their own bodies as a fluid medium through which they may achieve and channel something of the acceptance and love that they did not find in their early years of rejection and isolation. The result is a sort of perfect storm, a vicious circle in which desire feeds technology which in turn feeds desire.

It is no longer possible for many transsexuals to gain gender peace by the assumption of the role of the opposite gender. More is required of us; now we must attain gender perfection!

Now many of us, especially the young, are being coached by the lure of possibility to imagine themselves as the perfect artifact of another's desire or better still to be an icon of desire with a captive internet following. Suddenly the ugly duckling may become an empress in her own sexual empire. Then she may have the thrill of knowing that in the great silence of cyber-space, the men who might formerly have beaten her up are looking avidly at pictures of her in any number of provocative poses. They are following her blog and delighting in each tiny detail of her day, imagining that each possesses a unique position in her electronic harem. The end result is a sort of image-factory-in-the-medium-of-flesh now molded to a new and alien perfection which may now encompass the very acme of desirability by combining in one place exaggerated versions of secondary sexual characteristics.

The new post-modern version of transsexuals becomes a sort of sexual department store where any shopper may find something of interest. Can we then be far from the point of abandoning the archaic standards now in force and granting surgery on demand, for economic as well as for psychological reasons? How many bored and homely youths both gay and straight may imagine that they too may drive the polished and shiny body of an attractive she-male for the remainder of their lives? Why be stuck with an old Chevy-at-the-levee when you can drive a Lamborghini?

The body then becomes not what we are in all of our imperfections but instead becomes an investment opportunity. One will not then simply leave a gender role behind in order to assume the role of the other gender; instead one will leave behind the body as such with all of its messy and limiting factors (the world of modern plastic surgery become plastic indeed)! The desire in many is to become the perfect image in pursuit of power. The new transwoman falls in love with her own image, no longer like Narcissus by the pool, but as a new Lorelei singing from the rocks of the Rhine River to anyone who may type-in an entry code to her website. To see this phenomenon is already to see that it opens new areas to the transsexual and to those who for whatever reason wish to emulate the path formerly reserved for those most troubled and unhappy in their assigned gender. When the body becomes a mere artifact though, what becomes of the soul?

Is it possible to become a soul lost in one's own perfected body? Can beauty itself be the ultimate form of personal alienation? Will the pursuit of perfection create a new set of class distinctions within the transsexual community? Do such fantasies feed upon themselves so that what was formerly a pursuit of individual integrity becomes at last, what every transsexual of the past would have sworn that it was not, a form of high-tech masquerade after all? In this swirling ballroom of lifts and tucks and silicone dreams, of perfect labial folds, a world of color and flashing lights, are there really any transsexuals left at all?

We transsexuals may be in the process of witnessing our own demise. The new and youthful glitterati pushes us early ones to the sidelines with a sneer and a smile. We are rather an embarrassment, just like so many Edsels left over from the Eisenhower years. We may protest that we were the ones who brought transsexuals over the great prairies of distain in the covered wagons of our padded bras and daring use of eyeliner, but they will only smile in condescension as they purchase their tickets to whatever country becomes the new and lowest bidder for perfection of form and function be it Thailand, Iran, or even perhaps our own country that has lost industrial dominance in other fields, one last belated bid for dominance in something.

A Gender Aesthetic Theory

Recently a new male model took the modeling world by storm as a male who is modeling female clothes as a true female beauty. The astonishing thing is that the modeling world has been coming closer each year to an aesthetic based upon a univocal and genderless aesthetic ideal that unites the sexes at that point where puberty begins to create its own inevitable morphological gap. This exotic ideal is one of low to zero body fat, a sculpted face of cheek-bones, sunken and dramatically shadowed eyes, and a soft mouth. The universal appeal of this aesthetic transcends sex and a person manifesting this unique beauty might be called, if there were many of them and if their beauty could wear out the edge of time, "transcendsexuals."

While transsexuals are taking hormones and hoping to put on body fat in the right places so as to approximate the female fleshly ideal, genetic women have been indoctrinated for years to regard their bodies as having reached the perfection of hip-torso measurements at about the ages of twelve to thirteen. Young males on the contrary are taught to seek their ideal as the body that they will possess between the ages of twenty-five to thirty-five. For men the path is ahead of them while for women the ideal is passed in a fleeting glimpse and is soon behind them.

Transsexuals on the other hand by and large covet the most extreme version of female sexual difference from the male which is attained at about the age of twenty five to thirty five. After that decade the bodies of women usually take one of two courses. As they approach menopause women either tend to approach the male paradigm or they tend to lose flesh and become the prematurely old and brittle-looking individuals that we tend to associate with a witch-like demeanor. As the sexes approach a point of unity in old age these two types tend to merge into a sort of uni-sexuality. The female ideal then which is so often sought so that transsexuals will successfully pass as women may in fact require of them not so much hormones and surgery as it requires that their bodies remain pre-pubescent in appearance so as to approach the vogue in modern female models. The most attractive transsexuals are those who appear to still be in their teens when time and nature have yet to take hold of them to fully differentiate the sexes.

The force of nature as always thinks first of the species and only secondarily of individuals. The most beautiful things are those most rare and most transient. Our entire culture, particularly in the modeling world, worships that brief moment where the sexes unite in a single beautiful individual. We value that beauty because by its nature it is rare and in any event cannot be preserved because time will have its way at last. Time is pushing all of us towards the fate of eventual asymmetry, entropy, and decline. The blush of a peach lasts not for many days but is soon eclipsed by the hours that at first seemed only to make it more full and inviting. There is something almost frightening and disturbing in beauty and in those transsexuals who manage to achieve that beauty. They may be hated and feared by both sexes who see in the lovely male-to-female transsexual the final sterility of beauty, for perfect beauty invites contemplation rather than the mundane business of sex and procreation.

The paradox is that perfect sex is sexless. The loveliest models seem to instill not so much desire in us as envy of what we can never possess again (and perhaps never possessed at all). The business of advertising is to awaken desires that cannot be fulfilled. If they were ever fulfilled the need would be satiated and consumption of goods and services would cease. For this reason the ideal must remain always out of reach. Gender Dysphoria in its most extreme forms may latch onto this pursuit of the ideal, which unites the two sexes in an impossible beauty, a beauty as rare as gems are and as useless. When it does so, it can bring the all-too-familiar pain suffered by anorexics that can never be too thin. An entire industry is emerging to fulfill the dreams of transsexuals who may always feel that perfect love and acceptability may be bestowed by further incursions of the surgical knife. Vaginal lips are tightened, breasts enhanced to that perfect goal of fullness, hips or buttocks are molded and faces sculpted to remove frontal bone bossing or heaviness in the lower jaw.

Venus beckons us onwards and some few may attain, for a few years at least, a beauty that exceeds most genetic women for the very reason that true beauty resides in a mix of the sexes and not a single sex-type. It is precisely at the intersection, the sexual cross-roads of puberty, that the modeling industry has for some time located ultimate appeal which only serves to torture those who have made aesthetic perfection a personal goal to be sought and achieved.

Transsexuals then insofar as they desire to approach the female ideal may actually be closer than had they been born as genetic women. Real "passing as female" may actually be easier if the individual transsexual is less "attractive." Beauty is always arresting. It draws to the transsexual that enhanced scrutiny of the masses who find in beauty only a reminder of their own distance from that elusive formula that nature bestows only for a few short years at best. Beautiful is what many of us long to be. Perhaps transsexuals never prove how truly we are women inside than by this endless quest for an ever greater embodiment of "female perfection" whatever that may be.

Yet it is often remarked that many transsexuals are somewhat asexual when it comes to the actual procreative act. If this is so then transsexuals may be poorly named. Perhaps some of us should be called "aesthe-sexuals" whose only true intercourse is with a mirror. We are looking for an ideal to which we may correspond. Our medium is our own bodies molded by hormones and silicone. The unspoken sub-text for our lives whispered seductively is: if you are beautiful enough no one will ever care that you used to be a boy.

The Question of Passing or Realness

One of the most painful aspects of being transsexual is dealing with old friends. As invalidating as the comments of strangers may be, those of old friends are worse when it comes to that inevitable question asked of transsexuals, "Do you pass as a member of the sex to which you believe or wish you could belong?"

First let's take a look at a series of analogies:

1. You go off to college and spend years getting a degree with all of the expense of tuition, books, and denial of other pleasures assigned to your former job at a factory with its union salary your new degree may not even guarantee the same wage level as your former job, but you are studying for a life that was always in your dreams. Now you display the results and your friends say that not only should you have stayed at the factory where you might have been promoted up the pay scale but that you don't seem particularly smarter to them after all your study and in any case you probably won't find a job with your new skill set;

2. You have been overweight for some time and after years of dieting you manage to lose half of the weight towards your perfect goal. You are trimmer of course and feel better about yourself. You present yourself to your friends and they tell you that you're still a fat boy in their eyes. Besides, they used to enjoy going out with you and chowing-down on pizza while all you want to do now is hang out at salad bars with the girls;

3. You are a skinny-kid and you start a weight-training program and after years of work finally develop some degree of muscle-tone but are still short of the body bulk of the men in the muscle magazines and are still light for your size. Your friends tell you that you better keep your sweatshirt on at the beach.

All of these analogies, though imperfect, get at the situation of the transitioning transsexual. The question is always "passing or realness" whatever that means. Let me give you an example. I met with two male friends recently. Both have been through it with me during my years of dealing with transgender issues and deserve some thanks for bearing with me through hormone therapy and my efforts to achieve "realness." I had just come from Church where after many years I had finally created a sense of acceptance for the transsexual Catholic in their midst. During the week one of my friends had told me about a transsexual attorney he had met who was "dressed to the nines" and were it not for her slightly larger hands he would never have known that she was ever a transsexual. As further proof of her newly acquired status as a blue-ribbon trannie she was married now and to a man and lived full-time as a woman. Her husband knew of her former status but had no objections. In conversation she had expressed the opinion that she was no longer transsexual at all but "a real woman." She spoke disparagingly of some of her friends, those who still live in the gay community and who alternate their gender presentation depending on circumstances, as being "still caught up in "that life."This friend approved of this attitude. He seemed to be saying that it is mandatory to "go all the way over" which clearly meant in his eyes that I should present as female always and in all circumstances, settle down with a man, and presumably "dress to the nines" because that is what women do, at least successful upper-class women. The fact that the transsexual that he was speaking about is twenty years younger than I am and is inhabiting a world that is more accepting of transgender people, that protections are in place for her that did not exist when I graduated from law school and was afraid that when I told the admissions committee that I was transsexual I would be denied admission on one of two grounds:

A. That I followed a deviant lifestyle that was still criminalized in various jurisdictions of the country or;

B. That my condition was listed in the DSM-3R as a mental illness so that I was too unstable to practice law.

It had taken real effort then just to survive as a transsexual. But I was being compared to someone who had passed the ultimate test of "realness." She had bagged a straight-male who accepted her for what she was and married her. In fact so successful was she in her new role that she could look back and complacently pity those of her sisters who were still gender-conflicted and claim that she at least had arrived and is now a "real woman."

My friend had no problem accepting her as such because she had the status, income, and of a course a man, to prove that indeed she was real. This friend at least hung out the branch with the tempting fruit that I might also make the grade by taking a few more steps to join this perfect trannie by casting off any residual husk of maleness and stand there peeled like Chiquita Banana, all sweet and succulent, so that whether "dressed to the nines" or supine on a mattress in my suburban home with a pool and Jacuzzi I would be indeed, a woman.

I can't blame him for wanting "the best" for me, but just how sexist can you get?

Now let's take my other friend's response on the same occasion. I could see that he was disappointed that I was presenting as female for the day since I sometimes switch over (heresy) just so my friends will be comfortable in public with me and not be looking over their shoulders nervously to see if they are being read as "friends of a transsexual" and hence presumably as gay. My friend is not homo-phobic but I feel he still doubts, at least in my case, that switching over is a viable position and I am loathe to put him to the test by asking. At some unconscious level I think that I wanted to prove to him that, although I would never be real in his eyes, that a certain transsexual pre-op model is currently modeling women's fashions with great success. She at least might represent for both of my friends the very acme of "realness."

Since one of my friends had his I-Pad handy and the coffee boutique where we were sitting had wireless computer access I suggested that he bring up a site with her pictures. He brought her up for a minute or so but then switched over to the Sport's Illustrated Swimsuit Issue. It contained a bevy of the usual yearly icons to "realness" that dismays even many genetic females who cannot approximate or preserve such pulchritude. After my friends drooled over the site for a while it was time for us to leave.

As we walked out we met a group of people, average people of various ages, men and women, and I scanned, as I always do, for signs that I had been "read." It's something that transsexuals learn to do. You never really get over it (maybe not even if you have a husband who is willing to forget that you were "once a man in spite of your big hands)." I turned to my second friend after we exited and smiling told him that most people seemed to accept me, to smile back at me, not with ridicule or condescension, but as a human being and yes even as a woman.

I turned my head back to walk forward and heard him say behind me, *"Oh yeah...you blend."*

So I guess I've come a long way baby to get where I've got to today…at least in his eyes.

So the moral of the story is that to old friends and to family, transition may simply be impossible. To thread the gender maze and achieve legitimacy at last is often a lonely quest and for many of us it means losing what is most precious even if flawed within us … our past lives and associations. Another cause of discontent…

Acceptance by Others

But transsexuals actually begin our transition with the expectation of some level of integration with the rest of the world in the gender to which we believe that we belong.

I have written the above in italics for emphasis. As a bare statement of fact it is accurate. The entire transition project is predicated upon some manner of successful outcome – electrolysis, hormones (estrogen), breast implants, vaginoplasty, tracheal shaves, facial feminization, make-overs, voice coaching and practice, all of these and much more are designed to make the transsexual "acceptable upon scrutiny" to observers so that a minimum of social panic ensues when the transsexual person actually goes out into the world. To this end transsexual persons are sliced and diced, puffed and padded, shortened and elongated, molded like a gelatin desert, and yes then force-fed back into a society that by and large does not want to admit that such a thing is possible - a person who (for whatever reason at all, psychologists be damned) is unhappy in the sex they were **BORN WITH.** I have put *"born with"* in italics for emphasis. What I wish is that I could have chiseled it in granite because that **born with** is like a block of granite weighing down the hopes and spirits of transsexuals. It is one big heavy sentence of an irrevocable fate.

It is sometimes asserted that transsexuals ask for too much and that our demands are extreme and outrageous because everybody else just learns to adjust to their sex role and its socially imposed limitations. But that is just like saying to someone, "If you would only surrender or give up the very defining factor of your difficulty then we would understand you better." I on the contrary assert that this is simply impossible for transsexuals because if you are transsexual at all then it will be manifest in some way, even if only by and through taking people into your confidence and standing by your brother and sister transsexuals.

It does little good to my way of thinking to attempt to ease passage by adopting a studied ambiguity or by not "flaunting" your status. I have always been of the camp that advises existing "out and proud." To do otherwise is to preserve the binary categories relatively unchallenged which causes unspeakable anguish to those transsexuals who simply cannot pass as genetic females because of size or facial characteristics. The value of groups such as Transsexual Menace is that they are unapologetically trans-people.

I do not believe that most people understand what is really at stake for transsexual people to remain in their closeted lives, so I suggest that we feel like the victims of a social contract that we fail to sign at our peril.

If this was phrased in contract form, here is how its text might read:

We, the undersigned, live in a world of certain matters considered so essential and irrevocable that they do not bear question, of these the foremost is our primal division of all humans into males and females which categories are mutually exclusive.

Therefore this contract has been prepared, although it might have been considered by some parties to be lacking in contractual consideration, since where the parties to a contract already are obliged to perform there is no basis for a bargained-for-exchange of rights and duties.

However, due to the fact that certain unfortunate and maladjusted individuals, lately called "transsexuals," insist upon "changing their sex" and manifesting various mannerisms, habits, and sexual desires that are completely at variance with what nature has decreed and on which all social institutions rest, it has appeared wise to use the salutary means of a formal contract to reinforce the irrevocable decree of nature.

Therefore the contracting parties agree to be bound by the terms listed below:

In return for existing on this planet the undersigned person agrees to accept his or her sex as an action of irrevocable fate and to adjust to any personal discomfort as best they can. In consideration of this duty freely undertaken the undersigned party of the second part or its duly authorized representatives agrees to the following:

To not kill you on sight;

2. To acknowledge that the party of the first part is a human being;

   3. to allow for at least conditional membership in the human community as long as no behaviors, mannerisms, preferences, or appearance violates what are considered appropriate and indicative of one's real, actual, branded, and (for the religiously inclined) God ordained and commanded sex roles/characteristics by which we identify appropriate sex in every transaction of life.

In order to prevent the need for proof of special damages the following are included as general damages which can be levied at will in case of breech of the above provisions by the party of the second part.

[Note: This contract will seldom need to be produced since virtually all members of the species of Homo sapiens would never tend to question their sex or what that sex entails. But there exist various persons who insist that they are both human and "transsexual" so the following damages are meant to repair the social injury caused by their existence].

A Partial List of Remedies

- ✓ social ostracism and various manifestations of ridicule and contempt
- ✓ divorce on the grounds of mental instability
- ✓ denial of any prior relationship to the person
- ✓ deprivation of employment and ejection from places where other humans gather
- ✓ refusal to listen to their various absurd claims and justifications
- ✓ treating all attempts to aid them in their delusory belief as ill-advised, experimental, and/or cosmetic in nature
- ✓ And last of all (for the religiously inclined) to deny them eternal salvation

If the above appears to be excessive or even paranoid then I invite anyone to try a sociological experiment and assume the "transsexual lifestyle" for just one week in daily life. Use your imagination. The problem of course is that, even after the experiment is concluded and a general disclaimer of actual status as a transsexual is made, your life may be irrevocably damaged. People will never again be quite sure that you aren't really one of *them!!*

When even many flawless transsexual beauties are ridiculed when they appear on the media to discuss transsexualism and when the most tragic tales of the loss of transsexual persons to suicide or murder are met with responses like "good riddance," average day-to-day transsexuals may wonder when a place will be made for them to live their lives with peace, acceptance, compassion, and love. We all need a place of nurturance, respect, and understanding.

These have hitherto been in short supply for transsexual persons. But the tide is beginning to turn at last and though we have not all arrived at a state of sexual equality and human dignity there are many signs of hope and progress in the winds in this year of 2014 when this essay is written. Many school districts are adopting measures to aid in the integration of transsexual students into the fullness of student activities and not needlessly embarrassing them by treating them as members of a gender to which they do not belong.

The sheer numbers of transsexuals are larger than was formerly supposed. As the barriers to self-recognition and social acceptance fall, less people will be deformed by childhoods spent in rejection and quiet despair. They will be socialized as full members of society and be able to look forward to complete lives rather than to ones that offered only two options: silent disavowal of their most profound sense of self or coming out and facing a pariah status.

I cannot say what these new options may make possible, but I can speak from experience that the former course was brutal, lacking in insight and compassion, and simply an instance of social denial of the fact that many people are in fact transsexual.

We are not aliens from Mars or science fictional body-snatchers. Transsexuals are not simply examples of deconstructionism applied to flesh. We seek wholeness and balance in our lives by the only means that seem to remedy an unbelievably painful condition. We and others are attempting to write new scripts for what were formerly the tragic dramas of transsexual lives.

Transsexual rights are human rights. It is time that they were recognized. Even Iran can deal with us, how about America. Now is our time.

Do Cross-dressers in Afghanistan Wear Burquas?

It must be asked whether part of the appeal of being a woman, in western cultures at least, is the way that our culture has created the female body as a primary artifact that can be appropriated, not simply by genetic females, but by anyone who wants to acquire and to embody the technological certifiers of femininity and the sexual power inherent in them. Women are decorated with all manner of colors, textures, and enhancements that are simply not culturally approved for males.

The big question is why? Why such overkill if the female body is already inherently more complex and beautiful in line and symmetry than the male body? Or is it that no amount of frosting can disguise the bulky and angular surfaces of the male beefcake? Why do we allow women any variety of self-indulgence from pedicures to facials while deprecating these same procedures for men as a sign of being over-pampered and manifesting a suspect vanity?

Whatever the causes may be (and I am no more capable of a definitive answer than anyone else) the differences remain. It should come as no surprise then that male cross-dressers and male-to-female transsexuals may feel that they are reclaiming a more civilized and comfortable way of life when they are allowed to be beautiful, sexy, and catered to by the industries and countless products designed primarily or exclusively for female use and bodily enhancement. When there is added to this a greater freedom in women for emotional expression and communication and the fact that women are praised for efforts to cultivate their minds and sensitivities while men are confined to a pragmatic stoicism, and finally that women possess the fullness of the ability to bear, sustain, and nurture life within their own bodies, being male must appear to be a sterile substitute for the fullness of humanity that we allow women alone to access. The path being open, should we be surprised when some people with Y-chromosomes take it or cannot even imagine equivalent benefits or comfort in accepting maleness for themselves as a life-long sentence for a chromosomal deficiency (being one X-chromosome short)?

Back-peddling Sex-Change

It is called "purging" and it is not done over a toilet bowl but rather by giving away or throwing away all one's wigs and high-heels, one's make-up and clothing, or even one's books and TS literature while trying to regain lost ground in climbing the Himalayan path to manliness and a "gender appropriate identity."

I used to do this myself in my very early days. Nowadays though I still do what I call "breaking out." By this phrase I mean trying to find a time when being male worked for me or at least seeking a time when I first took the "wrong course" and ended up being transsexual. The problem is that I can't remember a time when I didn't feel this way, although I did on occasion manage by means of strenuous efforts to drive the consciousness of wishing to be a woman underground. It isn't that I want to be male as much as I want to be at least a non-transsexual. I want to be either so female that I leave little estrogen smudges like fingerprints on everything I touch, or if I must be a male, that I should be allowed to exist as a sort of sexless mind and noble spirit soaring above my body and all sexual desire. What I never want is for myself to be to be a sort of hairy thing with impressive phallic endowment and a chiseled face. At most I suppose I could stand being a pretty "Sean Connery type" ordering a drink at a casino "shaken not stirred" while saying to the voluptuous woman pleading for my attentions, "My dear girl, what I did I did for King and country; you don't think that I enjoyed it do you?"

What I do want in the course of my "breaking out" is to try, often by driving down to the sea or up into the mountains, to seek out and find within me a non-conflicted, non-transgender me to live the remainder of my life in either happy Catholic family bliss or as an English country-gentleman. I want to be the hero of my own saga, one nursed by all the heroic movies of my youth, which formed all my early expectations of life. The problem is that it is precisely at the moments when most heroic male figures in the movies receive the pay-off of enjoying the off-screen sex with the lovely leading lady that I find myself metamorphosing into her and find myself on my back in a slip with spaghetti straps with my blond hair spilling out over the down pillows and with my long carmine-red nails stifling a gasp as he undresses before me to reveal the delights that lie ahead for us both.

Yet I adamantly maintain that I don't really like men. What I seem to want above all else is either low-key, slow and loving "sex-between-pals" with a woman or to be mated as a male with a lovely but sexless "your ladyship" while I spend the majority of my leisure time with by coursing hounds or riding about the extensive acreage of my estate like Max de Winter the Master of Manderley. I guess I am afraid of being "just another" member of either sex. I was nursed on dreams of terminal upward mobility and these dreams remain with me to this very day so you can only imagine how painful it is to me to belong to one of America's permanent under-classes that of the transsexuals. Is it any wonder then that I never give up trying to break out of my silken cage with its bonds of iron? If I hold an exalted view of what it takes to be a man my view of womanhood is equally exalted and demanding, at least for the kind of woman that I would like to be. Both roles demand star-billing or at least that my role have the elements of tragedy rather than representing a simple decline into sordidness. I know that I ought to be satisfied to be just one more life on this planet and trust that I can be loved as an imperfect and average specimen of humanity, but I would feel somehow lost by being so, too likely to be swallowed up like all the vanished lives before me.

So am I just a flaming diva after all and is that my problem? If so I share this strange need with many others, from the older drag-artistes, lip-syncing lounge ladies doing their best Judy Garland or the suicidal young transsexual who may be seeking her moment of tragic glory and all too short-lived notoriety on the web of the internet. We all want to exist, to be recognized, and not just be what we may have always been, mere human beings looking for our little slice of dignity and respect in an indifferent world.

What if being transsexual is just one of the many individual traits that make us what we are rather than the single most different thing about us, that which determines everything else? Could we stand being normal after all? If I could endure just taking my place in the cafeteria line of humanity, then maybe the need to "break out" or even to break in to where I see others simply living would disappear and I could finally breathe an immense sigh of relief. I'm normal after all with no need to wait for applause from an empty theater at the spiral dance of my life and not need to back-peddle being a transsexual.

Transsexualism as a Meta-narrative

By the term "meta-narrative" I mean a plotted life story that unites past, present, and future in a single narrative thread that shows progress towards a set of stated goals so that one's individual life is held to have meaning and cohesiveness. There are many elements in this definition and all are important but the key point is that for many transsexuals the pursuit of a cross-gendered identity is the single most important element holding them together and uniting the diverse experiences of their lives around a central theme. Being transsexual then is not a whim or a caprice. It is something that is present in some fashion in virtually every period and changing circumstance of the life of transsexuals, something felt to be integral to what one is. This central importance is the best evidence that the transsexual imperative is rooted in brain structures or primal memories and probably both.

The problem though is trying to maintain a private meta-narrative without social support and often in the face of profound social ostracism and condemnation. These only add to the discontents that oppress transsexuals. That this opposition is based upon the supposed naturalness of binary sex attributions is merely a case of denying variation simply because it is a variation. To generalize from one's own gender comfort to deny the deep and anguished pain of others is both callous and simple-minded. But to this adamantine mindset transsexuals owe a great deal of the failure to construct a meaningful narrative out of our lives. Jobs, homes, careers, marriage, children, intact family ties with our family of origin – all of these are often compromised by being transsexual and seeking gender congruity through adapting the body and life roles of the other sex. In the face of this discrimination and rejection many transsexuals opt for a life without unifying concerns beyond those provided by the transition experience itself. When transition procedures fall away and the final end has been reached many transsexuals find that gender congruity alone cannot fill a life and give it meaning. It is these who often report regrets for having undergone gender reassignment surgery or other transitional procedures. One of the primary reasons that I am writing of transsexual discontents is to make it abundantly clear just what is and has been involved for transsexuals during the period since Christine Jorgensen first returned from Denmark. What was once considered to be a rare and idiosyncratic condition then is now recognized to have been all too common all along but hidden behind lives of terrible solitude and alienation out of a fear of rejection or the imposition of severe social sanctions. We are slowly emerging out of that period of denial, one that was represented even in the first gender clinics. We are beginning to realize how many lives have been marginalized and lost because of being transsexual.

To compose out of the diverse circumstances of a life what I call a meta-narrative is no easy task. Some may even argue that life has no real unifying themes or motifs, that all is mere accident and temporal succession. One of my objections to the advent of e-books is that the written word is being transformed into a transitory event flitting like fireflies across a plasma-screen rather than assuming the concrete form of a printed book. Words are cheapened by instant access and rapid replacement by other texts. The numinous quality formerly carried by books, the careful composition of proof sheets and the final embodiment in a bound volume was part of the human effort to stand firm against those eroding factors that undermine meta-narratives.

By implying that the process of elaborating such narratives is entirely subjective and of questionable validity our temporal culture questions human identity. This creates a sense that "my life matters to no one" and from this it is but a single step to "my life is not even meaningful to me." What cannot be united by significant loyalties to others, special feelings for a unique place or time, and a set of personal values and goals cannot be embodied in a meta-narrative and thus be made human.

Even negative experiences are at least a history and though they bring only a legacy of painful memories they at least imply a central unifying center to a human person. What I am saying here is that being transsexual is important but that in itself it is not enough. Transsexuals are not fungible commodities and however much we share in common we are each unique, valuable, and in need of affirmation both in our common character as transsexuals and in all the other parameters of our lives as individuals.

It is for this reason that I have appended an autobiography of sorts to the topical essays in part one of this book. I do not wish to imply that these short "verbal snap-shots" are the most important influences on my life or are adequate to convey continuity. They merely occurred to me as meaningful or amusing incidents or observations. They are simply data and should be received as such. No overall or cohesive argument to prove a point is intended to be achieved through them much less to serve as a model for others. Transsexual autobiography is swiftly becoming a genre and the temptation exists to tell an interesting story that is still representative of general transsexual experiences. I don't know if my story can meet these criteria so my autobiographical essays are meant to be the equivalent of songs on an album, lots of filler material and perhaps just a few hits.

Learning to Navigate
While Inhabiting a Woman's Body

It is no easy task you see to learn to navigate in a woman's body if one has spent twenty or more years in a male body. It is more than developing a wiggle in walking or to create a "head's up tits out" confident demeanor. One discovers that for the first time in

136

one's life that inhabiting a female body is to become aware that in doing so one inevitably acquires an audience. Living as female is, even for genetic females, a performance including costume and no end of accessories: bras, foundations, high-heels, nylons, earrings, purses, and other special-needs items that pertain to those who are not born chromosomally challenged and have that extra X chromosome. Women tend to occupy space differently, when they are both stationery and in movement, in a different manner than men. It is as though a woman is always aware of her body. She lives out of a center and her motions have a certain air of choreography even if she is not trained to be a model.

Consider the following points:

- ✓ When walking the head is held erect and the breasts forward
- ✓ The hip-sway, which should be present to some degree, is a result of the off-set of the female pelvic angle
- ✓ Feet should be planted as though walking a single straight imaginary line
- ✓ Length of stride should be shortened to shoulder-width
- ✓ Arms and hands should give an impression of fluidity and grace in movement
- ✓ The lowest part of the back is customarily arched
- ✓ This causes the breasts to be thrust forward and the buttocks to project backwards
- ✓ There should be an equality of projection forwards and backwards when breasts and buttocks are seen from a side view; head held back and aligned between the shoulders

These qualities of gait and demeanor convey a feminine posture and movement. But even when stationary a woman can convey her femininity by facial expression, posture in sitting, and by the face-to-face quality of her speaking to others, particularly to other women. Women tend to smile more readily and to convey a general atmosphere of care and involvement with others. Women's faces are more volatile and reflective of fine-degrees of emotion and meaning.

All of the above, when combined conveys a generally female impression to others. But there is far more to being a woman than mere structure, movement, voice, and manner. Where shall we locate that inner essence that yields identity and its social confirmation? How much is learned and how much is innate? Whatever the answer to these questions may be, transsexuals often have a lot to learn to before hitting the freeway on-ramp in a female body.

Learning to Navigate From a Woman's Mindset

One of the most destructive calumnies that transsexuals have had to answer is the accusation that the very effort to pass as convincingly female is inherently historically retrograde as though every transsexual wished to have her feet bound or to wear hoop-skirts. It was one of the tenets of modern feminism that gender is constructed as a means of female oppression by the dominant male sex. Of course this never explained the willing compliance of many women to the images and the culture of femininity that was supposedly foisted upon them. Was all of this the result of mere indoctrination? Is there no underlying substance in the dark strata of instinct? Is there no real vocabulary of desire?

To subsume everything into politics was an invasion of the cerebral every bit as artificial and oppressive as that which transsexuals were said to support by seeking to be accepted as women. The proof of this is the readiness with which the post-feminist generations of young women have rediscovered the source of the ancient and mythic powers of Circe. For every stern Ayn Rand reading monolith in a straight backed chair there is a college girl swaying to the lachrymose music of Lana Del Rey. If this latter image seems like permission to explore the trivial it seems to be a permission that is increasingly sought by young women in America for whom the prospects of careers in business suits may now seem far less enticing than standing by the picket-fence in her favorite sundress.

There is also a demand to young males in feminist rhetoric to feel innately embarrassed when they find the attitudes of a woman as represented by the lyrics in many of the songs by Lana Del Rey to be more appealing than arranging a luncheon date in an upscale bistro between business meetings with a sexual double of themselves. This rediscovery among heterosexuals of what the gay world calls butch-fem role play seems revolutionary today only because it is happening after a long trek through the sterile desert of feminist politics. If this revolution brings back the image of a muscled young guy in an old Chevy hot-rod and a girl in a skirt beside him smiling with her Revlon Fire-and-Ice lips is that to be condemned out of hand? Is this a less viable role for females than to explore the convoluted dialectics of oppression and resentment as feminists? Was late 20th century feminism a revolution that failed for everyone but those who could afford the increasing costs of college educations that led only to slavery to the very institutions whose women's studies programs vainly offered women's liberation?

Many women today are finding an answering response from across the vast empty dance floor that has separated heterosexual couples for forty-plus years. Some women are even choosing to have babies again and the abortion clinics, which were seen as the necessary adjunct to liberation from the home, are becoming a source of proper horror to those who are not being trained to adopt an instrumental outlook to their own bodies. The industrialization of women's bodies will come to an end when women are not taught to fear fertility as some sort of imposition of the fates, but the natural result of intercourse. Children are not a fate worse than death or a relic from some dark period of women's history, but are a unique female gift to the world and a source of justified pride. From this point of view the traditional loyalty of transsexuals to fem imagery may be seen as a gift from the sterile few acolytes to keep the candles burning until the temple is rediscovered by the former priestesses of Isis. There has been a lamentable tendency among many female vocal artists to assume that a mere displaying of square inches of female flesh is an innately freeing act and that eroticism is ensured by the extent of that display. They could not be more wrong. Eroticism has always been enhanced by a combination of concealment and revelation and that revelation is most effective which only hints at delights to come. It was this which made the pin-up art of the fifties more enticing than the most blatant of today's soft-core porn magazines. Eroticism is not reducible to power and liberation. Indeed many women are rediscovering the pleasure of the surrender implicit in assuming a softer image, the flowing fabrics, and all of those tried and true elements of hair and cosmetic usage that have never ceased to please their male partners. The failure of instincts to yield to the mere propaganda of cortical control or to a social agenda is proof that some things do not change and are not subject to control by simple fiat or political correctness. To rediscover romance may be the tendency of the next years of cultural development after a season when little more could be done with the human body than to slice it, dice it, and puncture it in various places.

State of the Art
Facial Feminization Surgery

I think enough has been written about *"the operation."* The penile inversion and dilation technique is well-known and its results both convincing and replicable. In the past it was "the operation" that was the conversion ritual that changed a male into a female. That a woman could be reduced to a mere vaginal opening never seemed reductionist to the early definers of transsexual legitimacy. Face and mind were irrelevant. It was the presence of a vagina that was the sine-qua-non for societal womanhood. But as many "tragic trannies" were to learn, society demands more than mere vaginal functionality before it will grant legitimacy to aspiring candidates for womanhood. It also helps if various chassis contouring and grill-work are in harmony with their newly granted classification as women.

The down-sizing from functional pick-up truck to a classy Sting-Ray requires more, so today facial feminization is all the rage. Careful observation reveals that the primary differentiating criteria for a female face include:

- ✓ Smaller head size
- ✓ High and prominent cheekbones
- ✓ Smaller nose with a slight up-turn at the end
- ✓ Shorter distance between nose and upper-lip
- ✓ Less noticeable brow-bossing ridge
- ✓ Rounded forehead from side to side
- ✓ Straight fore-head when seen in profile

140

- ✓ Fuller lips
- ✓ Larger eyes
- ✓ Lidded-eyes
- ✓ Long eyelashes
- ✓ Arched eyebrows
- ✓ Contoured jaw-line sloping upwards to ears without obvious angle
- ✓ Shorter jaw-bone
- ✓ Tendency to show upper teeth when smiling
- ✓ Tight smile musculature that deepens cheek dimples when smiling
- ✓ Tip of nose, lips, and chin project forward and meet in a single plain surface when viewed in profile. This latter factor gives the appearance when seen in profile that the upper face recedes somewhat when seen in relation to the lower part of the face

If in addition to these factors mentioned above two others are added, then the beauty that we associate with the female face comes into being:

Beauty is largely determined by two factors, symmetry and the diamond relation of the upper and lower quadrant of the face from the hairline to the bottom of the nose, bisected by the eyebrows. The beauty "diamond" is drawn by extending an imaginary line from the corners of the lips to the outside of the eyes to the outside of the eyebrows. The top half of the diamond should mirror this triangle to the beginning of the hairline.

What is called facial-feminization surgery is the process of altering flesh and bone to approximate these relations of facial structure. The face is the sexual equivalent to the sound of a language in terms of basic phonemes. When these are added to certain body-language gestures and modes of movement the gender-language spoken is perceived by the observer to be female. There is a certain degree of logic to these extreme procedures for those who can afford them. Faces are how we meet the world and communicate. Much of the ridicule meted out to those who do not readily "pass as women" is due to the retention of male facial features that no amount of electrolysis or genital surgery can alter. Indeed, facial surgery should precede all else from a strictly practical perspective. Once passing as a female the financial means for expensive genital reassignment may be more easily obtained.

A cute guy is still able to revert to the male if circumstances make this essential whereas a male-to-female transsexual who is genitally corrected but otherwise indistinguishable from his former male self may be forced into a life of extreme social isolation precisely when she most needs confirmation and support in her new role. Means must be found through medical insurance to help those who require complete sexual conversion including complete cranial-facial work in order to live full and productive lives in their gender of choice.

Through the Looking Glass:
Living in a Post-gender world

On the other side of the mutual deception practiced by those with traditional polar-opposed gender roles lies androgyny. Recently I had occasion to attend a three-day convention held in the Capital Hill area of Seattle, a neighborhood that is known for its LGBT presence. It is a unique feeling to be walking around in an area where republicans are almost as rare as escaping radon gas and where sexual reality is less determinative than declarative. The entire atmosphere is one where an awareness of global warming prevails, where anyone can be seen holding hands with anyone without a second look, and where you can't tell the players without a program. In such a world old style transsexuals like me, who still use the politically incorrect word, "trannie" (with my own idiosyncratic spelling of the term as well because it is cute, short, and familiar,) seem at times to be out of place. With the new profusion of gender and sexual nomenclature it may seem quaint that tortured persons of my generation felt a need to convince skeptical physicians that they should provide hormones for us and refined surgical procedures to help us to approximate the gender presentation that we felt essential to our mental peace of mind and sexual appropriateness. Looking about me I began to wonder if a new naturalism is in the process of being instituted, one in which people could flow in and out of gender classes and adopt various contradictory signifiers at will without social opprobrium being exacted or condemnation being applied to these behaviors.

I attended college in the same neighborhood where the conference was being held and at night I found myself walking back to my car where it was parked at the school. Some of the buildings I had known were gone now or had been cleaned up since my student days while others remained startlingly the same. I kept thinking back on the lonely and alienated student that I had once been, one who escaped his body and all of the stresses of his emotional life by living in a world constructed out of various fictional narratives rather than trusting that I could abandon the social role-playing of my parents' generation and might dare to make inquiry among my peers without fearing their rejection or ridicule.

Was part of my Gender Dysphoria a legacy of the "I like Ike" Generation, that generation where any non-conformity might earn one eternal exile from post-war prosperity? Whatever challenges this new tribal group might face, could they possibly be worse than the stolid, tight-assed repression of the world that I had then known as I tried to find my place in the world? Were even the excesses of my own generation's coming-out party traceable to the grand masquerade of uniformity that had preceded us in the 1950's? Would there have been gay bathhouses, AIDS, and s-and-m crypts if those who sought out and inadvertently discovered the price exacted by fate and circumstance for sudden and radical sexual experimentation had not been preceded by an era of such outward conformism and inward hypocrisy?

What advice would I render if as a ghost I encountered that tragically earnest young man who still exists at some level within me? Would he be appalled at the cross-sexed and sexually indeterminate creature standing before him now, one who is the production of that young man's choices? Or would he condemn me for failing to live up to his fantasies of a life of future money, power, success, and independence? Surely it could not have all culminated in this! Yet, for all of that I might well have done worse and "he" may have not realized what snares still lay before him. He did not know that time for instance was a far more limited commodity than he imagined it was. He did not know that he was living in an American version of the Belle Epoch and that a deluge or rather a series of deluges was to beset the vast certainties of his limited grasp of life.

I might say in defense, "Well, could you have done better?" Obviously not because once again, here I am – if he could have done better he would have done so and a different me would stand before him now. Or is it rather the "present I" who condemn him for being so lonely and so lost and for having wasted resources that he did not even realize that he possessed, for daring so little, for not rebelling enough, for not looking for happiness in better places and seeking relationships from other people than those who have been important to me? It is not only this one other who is younger than me but rather a whole succession of similar incarnations that wander about like ghosts on that same campus that has been known in turn by each of us. I could fill a small stadium with each one of us assigned a separate irrecoverable day or night of my life.

"Who are these people?" I ask myself, "And why do they all share the common fate of being condemned to be … me?"

They are all silent. Worse still, they do not come out of the shadows bodily to reproach me with their startled young visages aghast at how old I have become. No, there is instead only this place and the scenes of the drama still existent and standing silently in brick and mortar in building and in street. These new denizens of the university seeking an education will in turn come back in later years and wonder even as I am doing where their dreams took strange turns and their professors in turn will be dead. These students also will someday discover that time, to whose stern mandate they believed themselves to be immune, has triumphed once again, as it always does: "Move along now," it says," Others are coming and they will need your place."

So just what is Transsexualism?

I still don't know the answer to this question and maybe just possibly nobody does. I only know that the questions raised by being transsexual are significant ones and that the answers matter in people's lives. I don't see transsexuals going away anytime soon. I think we have always been here and that we are not unique to our media-obsessed culture. I also don't think it is possible to decide once and for all what parts of who we are have a gendered basis rooted in biology. We are cultural and expressive creatures. Artifice is as natural to us as living. Even if LGBT culture feeds on urban ghettos and takes various tribal forms in 21st century western life, it is found in some form in every culture and region of the world. I think my experience is relevant if just to show how unpleasant it can be for transsexuals to openly live our lives. I might have been spared much if I had been less determined to legitimate my life by living openly and without apologies as transsexual. I wouldn't want to be anyone's model for the best way to do a transition. But this is my tale, so I have set it down here just as it was. So while in a mood of reminiscence some essays from my own experience as a trans-woman may carry our discussion into those remote regions when my own struggle began to decide which way to go in my one and only life.

An Autobiography

(Allegro con Lacrimoso)

Writing of Myself

Many transsexual autobiographies seem to be written with ease as though speaking of the self can ever be easy to one who for significant periods of her life has not had a persona or personality that could be socially validated. I cannot share this ease of composition or portrayal. My title for this book is a deliberate one for the simple reason that for the most part for me to be transsexual has been a source of rejection, limitation, marginalization, and as a result I am angry, not merely with social norms, religious prohibitions, and the ever recalcitrant body, but with myself for ever desiring more than what was implied by possessing a Y–chromosome. Since my own past is now irrecoverable, and may not be reformed along other lines, I can only report my own lived dismay and sense of alienation. To relive these times is painful, but worse I find that I have so long maintained various fictional substitutes for an identity that to ask me what I actually feel or desire is often simply a meaningless question. I learned early on that as regards my essential self the world had one clear message, which was not to be. So it was that I always looked outside of my own being to various structures in order to say what and who I was.

So much has this tendency grown habitual within me that my first instinct is always to define the situation rather than to simply respond in a natural and sincere manner. The question of preference or desire is always subsequent to the possible danger posed by the surrounding criteria for evaluation. My response in recent years has not been to yield to this uncertainty though but to use it to blast through all perimeters. I have a tendency to see opposition everywhere and to seek the point of weakness in any citadel, the better to storm it and to take it by force. It is not that I enjoy victory but rather that I fear defeat and what will surely follow, dismemberment and pain.

So it is that I am an aggressive character, one who weaves a spell about me, one who tries, insofar as I am able, to bend the force-lines of any pattern or situation in my favor, much as gravity is said to operate by literally causing space to bend towards any center where a mass exists. This seeking for an edge and advantage is very typical of certain martial arts principles. It is in me the fruit of being alienated and of believing after much experience that one must be ready to shift one's ground at any time and never to establish a permanent abode or fixed position lest it should be overrun and the emotional slaughter commenced.

It is here if anywhere that the transsexuals of my era may also manifest what is called Borderline Personality Disorder, a condition that often follows abuse and trauma in early life. To be transsexual is often to be in recovery. What I needed above all to recover from was the systemic abuse inflicted by the denial of our inner sense of self by an intolerant and ignorant set of social institutions as the following essays will explain.

Lipstick

I grew up during the days that knew the height of female artifice, the 1950's and the 1960's. Every woman was a potential priestess then, enacting the sacred rites to herself as Aphrodite. Each day she would construct for herself that version of her own sacred mysteries that she would show to the world. That which was most secret was hidden while that which symbolized the approach was formed, molded, padded, uplifted, and pointed, like so many Cuban missile silos, towards the men in grey flannel suits, ties, and hats that would watch with fascination and worship the result.

Men might wear underwear, but women had *foundations*. She was built from the ground up to the top of her hair, frozen by hairspray into impossible waves. Every item of her appearance was directed with un-erring accuracy to zero-in on the male libido and to both offer access to the imagination while yet forbidding entrance to the temple. The most female attributes of her body were kept under secrecy as though each woman had her own Secret Service Agents to protect her. For all of her open sexuality she must appear as glacially uninterested in sex itself.

Her appeal came from suggesting that it was only the male, the ever hungry male, who was burdened with sexual desires. If a man were to understand how much was at stake for the woman in the proffered transaction between the sexes her market value would fall overnight. Her appearance must then go hand in hand with a strict moral code that had less to do with religious strictures than it did with making sure that when she finally said, "I do" and then, "I will let you," that she had some future security and prosperity ensured for the long years ahead.

To a child of course none of these complex sexual politics were apparent to me. All that I as a young transsexual of the time knew (and perhaps knew more at this time than at any time in America) was that women were special in fact they were goddesses to me. Gender non-conformity in those days was surrounded by more than the usual gender police of societal expectations. Gender non-conformity was the equivalent of a young slave boy who sneaks by night into the harem and dares to dress his still undifferentiated flesh in the seven veils and to light the incensed lamps only to see himself in the mirror with unevenly drawn and exaggerated lips but still joyous and awestruck at the transformation.

Lipstick was an easy and accessible way to say who I was and carried the entire weight of the cultural definition of femininity. What was a more familiar sight than to see a woman reach into her purse and abstract her compact, that golden jeweled treasure which would snap open to reveal the pink pressed powder with which she would first dab her nose and chin before reaching again into the mystical reaches of her purse to abstract the canister that when opened would reveal a gradually emerging tube of glorious red lipstick. She might hold it first for a moment meditatively before removing the cap. Then she would turn the base with her long nailed fingers and slowly the budding tube of color would emerge all wet and glistening with, as the ads said, "Extra moisturizers and emollients to give your lips that soft and inviting look."

If the lipstick was new (and what woman ever has enough lipsticks) then it would be beveled so that she could paint her mouth to a razor's edge of accuracy from a Cupid's bow top lip to a pouting and shimmering bottom lip. She would proceed to paint her lips while (if she was young and attractive) all activity about her would cease and men would look over fascinated, as though someone was performing impromptu brain surgery at the next table. Slowly the color would be left behind and her mouth would assume that perfect curvature that only a bright new shiny red Cadillac might hope to rival. She would press her lips together and then carefully blot her lips with a discrete Kleenex tissue and dab with infinite care a corner of her mouth where the line might have slightly exceeded the demarcated region of her lips.

What a fascinating device the modern lipstick was to me as a child. But even this complex initial procedure was not enough. She must now use a small tube with a retractable brush to smooth the tiniest details of her lips so that each crevice would show a smooth richness of adhering color before she smiled as one does who has just accomplished some great mission with success. She would then close her lipstick, snap her compact shut, and return it to the dark confines of her purse once again.

It was not only young adoring transsexuals like me who were prey to the many charms of lipstick. Lipsticks always had such marvelous names, each promising to a woman that by purchasing it all her dreams would come true. This practice of naming lipsticks has never ceased to this day. It would be easy to parody their names here. They seemed always to carry a message:

Blushing Bride Pink, Get You to the Altar Red, Don't Let Him Stray Mauve, and Pile Him Up on a Coral Reef Orange!

Then there were those names that flirted with temptation:

Don't Say No Pink, Keep Him Guessing Gloss, Do it in the Backseat Red, Tempestuous Scarlet, or Luscious Dripping Peach.

Or you could really walk the edge with names like:

Coral Crash Crush, My Mouth is Bleeding Red, Open Blossom Pink, Make Me Shudder Scarlet, Climax Coral, or No Yes No Yes.

You could even strike a somber note, a sort of pre-gothic aura with:

Maybe Tomorrow Pink, Sighs and Regrets Red, or I Should Have Known Better Bronze.

But what woman could resist that most quintessential lipstick of its day or the sight of Dorian Leigh with her wide open eyes and spread fingers gazing at herself in her tight spangled dress with an impossibly rich bright red mouth as she asked American women the daring question, "Are you ready for Fire and Ice?" Could any name of a lipstick better conjure the image of woman in the fifties than the phrase "fire and ice?" (Of course the ice always should come first).

A proper woman was supposed to be unaware of how sexual she was in the fifties. Yet how could that be? She was never out of dresses or skirts (no Levis unisex look back then)! Her breasts were molded by bras that gave them that unique pointy look that was only to be rediscovered and parodied years later by Madonna. A man who danced close to a woman in those days must have never be allowed to forget, as he felt those pointy things pushed against him insistently, of what might await his straying fingers later that night as he dropped her off and stood before her on the stoop of her apartment for the obligatory goodnight kiss. He would know his future with her by how long she allowed that kiss (and there was only one) to last. Then with a sign and a little laugh she would turn away and he could watch as her tightly girdled and streamlined behind beneath its skirt or cocktail dress would sway away from him, catch a last glimpse of the seams of her nylons, and hear the click of her patent leather high-heels before the door closed upon her ... and their date was over.

This was the image of the sexes that you saw in movies and sometimes enacted in real life. It was all based upon a stringent code, a code no less stringent in its way than Sharia law. It made a woman magic though and everything associated with women was vaguely suggestive of some unimagined climax if ever one might thread the maze of thorns that guarded the castle's treasure.

To a young transsexual of course this very set of aids and adorn-ments suggested that if they might be purloined and applied that the little boy who saw his own body as just a skinny male thing and with no one to imitate other than the silent and ab-sent fathers that abounded in that era could become what he so longed to become: first a little girl and then like the young goddesses who babysat him, a woman. How many young boys of my era playing in the outfield in their Little- League teams or sitting around in their cub-scout dens would have wished that they were learning to bake cookies and watching older sisters getting ready for dates? How many would sing along with the girl voices and wish it was their party and they could also "cry if I want to?" How many would love to tell the bullies at school that called them sissy that, "My boyfriend's back and you're gonna be in trouble?" How many were in the bathroom scrubbing their lips raw to remove the indelible stain of having gotten into their Mother's lipstick once again in spite of the heavy and repeated prohibitions?

I at least was finally given my own lipstick by my exasperated mom, my own lipstick to keep as long as I promised to never use it. Just owning it was enough for me. One of those tiny precious ways that (in spite of the prohibitions at school, at home, and in the silent era in which I grew up an era that denied gender and sexual variance) I could look at my lipstick, my very own lipstick, and know that I was secretly a real girl after all. There was only that and the greatest resource of young transsexuals of that era of denial, our imaginations. Young transsexuals of that era were still allowed to dream. They could imagine that the tiny rituals that they had devised with items more available to them such as color-crayons or water color painted nails, wearing girl sneakers, or some other small but hidden ritual would be the equivalent of a sex-change and as effective in their magic to transform them into the girls they so longed to be as the magic of Lipsticks were for us.

Of Nancy Drew Books, Monster Movies, and Criss-cross Vacations

Transgender children like other children tend to look everywhere for role models but especially those in my generation of transsexual silence we looked to movies and to books. I was fortunate in receiving a gift when I was eight of the cast-off books of the daughter of a friend of the family which included several Nancy Drew mysteries and a wonderful book about a shy blond girl named Morey Winters who takes a vacation one summer to Vashon Island in Puget Sound. I was living in New Jersey at the time and by no possible effort of the imagination would I have ever known that fate would eventually lead my family to Washington State and to a town separated by only a narrow arm of Puget Sound from Vashon Island.

It wasn't that I didn't also read the Hardy Boys Books, but I always thought it would be more fun to be with Nancy, Bess, and George rather than with Frank, Joe, and Chet Morton. What could be more adventurous than carrying around a flashlight in your purse and taking off your high-heels so you wouldn't make a sound in the dreary old mansion you were investigating or upon hearing a sound to reach up to your perfect red mouth a perfectly manicured hand and after a short gasp to knit your pencil thin brows with determination and to press on with the investigation in spite of a danger that would send most girls running back to where faithful Ned was keeping a lookout on the sagging front porch for the foreign spies who were using the place as a hideout while they broadcast coded messages to their confederates?

I have always thought that a strict Freudian could make a great deal over the fact that Nancy had no maternal rival for her father's affections? Can we say Electra-Complex here? Nancy could always be brave in these tales because as a mere girl she wasn't expected to be brave. How pleasant for a little trannie-boy to inhabit a world without the need to pretend to a set of alien gender feelings each day. There was also a marvelous British book entitled, "Five on a Treasure Island," which included a girl who insisted on being called George. She had a stern scientist father and a big mongrel dog and made friends with a family of

London vacationers named Ann, Dick, and Julian on the coast-line one summer. I alternated from trying to be like Julian while feeling more like the girl George (for Georgina).

To say that these books were real to me would be to understate the case; they were archetypal! Apparently there was at least some acceptance of gender rebellion then (at least if you were a girl who wanted to be a boy). Maybe that was what I was, really a girl who on occasion could be brave and noble, but could always withdraw if necessary into my true gender, my deep and secret girl-self. It was the same impulse in its way that would make me later wish that I could be the yummy starlet in the white bathing-suit. She was abducted by the Creature from the Black Lagoon and was carried with her head flung back with her breasts pointed upward at the trees of the Amazon jungle, while the creature carried her away to his cave. Oh help!

Even in our diversity aware culture the offspring of that union would have been aliens, great on the swim team, but always needing to rush to the aquarium in the biology lab or to the drinking fountain for a quick drink of air. No worries though because she was always rescued and the Creature, poor thing, had to join the league of disappointed monsters with impossible crushes on human females that just had to die. Take King Kong for instance...I mean think about it; could it really ever have worked out?

My childhood had its share of misfit girls too though, from the Fifty Foot Women running amuck, to various amorous scaly creatures, to Frankenstein's Daughter. The message was that even impossible loves and out of place desires do at least exist so perhaps there was even room for me. To this day I doubt that Hollywood has ever created any image of women more glamorous than the typical B-Movie heroine like Allison Hayes. In those days no one did anything more than kiss in the back seats of cars and wait for the giant tarantula to arrive, but what could be sexier? The scenes went sort of like this:

"Oh, Steve, when can we get married?"

"Susan, I thought we had talked about that. You know that I am working with your father on a growth serum to make giant bananas to feed the world. We are getting closer every day."

"But Steve what if something does wrong? What if an ant or a grasshopper, or, or maybe a tarantula was to eat some of the compound? It could destroy the world."

"Tush, tush, Susan, your Father and I are exercising every precaution."

(Little does Steve know that the Romanian janitor at the university, Anton Radalescu, has stolen some of the substance and is feeding it to Tarantulas who will soon menace Fairview!)

"Oh Susan, I do love you, you know that um… your hair, your lips, your…"

"Steve, what was that?"

"Nothing Susan, like I was saying I just love your…"

"Hush, there it is again!"

Pause.

"I don't hear anything; what did it sound like?"

"Well you would hear it if you weren't breathing like a horse. It sounded like (now don't say that I am being a hysterical woman) it sounded like a tarantula walking through the rhododendron bushes that are surrounding our car."

"Nonsense Susan, you are just being hysterical; what you need right now is to be caught up in an embrace of iron and kissed unmercifully."

"Oh stop that, listen! It's coming closer! Oh Steve, take me back to my dorm at Fairview University before…"

"Oh alright Susan but you are being perfectly ridiculous, what would a giant tarantula be doing in boring, predicable, and of course Republican Fairview?"

{Sound of car starting}

"Oh thanks Steve. I'm really thinking of you. I just couldn't face life if something happened to you now, just when you are getting so close to growing a giant banana."

154

I was raised on stuff like this. I wanted to be the girl in the car. I wanted to be Morey Winters whose father in the city gave her a Criss-Cross book to mark every time that she was brave that summer. Nobody ever cared if I was brave. Nobody cared about what it was like to pretend every day that I wanted what other boys wanted or related to objects in an impersonal way rather than as I did giving names to them and imagining that they had feelings so that I cried when I left the cord on my steam engine plugged-in and it was ruined. It overheated and its lovely silver face grew brown and tarnished. I cried then, not because I had lost a useful toy, but because I had through my own irresponsibility caused it to lose the one precious life that it had; it was broken now and would never be the same, broken just as my life was being broken every day so that I could learn to be a boy.

Learning to be boy made me very hyperactive. I felt as though I was trying to climb out of my skin all the time. At other times I would get depressed and hide in the fort that I made at the side of the house. Transsexual children have a horror of being observed too closely because they fear that their terrible secret will be discovered and then summarily dismissed with a "You'll grow out of it." So I lived a strange girlhood/boyhood and wondered if other boys wanted to paint their nails and wear pretty things and have a book filled with Criss-Crosses because they had been brave for that day. Did they want to wake up on Puget Sound and walk on the beach poking sea anemones to make them close and wake up in the morning each day and shake out their long blond hair before putting on a frock top and shorts and slim girl sneakers? Did they want other boys to look at them in a special way instead of treating them with scorn and incomprehension? I wanted to go to clambakes and eat clams and roasted corn and potatoes that had baked on the shore under a blanket of seaweed and then walk home by starlight with an older boy's arm about my waist telling me how brave I had been that day to walk down the steep gangplank at low tide to the beach.

I hated these desires though so I would do everything I could to be the hero I wanted to become, even if no one noticed it. It was I that demanded it. I must be brave and fear nothing, need nothing, least of all understanding or sympathy from anyone for

155

my shameful cross-gender desires. What could be worse anyway than a boy who wanted to be a girl? It is a strange thing to live side by side with another you, especially if she is the opposite sex and seems to come out at different times all on her own. Is this analogous to Multiple Personality Disorder or to other dissociative states? More research work needs to be done in this area. I can only report here my own feelings and history, trusting that they will be validated by others who have experienced early gender discomfort. I was always flashing in and out of the two me's, the girl that I felt I was and the boy that I was trying to learn to become. But the path was always uphill. It was like seeking some outer validation to a false passport that I longed to replace with a real one. That's what my early childhood was always like.

Kick-balls, Marbles, and Jacks

My first years at school were hard for me as they are for many transsexual children. I used to feel like I was going to be sick everyday before leaving for school. I wasn't good at recess games. I didn't really see the point of most of them. They seemed like some invention of adults that they had cunningly devised to exhaust us and make us more pliable when school resumed. I liked jacks though and for my own unusual reasons. Not only were they subtle gender identifiers, but they allowed me to play with the girls without risking the rejection that the more team-like game of jump-rope would have entailed. It was social suicide that would never be forgotten for a boy to play jump-rope. But I just liked jacks per se. I liked their bright shiny colors and the way that you could spin them. The hard yellow ball could bounce amazingly high and I loved the round shape of the ball in its perfection. For the same reason I loved marbles, particularly the large aqua cat-eyes. There was always something jewel-like about marbles and the black box with an imperial crown on top (which alone out of all my childhood toys I still possess). I also liked puppets because they were the only "dolls" that were acceptable for boys to possess.

I had the most amazing thing for kerosene lamps (my Victorian preferences surfaced early). But to be fair, I also loved chemistry sets and what were then called erector sets (get your mind out of the gutter). I liked making robots with the latter (again dolls in disguise). Chemistry sets were like magic. To this day I recall how mixing what I believe was called Ferric Ammonium Sulfate and Sodium Ferro-cyanide to make this beautiful blue ink. Then there was Cobalt Chloride which made an invisible ink that turned blue when it was dry and heated over a light bulb.

I also loved the tiny dinosaurs that came with corn chip six-packs as a promotional prize. I built them their own swamp, which was subject to periodic dry-spells. By turning on the hose I could restore them to peace and plenty (such God-like power) which I always did. Pretty boring when compared to today's video games, but they worked for me. I even liked looking at clocks and the intricate gears and springs within them. I showed an early fascination with the intricate that indicates the future philosopher. Or I may just have been unusual and as everyone knows so well, children who manifest difference are just so welcome in a world of strictly enforced rules that children learn to enforce against each other.

Still there is always hope for the unique kids. Who can say what use their toys are to these children or what creative ways they will devise to subtly tell us who they really are if they are only listened to and respected?

Desert Destination:
Of Flappers and Rodeo Cowboys

In 1960 we moved from New Jersey to Arizona and my lipstick that had I had always kept in the top right-hand drawer of my dresser suddenly disappeared. When I asked my Mom about it I was told, "You're too old now for that." I never could figure out what age had to do with it. I could at least enjoy the make-up commercials on television and those wonderful cigar ads featuring the lovely Edie Adams. She would always end them by smiling coyly and holding a cigar cradled softly in her hands as she said in this sexy voice with her wide eyes and pouty lips, "Why don't you pick one up and ... smoke it sometime?"

In the early 1960's there was also a show on television called, 'The Roaring Twenties.' The opening credits showed the actress and dancer Dorothy Provine as a flapper of the gangster era. She was an early role model for me. I so wished that I could just be her. She would dance in a short, spangled flapper dress while behind her a panorama would show gangster cars and all the action of that exciting era. It may seem strange but I was also mad about Jack Lord who played the rodeo cowboy, Stony Burke, in the series of the same name.

I was in the fifth-grade and I was eleven years old. I already knew that I identified with all of the girls in every TV show that I saw and that I had an unspoken crush on Robbie of "My Three Sons." The rest of my childhood was an effort to forget that knowledge and to bury it as deeply as I could. The awakening of our sexual and affective being is spontaneous and natural, even for those of us whose sexuality or gender identity conflict with the heterosexual norm. The problem of course was that in the sexual Jurassic era when I was growing up there was simply no place for these feelings. The chart or scale of the composition could not be recorded on the paper provided to us and present in the gender-normative roles that surrounded us. The result was that certain feelings were not so much forbidden as they were simply inconceivable. It was as though we could hear the sound of a dog-whistle that was supposed to exceed the range of human hearing and nobody else could. So it was that nobody, not our parents, not our teachers, and sometimes not even we ourselves could hear our silent screaming.

Maturity becomes impossible to model when it is formulated on an alien gender. The result is that GLBT youth learn early on to fake what they are supposed to feel. European philosophers have a word for this; it is called inauthenticity. I spontaneously identified with every girl-star in every movie from Shirley Temple to Hayley Mills to Patty Duke. I would walk out of the movie theater and for a while I just was her, I can't explain the feelings better than that, but I know that most transgender people will understand. If I were to name this strange inner experience I would call it a process of ego-glide. It was as though each personality cast a sort of glow or penumbra within me so that I would find myself *becoming them*, not imitating them but literally feeling their own character and gestures spontaneously emerging from within me as though they were my own or as if I were a wandering ghost looking about for an appropriate gender house to haunt. Psychologists speak of depersonalization as a sense of the loss of self but this experience was the opposite from this; it was one of acquiring a self by absorption and re-emission of the image on a slightly altered wavelength, just as a florescent bulb glows when the mercury particles are bombarded by an electric current.

I didn't ask my friends if they were becoming Marilyn Monroe when they watched "Niagara" or the girl in the swim suit when they saw, "The Creature from the Black Lagoon." I didn't ask if they wanted to be Dorothy Provine as a flapper in "The Roaring Twenties" or be any of the pretty extra's starring in guest roles on "Bonanza" or "Perry Mason" – *but I did.*

When I was in the fifth grade, a pivotal year for me as a young transsexual, Alfred Hitchcock's great film, "The Birds," came out. There was a big spread in Life Magazine all about it and pictures of the young and lovely star Tippi Hedren. I naturally wished that I was Tippi Hedren. I wanted to wear bright orange nail polish and have Rod Taylor hold my crossed hands down over my breast when I emerged back to consciousness after being attacked by the birds in the attic bedroom. I wanted people to care because a gull had hit me and a long stream of blood was winding down my cheek in the café. I wanted to be cute and sassy in the bird shop at the beginning of the movie and later when we were falling in love I wanted to tell Rod Taylor to "be careful please" when he went out to the Foster place while I tended to his mother and picked Cathy up at the school.

I have seen that film by now many times and I can still see its unique and mesmerizing appeal for me at the time. The rather boring life of Bodega Bay seemed to so encase one against the backdrop of the inevitable destruction wrought by the coming bird attacks that one becomes a resident of the town. Each hour of that magic weekend seems remarkably important when set against the budding romance of Melanie and Mitch. I remember feeling how wonderful it would be to have someone care about me in that unique way. The strangest thing of all though, for a

159

young boy, was how intensely I wanted to be Melanie and to have her perfect nails, her pert expressive face, and to know that I would be protected and taken to the hospital, even after being shredded by bird beaks in the attic that I would still be beautiful to Mitch and be part of his family.

I always like the beginning of the movie best though, which is to say that I like the long boring buildup rather than the climax of the bird attacks (seemingly wrought as some sort of cosmic retribution against Melanie for being so wicked as to jump into a fountain in Rome without any clothes on). Melanie, the lost motherless girl whose father is always busy with his newspaper and can only show his love for her by providing Melanie with a mink coat that she will even wear in an old rowboat without worrying about getting it soiled (think about it), Melanie who drives an Aston Martin and can wrap Charlie at the news desk around her little finger, Melanie, whose unique up-do hairstyle just screams "muss me" so that even seagulls cannot resist hitting on her; that is the Melanie who I wanted to be with my wide open eyes reacting in horror to all the chaos surrounding me.

Maybe the lady in the café had it right after all and Melanie is some sort of locus for disaster drawing down the bird attacks for tempting nature with her intense virginity, her whole "I'm-too-rich-to-touch" non-availability. After luscious, meaty, Marilyn Monroe and gushy, busty Jayne Mansfield, America had found a blond who was so pretty that she was like a cool shining ice-sick-le, glinting like a diamond, while teasing the helpful post-master (as she no doubt teased everybody but Mitch whose mocking smile lets the audience know that he is up to all of her tricks and pranks and practical jokes). Yet her mischief and its motivation appear to lie in her own anger at her own abandonment so that the entire film seems to be a search for acceptance and a secure home. In spite of the bird attacks Bodega Bay seems to be a very safe place, a harbor in a greater storm. Is Melanie channeling the bird attacks out of some strange guilt complex? Where is her all-powerful father, who even after she reports the bird attack on the school fails to even send faithful Charlie or some other employee to drive up from San Francisco to rescue her? Instead she is forced to accept the kindness of strangers and in the end finds a new mother in the formerly rigid Lydia, Mitch's mom, who sees in Melanie perhaps a younger version of herself, looking for a man to protect her.

All I know is that I got so caught up in the film that I didn't want it to ever end. I simply had to go on down the road with Mitch and Melanie, part of their romance. How often in later years have I done the Melanie thing of asking for help and rewarding my benefactors with that same smile whether they were pulling my car out of the snow or carrying gas cans for me and filling up my car if I ran out of gas. "But it is just a movie!" you will say. No, like all art it was iconic and worked upon my unconscious mind on multiple levels. I know that I found an early role model in Melanie Daniels, perhaps a female version of the early apoc- alyptic prophet Daniel.

Living now as we all are in the shadows of ozone depletion, global warming, and terrorism I still feel that I can conquer all with only a rowboat, a green suit, and a mink coat. But instead I became a lawyer like Mitch and I also became a blond- haired girl like Melanie as well. I am still looking though for my own Bodega Bay where there is lots of time and I can drink Brandy with slightly butch and sexy Annie Hayworth the school teacher, knowing that Mitch will always be there to put peroxide on my wounds when a sea gull hits me or to watch this time when I bathe again naked in a fountain in Rome.

California Girl

We moved again after three years and I had to leave my two best friends behind me, Mark who was the handsomest boy in the school and Wally who seemed in some way to understand that I was really a girl. In retrospect I see now that I had hidden crush- es on both of them. It was hard for me leaving Arizona but it was in northern California that I met my best friend Michael. I have often thought how unique it was that in a little country school on the first day, the one little gay kid met the one little trannie kid in the school. Both of us had metal lunch pails instead of brown bags (it should have been a clue).

We sat on the bus together everyday and Michael would make me laugh by catching imaginary and invisible leprechauns (always a symptom that should be referred to the guidance counselor ... but we didn't have one, thank heaven). Michael had smooth olive skin and long nails that I wished I had the courage to grow instead of modeling them with play-dough alone in my room. He had a tiny moustache of black fuzz on his upper lip and a pretty mouth and I thought of him as a little immigrant French boy. Nobody seemed to notice our girl-like friendship of laughter and gab and we rationalized our difference (if we perceived it at all) by referring to everybody else as peasants. We alternated between being Dracula or the Wolfman and shared a common passion for Halloween and make-up.

Halloween was our generation's disguise for unique sexualities. We soon developed our own unique struggle for dominance by wrestling all the time. I think we both wanted to be boys very much. Michael would tease me to distraction simply to watch me bite my lower lip. His marvelous enthusiasms for art were compelling and he in turn seemed to relish my own unique enthusiasms. Michael made my life tolerable and I do not know what I would have done without him as a transsexual child. After two years we moved away again and I came north to Washington expecting that I would find someone else like Michael in my new school, but I never did. It was not that we talked about our unique feelings openly. Certain things were just understood, like our exclusivity, the space that existed around us that was ours alone. What else can one expect to know at twelve?

But by fourteen the human brain expects certain things when puberty arrives and when the contrary happens the inner stress can only be imagined. Our society has made little provision for children who are differently gendered or divergent in sexual attraction. The result of course is the systemic lies that children must learn in order to silence what is not simply within them but which is aching to burst forth. The damage done in these years may be well nigh irreparable. In fact I would go so far as to say that much of transsexual discontent is a product of a deliberately maintained ignorance of the complexity that is actually present in human sexual development and the mystery of the person. Whatever the justifications for these past practices may once have been, they are inexcusable now. We must in some measure take into account the very real suffering of gay, lesbian, and transsexual children (and those who lie between even these distinctions). But that help was not available for me.

As my year in the seventh grade ended I neared an age when many young transgender kids take their own lives. As I look back on my life now, armed as I now am with philosophy, history, and the law, I can only imagine what it had been like to survive my Catholic childhood in those pre-Vatican Two days when I was at the mercy of persons and institutions that combined intransigence with ignorance and added to both that singular lack of care or empathy with which age is pleased to treat those at the more vulnerable stages of psychological existence. It seems strange to me now that the good sisters at the Catholic school that I attended had no problem telling my parents that I would end by "destroying myself" yet were unable to put a stop to the daily bullying that I was subjected to. I recall once silently weeping at my seat in class as I remembered how I had once believed that to be among members of my own faith would be to be surrounded by angels seeking God, founts of charity and good-will. I was asked pointedly by the Irish sister after class why I had been "crying around" as if I was weeping to make a display of my distress rather than at the failure of charity in my classmates and the impossible standards imposed upon us backed up with threats of damnation in the standard Catholic pedagogy of the times. Even the imagery in prayer books and later on the images that were displayed on the walls of the novitiate I was later to enter conveyed a vision of sanctity that bristled with a love of pain for its own sake, more a vision of the Marquis de Sade than of the stern but practical St. Ignatius of Loyola who spoke of the active love of man in return for the all-abiding love of God. I think that many people lose their faith because of the bitter wounds inflected upon them by persons who have been shamed in their own youth into believing that God despises humanity rather than finding in our deepest affections proof that God exists in the human heart.

Even young children in those days who had reached what was termed "the age of reason" were presumed to have with the first dawn of freedom have stumbled into sin so that their first experience of God was as a taskmaster in a dark confessional before they could receive their first communion. It seems to me that Jesus once told his apostles to let the little children come to him and not to hinder them because it is such as they who make up the kingdom of heaven, just one more gospel passage that seems to fall through the grate. Thus prepared to fear their creator they could now face a lifetime of going down on their knees and saying thing like, "Bless me father for I have sinned. I beat my old woman again last night but I had been drinking you know and the kids were screaming and well you know how it is, but no I guess you don't do you." Many people carry these wounds about with them and the bitterness that they engender forgetting that their teachers received in turn the same poisonous pedagogy. One of the greatest tricks of the devil is no doubt to make us think so much about him that we forget that God exists too.

Meltdown

In my eighth grade year my family moved to Washington and enrolled me in a Catholic school there. It was a horrible time for me. The experience of going to any school had always been difficult for someone who felt she needed to adapt rather than to express how she felt inside. I always received excellent grades but I simply did not understand the other children. The constant switching between school systems only added to my confusion as a nervous child always needing to make new friends and establish a new acceptance for my differences was very difficult. Even my summer vacations were usually spent elsewhere than where we lived during the school year.

Puberty was approaching rapidly and I simply did not know what to do with it or about it. Added to this was the stern instruction that I was receiving daily that virtually anything having to do with sexual feelings was sinful, and not just bad but backed up by visions of hell should a sexual thought be entertained or allowed to linger unduly. This was called, "morose delectation" in the old manuals of moral theology that carefully listed all the many sins. The phrase sounds like it might be applied to licking an ice-cream cone that has first been dipped in sand. Only in the case of the 6th commandment was there no "parvity of matter," which meant that any sexual sin was automatically serious matter and if knowingly engaged in and with full consent of the will was always a mortal sin. How was I not to take these people seriously and therefore to live in constant terror?

My endurance for change anyway was at an all time low that year. I was dreadfully skinny and growing like a weed. For Halloween that year I had purchased a lovely braid that when unwound I could function into an acceptable wig, just in order to be a monster of course because I could not admit that I really wanted to look lovely and exotic while wearing it like Jeannie or Ginger on television. I could be excused for wearing make-up as long as I was being a vampire and not Mortisha on the Addams Family.

After I started school I noticed that unlike the public schools that I had attended strict gender segregation was the rule here. The nuns still wore the habits that framed their faces and prevented any peripheral vision (something symbolic in that surely). Not since the first grade when I had also gone for a few months to a Catholic school had I been so immersed in a Catholic cultural atmosphere with its omnipresent bleakness and its dread. I reacted to it with what in retrospect seems a sort of allergy. I felt that I was living over an abyss and that various actions might (should I die) plunge me into eternal exile from everything bright and beautiful. God was filtered through a web of complex legal strictures to which only priests had the key. The little bits of knowledge that were allowed to trickle through to the laity were bad enough. Everywhere were the favorite images of Catholicism, ascetic saints and a mixture of torn flesh and admonitions. Our pastor used to lean upon the pulpit and in sonorous tones regale us with observations that were alternately sour or ironic and never delivered with a smile. All in all it was not ideal for a young transgender child who a year earlier had been doing imitations with his gay friend Michael of Dorothy and her troupe on the way to see the Wizard of Oz.

I soon fell apart with a severe variety of Obsessive-Compulsive Disorder called Moral Scrupulosity. That I did so should have been no surprise considering the stress of being a young transsexual and having learned so early that the world around me had standards that were inflexible and indifferent to my deepest sense of myself. The teachings of the Church were merely a more universal version of American pride and callousness (for I did not grow up in the Roman Catholic Church but in the American version of the Roman Catholic Church). It was this same American church, the most visible spokesman of which was Cardinal Spellman, a man who could advocate making war on Vietnamese Catholics because he hated communism more than he loved little brown people in South-East Asia, even if they were of his own faith.

The message that I learned growing up was to measure up to the code of that church or go to hell. I was convinced that the Code of Canon Law must contain innumerable additional commandments which when added to the ten I already knew with their endless ramifications would create a virtual Catholic Talmud of complex calculations necessary to avoid constantly committing sins. It didn't help that in that very year my body began its male adolescence and I was hit by an assault of male hormones. How would I ever succeed in becoming the lovely Mrs. Emma Peel, played by Diana Rigg on my favorite T.V. Show, "The Avengers," if I was being turned into a man? It was bad enough being a boy but a man?!!

When a nuclear reactor melts down the core gets so hot that the containment cell cannot contain the fuel. Well I just wasn't meant to run on high octane testosterone and my own containment cell of Catholic doctrine, one taught with no soft edges of merciful exceptions but only as law, law, and more law, simply did not give me the means to deal with what I knew about myself. The result was that I stuck to the commands as well as I could understand them and everyone thought I was crazy (and I was but just not in the way that they supposed I was). I knew what was really wrong with me and I even told my Mom why once again but I couldn't tell anybody at school so I just coped as best as I could.

The nuns told my family that I might kill myself; but I knew that to do that would mean instant hell. Besides, I loved life! I just wanted to spend it as a girl. Each day, regular as clockwork, a group of four or five boys would spend their recess in tormenting me. I couldn't seek refuge by joining the girls of course because there was an informal code of radical gender segregation in Catholic schools. The worst part was that everyone knew what was going on and nothing was effectively done about it. It was there that I learned about what being trained to embrace a Catholic ghetto mentality entailed: conscious duplicity and subterranean resentment towards the silence and shame attached to sex that was pervasive in Catholic culture.

There has always been an aura of subtle sadomasochism in Catholic life, a nauseous blend of pastel innocence covering a darker reality. It was therefore no real surprise to me to hear of the clergy sex abuse scandal. In the rigid power hierarchy of religious institutes and the bitter immigrant Catholic ghettos, where poverty and alcoholism so often went together, it was only natural that predators would be formed and that secrecy would provide a perfect culture medium for the growth of their victims. It has even occurred to me that some of the victims walked into the fan like zombies because they had always been told that priests knew everything and you always did what they said or you went to hell.

I was happy when in my next year I decided to skip following the males of my class into the local Catholic preparatory high school and instead decided to take my chances in the secular public school. It was only with the help of an understanding Jesuit that I made it through that year. The result is that I do not blame the Catholic Church but American Catholic Culture for the pain that I endured. If you want to know what it was like, look at the representatives of that mentality that still exist among us; take a long look at the snide smiles or perpetually constipated frowns of certain members of the Supreme Court.

The First Magic Year: 1966

Maybe everyone is haunted by one year that they would like to go back to if they could. For me that year is the year of 1966. It was the year that a Jesuit priest helped me to realize that the Church was not as grim as I had thought and who helped lead me out of the maze of my own doubts. The Jesuits have always been the most intellectual order in the church, the most dedicated to social reform at all levels from the missions to the aristocracy and the ones who, while not neglecting Augustine or Aquinas, have never lost sight of the human equation. Their so-called militarism is actually a systemic method of mysticism based upon the love of God and an effort to make a return for that love by doing good things in the world. Their humility has always tempered their undoubted excellence so that the mindless rigidity that has already given Opus Dei a bad name and the inquisition of the Dominicans a well deserved infamy played less of a role in Jesuit history. I have a soft spot for them and also for the religious orders of the Discalced Carmelites and the Trappist monks.

Nineteen sixty-six was the year before America fell off into the deep-end of the pool of the ripening conflict in Viet Nam. It was the year that I emerged from the mental meltdown of January through April and began to live again. That spring, my father purchased a lovely white Fiberform ski-boat for the family. We had never seemed as young and vital as a family as we did then. My Mom and I used to go skiing together and I would make her laugh by pretending to be from Austria. All of life seemed to blossom with the daffodils and tulips of that year. (This was also the year that my beloved "Dark Shadows" premiered with its vampires and haunted houses).

I had emerged by June from my first major attack of Obsessive-Compulsive madness. I was alive again. The demons of doubt and fear were temporarily silent. The shadow cast by Viet Nam was lowering though on the horizon but it had yet to goad the country into madness and division. My high school years were still before me and un-sullied by any reality consisting in my mind of dreams of the dances, soda-shops, and dating I had seen in the movies and television, all the visions that I had imbibed from watching re-runs of the Patty Duke Show.

That year of 1966 was the pivotal year between the imagination of my childhood with its toys and the pretend world and the dawning of the real world with its responsibilities and disillusionments. The reality when it finally dawned was solved by me as for many transsexuals by creating an impenetrable wall between my public self and my private self. The latter was confined to our neighborhood which was transformed by my fancy into an exclusive and privileged citadel against the outer world. Secret agents were not far away and I could imagine myself as inhabiting various roles. The various goddesses of television, Ginger on "Gilligan's Island," Jeannie on "I dream of Jeannie", Mrs. Emma Peel on "The Avengers," Agent 99 on "Get Smart," and Julie Newmar as Cat Woman on "Bat Man" provided for me models of the unattainable. It was not so much that I identified with them as I have explained but rather that I wished that I simply *WAS* them. This wish was silenced though by a blanket of effort that if not denial was at least a heroic effort towards denial. But none of this mattered in 1966 because everything was clean and fresh for me in a way that few later years since have ever been.

If a person's inner orientation to her body is female, it is ego-alien to the extreme to go through a male version of puberty. Is this surprising? Strangely enough even now I hate reviewing my life because the only parts that I really liked were the fictional parts mediated by books or movies. I used to put on characters to cover the fact that no spontaneous impulses of my own could ever be trusted. Instead I just thought up a version of myself and lived it out. The rest was just adaptation to whatever was expected of me. My attitude was *"Who do you want me to be? What are the rules? Okay, now get out of my way and let me keep them (but resentfully. I must at least be entitled to my resentment; what else do I have?)"*

Keeping the shadow of femininity out of my life was a full-time job then and the really funny part was that it wouldn't have been so bad being a boy if I just was one inside (and I wanted to be normal) but it was all externals and effort for me while a real gender identity should be as natural as falling backwards onto a feather bed or a warm pool of water, not an ascent of a high mountain undertaken without enough oxygen. The result is often the slow-burn of transsexual anger and self-hatred. It is as though the entire world is determined to keep one on the rack of gender pain and as though one were in a state of perpetual exile.

The need for pretense never ceases. Denial and reaction formation become after a time second nature so that in the end one succeeds in adapting more or less to one's assigned gender and may even scorn the very idea of crossing-over, but always there is that still and quiet voice that reminds one that it is all one great and unending effort to bend a material that keeps springing back to its original shape and that shape keeps whispering, "You should have been female."

Scarborough Fair

My favorite song then was by Simon and Garfunkel. I lived in the times when American youth was given to the grim reaper with reckless abandon. Politics were not important in my home and we may have been one of the few families in America that was not divided by the war, but it was there still like some grim and growing shadow nevertheless. Raised as I had been in a world of obligation and heroism and the belief that America could do no wrong I sensed at the most a whiff of betrayal in high places. There was a feeling that we would all we whisked off soon to the jungles to a smell of vegetation and jet fuel and there was nothing to be done about it.

My political awakening came with reading Thoreau's "Walden" and Father Dan Berrigan's book, "America is hard to Find," in my later years. I only knew that I did not buy into President Johnson's speeches and that I was very glad when he announced that he would not seek another term in office. By then I was a rebel in every way that I could imagine except for drugs and sex. My pride was such that I considered my body as inviolate. I filtered perceptions the way that baleen whales filter krill. Had I been drafted I doubt that I would have survived. My world was a combination of gothic novels and the optimism of a Broadway musical combined with an Anglophile belief that England was a paradise of civilization, my version of Mecca. I kept my balance through constant vigilance and spent the time when my mind was free of the dread that was at the time my only sense of God by seeking repose in escape and delusion. Above all else I was lost and sad, alienated beyond being surprised, when Martin Luther King and Bobby Kennedy were killed. If you were good and tried to do something for the world you just died, that was all. Each year of my senior high school experience seemed to manifest some major change in the national consciousness from the summer of love of '67, to psychedelic '68, to the revolution years of '69 -'70. It seemed as though as the country grew more disillusioned and bitter that my attitude kept pace with the changes so that I withdrew even more into a world of fantasized escape. Like many teenagers current songs could capture the mood of an era. These are now my time capsules to the past. As always it is the artists who reflect the reality beneath historical events. The changes in the country then have born the bitter fruit of our various wars of intervention. These have been costly, but never since the end of the draft has our nation watched as an entire generation of young men was led to the slaughter with such cynicism and for such shoddy reasons. It was all part of the business as usual of vast organizations, the brutal manifestation of an antiquated mindset. It was all so disgusting, so wrong, and so ever-present. As for my own fate, I expected to get a college deferment. I would figure it all out later.

In the meantime I was learning karate so that I would never be bullied again. I drove my motorcycle on warm spring days and dreamt of summer on the lake where we lived and once swim team season was over I could get home before dark and resume wishing that I could just step into the world of the serial TV show "Dark Shadows" and live in a big mansion on the seacoast of Maine.

"Dark Shadows"

It is a sad commentary on my high school days, spent in one of the most exciting eras of youthful rebellion and rock music ever known that the real love of my time in high school was probably getting home to watch the ABC gothic soap opera, "Dark Shadows," on television. My Mom always warned me that it would warp my mind to watch that show with its scary music and maybe she was right. At the very least I wanted to be Victoria Winters although Carolyn Stoddard and even working-class girl, Maggie Evans, were sexier. I liked Victoria though because she was always getting rescued and her dark hair, embellished with a long fall, and her deep and tragic eyes seemed far more "me" than petulant Carolyn or sassy Maggie. On this series even the boys got to wear eyeliner even if they weren't vampires. I thought it would be wonderful to be a fearful vampire or witch and to live in an old ivy covered and moss-enshrouded mansion, to wander abroad on foggy nights through fragrant apple orchards, like the one surrounding the abandoned asylum building above the grounds of Western State Hospital, and to have any number of diverse means at hand to defeat bullies or anyone who dared to judge me.

The world of "Dark Shadows" with its storm-wracked location of Collinsport and the great mansion of Collinwood by the sea enthralled me. It should not have surprised me later on to discover that the series had a gay presence among cast members and a substantial young gay audience as well. I think that like the many drag-queens who later followed the television show "Dynasty" religiously, dreaming that they were the Joan Collins character, that my own devotion to the world of Collinsport was an act of what might be called imaginative displacement and fantasy identification. I loved the closed-in atmosphere of intense human relations in the tiny community of Collinsport. Somehow the Collins fishing fleet managed to keep packing sardines while any number of supernatural events, which might have distracted most communities, still allowed the denizens of the tiny and remote village in Maine to go about their everyday life and somehow make ends meet. What would life be without vampires and werewolves to add variety to Chamber of Commerce gatherings and PTA meetings? It definitely beat out pale suburban housewives like Samantha Stevens or Lily Munster whose husband, Herman, could barely bring home the bacon from his job at the funeral parlor. I always liked my role models to be aristocrats. The main point though is that along with many transsexuals of my time, who were denied today's ready access to an early transition, I relied on fantasy to make up the difference between the necessity to maintain a male persona at school and who I really longed to be. I was in a state of almost constant depression in those days that was relieved on occasion by bouts of exquisite joy entertained for the most subtle of reasons. It was as though seen against the dark background of my deep sorrow at being a male there came occasional starbursts of delight. These were often associated with subtle symbolic ways of being female by indirection or symbolic means. It was not unlike the prisoners of the Nazi era who expressed their rebellion by whistling the tune of the song "Die Gedanken sind frei" [our thoughts are free] whenever occasion offered. Until the Nazi's caught on and would beat people up just for whistling. There are people like that today who bristle like porcupines at even the suggestion that transsexuals have a right of self-determination.

The problem though was that I was denied the normal opportunities to experience being female in the real world and to hone a stable adult female identity in the process. This has left me with certain deficits which persist to this day. It is not too much to say that transsexuals who were brought up in those times of intense denial often display certain long-lasting areas of emotional damage that therapists mistake as showing that simply being transsexual is a mental illness rather than manifesting the result of a difference rooted in the brain itself that may have existed from before birth. Only the future will show whether the early treatment of transsexual children will spare them the necessity of living a displaced existence in a world of hiding the deepest truth of their nature in a world of dark shadows.

Western State Hospital

In my senior year I quit the swim team which I had joined for the sake of getting a boy-badge, a sort of gender certificate, a varsity letter to prove that I wasn't a sissy after all. I wore my letterman's jacket every day like a suit of armor but I lived in another place inside my head, inside my books, and in what I wanted but could never have. It may not be necessary now to threaten acts of self-mutilation in order to get surgery, but you still have to leap over most of the hurdles that were promulgated then in the Harry Benjamin Standards to get what is still referred to in insurance company language as "cosmetic surgery." So I guess we still don't fit in and isn't that the social definition of crazy? If you're a boy, you can't possibly really be a girl. Everybody knows that.

Two miles from where I spent my Junior High and Senior High School years is the Western State Mental Hospital. It is a complex of huge three-story brick buildings, green lawns, and even an old public golf course. It was here that Frances Farmer, the lovely movie star, was incarcerated for so many years. Today her particular form of madness might be classified as a personality disorder rather than as a psychosis. She was a combative alcoholic and a victim of a strained relationship with a controlling mother who despised her daughter's independent patterns of thought and contempt for the culture of the Hollywood studio system. Though Frances may have been rude and abrasive, particularly to authority figures, she was a woman who dared to question the way that her beauty and talents could be co-opted by a society that thought that it knew how women should behave. That was her crime: that she dared to self-define in a society of rigid definitions. The result was that she went head-to-head with a system of targeted violence by questioning its right to treat her. The harder she struggled the deeper she sank in the quicksand of the psychiatric establishment of the time. No one will ever know the full extent of what was done to her during those years in that place. When she died of cancer years later after a time spent in Eureka California she was obscure and largely forgotten. Today she is remembered as an early rebel who took on battles with all comers rather than realizing when it is best to just step aside and allow the thundering bull to run past.

It might be thought that I would, during my growing-up years, have had a horror of the old asylum just down the road, but instead I found its presence vaguely comforting. On misty winter nights when the school-bus would drive down the two-lane road of Farwest Drive to Steilacoom Boulevard where it would take a right turn and head towards Lakewood. If the bus had turned left it would have gone down a steep hill to the little town of Steilacoom, the oldest settled town in Washington. The road at that time was cement rather than pavement, narrow and with seams that would click rhythmically beneath the bus tires. There was also a stone fence along the road built of natural round rocks. The place looked like my vision of an English college like Cambridge. The yellow lights in the wards looked vaguely inviting. I always felt that if I ever went crazy that I would have a place to which to go. In fact to be crazy seemed like a sort of gift. If you were really crazy, then people would listen to you, at least your psychiatrist would once a week. Your case would be fascinating and wise and thoughtful people would match wits to solve the problem that was you. You would not be just ignored. You would not walk home alone from the bus stop keeping your secret deep within you, that you still wanted to be a girl and what could be more crazy then that?

I felt a sense of sympathy then with the patients of Western State Hospital. Maybe the difference between me and Frances Farmer was that I knew when to shut up. I was a rebel too, but I seemed to know instinctively that if you rebel in certain areas you risk confinement or even death. When the Stonewall Riots happened in New York City in 1969 I was still in high school. I didn't hear about it then but I do recall the issue of "Look Magazine" that told about transsexuals that appeared in my senior year of high school. I longed to open it at the time but took just one quick terrified glance and then decided that if I read it I might never be able to put the genie back in the lamp.

My high school allowed us to volunteer to visit patients at Western State Hospital. I used to go to North Hall which was a three-story building that now no longer stands. It was old and was made uninhabitable by the last Puget Sound earthquake. I remember that the place seemed to smell of mental illness as though the many people who had occupied its halls had left something of themselves there. There was a smell of stale sweat and cigarettes that went with the brown floors, the iron bedsteads, and the high ceilings leading to the nursing stations. There were arm-chairs in the day room that looked out on the lawns below and the winter-bare trees of the forest in back of the hospital.

The young man that I visited used to keep his arms down by his side and shuffle forward and backwards in a sort of line dance and sing a song about being "with Ray now" when he was happy. It was his private language for peace and I never found out who Ray was. In later years I also met with an old blind man name

Jack, who never seemed psychotic to me, just blind. He always loved it when I read to him. I wanted to do something nice for somebody and I felt guilty if I didn't go.

I went one time to one of the women's wards and saw a young woman who had scratched her arms and her face with her nails. I remember that she stood up and tried to hug me. I took her arms gently down from around my neck and told her that I had only come to visit on the ward. I never saw her again but I remember thinking that she was too young to be crazy and locked away like this, scratching her face and smoking endless cigarettes like they all seemed to do. She should have been in a lovely dress on a spring day walking by the sea. In those days you see I thought that you just couldn't be beautiful and unhappy at the same time. Whenever I left Western State the smell of the old buildings seemed to stay with me and I could never understand why some people's lives carried so much suffering. I used to walk home thinking of the two worlds, that of the sane and that of the insane, of the rich and the poor.

When I would get home I would put on my swim suit if it was summer and dive into the lake where our home was located. I would come to the surface clean again from all of the craziness except my own. I would see the water-ski boats driving past and smell that lovely smell of water and feel my strong swim-team honed body bobbing in their wake. I would shake the water out of my hair and dream of a non-gender conflicted life ahead of me as a young man. I still had the androgynous body of the young, but the gap was closing fast for a time when hormone therapy could push me in the desired direction of female. I couldn't finally get on hormones until I was thirty-four, which is still better than forty-four, but every year counts for transsexuals. It is impossible to remove the bone and muscle and bulk that still make many of us appear top-heavy in the shoulders and narrow in the hips. I was still swimming upstream then and away from being transsexual...swimming as hard as I could. I think I would have readily changed places then with the girl on the ward who beneath the scabs on her arms and face was at least a woman. Maybe she got out one day soon after that. I like to think so. How sad it would have been if she grew old and came to resemble at last the old woman who used to walk in a counterclockwise circle with her head down carrying on an interminable conversation with herself (and an angry one at that) with someone who just wasn't there. But then we all have our regrets, and our ghosts.

My Short Military Career

College was horrible. I never dated. I just did what I had always done: study, get good grades, and envy girls. It was at least fun to move to a co-ed dorm for my junior year. The year of 1974 was when I graduated and when Candy Darling, the early transsexual icon, died. I was about to try and bury my sexuality in a Jesuit Novitiate by studying to be a priest. Things were happening for transsexuals already, but they were far away from me. As far as I could see, I was alone and unique. The Viet Nam years still haunted all of the young of my generation but so deeply did I exist in a fantasy world that I did not think much of that far-off conflict while I was still in High School as I have mentioned but after I graduated with honors and went away to college the horrifying prospect of military service reared its ugly head again. Military service in those days was considered a universal fact of male life, something owed to the country by every young male. So it was that I simply assumed that I would have to serve sooner or later and the only question was in what capacity. It was not until college though that I took time to thoroughly explore my alternatives in the various ROTC programs that were offered on campuses. I must be an officer of course. I always had a sense for more comfortable accommodations. The idea of an enlisted barracks filled with sweaty enlisted men did not appeal to a fastidious girl like me. Are you surprised? (I also do not find appealing the idea of groping under red lights in back-room bars). You would not have found me in the leather bars of the '70's.

In my case I maintained a certain hierarchy of the various branches of the military in their appeal to me. At the bottom of the list could be found the Marine Corps. Hitting the beaches unless it was for a swim-suit layout for Sports Illustrated just had no appeal for me. Although I found the idea of wearing a green beret to be rather chic I thought that counter-insurgency sounded more like what a girl needed to know to keep her virginity in a parked car.

The Air-Force was at least clean and somewhat heroic because it brought to mind gallant young chaps manning Spitfires and Hurricanes and shooting down Zeros over a clean blue sea. Then there was the Navy with their white uniforms and crisp salutes to grizzled Admirals on the Bridge of some grim grey-painted hulk of a battleship. But all in all I liked the Coast-Guard best of all. It was small, elite, and busy giving citations to yachts for not having aboard enough life-preservers. That was alright, but nothing to write home about. The Army meanwhile was only a step above the marines for grunginess. But alas, that was all that my school offered in ROTC training so that was where I signed up in my freshman year of college.

(It never occurred to me that I had a built-in passport around military service by simply being transsexual, although in those days to be branded with a 4-F by the Selective Service was the kiss of death for later life).

Just to show you how un-ready I was for Viet Nam (not that anyone ever was ready) my whole idea of military life began at the level of generalship. I was totally into left flank, right flank, and pincer movements at the regimental level, but when it came to grungy platoons, backpacks, and cleaning the carbon from old M-16's, well just forget about it. Unfortunately that was the level at which they insisted that we begin our military careers. Not that we had no spiffy decorations at all. We were entitled to these tiny little brass things which we had to polish constantly and they insisted on what they called "spit-shined" shoes, icky. Not only were the shoes big and ugly and slippery when marching on Astroturf at the gym complex where we met for early-morning drill but they seemed to be cursed by whatever guy (now off in Viet Nam) had owned them before me. They came with the curse of clumsiness. I simply could not march in them. I could never figure out what this whole "to the rear...MARCH" stuff was all about. I mean make-up your mind! If you don't know where you are going, then I am not going to let you lead me into battle!

"Uh, listen up guys. We're going to take that hill over there. I'm going to call in our coordinates and have the hillside strafed."

{Yeah make sure you get those coordinates right Mr. Map-reader cause I don't want to be a friendly-fire casualty}

"And then we're gonna move up country. Ready GO! Oh oh…"

{What do you mean oh, oh?}

"Ah, company to the rear March!"

Any way you get the idea. Drill was a perfect nightmare for me. This was Seattle and here we all were looking perfectly ridiculous in our clear plastic cap-protectors {think cap condoms} running towards the gym in our rain-shined shoes. Just getting up so early was bad enough but the "officers" had an even worse attitude that we budding recruits did. Let me give you an example. One of them kept insisting that my gun was a weapon. Now how dumb can you get. First, the gun was unloaded and I doubt if it even had a firing pin, and second, weapon is a generic term covering everything from sling-shots to nuclear warheads. I can understand making a mistake and calling my gun a weapon once but would you believe that this student officer kept making the same mistake every day and having the gall to correct me when I called it a gun? I mean I tried to be tolerant but really. Then we had to stand there and be inspected. How "pervy" can you get? Talk about don't ask don't tell…

Anyway drill was only two days a week and I figured that if I was just patient sooner or later he would get his act together on weapon/gun nomenclature. Meanwhile I was doing splendidly in class and had an A average going. I even liked the little tan manuals telling us about various military subjects. It was all so like the official Red Cross Lifesaving Manual. Anyway, I don't believe in doing things by halves. I thought that I should go them one better and join some voluntary ROTC organization. There were only two options: "Drill Team" and a gung-ho group called "The Raiders." Well drill team was out; who needed more of that "to the rear march" stuff? "The Raiders" though sounded like fun. So it was that I went to their organizational meeting in the basement of the brick ROTC building. We all sat down at bare wooden fold-out tables and I was waiting for things to begin…the welcome, the cookies, and the other advanced scouting stuff when suddenly some guy threw in something like a string of firecrackers and someone else called out, "Hit the dirt!"

Well everyone else did so while I remained quietly, sitting in my chair reading Chaucer's Canterbury Tales for my English class. Why should I encourage such sophomoric pranks? This was long before the days of improvised incendiary devices and I felt pretty sure that I was in no immediate danger so why should I join the others groveling about on the floor? I thought that I had shown my officer potential by quickly assessing the situation as a phony one. I was about to say, "It's all right there chaps, just a false alarm, part of the enemy's plan to demoralize us, try not to be so nervous, damn pity to dip the regimental colors at the first sign of danger, stiff upper lip, over the top and at them, and all that," when all of the other guys climbed back into their chairs. I was disgusted by the whole thing but decided not to embarrass them by dwelling on it but in that split second I had made up my mind that "The Raiders" was just not my kind of crowd. This impression was hammered home further when the whole crew and I began running about the streets in our college preppy outfits singing these stupid army songs, only one phrase of which still remains with me, "I want to be an air-force ranger; I want to live a life of danger."

It was about then that I began to suspect that this whole military thing and I were not going to work out. I might have to figure a new solution to doing my mandatory two to four years of military service. There followed a period of inquiring into every other way that I could serve. I received tons of descriptive literature from the U.S. government. There seemed to be an inverse ratio between the obnoxiousness of the branch of service and the time that one had to serve. I was more or less gravitating toward some combination of National Guard and Coast Guard when I decided that Army was out for sure. I liked our Colonel though and I went to see him. He tried to dissuade me because he knew that my grade average was an A in all subjects and he hated to lose me but I was adamant. I did feel sorry about not finishing the Biography of Patton that I was reading but in any case if he had been present I might have added a Trannie-slapping incident to his record. But then again he might have liked me. "Men, you should all be like this fine young recruit. He is advancing constantly. He doesn't even know the command, "to the rear march." "Oh and another thing, I would be happy to lead you wonderful guys into battle, anytime anywhere (and by the way the word is gun not weapon)."

My draft number turned out to be 183. It got to be December and my Mother heard from an officer one day at the grocery store that he doubted if they would get through the 120's. He recommended that I go 1-A for the month and if they didn't get to me I would be classified as what was called 1-H and I would likely never have to do military service at all! I chanced it. They never got to my number and I was spared an ordeal that I now know I could never have endured – gym class in high school was bad enough.

The Second Magic Year 1972

I had already come out to myself as a transsexual in the fall of 1972. I still refer to this period as the great thaw as though a glacier had suddenly melted and life began at last to flow in its proper channels. I had spent the summer in Cleveland, Ohio working on a driving-range at a golf course and memorizing a new poem each day. I was obsessed that year with Leonardo De Vinci and wanted nothing more than to have a renaissance mind like his. I also became obsessed with Tolstoy's "War and Peace" (I said obsessed not read). Instead that fall I read "Wuthering Heights" and became both Cathy and Heathcliff by turns. It was then that I developed my unique method of lining up opposing viewpoints and seeking resolution by seeing which one would prevail in a head-on-head competition. This was also the period when I became obsessed with the Olympics and when I bought Ralph Vaughan William's Pastoral Symphony, which became the very voice of autumn in my soul that year. This was the season when I first read the poets Wordsworth, Shelley, and Keats and that early classic of adolescent freedom in education, 'Summerhill.'

As the autumn progressed I read the romantic poets and lay back as the paradise of the autumn leaves falling yellow and lovely from the three poplar trees in the backyard. I dreamed then that all things were possible and that my own identity was infinitely malleable to fulfill any desire but above all to finally emerge as a girl at last. I began to realize only then how very resonant a contrary sexual identity was with my deepest inner feelings. I discovered then in the music of Ralph Vaughan Williams a mirror of my own spirit. At first it was only his London Symphony with its deep tragic themes which seemed to mirror all of my unspoken feelings. Later it was his Pastoral Symphony and the shorter orchestral pieces. What an addition he was to Dvorak, Brahms, and Paganini! Vaughan Williams seemed to be the voice of my very soul. What kind of autobiography is it that reflects loneliness so great that one adopts almost psychotic ideas of personal reference to fill the emptiness and then calls this happiness? But all of this set the temper of my future life. It was only an extension of my childhood, surviving by the use of imagination.

My "Russian" Period

I was late in discovering David Lean's great films. That same autumn our tiny local suburban movie house had a film festival and showed in succession "Lawrence of Arabia," "Dr. Zhivago," and later on "Ryan's Daughter," the latter film was about a young woman discovering her own sexuality during the struggle for Irish freedom. All three films deal with sex in an almost convoluted way and for me at the time simply to raise the issue was an awakening. So well had I succeeded in stifling all my sexual feelings and impulses that this was the period of my real adolescence.

That winter of 1972-1973 was what I call "my Russian Period." I lived on the steppes of Russia and dreamed of Julie Christie as Lara and of Lara as who I wished I was, but I would settle with being Dr. Zhivago instead if I had to. I became convinced that I was an immortal poet and that years after my tragic early death scholars would seek our any remnants of my past that could be found and debate over whether the undated poems were from my "Russian" period. Is it psychotic when you live in a completely imaginary world but still function as an everyday, boring, typical college student of no real interest to anybody let alone thinking that you are one of the immortals? But I needed to believe this so it became quite real to me and the slide in and out of identities was perhaps natural because I had never been approved for being simply me and I had been taught that I could never trust my own instincts.

At the end of 1974 I moved out of my "Russian" period. Instead I became a St. Francis of Assisi "wannabee." He was among the most androgynous of saints, at least as he was portrayed in "Brother Sun Sister Moon." But I liked the academic Jesuits better still so rather than be a Capuchin with a hood I opted for the stern intellectualism of a Jesuit vocation. I graduated with honors from college while not knowing a blessed thing about myself or what real life entailed in the world entailed. I simply tried to avoid various panic attacks and the onslaught of depressions. I knew that I was transsexual but the gears were already in motion and I did not know how I could tell my family that I would rather be a girl than a priest so I spent the last summer before entering as a novice reading Oscar Wilde's "Picture of Dorian Gray" and drinking Brandy and then left I home for the novitiate in Oregon and a life devoted to poverty, chastity, and obedience. I was as virginal as a white rose and in full flight from my feelings.

Driving my Chevy to the Levee

As a brief retrospective at this point of my story, my college years were the age of "Godspell" and the Jesus Movement, of the anti-corporate book "The Greening of America," and of the Jesuit activist, Dan Berrigan and the Catonsville Nine, the age of Don McLean songs, and the advent of Watergate and I was looking for something desperately. I knew nothing of life and less about myself but it was time for me to cast off and somehow live up to the American ideal. I knew that I wanted to be a girl and that to be one was impossible yet I wanted my life to count for something. Disillusionment seemed to be everywhere about me. I knew though that I admired the Jesuits and I still do. It was years before I was able to understand that what is today referred to in the DSM as Gender Dysphoria (all that remains of Gender Identity Disorder) had in my case made me show many of the criteria for BPD (Borderline Personality Disorder). Many theorists believe that BPD stems from traumatic life-events or from hypersensitivity to emotional events or perhaps from what might be an over-active part of the brain that deals with panic and fear. I only knew that I had been in a sense "shopping about for an identity" for some time. I would find people who seemed like me and read all about them. I had this tremendous bond with Vincent van Gogh and with Lawrence of Arabia. I would go to movies and walk out as one of the people on the screen.

I could have gone in any direction at this time. I avoided drugs because my mind was already complex enough and keeping my emotions balanced was a full-time job. It was probably lucky that I couldn't afford transition and was scared of it because at that time a pretty face and a pair of high-heels might have turned me into a transsexual version of Gia Carangi or just add a South American Dictator and I could imagine myself as another Evita. I now know that for someone with BPD surviving drama is the task of our twenties and I did it by hanging out with the holy guys who were my brothers in the novitiate of the Jesuit Order of the Catholic Church.

I was unhappy at the time because I thought the world was mine (that is when I didn't feel that I was nothing at all). The Jesuits gave me a reality check. That experience may have saved my life; it deflected me and delayed further confrontations with the world that would have been more brutal for me still. So what seemed like prison at the time was instead the very "holding environment" that I needed to keep me together instead of allowing me to run off the table like so many globules of mercury if spilled from a laboratory flask. My frenzy for life was tempered and my manic belief that I could somehow be all things and be in all places simultaneously was blocked for a time. Reality was allowed to penetrate slowly and in company and it may have saved my life.

Novitiate

Most transsexuals have a period of running from what they are. Some choose the macho military. I chose to join the Jesuit Order of the Roman Catholic Church by becoming a Jesuit novice. It was not denial alone that motivated me however; it was a genuine love for the Church itself, an actual love-affair that will be familiar to many who have known what it is like to enter upon a real conversion or the later activation of a latent faith. There is nothing like a clerical life to provide an identity to those who do not have one and I am sure that the path that I chose then is a common one. I will say that I have never known more camaraderie than I did in those two years, which seemed like prison at the time, but that now seem to have set a pattern from which I shall never completely emerge: one of order, grace, and peace. Considering the sexual pressure-cooker atmosphere of any sort of sexual segregation during one's twenties it may seem strange but I never heard of or saw any direct sexual acting out in the novitiate. In the old days young novices were cautioned against what was then termed "particular friendships." "Custody of the eyes" was stringently inculcated so that many older priests of the order never met one's gaze directly because they had so internalized this practice.

Our novitiate building was in an old convent and girl's school that looked like the House of the Seven Gables. I like to think that I played a certain mascot role while I was there by making the other novices laugh and composing birthday poems for them. I grew my hair very long and wore tight black polo shirts rather than the usual regulation button-down clerical shirts that everyone else wore. I baked cookies in the huge industrial kitchen and I excelled at volleyball. But just to assert that I was male I brought my huge karate kicking-bag down to the novitiate when I moved in and spent some time at it from time to time to demonstrate how really fierce I could be. I was also the only novice who enjoyed bathing in the freezing Oregon coastal surf that is notorious for its treacherous rip tides.

When we took our summer vacations to the Oregon coast I avoided the communal outer-buildings where most of the novices slept while we were at the ocean. I preferred the main cabin which alone had heaters. I was usually chilled to the bone by my day of body-surfing and from reading alone in the dunes at the end of the great sand-spit across the Nestucca River that separated the lush green hills from the sea. I remember thinking that I worked for the same God who had formed the earth and the ocean. I would stand gazing out at the bleak rock around which gulls circled all day with its huge expanse. We used to build fires among the driftwood logs each day and boil fresh crabs caught from our little motor-skiff at the head of the estuary. We would only head in for supper in the old refectory as the sun began to incline and the night breeze to pick up with the late afternoon. The old wood refectory with the nearby primitive wooden chapel and the main house were collectively what was called euphemistically "the ocean villa." I shall never forget those days that set up a lifelong love for the Oregon coast.

But if summers were paradise the long winter days and nights were grim. Our days were divided between various periods of prayer and study and various outer missions of mercy. In the first and second years we were also sent out on what were called experiments. The first year experiment was common to all and consisted of living on the city's skid-row and working in either a soup-kitchen for street people or doing admissions at a settlement house for alcoholic men. One of the least savory aspects of this was sharing one stall-less open toilet with all the residents. For someone as fastidious as I am, one who constructs an elaborate bird's nest of multiple overlapping sheets of toilet paper in a patented and non-imitable pattern that combines origami with practicality, sharing one nasty toilet with a long hall fronting it, around the corner of which anyone could come at any time is so horrifying to me now that I am surprised that I ever managed to tolerate it as well as I did. Then there were the delightful little cockroaches on the shower curtains in the moldy shower stalls. The whole place was probably an asbestos haven and sad to say I spent my days there engaged in repairing the ceiling with spackle so as to feel that I had at least accomplished something – no lung cancer yet but in any case it's too late now.

I brought along a huge bottle of pine oil disinfectant and some Lysol from the novitiate but how does one disinfect an entire world so I just stayed contaminated during all the time that I was down there. Strange though as it may seem, it felt good at night to leave the bleak streets and climb the urine-smelling stairs because the wet December cold stopped at the doors and once you were upstairs in the communal kitchen it seemed good to be warm and safely inside. We had no security protocols or education to prepare us to deal with any emergencies. I guess now that we were simply expected to wing-it. The result was that I quickly developed the same street-smart attitude that many of the tenants of the building had. I considered that I and the other novice paired with me were on our own and that no outside authority gave a damn about us.

I had a terrible cold while I was down there and may have acquired the tuberculosis exposure that later laid me low in 1980. The general health conditions were abysmal. I still recall one of the one-dollar hotels in the neighborhood which consisted of wooden cages with chicken-wire ceilings so that if anyone threw bottles over the partitions it would not hit other roomers on the head. I went up to one of those rooms in the hotel one day with one of the tenants who was visiting a friend to see how he was doing. Bottles of Tokay wine were stacked into a sort of longitudinal pyramid and the wooden floor was covered with various unmentionable blankets. The life of a street alcoholic consists of waiting for one's social security check and being kicked out of various low-life hotels. I recall resenting the nearby middle-class department stores and the whole society that allowed such places to exist. Who was going to care for these people and where would any real reform of these conditions even begin?

I remember talking one night to a young guy who liked sniffing paint and warning him of the health hazards and not understanding that he just didn't care. At the same time there was something refreshing in dwelling in an environment that was so appalling that all one's fears and loathing were present realities rather than some distant fear of what could become to one in our competitive society. Down the street there was a famous drag-bar in Portland. I longed to go in but I would walk by its posters of the girls with averted eyes because I knew that I wanted to go in and talk to my own people but that I had charted a different course for my life. I turned away from temptation.

When I returned to the novitiate for Christmas after the longest twenty-five days I have ever lived through I was joyfully welcomed home by my brothers. I knew that my street life was over and that I had survived its nastiness. They hadn't shaken me loose and by that I mean that my privileged and sheltered upbringing had been overcome to this extent at least that I did not just call home and leave. The result was that I survived into my second year and only left when the departing Novice Master had a general purge of unsuitable novices prior to surrendering his post to another. I left just before my second summer and vows. I spent the summer after I left working for relatives and still with no idea what I would do now that I was back in the world outside the novitiate. I had cut all my strings to my former life. All I knew was that I still wanted to be a girl.

Detroit

I didn't do anything specifically wrong to be shown the door of the novitiate besides manifesting a general spirit of rebelliousness to religious discipline. Of course that was enough. But above that reason I think that what was really involved in our rather forced agreement to part company was that I did not manifest the definition of what my superiors thought should be the values and image of where the Society of Jesus (official name of the Jesuit Order) was tending as it struggled to enunciate a collective image of its own mission and vocation. I did not want to leave but I was tired of shouldering uphill against what I felt at the time to be the scorn and personal disapproval of our novice master. This conviction was probably only partially true. I think that in his own way that he was trying to spare me a greater disaster later on and that if it had been strictly personal he would have been more willing to support and encourage my vocation. In many ways I have never left the novitiate and granted a higher level of maturity prior to entrance I no doubt would have managed quite well. The real problem was that without the structure of religious life I simply did not know then what to do with myself ... nor did my family. Thus began a life of "boomeranging" away from home and then back again, never getting a sense that I had pleased my family and yet never failing to achieve any goal that I set for myself.

I missed my community and felt that I was somehow in disgrace for even trying to be a priest like some sort of deserter on the field of battle. I valued the brotherhood and the goals of the order too much to compromise its values and my own to do anything that people may imagine takes place in a sexually repressed and cloistered all-male environment. I did find one novice particularly attractive but we were not particular friends and for the most part I avoided his proximity because simply seeing him was enough of a draw.

After leaving, or rather being shown the door of the novitiate like Fraulein Maria, I didn't know who I was anymore or what I still believed. I needed work though so I packed my books, my motorcycle, my new green cardigan and matching gaucho pants-skirt, and my one Coty Ultra-Red Lipstick and moved east that fall after working over the summer in a family owned business. It was already early autumn and my life had gone through a revolution since January when I had made a three day private retreat at the Trappist Abbey in Oregon. I had spent my time there reading Georges Bernanos and had more or less decided to stay in the order. That was not how things had turned out though and now I was a strange sort of caravan crossing the broad prairies. The aspens were turning into yellow flames in Wyoming. Amazing as it is to me now I appeared in full female regalia in Casper at a gas station and did so without any fear, a true testament if there ever was one to my budding confidence as a proto-woman.

I arrived in the last weeks of Indian summer to my new home in Michigan. The brief mid-west autumn of the year was soon in full force just before the bitter cold of early November set in. I would not be living just outside of quiet little Franklin Village and just north of the large community of Southfield. Both were well outside the grim limits of Detroit proper. It was here that I began to feel the full import of being transsexual. This was the first time that I could explore living as a woman. I was only twenty-four. Could I ever have been so young? Yet even then I was engaged in mourning for my lost high school and college years when I was not able to live openly as a girl.

I loved the snowy nights that winter and the sense of living in a "Dr. Zhivago landscape." I learned to bake bread and drank Stroh's Bock Beer. I worked by day in the inner city and came home at night to read while curled up in a big modern leather arm-chair. At work I read from my 18th century literature text to the firm's truck drivers eating greasy food in their lunchroom during what I called, "The Culture Hour." I suppose it was a kind of gay thing to do but I thought it was funny amid the grim industrial setting where I worked and I needed humor to survive. Detroit is the very archetype of a gritty early 20th century industrial city of power and steel. Nothing natural seemed welcome amidst the pollution. Only my innate romanticism and ability to identity with the sentiments of F. Scott Fitzgerald, William Faulkner, and D. H. Lawrence sustained me through the long solitary winter nights once I got home from the inner city. I would leave my greasy clothes on the floor at the entrance to my apartment and after a long bath emerge as my twilight evening self, a young ingénue. It was then the age of high disco but with only a few exceptions I stayed home and my night life was confined to Friday nights spent at a tiny Irish Pub in Rochester, a small suburb up north. Only a few times did I venture into the city as a girl and that took of all my daring. I felt like I was about fourteen (which I probably was inside). I was a naïve suburban princess and one subject to insult and injury when I came out, but youth is always on the side of a feminine appearance so I was never called on my gender. But in retrospect, the danger may have been more real than I ever realized at the time. At the time I had no idea of the entrenched animosity than can follow the discovery that someone is transsexual.

Then there was the issue of being "read" in daily life. I thought then that I would always be presumed to be straight and male whenever I wished to be read as one, after all I had worked so hard at hiding my secret through the years, but people in my life have again and again manifested evidence that my closet was really only a transparent one. Secrets will out and that's not even counting those tell-tale remnants of nail-polish that adhere to cuticles or lashes that weep mascara for hours after I would have sworn that none was left. There is also a strange compulsion within many transsexuals to court suspicion, something inside us that wills to be out. I can recall many times when the same declaration needed to be made and the same risk of rejection faced by explaining that the clues were in fact an admission.

In retrospect the Detroit years seem to me now be have been a sort of glacial exile. During those first months of my exile from religious life, with my friends and brothers now thousands of miles away I actually found comfort by holding a knife blade pressed against my breast knowing that one sure thrust would bring me release from my horrible loneliness. Later when a sense of hope had returned (as I assure my sister and brother transsexuals that it always does) I was glad that I had refrained. Death is nobody's friend. I have learned never to trust my sense that everything is falling apart. The margin of survival is often attained by simply waiting for the inner darkness to pass, just one more hour, just one more day. Strength gathers like water that fills a hole dug in the sand by the ocean. Never give up! I soon adapted to industrial life and I appreciated the chance to have my own dreams again and not to gage everything by the rigid daily regimen of the rules of the Jesuit order. Now my life was up to me. The problem was that I didn't know how to pick up the threads of my life again, in many ways a life that had always been handed to me already planned for me by other people, with the sole exception that I knew that I was transsexual and I knew that I loved literature. So that winter and spring I explored both and tried to put my new and unexpected life together, now that I was not to become a priest.

It was so cold that year for someone who had been raised in the Pacific Northwest. After a long day spent in an industrial setting it was such a relief to simply be clean and warm and lovely at the end of the day. But it was also a solitary and painful time for me to be so intensely closeted, as befitted that era. To be transgender then was not to be part of a generally recognized group with protections and legal standing. Every transsexual in those days stood alone. We were unaware of where to even begin to look for others like ourselves. So Detroit that year was a gender and sexual Siberia and it lasted for a year until I finally decided to leave my job, pack everything away, and simply be another "American in Paris." It was what young writers were supposed to do, a general rite of passage whether you were James Joyce leaving Dublin or Hemingway leaving the mid-west. I thought then, as I always did, that I could leave my identity behind me and forge a new by the sheer extremity of distance and as always I was mistaken.

Europe

After my year in Detroit I decided to do as I had always dreamed of doing, to go at last to Europe. My journey was a familiar rite of passage for American writers. Many of the writers that I had long admired had done the same thing, sought in the old world the experiences that would allow them to see their lives and their country in a more balanced context. I half-imagined (such was my vanity) that future generations of grad-students would some-day refer to this as my European period. I was still young enough to assume that my particular life and fate would be of interest to anyone but me.

I was totally unprepared emotionally to make a trip like this one alone. I felt like a lost soul when I arrived in Luxembourg with no one to meet me after my long flight on Icelandic Air-lines, which had the cheapest fares to Europe. Strange as it may seem I had not fully apprehended that with only a smattering of remembered German from high school and no capacity in French at all not even having brought along a French phrase-book that I would find it difficult to manage at first. I was totally culture-shocked and appalled by how *OLD* everything looked! What had I expected? All I had with me was one suitcase that remained at the airport in a locker for the entire six months of my stay in Europe, a backpack, a sleeping bag that I never used either not wanting to camp out in sheep pastures, and of course more books than I had time to read.

I also had a paper bag with a sandwich that my mother had packed for me, which seemed more than just a familiar article from home; it was like a link to another world. I know that it was very traumatic for me because that day old sandwich and the dreary look of the room I finally found by pointing to an address in my guide book is all that I can remember about my first day of the grand tour. I have a vague sense that I even had to share my room that night but that is all that I can recall. I do remember making it to the train station though the next morning. I knew that my resolution of the previous night to simply go home was out of the question; at least I should see Paris since I was here. So it was that I was soon on the train going south west. I talked to someone who spoke English on the train and I was soon re-oriented. I got off the train in Rheims and saw my first Medieval Cathedral and from then on I was hooked on Europe. I ordered a pork and mushroom pizza by using sign language, my first real meal in 48 hours, exchanged a traveler's check for some francs, and I was on my way to Paris. I traveled then for two months before heading east to Graz, Austria for my fall term spent learning German in an intensive-language course. I grew my hair long in Europe and I bought horrible English lipsticks that were cheap and almost as stiff and useless as color crayons. I often spent my time on the train as a girl while traveling but reverted to being a male when I finally settled down in Austria to study. For companionship when traveling I read from Dickens' "Bleak House" or Mann's "The Magic Mountain" and tried not to have panic attacks when it was night and the train was my only link to the comforts of a home, a sort of traveling domicile. It was at least a warm and moving place, and I often felt as alone as any human being can feel who has no real sense of herself, only a padded bra and a few turtleneck sweaters. I am just not cut out to be a refugee. I loved Europe though and felt like I belonged there in my life of trains and cheap hotels, of castles and cathedrals, following in the long abandoned paths of artists and the great writers I had read. I felt like a girl completely now and thought that when I returned home I could swiftly have my sex-change and begin life again with everything all right at last before I turned thirty.

But that was not to be. Those were the days when the formerly chic gender clinics at the universities were closing-down after John's Hopkins closed its doors to the many desperate sex-change applicants. Thus began a ten year search for medical help which in the period before the internet was humiliating and usually led only to simply being told, "The doctor does not see *those people.*"

But that was all ahead of me then and Europe was simply like one great volume of history now lying open before me. I lived on sausages and kraut salad and bread and rode the street cars around Graz past the Franz Joseph Platz to the Hauptplatz. I met the figure-skating champion of Austria and went with him and his girlfriend to a strange eastern European institution that served only thick bread smeared with the equivalent of bacon grease. We drank apple cider and shots of slivovitz.

Most of my fellow students seemed to live mostly on beer while I being four years older preferred to dine alone eating Raznici or Wiener schnitzel at a lovely family restaurant that was just down the street from the Gasthaus where I lived. I had lived alone for so long that I did not know how to reconnect to student life. I still lived in this intense but disconnected life of literary fantasy. I was reading Sinclair Lewis and a biography of James Joyce each day and growing accustomed to the vaguely post-war feeling of Styria. Tuberculosis was very common in Eastern Europe and I could see why Franz Kafka had died so early of what seemed to be a universal disease. It was treated at state expense at the nearby Landeskrankenhaus which was a grim place where the consumptives lined up in their bathrobes to receive their daily medications. I had to visit there just like Hans Castorp to get some medication for a lymph gland infection that I had in my throat. I may have contracted tuberculosis while in Graz since I was often sick in Europe. I learned that the war still cast its long shadows there, even into the present. We were on the very borders of Yugoslavia and on the fringes of free-Europe. There was something dark and sad in Graz and for the first time I appreciated the speed, the cleanliness, and the modernity of America. I was anxious to begin traveling again when my new rail pass arrived that had been sent to me from home. It was December and I went at first to England and then traveled through Trier and Aachen in Germany and then south to Switzerland and Italy.

In Italy a young, gallant, and handsome Italian offered to carry my backpack for me between the two stations in Milan and I will always remember his kindness. I was horribly tired that day and rather at the end of my rope after a night spent wandering the streets of Strasbourg because it was Christmas and everything there was closed. Grim and bleak Strasbourg was like a frozen nightmare and I walked about the town simply to keep warm because there was no second-class waiting room at the train station. Today I only recall the chill night, the empty streets, the darkened windows, and the great back silhouette of the Cathedral. I got to Piacenza at last and slept round the clock in the nicest room I was to find in all of my stay in Italy. I was glad that I had finished with my studies in Graz and it had been lovely to flee after seeing Italy across the continent to my beloved England for one last look at the land of the great poets and novelists. England was always clean and civilized with lovely bed-and-breakfast establishments; no more nasty, sewage-smelling, continental water closets with a dead drop to a malodorous underground tank. Lovely Brit-Rail trains took the place of the standing-room-only grey carriages of France. The pubs served Guinness Stout in great foaming pint mugs. There were delightful fish-and-chips shops at every corner and even British money was hearty and substantial. I knew in those last days that I must soon leave for home so I soaked up my last days in scenic Dover before setting off again for Luxembourg to catch my return plane flight to Chicago and then home to Detroit for a job interview. I was out of money, sick with a desperate cold, probably somewhat malnourished, and at the end of my physical resources. I was lost and triumphant at the same time. I had done something alone in spite of my fears and for me this was special.

I even trusted people a little but now. Europeans were always so kind to me. It occurs to me now that lake many male-to-female transsexuals I managed to convey my inner gender without announcing it by subtle expressions and body language. I certainly looked enough like a girl by then to occupy that middle ground of androgyny that broadcasts a universal appeal because I really was lost inside. So much did I feel like a girl that it did not seem daring or inappropriate on my part on my last night in Europe to share half of a big double-bed with a Belgian girl that I met only by necessity when my hotel was overbooked. The hotel was full and we all were going to be bused into Germany unless we paired up. I wasn't going to take a chance on missing my flight home in the morning by having to catch a bus back to Luxembourg from Germany. The whole thing was very simple and pragmatic and it seemed only natural that I would room with a girl and not a guy. The next day I took one last look at the rail station wishing my trip was just beginning and then went to the airport to return to America.

Dust in the Wind -1978

The year 1978 was my third "magic year," if a somewhat grim one. As I stood in the railroad station in Luxembourg on that last day and I looked up at the posted schedule and thought that it had all come to an end I knew that I would if I had the funds on hand begin it all over again. I had grown acclimated to the European landscape and mindset. Why then was I returning to America? Was I an American in spirit after all? Did I even know my own country? I was returning as I told myself that last day to re-build my base. It was in America I told myself that I would become a writer and it was there that my gender transition might at last be completed. My last week in Dover as I have mentioned was spent living the idyllic life that the swift pace of my travels had hitherto precluded. I spent that week in the town's library feeding my obsession with Virginia Woolf and Dylan Thomas. I would walk through the streets beneath the softly misted Dover Castle each day eating apple turnovers and waiting for the pubs to open. My evenings were spent in the gentle haze of pint after pint of Guinness Stout and as much fish and chips as I could consume. It is lucky that I needed to come home because I found that way of life so satisfying that I might have simply drifted off into oblivion like many other young expatriates have done before me. I was ill when I left. I don't know how much Vitamin C there is in fish and chips and stout but I doubt if there is any at all. Like many transgender people I had grown up divorced from my feelings and not particularly careful of my health. I can still see the lights of Chicago that lay below me as I circled down out of the night aware that I had left Europe behind me, perhaps forever. I caught an immediate plane for Detroit where I arrived in a sort of coma. I was beyond tired. The walkway to the baggage claim actually heaved beneath my feet like a boat adrift in the middle of the gulfstream. A friend who I called from the airport was kind enough to pick me up there and drive me through the icy streets of Detroit to my family's apartment located in a lovely suburban high-rise with a doorman. My parents had sub-let the family apartment that year to a hockey star. I would usually take over the apartment and pay the rent in the winters when my father began his long period off from his job. But this year it wasn't mine. I didn't care. "Go ahead and shoot me," I thought.

I talked the door man whom I knew into letting me into the apartment. I took the elevator up and hoped that the new renter would be off on a tour. I knocked and no one answered so I had the doorman let me in and collapsed on our big white coach. I was not disturbed that night. The next day I was given a guest apartment on the first floor. My hair was luxurious, clear past my shoulders and heavy in a way that it would never be again. My mouth though was so chapped by the cold that the lipstick that I wore behind closed doors left tell-tale red veins in my lips. I thought that I looked awful. I knew that I needed to interview with the same company where I had worked in order to seek a job before I left for home in Washington so I had my hair cut in one of the barbershops located in the business section of the apartment complex.

I met with my old boss and he mentioned that a job as purchasing agent might be open soon. Until then I decided to head back to the family home in Tacoma, Washington. So I wrapped up my girly-life and headed home to wait for the opening. I don't know what I expected after all my adventures but I was welcomed home as though I had barely been away at all. No one wanted to look at my pictures or hear much about my trip. As the weeks passed with no news from back east I went into a deep depression. I was reading Virginia Woolf's first novel, "The Voyage Out." It seemed to describe my feelings exactly. The song, "Dust in the Wind" by Kansas was very big at the time. I used to listen to it over and over again. Only when you are young does death and dissolution seem to be so sweet. I loved to think that I and everyone about me was only dust in the wind. It brought me a sort of dark joy. I know now how typical these symptoms were for someone with Borderline Personality Disorder, a disorder that had not yet been clarified even among psychologists. It was not until 1980 that the DSM III clarified the diagnostic criteria for this mental illness. So I faced my symptoms alone. I drank dark beer every night and went to a few gender support-group meetings in Seattle. I don't know what would have happened to me but just as I was about to settle in again in the old family business in Spokane I got a welcome call from the east. The job as a purchasing agent back in Detroit had materialized at last. I would have money coming in again like water in a desert. But I would have to wear male business clothes by day and only be myself at night.

Winter brought the usual snow and dry cold to Detroit but there was ice-skating again for me and that kept me alive. Ice rinks were my comfort and my joy in those days and I knew the schedule at every rink in greater Detroit. I was still isolated though by the sheer size and threat of that strangely divided city. My books were still my best friends and God my only confidant. I still dreamed of a career in law or psychology so I collected a huge library of existential and phenomenological books many of which I have yet to read. I may go to my death without a firm grasp of Paul Ricour!

I went to a gender support group the following year that was run by a doctor who seemed to hate all transsexuals. I caught the last gasp of the message of the old gender clinics that specialized in telling desperate people that they were only cross-dressers after all. "So just snap out of it; no hormones for you girl!" They took your money though and took their own sweet time about answering you. Oh, and as for follow-up (after they had skimmed off the creamy-dreamy types, the Miss Transsexual-America type queens who would do honor to their surgical skills by appearing real) forget it. So narrow were the surgical criteria at that time and so reluctant and few were the doctors still treating gender issues that most candidates were simply sent packing after their initial consultation fees were paid.

That was the transsexual world of the late '70's and '80's. Transsexualism just wasn't hip anymore and gender clinics were following left and right in the wake of the Johns Hopkins closure of its own gender clinic. No place for us, no rights, no diagnosis, no surgery. "Go away! It's your problem after all and nothing makes you people happy anyway." Maybe transsexuals were viewed then as simply poor candidates for any intervention at all on our behalf and not worth a research protocol. "Besides there simply aren't that many of you anyway, so learn to adapt, play the cards that you were dealt; shut up and go away." That was the message that so many of us were given at that critical time. I, like so many others, just couldn't make the grade to qualify for a vagina, so I was cast adrift once more. But by the year of 1979 I was ready again for another type of change as well. I didn't like the business world and I didn't want to get stuck in the east alone if my family left. My roots were always in the west anyway. Besides, I had caught a bad case of California fever, as much as anyone had during the gold rush era of 1849. I wanted to resume my education at last. I dreamed of pursuing the humanities or studying law before getting any older and ended up by taking a degree in both areas and getting an M.A. and then a few years later on my J.D. degree to become a lawyer.

California Reprise

In 1980 I began a new decade imagining that I had made my last mistake of indirection and that now my life would unfold clearly. I was reading Thornton Wilder, Henry Miller, Lawrence Durrell, and Anais Nin at the time and was still in love with writing. I began my love affair with California and particularly with the sleepy towns reaching south of San Francisco from Santa Cruz to Big Sur. It was my year of eating calamari on the dock at Santa Cruz, of reading Jack London and Robinson Jeffers in Carmel or the beach at Pescadaro. I loved the breakfast bistros in Palo Alto and the sleepy bookstores serving coffee and giant chocolate-chip cookies. I became obsessed with Carmel and the Big Sur Highway with its hamlets with magical sleepy names like Nepenthe on the way to San Simeon. I used to drive up to the city as well through the lush green foothills.

It was the San Francisco of 1980, just before the AIDS deluge was about to hit the city and turn it from paradise into a city of perpetual mourning. 1980 was the last clean and perfect year when everything seemed possible for gay people, just as 1963 had seemed to me before President Kennedy was shot. I remember two main things about that year: dreaming of literary greatness and walking along a beach crowded with too many people and vowing "no compromise" by which I meant that I would find my own way to live and never accept an existence mediated to me by others who would tell me who I was. Writers are like that. Shelley once said and it is probably true, "Poets are the unacknowledged legislators of the world." But like Jack London and Ernest Hemingway they often end up dead after years of self destruction in trying to forge an independent self. I know now that sometimes a mediated existence is the wiser choice – it can bring you money and a condo in Palm Springs if nothing else. As I mentioned above, I loved Lawrence Durrell and Henry Miller at the time. I was obsessed with the search for the perfect form for my writing. I liked the seeming spontaneous prose of Henry Miller and the dark romanticism and exotic locales of Lawrence Durrell. Both authors seemed to know the importance of place and time, how important it is to capture a fleeting impression before it is lost forever. Both seemed to know that it is our personal history that is important rather than universals.

I have spent my life bouncing back and forth like a ping-pong ball between the classical and the romantic spirit. California in 1980 was one of my romantic periods. That was the year that Mount St. Helens blew up at home in Washington. I had to wait until the fall to travel across the state and see the piles of ash there, piled up like great snow drifts. Who would have thought that so much molten anger lay beneath the great snow-cone that I had known? A similar secret was working in me that year. I developed a terrible cough and a sense of lassitude. I got weaker and weaker until I was fired a month early from my summer job and suddenly everything collapsed. I went and saw a doctor and discovered that I had a very bad case of tuberculosis. It took me a month to regain enough strength to make it home to Washington. My applications for graduate study to Stanford and to the University of California at Santa Cruz, both small scholarship funded humanities programs, had been turned down. I decided to go back up north and apply to the University of Washington for graduate work in literature.

My dreams of California had come to nothing and I was home again just like I had been in 1978 after my studies in Europe. But I was deathly ill now with tuberculosis. I had that in my flesh that the great artists and writers had known before me and many of them had died of it. I was almost happy to be ill; it was a strange bond of sorts with my favorite writers for me. Like many people with Borderline Personality issues I had always felt a sense of romance with oblivion, something one can afford when one is young. This attitude seems very foolish to me now when I know the high price exacted by time, but then it was a joy to be one with the falling yellow leaves at home because I knew that I would eventually recover. There was at least a cure – unlike with AIDS which in that very time of 1980-1981 was about to emerge in all of its hideous strength as its dreadful and stealthy presence had eluded notice spreading far and wide. It was about to become the new icon of death among the young as tuberculosis had once been. If I thought that my disease made me iconic I was not alone. An old High School classmate of mine soon became known as the "AIDS poster child." The following years were to demonstrate however that diseases have no favored children; they embrace multitudes.

Consumption Year - 1981

It took me a full two years to recover from tuberculosis although I ceased to be contagious after going on INH and Rifampin. It may sound strange but in my little private world of books and writers my sickness seemed to be a promise that these men and women whom I felt that I knew personally through their writings and published letters, many of whom had also suffered from the dreaded "white plague," were in fact my brothers and sisters. I still thought that someday avid biographers would scour up every scrap of paper that contained a sentence by me to write my biography for eager readers. After all I was one complex cookie! This delusion that I was secretly one of the immortal writers of my age was a compensation for my utter poverty and anonymity. Yet there is something romantic about the disease. Having had tuberculosis is to understand at first hand what the word "consumption" means. Tuberculosis feeds on you. It insinuates itself into every breath until you can't take a single breath without coughing. It lives with you for years with the intimacy of a lover and always it whispers softly, "You are mine and I am killing you little bit by little bit." I was treated at home in Washington by the county's public TB Clinic that was already treating hundreds of Cambodian refugees, the survivors of one of the worst holocausts that our era has ever known. We all stood together in line for our pills, INH and Rifampin, the latter of which makes you pee orange. (Just thought you'd like to know). As the weeks passed my physical strength gradually began to return. I spent my days of recovery drinking dark beer and reading the Letters of Thomas Wolfe before the fire at a local pizza parlor and dreaming of writing my own version of "Look Homeward Angel" someday. I later learned how hard INH is on the liver and I shouldn't have been drinking at all, but I lived in a strange sustained fog in those days just hovering above the earth. So I spent the spring of 1981 sitting in a window-seat looking at the fire, smelling yummy pizza smells and listening to "Open Arms" by Journey and "Harden my Heart" by Quarterflash.

By summer I was healthy enough to drive my little Chevy Monza around the west on an epic 8,000 mile journey. I bathed in lakes and streams and camped out for two months as I got to know my own country once again. By fall I was working on my Master's Degree in literature taking a seminar on the Decadent Movement of the 1890's (are you surprised?) and one on World Mythology. On my GRE I had placed in the top 2% of those taking the test on my knowledge of English literature and now I was in academic harness again so I thought that I had found my path in life at last.

I even fell in love and for the first time had my love returned. It was short but complete and without a dénouement. Even in these days of reunion-made-easy I have not sought out the following story of that first love with a lovely blond bi-sexual female writer. I prefer to leave it in the ashes of that dark autumn when I met her and the year that followed when I listened again to all of the old songs in all of the old places. As with all such early losses there is a part of us that is lost forever and best remains so. Like Wordsworth I can say that succeeding years have brought with them abundant recompense. I recovered from my early heartbreak and the folly of too easily relinquishing my long cherished virginity and I spent 1982 and 1983 after the break-up reading James Joyce's "Finnegan's Wake" and all of Virginia Woolf completing my literary studies. By 1984 I had decided not to go beyond the M.A. I decided that it was time for a practical degree in the real world so I applied to eight law schools and was accepted by seven of them. It is only upon reflection now that I realize how similar my life experience has been to that of the Victorian British pattern for England's upper-class sons: either go into the ministry or go into the law.

Law School

I was now living as a woman again. I suppose I owe it to the bigoted police actions extended to transgender persons in my home town in Washington and from the vigilant mall security types in those days that I decided at last to do what I had always intended before I entered the novitiate – to choose the law for my career. I now would become a lawyer! (Say what you will about lawyers they do draw attention). Lawyers are hard to eat in the same way that porcupines are; we are inherently indigestible. Nobody likes to mess with a lawyer if they don't have to do so; the next thing they may know is that they are up to their chins in nasty papers: subpoenas, motions for discovery, interrogatories, depositions, and worst of all trials. In the last analysis our entire legal economy has less to do with the substantive law and the merits of the case than it has to do with the ability of a rational human being to endure the presence in his life of close and intimate contact with lawyers. In fact many people would point out that lawyers are so obnoxious that they do not even enjoy one another's company. What could be better then in that era of transsexual invisibility and oppression than for me to become a lawyer? "Transsexual … oh and attorney hmmm, we'd like to throw her in the drunk-tank so she can be raped by morning but the bitch could sue us and if she can't maybe her friends, top-notch litigators all, will do so on her behalf." (Anyway that's what I figured).

The thing about law school is that there is no time to have personal problems because to have personal problems you have to have a life and a concept of happiness and for me during those years there was neither; there was only the law. If it wasn't in a big volume from West or Foundation then it just didn't exist. Life as life was not capable of judicial determination so naturally as a good law student I assumed that life as life did not exist. It wasn't that I really liked law school, but there is a compelling anesthetic in constant study that can distance one from all other painful life-choices. Happiness becomes irrelevant. One has no standing to bring a case for disappointed hopes. It just doesn't matter. So strangely, not since my days in the novitiate had I felt such peace. For my first two years I lived as a woman everywhere but at school. Only in my last year I thought it was time for a change. Law students are notoriously conformist and fearful. Class standing is so important and lawyers are still members of a profession that is overly identified with the status quo. Walking into class in a big amphitheater with one hundred other very bright and aggressive people is intimidating. I will never know how much good I did by walking down the aisle each day and taking my seat wearing my fringed white "solid gold dancers" go-go boots, but I like to think that, sitting in their plush offices serving corporate clients later on, a few of my fellow female students may have wished that they had worn their own snarky boots when it was still permissible in the comparative freedom of law school.

In my last year of law school I had my breasts done at last. No single feature besides the genitalia is as indicative of femininity as is the presence of breasts. As such I had always coveted them and felt my deprivation not as mere aspiration but as the loss of a birthright. I have told many transsexual friends through the years that the vagina and surrounding structures are virtually useless when it comes to negotiating gender reality, whereas breasts are immediately evident signifiers and as such have what might be called "a gender indicative currency-exchange value." A vagina by its hidden nature in contrast is only relevant to lovers and to the police if one must submit to being strip-searched. There is a very real economic component to being transsexual in our society and it is important for psycho-social survival and public acceptance to manifest as many cohesive gender-weighted traits as possible for a successful transition to take place. I have for instance seen some pretty butch numbers among the genetic female population through the years (and not all of them were lesbian) but breasts still carried that universal exchange value. In gender terms, breasts are as good as an American Express Gold Card – they are recognized and their possessors usually granted the status of women by the passing crowd wherever she may go. By contrast many very attractive drag queens are recognized and then despised, not because they look like men (they don't) but because pretty people often elicit that second appraisal that manages to detect some tiny residual male gender clue; when one is discovered it is just like a credit machine at the grocery store that processes checks. People who are "read" are targeted for their gender divergence. Not that most transsexuals want to look like heavy-set but maternal women if they can be slim young things, but in any case breasts are worth their weight in gold to transsexuals. Much of gender passing is directed to removing male signifiers such as facial hair so that one may begin to occupy that middle zone of androgyny before ultimately crossing over full-time. The presence of breasts can add that extra weight that tips the balance beam in a decided direction; the rest is in doing face work and female voice development. I had always wanted my own "Barbie-Doll Bust," my little gift to the world. It is amazing how happy a low-cut dress can make people. Breasts are the world's lingua franca. I guess we never really got enough nurturing as babies. So I have always been happy with my breast implants and willing to make the world a happier place wherever I go.

Wishing I could be Sheena Easton

My early transsexual ideals were the female singers of the eighties as I entered a long delayed adolescence and started on hormones. I loved what were called the "solid gold dancers" and watching "Night Tracks" on TBS. I loved to see The Bangles, Stevie Nicks, Bonnie Tyler, and the lovely Sheena Easton (if she called me on the telephone I would be sure to be home). It was the era of short hair and pouty petulance in female soloists with their flashing and defiant eyes and disappointed diva attitudes – great music for new teen transsexual lip-synching.

My older straight male friends watched in horror as a sixteen year old in a thirty-year old body sprouted among them tears and all as exemplified in the anecdote below when I became the Zebra-Lady on a memorable Friday night, an episode that appears consistent with the era of my transition but is a little embarrassing to the much more conservative comparative dowager that I have since become. But just play "Telephone" by Sheena Easton, "Self-Control" by Laura Brannigan, or "Total Eclipse of the Heart" by Bonnie Tyler and the slumbering "Zebra-Lady" stirs once again to life.

I guess you can tell that I love the sad songs best, songs of sorrow and release, songs poised on that bitter knife-edge where I have spent most of my emotional life. I am most likely to bond with pain, with one who knows what it is like to feel everything coming apart inside in tiny little shattered bits. I don't fall in love, I send out tiny green tendrils like ivy, I climb and interweave and blend into what I love. My desire is to create a shared space and time, an identity so charged and intense and yet so peaceful and eternal that I could stay there forever.

If it is true that transsexuals are denied affirmation in themselves, then this sort of vicarious search for bonding could be expected. I don't know what sex would be or even if it could ever be an appendage to love. It has always seemed to me to be a minefield of role-playing with rejection and humiliation ever present. I always keep something back well within a citadel that will not be moved. I can't blame the Church's teachings alone for what I am where sex is concerned. It might have been different I tell myself if I had the razor glance and incipient scorn that Miss Sheena has when she accuses her absent lover with, "I call you on the telephone, but you're never home." But I am far more likely to be like Bonnie Tyler brokenly confessing, "I really need you tonight ... once upon a time I was falling in love, now I'm only falling apart, nothing I can do – a total eclipse of the heart."

I don't know which sex does the abandoning thing best or which sex leaves their lover feeling most bereft of any dignity or residual self-worth when they leave. I only know that anguish and loss are things that I know and have known well. These feelings

206

draw me to the lost ones, those who know what it is to feel everything fading away like a withdrawing tide before a tsunami and the terrible wave of desolation that inevitably follows that withdrawing tide.

My First Coronation Ball

After I graduated I began to explore my new life as a girl at last. I was about ten years late but I tried to make up for lost time. I had by this time been on hormones for three years and had the only surgery that I could afford. I needed now to find my people. I began with what is called the "Imperial Court System." My first coronation ball was one staged by the local branch of the gay court system with its kings, queens, and other royal titles. It was a most significant event in my life. I had by then received my law degree graduating in the top third of my class. The ball was held at the old lodge of a men's club downtown in a great aqua-painted, antiquated, and semi-empty building. I was too afraid to come that night as a girl so I appeared instead as a hopelessly frightened sort of ghost-boy who managed to be admitted for free by name-dropping the name of my former Empress friend who had already arranged beforehand for my admission if I showed up. I had spent the afternoon circling through downtown and watching the arrival of the drag queens at M----'s apartment. My question was how I could enter as a mere observer and get past the gate to a safe place in the wings of the upstairs theater venue where the coronation was to be held. I suffered then and now from OCD and I was petrified of this then mysterious disease syndrome called ARC or GRID and finally AIDS that was already emerging in pockets even in Washington. But I couldn't stay away. I walked up the old stairs and a man with the gay clone-look of San Francisco, who had heard from my friend that I would be coming, motioned me through. The next minute I was in a corner looking out at the tables and seats and stage and reflecting, "I can't believe that all of these people are gay!" The beautiful women were all really men and only the short women with their short haircuts and black-tie-and-tails who seemed comparatively invisible, were actually women (and they liked other women!!!) It seems so simple now, but at the time and for "sheltered me" this was a revolution of consciousness. Later that evening when G------ sang that immortal song from "Dream Girls" and the whole room came alive with "And I'm telling you I'm not going … and you and you and you, you're gonna love me," I was just…well it was a revelation. The energy, the smell of the old theater, the warm sweet air with all the men, the sheer unapologetic affirmation of each other as gay, and me in the background like a silent wood-nymph was thinking, "Tonight all this energy, all this life, all this effort to find love and to bond and to preserve the silent gay culture that flies just under the straight radar is all so lovely."

But it was also so doomed by what was coming. That night is just a memory now and I often feel like Ishmael at the end of Moby Dick. I keep repeating, when I think of the many lost ones, that phrase, "And I alone am escaped to tell thee." Soon it was as though a great wind had blown through a grove of poplars with their yellow leaves, just now shimmering in the sun, leaving them fallen and the branches barren and empty. Where had so much life and color gone? If their lives were hectic and frenzied in their way, they were no less precious, but few seemed in that dark and negligent era to mind their passing.

The Pageant Years

In all my years as a transsexual in pilgrimage I had not known the gay community before. But in the late eighties I heard from a friend who was a cross-dresser about a secretive bar in Tacoma that had once been known as The Barbary Coast. It was located a block up from Pacific Avenue in a strange triangular block. Tacoma at the time still showed the remnants of the decline in its downtown fortunes that made it, in certain neighborhoods at least, something of an urban ghost town. Even now I can see in my mind's eye the old Greyhound Bus Station and the seedy area across the street which housed a decrepit tavern and a local adult bookstore. This whole area of town had always frightened me because in it I read a symbol of that darker side of life that was waiting to embrace those who had fallen from the clean and pristine world in which I had been raised. Yet I was seeking something that day as I drove into town. I was attempting to find the gay bar called "The Barbary Coast" and to glimpse something of those strange creatures that had created in its lavender and violet depths a rare and scarlet beauty. I recall now how appropriate the name had seemed to me with its evocation of a lost San Francisco, of pirates and miners embracing chorus girls with powdered and rouged cheeks appearing like ghosts out of the mist on foggy nights.

There is something in the gay spirit that delights in ruins. There was a trend that gay bars seemed (in those days) always to inhabit the slummy parts of town. This was due not merely to the desire to be invisible and free from police attention or to obtain the lowest rent possible; rather, the locations were chosen to confirm the entire world-view of gay men at the time, to confirm their love for seedy grandeur and Victorian facades. Gay men often used at that time their unique creativity to embody the erotic in various dark and precarious forms so that the world became a stage on which to project and embody their hidden dreams and fantasies. There was among other things a certain love of the tragic, particularly when it was embodied in women. The gay icons of the age included all of those women who seemed most tearfully over-the-top, women such as Judy Garland, Tallulah Bankhead, Bette Davis, Joan Crawford, and Marilyn Monroe. These women seemed to share the need that gay men felt within themselves to create and re-create new versions of themselves in pursuit of that strange and elusive gesture that might sum up in an instant all the pain and rejection of an entire life. That these women also often had a hidden masculine edge appealed to the drag queens who lent themselves to caricature but also to admiration. A talented drag queen could turn from tragedy to comedy in an instant by going just a bit too far. In laughing at herself she could rediscover a deeper sanity that made the tragedy of all of their lives bearable. These characteristics of gay humor known as camp were never better portrayed than in Jackie Curtis' plays "Glamour, Glitter, and Gold" and "Vain Victory" during the Warhol drag-diva era of 1967 – 1974.

In the hinterlands of Tacoma though there was only the dim reflection that day of the gay universals as embodied in the boarded-up and closed face of what had once been "The Barbary

Coast." It was out of business, closed perhaps a year or two before my return from the east. I had missed it. The pictures that my friend had shown me of black painted walls with silver stars were now no more. I got out of my car and walked over to the door now posted with handbills and graffiti. A substantial padlock guarded the door, and the windows, such as they were, were also boarded over. The whole impression made upon me was that I had missed the halcyon years and that while I was living in Detroit a renaissance had come and gone at home and it might never come again.

My twenties had swiftly faded away and I was yet to know the thrill of being young and painted and admired, to immerse myself in the black waters of gay life, at least to the extent of joining these fireflies of night for even a single evening. I could not know at the time though that in the years ahead I would become a sort of phantom presence at other gay events watching always from the outside. It was perhaps these very fears that saved me from the disease that was to ravish that vanished world of early gay life.

As I sit here typing I am aware of how many of those lovely creatures I had known so well were to die in the late eighties and nineties so that what I was witnessing was not a renaissance after all but rather a long drawn out aria to vanished youth and beauty eclipsed too soon. I think now of the successors to "The Barbary Coast" in those closeted days. All of these I have entered as though I were entering the core of some nuclear reactor, amazed that between those walls was present an obscure African virus that was engaged in killing many of the men about me. Had it been another time or another place, had I not been Catholic to the core of my being, I might have joined the passing carnival of their lives. As it was I was to become a mere observer at once of them and yet still apart as a transsexual. What I desired for everyday was for drag queens but an evening of glamour. Not for them a sweater and blue jeans drawn tight over hormone and silicon enhanced breasts. No, for them there must be floodlights and sequins and color, the homage paid to the empress as she takes her last walk in a diamond tiara signifying that her year of rule has ended.

The court system funded various charities. Each year it had its series of drag balls. They were called: Closet Ball, The Miss Gay Tacoma Pageant, Imperial Prince and Princess Pageant, The Empress Ball, and Mr. and Miss Gay Washington, held in the late spring. Often these were staged at the same lodge I had first visited, a vast ruinous building painted a faded aqua color on the outside. There were balconies that overlooked Commencement Bay and terraced walkways where the drag queens would cluster on a warm spring night to smoke and gossip between their acts.

I can still see D------, tall and dressed in a skin-tight pink jump-suit and silver heels shimmering in a cloud of blonde air. I can recall how G------ sang a song from Showgirls on an evening just like this and brought the crowd to its feet. I can recall the strange and sultry air of old leather seats and damask draperies, of perfume and of scented bodies in a closed space.

Later still I was to join them at more glamorous venues held in better parts of town. I used to stand all evening in my high-heels and my tacky trannie-glamour (for in those days I could not afford to buy the gowns that the drag artistes had made themselves with endless beading in living rooms while watching Dynasty and imagining that they were Crystal or Joan Collins).

I watched as always from outside as these beauties sought to ambush the perfect turn of a lash or the scarlet and disdainful mouth of vanishing stars while I, like a clumsy Afghan Hound wearing my shaded, ash-blond, "Tina Turner" spiked hair that was in fashion at the time ran about paying homage to what I dared not claim for myself, dared not for I knew that to embrace it was to embrace fatality as well. For many it was too late for caution. The virus had stolen in amongst them in the late seventies and early eighties while I was in Europe or Detroit from places like New York or San Francisco, from Fire Island or the Russian River. It was too late for these people and in a different way too late for me as well.

So it was that I merely watched and listened and admired then so that someday I could record what it felt like to be among them, when the outer doors would open at last after the ball, long after midnight, and the wet rain-drenched air of Puget

Sound in autumn would flood the hall. The tables, which had been pristine in the early evening, would by then be littered with the remnants of drinks and the air fogged with cigarette smoke. The great florescent lights would come on and the glamour of the evening was over.

I would see the tired eyes of the men in suits who would escort home the skinny youths who for an evening had been like the most desirable of women but were then revealed, in the late evening lights, as simply skinny kids who often worked by day in a sandwich shop or in a beauty parlor, what was called in gay parlance, a hair-burner. The elegant gentlemen would return to their antique shop trades or other occupations. I would climb into my car then and seek the solace of the suburban west-end of town which was all heterosexuality except for the one lone transsexual, the one who was now frantically trying to wash off her makeup to erase the aura of an evening spent among these very people whom she both admired and feared.

Tribes

I had the advantage of having been raised in the era when to be homosexual was such an arcane and subversive designation that to "come-out" was a revolutionary act. By contrast the present period of gay visibility seems at times shocking even to me. I had come over time to consider members of our community as fundamentally different from the average members of society who were both gender and sexually orthodox by being heterosexual and comfortable with their assigned gender role. Bisexuality therefore seemed to me to be rather like polygamy in that no essential and final choice between limiting extremes needed to be made. For this reason I have also caught myself being impatient with the vaguely incestuous character of any gay relationship in which the parties are not within a fairly close propinquity in relative age. I prefer a certain tension to exist between two individuals engaged in a sexual relationship and if that tension is not provided by sexual differentiation then I prefer that an almost mirror-like identity be present.

My problem with a gay sexuality between individuals of diverse chronological ages is that it is not "homo" enough. It looks more like incest between a substitute father and a substitute son. The categories collapse so that my general disapproval of incest prevails over whatever loyalty I might feel to the gay liberation of the individuals involved. Perhaps this disapproval stems from my own need to separate from the parent of the same (at birth assigned) sex. I share with Freud a belief that the father/son relation is one of essential competition and conflict. I envy the approval and warmth that some Jewish men show for their sons, but that very closeness is preserved by a firm heterosexual emphasis upon eventually contracting a viable heterosexual marriage and expanding the Jewish community by bearing and raising offspring. The innate sterility of homosexual relations never seems more pointless than when it is less a political designation and when it approximates basic family ties while failing to embody those ties in a traditional and procreative heterosexual marriage. Coming of age when I did, gay simply meant political rights to me and all else was subservient to that struggle. I rejoiced then in the fall of the anti-sodomy laws at the very same time as I found its actual practice to be abhorrent to my own sensibilities. Some may say that I thus betray my own shame and repression and I plead guilty as charged. I am far too inherently "a bottom" to imply that I would find certain passive positions as fearful or unpleasant as they seem to me. But it is hard for me to ever leave the alpha role. Along with many transsexuals I am profoundly uneasy with sex. I like knowing about it and enjoy being able to show a familiarity with Baudelaire and de Sade, to know all about The Everard Baths and The Mineshaft, or the Meat-rack on Fire Island while being appalled at the idea of fornication in any form. If I have a sexual preference at all it is for long, languishing, and tortured relations between two tragedy-racked souls like Heathcliff and Catherine in "Wuthering Heights."

I am similar to the poet, John Keats. I usually prefer the still cold charm of an ever elusive La Belle Dame Sans Merci to a warm Ianthe. Worse still I love the Liebestod of German lore over the warm Mediterranean loves of healthy lovers. Love that is not anguished and indefinitely deferred seems shoddy and lacking in true romance. May Sleeping Beauty always recline behind her thicket of thorns! These become her more than many a panting session followed by a trip to the local convenience store for a six-pack. Lovers that do not drink poison and plunge "happy daggers" like Juliette into their breasts are missing out on something wonderful! What they are missing I do not know, because I never reached that hour of desperate fulfillment in my preoccupation with the pursuit of equally tortured fellow sufferers. I am one of those who fears to lose what their own terror of rejection or commitment always keeps in any case infinitely at bay. I am rather like Henry James in this disposition. The prose of Henry James is disjointed by constant qualification and requalification as though any simple declarative statement must always entail some degree of oversimplification. Poets have written many lines about the charms of intellectual beauty and I have nourished a long life at the pale fire of their words while the outer darkness pulsed with the voodoo rhythms of variously coupled bodies. I prefer a more Augustan and classic model for love, one of two marble statues or figures on frescos with the two lovers engaged in an always deferred pursuit through an olive grove. Eroticism is at its height of passion when unfilled by climax. Suggestion is always preferable to full explication.

I believe that the genius and displacement that often made gay men the arbiters of fashion and of taste in past eras was due to the comparative unavailability of actual homosexual experience. I still value the witness of that prior era and the subtle rebellion of gay bars hidden in the depths of every big city when the torch of smoldering rebellion was carried proudly by the drag-queens. Maybe sex is all about tension. What, after all is sad and done, is more prosaic than naked bodies coupling? The real problem with pornography is that it represents a real failure of the imagination. Most of the art of the western world is made of imagery that seeks to explore ideas that are either unexpressed or inexpressible by other media. Beauty is all about invitation made from across a border of thorns. Free love is not love at all. Love must always exact a price of some sort if it is worth pursuing. The tribes of gay men and lesbian women used to know this. To suffer is the price of being who we are and resistance is what makes any political struggle worthwhile in order to build a sense of community cohesion. Nothing will disperse our tribes faster than joining the dull mainstream of middle-class American culture.

A philosophy teacher of mine once said:

"Happiness is the acceptance of human conflict, both within your own life and in and with others. So if you don't have any conflicts in your life; go out and find some!"

GLBT people have historically never been lacking in conflicts and it may have done us good by making us who we are. I remember once talking to a man who said that homosexuality was the cause of the decline of western culture. I wanted to tell him that gay men like Socrates, Michelangelo, and Whitman had made western culture while men like him already *were* the embodiment of the decline that he was prophesying was soon to come. So perhaps we had better main tribal after all rather than seeking out too much acceptance.

The Plague

It is difficult though to form a community on the foundation of exclusion or destruction. The members of my generation of GLBT people who have survived thus far free from HIV infection must look backwards at times with a sense of gratefulness that the great scythe of death by AIDS has thus far passed them by. For me that reflection involves the memory that I was living in the San Francisco Bay Area in 1980 just before the first cases were diagnosed and the warnings went out about the strange new disease affecting young gay men. I skipped Polk Street and the Castro and used to go on my visits to the city to an Irish bar off of Geary and drink Anchor Steam beer and listen to Irish music. If I had proceeded eastwards I might just have found a drag bar and a friend and walked away with the virus. It is like having visited Mount Saint Helens and Spirit Lake just before the volcanic eruption that occurred in that same year.

I remember first hearing about AIDS on the Donahue show and thinking, "Oh, oh, this is going to be big." Well it was even bigger than big and it tainted the whole experience of coming out for me because sexual love equaled death for most of my early transsexual years. No one really knew just how much saliva in even a wet kiss might be deadly. As a result, what admiration I did share was from afar and within two years many of the pretty ones I had envied for their beauty were wearing the tell-tale lesions on their backs or legs visible at the annual Freedom Day Parade in Seattle.

I appeared on an early AIDS discussion panel with HIV positive people, but I was afraid to undertake those more intimate services of cleaning and meal preparation for AIDS patients like the volunteers with The Chicken Soup Brigade. AIDS was a great dark shadow hovering over entire neighborhoods so that when I heard that G----- was dying that night after M---- had quit her job to take care of her for her last months I felt involved but safe behind my own wall of celibacy. After a time I simply assumed that everyone that I knew in the gay male community was HIV positive and for the most part I was right. There seemed to be a sort of "AIDS look" and after awhile it was added to one's innate "gaydar" so that even in a crowd of gay men some stood out as being further along the road of their T-cell devastation. In the tragic grand opera of those years I had a balcony-box seat and even spent time milling among the crowd in the pit. I was like a skier going down a giant slalom course but I never lost sight of the grim reaper that was weeding out the community year by year and even month by month.

Today AIDS is just as present and even more insidious as a threat but no one talks much about it thanks to the new AIDS drugs. But for one who recalls the plague years this attitude is foolish because we are only witnessing a brief reprieve rather than a cure so far and the virus could easily mutate at any time. Those who lived through the dark days of the middle 1980's will always recall above all else that no one seemed to care as long as they were not exposed to the communities that were hardest hit. It was the period of triumphal televangelists who were using the new capacity of cable television stations to reap record profits, passed on as high salaries to people who often used AIDS to swell their coffers by pointing out how deserving of God's wrath were these practitioners of unnatural coitus. My memory of the period is of anger and fear in equal mixture as well as a sense that something historical was happening around me. There was something in this, in the knowledge that a generation was being winnowed out, not by the war in Viet Nam as the last winnowing of my generation had been, but by an alien monkey microbe from Africa. Who would have thought that such a thing could ever happen?

Anyone who recalls the hatred for gay people of those days, and I as a transsexual was the proxy recipient of much of that hatred, will never forget the sense of isolation and abandonment. I recall walking through the autumn leaves one night to climb up the stairs of one of the old North-end apartment houses and being part of the group gathered in the living room around a large table. My friend D---- who I talked to every night lived in the same complex. Everyone was painting up for a night at the bars. All the skinny queens who were so pretty later always looked like plucked squabs out of drag, except for plump and pretty A----. The drag queens lived mostly on bad food and crystal meth, so that even had AIDS not come around many had already charted out a short life course. But they all had a frenetic energy and beauty to me, like colorful orange moths flying into a fire. There was a sense that time and life were only granted for tonight and the task was to dance and make love now, now before the final curtain fell.

When I left later that night to walk to my car and looked up through the Tacoma mists at the warm bright windows I had just left, I wondered whether I should be up there with them ... or was there more life after all to be found in the lonely transsexual walking away alone through the wet and fallen yellow leaves.

Night of the Zebra-Lady

I am not sure that the literature on Transsexualism has commented sufficiently on the phenomenon of spontaneous age regression in transsexuals. Certainly it has been noticed that many transsexuals attempt to catch up on their past by choosing clothes a decade or two below that associated with their current age. Some of this is simply attempting to be as attractive and feminine as possible through what might be called feminine overkill. The theory is that gender identification is a matter of the number and variety of gender- specific clues: breasts, butt, hips, and mannerisms that one may adopt.

The ultimate goal is to avoid being "read" or "clocked." It takes years to realize that most women feel comfortable with a certain number of masculine insignia without fearing that they will compromise their identity as female by adopting them. Ordinary observation reveals that many women display a certain lumberjack quality and yet never get called by masculine pronouns. Perhaps society has an unwritten rule that the more masculine and bulky a woman may appear, as long as she retains some fragmentary sign of her actual female gender, will be read as female; whereas many a drag queen who looks as though she has just stepped off the Red Carpet on Oscar Night will still be called sir. Go figure! Anyway that is not what I am talking about here. I am talking about the emergence of a younger emotional and mental self, particularly under stress as spontaneous age regression.

To dispense at once with any unnecessary mystification: the Zebra-Lady in question c'est moi. I had bought myself two skin-tight jump suits as befitted a trannie in the 1980's. My identity at the time alternated between Sheena Easton and Dolly Parton with touches of Madonna and of course the Palmer clone-girls. That night I was going to the TS support group in Seattle escorted by my two old high school chums who were less than thrilled by my choice of a garment for the evening, one that was light-weight enough to be stirred by a sigh. I on the other hand thought that I was one hot cookie and I must have been right because traffic slowed, even along gay-sophisticated and therefore one would have thought bored and jaded Broadway, the street in Seattle that bisects Capital Hill in Seattle's main gay ghetto.

"Who needs to wait for a Freedom-day parade to prance," I thought. I had always had a hard time with trannies who looked like they had just come home from voting for 'Ike' Eisenhower. I was more sixties-chick crossed with eighties new-wave, and with just a touch of the Playboy Club without the powder puff tush.

The plan was that they would drop me off on Broadway and Pike and pick me up again at 8:30 when the meeting ended. The meeting went well and I enjoyed showing off amongst friends at the break when we all filed out into the hall. The center closed after the meeting finished at eight-thirty though and I found myself standing on the street corner, freezing my tush for fifteen minutes while I waited for my friends to show up, which they finally did. I thought I was being more than gracious to overlook their lateness knowing as they should have known that I was a trifle exposed standing on a street corner in the dark on Capital Hill on a Friday night in a Zebra striped jump-suit. I wanted to be seen as cute but not as a public convenience.

Anyway, the plan was to go to a popular straight watering-hole on Lake Union, upscale, maybe even a little stuffy, but modern, all glass and chrome. My two friends dropped me off at the door while they supposedly parked the car. I was still a little huffy about their lateness in picking me up so I thought I would wait for them in the seating area before being shown to a table with my two escorts.

It was then that things began to go terribly awry. The minutes began to tick by. I began to wonder why it was taking so long for them to park the car. A certain low-grade suspicion began to gnaw at me. Their earlier sullen discontent, combined with their lateness in picking me up on time began to seem less an oversight and more of a dark and subtle plan to teach me a lesson. The mere thought that this might be so soon grew from suspicion to panic. I am not sure how familiar you may be with Zebra Jumpsuits but they do not have pockets. Besides, it simply spoils the entire impression of just having stepped off a catwalk in Milan if you are carrying a clunky purse along. In other words I was in Seattle on a Friday night with only a slim film of nylon between me and the cruel and naked world, which now began to seem to me to be utterly strange and hostile. It was about then that the spontaneous age regression I have spoken of really came into play.

I was an abandoned woman miles away from home, chilled and sitting in a fancy upscale restaurant without an escort or a dime to my name. My mind began to race. Who could I call? My panic was seasoned by a healthy helping of surprise and a sense of betrayal and outrage. How could they do this to me? Had I never really known them? Sudden abysses of latent male evil yawned before me. My rising panic soon began to manifest itself in signs of acute distress.

This was in the days before cell phones and no public phone was available without a walk out into the even more threatening night. I asked the maitre'd if I could use the restaurant phone and he graciously agreed. After several frantic calls I reached no one.

It was then that things really got interesting. My panic began to spread among sympathetic waitresses who began to leave their stations in shifts to come out to the foyer to comfort me. To this day I can recall few instances that better showed me the basic goodness of the human heart. My abandonment had assumed epic proportions. I was every woman who has ever been left alone and without recourse. I only wished that feminists and people of goodwill from every era of female exploitation could have been there to witness the perfidy of my friends.

My personal trauma was now spreading further still. Patrons became aware that there was a reason why their shrimp-puffs and linguini were being held up through a shortage of waitresses. Who was this Zebra-Woman and why was she in tears? What nameless dread had clasped itself upon her like a viper to her hormone induced bosom which rose and fell in hyperventilated angst? What fiends had added to their earlier caprice by leaving her in Seattle to thumb her way home, the prey of lustful long-haul truckers or wrapped in a borrowed rain-coat to solicit quarters on the chill night streets? Where was the Greek recorder of elemental tragedies to record the hour? What were the sorrows of Dido or Clytemnestra to that of the thirteen year-old me who was sniffling in the vestibule? All of this had occurred over the space of about twenty minutes since I had first walked into the restaurant fresh from the cat-walk in Milan into a Shirley Temple movie.

During all of that time the dark souls who had been my friends earlier in the evening, with the sympathy and foresight of most males of the species, had decided that the smells from the local McDonalds across the street were too good to resist and after parking the car had purchased some burgers and fries and gotten involved in "boy talk" in the car. Just what they thought that I was doing while they dawdled is a mystery that will never be solved. In any case they were about to pay for the oversight even if it was merely due to a genetic flaw of their sex chromosomes. They entered at long last to find a comely waitress holding my hand while I cried with that peculiar wholeness and completeness that leaves us all at the end of adolescence. Not even Shirley Temple addressing Captain January could have had more pathos in her voice as did I when I stood up and said, "I thought that you had left me."

As suddenly as the storm had come upon the unsuspecting eatery a solution had been reached. The thousands of accusing eyes focused upon the cads caused them to secure a swift retreat with the Zebra-Woman, still weeping freely, more freely than she had yet done now that rescue had come at last, even if it was offered by the unworthy, by the very ones who had so callously abandoned me. They were now condemned to suffer my tears all the way back to Tacoma, tears which like the pent up Nile simply would not stop.

It was only after they had dropped me off and finally driven away after suitable apologies two hours later that freshly bathed and comfortable in my warm duplex apartment in Tacoma I attempted to explain to my roommate and even to myself what had just occurred. That it had been real, I could not doubt. I simply could not have acted a part so completely, not even as a method actress. Brando would have been impressed and Susan Hayward would have looked to me for tips. No it had been real alright. The Zebra-Lady had been in reality the long suppressed little Zebra-Girl, the tears shed had been for the long abandonment of the little girl I had once been but could not express in due season because there was no name for Childhood Sexual-Identity Disorder at the time. My older self had simply disappeared and everyone around me seemed to know it. I had received a rare glimpse into the latent compassion of humanity, which had I trusted it as a child, might have brought me the understanding, even in that more ignorant time, that I had once needed so badly and never found.

221

Behind every transsexual is an ocean of hurts, born at the time by a child who needed to keep silent about all that was closest to her or to him, a stranger even to her own soul. Is it any wonder then that when the time is right that lost child may rise again to the surface as mine had done that night in Seattle, when an unwitting bistro that had witnessed drunks, catfights, fits of jealousy, and all manner of other situations was knocked off its certainty and routine by the advent of the drama of the Zebra-Lady?

A Transsexual Intellectual on the College Lecture Circuit

I didn't rush right into law practice when I graduated. Jobs were few and the interviews for budding transsexual lawyers were if anything virtually non-existent. In any case I didn't go to law school to practice law in the final analysis – I went to law school because I wanted to understand how the world worked. So it was that after law school I wanted to understand systems theory and went on to study the systems theorists. I became convinced that the reason that things went wrong was that they were approached at the wrong level of analysis. I now went in search of some vast and greater synthesis, a search for an uber-methodology that could resolve all questions by defining the conditions imposed upon questioning as such. I am still on this quest.

After graduating from law school I did a few television shows and radio shows in which I would simply talk about anything that occurred to me. The idea of course was to show that simply being transsexual was not a disclaimer to having a mind. I was a sort of performing seal. In retrospect I am embarrassed that I went into classrooms more as an exhibit than as a person, but it did allow me to have my say in many arenas for a few years and for this reason alone my appearances may have had value. A moment of reflection will reveal that most public celebrities are given extensive air-time, not for their insights, but simply by virtue of being press-worthy. I got used to being able to rivet attention long-enough to get my message across. Like many public speakers I learned how to read an audience and to pull people into the lecture. Once in America the Chautauqua circuit provided a venue for people like me to entertain with ideas.

After all, ideas make great entertainment. I carry around a vast and diverse body of knowledge in my head that allows me to comment and trace ideas across many disciplines, but above this is the ability to show how ideas can relate to human experience and values. The telling phrase is the key to successful legal advocacy and the mutually agreed consent to form a contract is the basis for most human progress.

What all of this has as its basis was my desire to have an impact upon the march of events. If I have been marginalized as a transsexual person I have also been granted a unique perspective on one of the great givens of human life – sexuality. From this unique outsider viewpoint I have been selectively made immune from many of the ways that people surrender their sovereignty and accept the complacent generalities of life. I practice what might be termed "creative anarchy" as a basic style of life. A friend once summed this up as saying that I behave as a combination of an entitled heiress and a moppet.

It works! In a world where everyone is adjusting to reality much is to be said for those who succeed in ignoring it. So much of what we call real is after all simply projected images of our hopes and fears. Obstacles that appear to be solid walls are often mere stage-settings made of thin cardboard.

So it was that after law school, when I might have been learning to claw my way into a law partnership, I became instead a general critic of what I had just learned. What had happened was that I had already come to see law itself as simply a method of justification for often foregone conclusions. The real task of an appellate court is to learn to weave prior decisions into as seamless a web as possible while still reaching the decision that is dictated by the prior world-view and values of each judge. The same critical method that I applied to the world of law I now applied to Transsexualism as a whole.

What was this whole enterprise of gender change? What were transsexuals really searching for in the contra-body of the desired sex? After all of the interventions had taken place were we ever happy? Was I happy? Could I ever be made happy? Had my history been different, would I have been happy? Or was it like this: if Descartes had said, "I think therefore I am," my characteristic mantra was, "I am, therefore I bitch at things until they give me what I want – because of course I am right."

So I proceeded to become first a wandering lecturer and then a professor of sorts. I taught college for several years and learned that there are few more cynical professions than being a college instructor. Finally, I had seen enough of educational duplicity. I was ready for my own "total eclipse of the heart."

I Move onto the Sea

I moved onto the sea for the same reason that people have always gone to sea, to escape the land, to leave my old self behind. I was thoroughly sick of everything. My beloved mother had suffered a stroke and my hopes to re-unite our family in the northwest and perhaps to recreate the life that I had known but with a different outcome was now impossible. Now began my darkest period. Who would have thought that everything that is now precious to me would begin with the decision to move to a little village on Puget Sound so very close to the Vashon Island that I had once dreamed about after reading "Criss-cross Vacation?"

I had always had a thing for boats. There is something about escaping the land and looking back upon it from the sea, which has no set lanes and traffic lights that means a sort of ultimate freedom. From my very door-step I can theoretically sail to China, Africa, or Europe without touching the land again before arrival. My hope was that by going to sea that I could definitively escape having a body at all. The metaphor of voyages and the common experience of trial and travail seemed to merge all gender differences into the more overriding question of how human beings have survived the encounter with wind and wave in the various frail crafts with which they have ventured out upon the bosom of the ocean. I developed in short order an extensive nautical library containing accounts of precisely these experiences.

Living on the water takes a certain degree of endurance and ability to reduce personal space to a minimum, but since I love tidy cozy nests and live sort of like a hamster, this part wasn't bad. I don't get seasick and I quickly adapted to the perpetual wind-chime effect of loose sheets and halyards banging against masts because they are too loosely tied down. I loved having the water near and watching the blue herons fishing on the dock beneath the lights at night and hearing the river otters making their strange squeaking noises.

In my time living on a boat I have learned to navigate gang-planks in high heels, to paint my bottom myself, the boat not my body, and to navigate by compass and charts. I have been in every bay and inlet between Puget Sound and Campbell River on Vancouver Island. To live on a boat is to know an intimate relation with wind and weather that no householder may ever feel. When the elements howl about you on stormy nights and various drips and drops find their way even into your most reserved dry private spaces and the heat that your tiny heater throws out is swiftly obliterated by various drafts, any shelter is appreciated even if it is moving about with every new assault of wind and wave. To bond with a boat is to know a connection that must meet the various conditions of the sea and even those who have not known real peril can speak of times when one's old friend turns against one and the danger is quite real.

I will keep my sea tales for another book though. Suffice it now for me to say that I would not have missed this rather unique context for living. It has shown me how spare and sparse our needs really are and how artificial, elaborate, and unnecessary is the bondage to house and mortgage that so often absorbs most of one's earnings and the time spent in generating them. I may have caught the last of an era though because my moorage fees have tripled since I first moved onto the water and I have tales to tell of port commissions that are as objectionable as a pile of mussels left beneath a boat after a boat haul-out: wet, slimy, and smelly. Regulators as a class are like barnacles: ever-present, sharp and cutting, and hard to remove from wherever they have attached themselves.

I do not know that I shall never choose another mode of life. Warmth comfort and social life increasingly play a larger role in my life than the pursuit of adventures. Nor do I find myself as ardent to prove by dint of sheer physical endurance that being transsexual need not mean that one is a sissy. I was raised to assume that showing any sign of weakness, emotion, or to long for comfort was shameful for a male but permitted or even encouraged in females. I have never been able to relinquish the need to push the envelope of mental and physical endurance in order to keep my confidence intact that I was worth something after all. It would be nice if admitting to a cross-gender identity spared me this desire but it has not. In fact I have never accepted a transsexual core and destiny but have spent my most stringent efforts to escape what has often proven to be a quagmire and a dilemma. It has been a struggle that has left me a ball of tangled contradictions like dried thistles or prickly tumbleweeds blowing before the wind. These contradictions are of the essence of this book and of my story as presented here, therefore I do not apologize for them. As with any life story the question is always present: might things have been different? To trace causality in a life is in the last analysis a futile pursuit, there are simply too many of them. What finally emerges may better be reduced to chance interacting with character. In my life it has been the word "pursuit" that sums everything up. I have been driven more than many to test pre-existent ideas and attitudes, to melt down categories into their ever finer constituent elements. My story must now merge with the transcendent as actuality is displaced by symbolic meanings. W all merge at last with the hunt to relate first to ourselves and then to something far greater than ourselves. In this realm I am Catholic and will always remain one. But I have at times probed the parameters of my faith in trust that doing so is in the last analysis an act of trust that it is able to resist my probing and to ground my doubts in even more solid ground.

Fern Hill

I began as a writer with a preference for poetry over prose. As we grow older though our perception of time lengthens out and soon the years become indistinguishable from each other. When that happens only prose is adequate to express our refined sensibilities, ones that know many hesitations and qualifications. At the time of which I speak the universal prophesy contained in

Dylan Thomas's great poem, "Fern Hill" moved from premonition to reality.

By 1997 there could be no doubt that I had lost my way. While in law school I could still imagine a glorious future and teaching, however unsatisfactory it had been, was at least something. But by 1997 all signposts had disappeared. The past was dying all around me. To wake up suddenly to age and the gradual descent of change is the theme of "Fern Hill." But the age that he was speaking of is childhood; how much worse is the loss of the young adult and the beginning of real aging? Without marriage and children it is easy to fool oneself that an eternal reprieve has been granted, that one can always begin again and recapture vanished dreams. The owls had yet to bear the farm away. Each year fell into a pattern of voyages to Canadian Islands or motorcycle trips down the Oregon coast or up to the mountains. Between times I began the study of organizations and delved deeply into the primal social problems of the globalized world.

My library grew in size to amazing proportions, each volume of which was an essential stepping stone toward some vast synthesis. I was too diligent to be merely manic, but still my efforts were inadequate to fulfill my aspirations. Until one day I began what was to grow over six years into a novel of seven volumes and 830,000 words. It may be the only pension that I will ever receive.

In tandem with it I began this book, the harder of the two projects because it has forced me to look at myself with fewer illusions, to step into my own flesh shorn of adornments. To be condemned to look at our delusions and wasted opportunities is not a pleasant task. Worse still is the admission that at each stage of our lives each choice seemed to be almost inevitable and that nothing else was possible from that limited perspective. If nations and history are prone to the follies that kill millions can we hope to do better as individuals with none to effectively gainsay our mistakes?

So when I hear music now from Chicago, Fleetwood Mac, or Journey I can feel again the tenor and theme of those times still alive within me. I am the gypsy and mine are still the open arms.

To lose someone still takes away a big part of me. There have been losses and I mourn them still. Can what remains be other than an epilogue? Or like a Shinto devotee shall I seek out the graves of my ancestors to make amends for simply becoming who I turned out to be?

Ocean Therapy

In therapy they call it taking a geographic which means thinking that if you can just move away from where you are, you can re-create yourself, leave behind all the garbage of your life and start again. The subtext is that this is an illusion, that a new lover, a new set of friends, or even a new self will probably, within a year or so, resemble the self you have just left behind. This may be true but I believe that each of us requires a place where we can go to escape our lives and to imagine that there at least everything can be different. For some people death is that place. I don't think people commit suicide so that they will cease to be but so that they can take what might be called an ultimate geographic. But beware! I for one always keep in mind Hamlet's cautionary line, *"But in that sleep of death what dreams may come?"*

Besides, there was always the ocean for me, to restore my faith and confidence in life and to help me imagine that a healing might occur. What infinity might surpass those vast waters or what reflected light make dim the summer sun upon the green and purple billows that swayed the great kelp forests beneath Cape Foulweather, my favorite destination on the Oregon Coast.

From there I could once gaze down upon the secret pirate bay where my family once owned land, land that has since been sold I regret to say. It was only an asset after all, not a tradition. Whoso-ever lives long enough will watch as the general liquidation of our elders leaves us alone.

My family always savored most the transient joy that follows purchase with real sharing and enjoyment indefinitely deferred. It is a habit of mind that I absorbed unconsciously. I still have fa-vorite books that I have never read. As our socio-economic status increased a certain class division began to exist among us. Our generational search for various forms of freedom from needing to exist beneath the judging gaze of the groups that had treated us as unworthy were seen as contrary to the values of our parents who had grown to internalize the oppressor. Even religion was more a matter of formality than of substance. I of course did not realize this. I once thought that my parents would value it if I became a priest rather than viewing it as a déclassé occupation. I had not realized how much materialism really was our religion. I am not immune to snobbery myself by the way. It is only that I think that even American aristocracy is rather crude by world standards. I enjoy the quiet arrogance of Emerson and Thoreau and look down my nose at billionaires.

Nothing is ever finally cherished or retained in our family mythos. We celebrate the transitory and scorn the permanent. We take pride in being a mere passing link in a chain of custody. Tears must not be shed over losses. We also don't believe much in funerals or in asking even the Church community to intercede for us. We prefer to face God alone with ceremonial certainty. We followed the rules! We are solitaries and Pelagian to the core in our beliefs. Like everything else heaven has its price. We believe in carrying adequate theological insurance of course just to cover any deficiencies. Faith is measured and weighed at the toll booth of heaven so it is best to play with the deductable but still keep the overall coverage amount high.

Even our parent's friendships as they grew older were based on business contacts rather than personal intimacy. As for God, as we grew up, the message was that we were all alone to work things out with that scary guy. After all who should ever trust God? This would require imagination and to feel our neediness. It would mean not having a ready answer or excuse for everything. It might mean being weak or of finally daring to speak what we feared to know about each other. No, it was better to remain largely strangers, as in the word "estrangement."

I don't know how we got to be like this, we just always were. We grew to be like workers who clock in each day and nod to each other before going to their separate tasks. The habit of secrets finally becomes like a pall of silence over everything. We don't talk often or share much today as a family. As a result the new generation will be one without memories of the prior generation and maybe they will be the better for it ... fewer ghosts to exorcize. They will not need to forget past longings and to regret unfulfilled promises.

In closing I submit the following passage written in the present tense as a tribute to what once was for me a vision, knowing now that it was really only a dream...

***

I can glimpse the lighthouse of Yaquina Point in the distance and watch the fog wreaths coming in from the lemon-tinted sea. Each hour the ocean may change its mood and I find in variation relief from its constancy. Its vast indifference to my admiration is matched with a sense that for all of that, it is waiting for me to return to it whenever I am away. Through the years I have imagined that I would someday people it with friends or with family and see figures that were not strangers running along the beach after the gulls or sandpipers and peering into the green depths of the tidal pools. I imagined a summer that has not yet come when I would repair to paradise, but not alone, that others would sit beneath a tree on our land and listen to the sea grasses that shake in the wind blowing in over the great grey rock with serrated edges that remains from an ancient lava flow.

The place is shaded by trees with many dead limbs that I call, the Haunted Grove. Many years ago a man claimed to have been set upon by fairies or gnomes of some sort near there. I have seen the haunted grove by July moonlight and walked down to the beach and felt the sands blowing about my bare feet. Once the beach is reached the view of the cove opens. The gradually crumbling ruins of Sentinel Rock and the ridge that I call Water-fall Rock appear through sea mist. At high-tide the waves climb up the long mussel-covered slope of the ridge and cascade over in waterfalls.

But above all else there is Cyclops Head that stands against the full strength of the southerly winds and shelters our little bay. If you look on a travelers guide for Oregon you will not find these names for the rocks and headlands; they are mine alone, parts of my own intimate mythology of the place. To name things is one of the few prerogatives of ownership it seems to me. No Lincoln County planning commission can tell me what I believe about this place or deprive me of the illusory home that stands here while I sleep up north through the howling storms of winter.

The entire area is what is called a Seismically Active Area which means that the land is buckling and moving northward and also westward and thus outwards into the sea. There was a great landslide there one hundred years ago and the planning board feels that any house built there will topple over with time or have its foundations ripped asunder. My answer to them of course is "What do I care?" My own foundations are being ripped asunder and in thirty years or less I will be dead and quite content to have a ruin above my head. I would like the planning board to go to Ireland and see the ruined castles and abbeys that crown the shores of Antrim, Kerry, or Donegal and realize that all things pass. If I was Robinson Jeffers I would build my own house of stone there but perhaps even then I would need a building permit, a septic drain field, and set-backs. Perhaps the land is unbuildable after all but I ask myself is that so bad. Perhaps it is destined to simply be a private park as it has thus far been in those summer days when I sat reading on the bank forty feet above the beach and saw the artists below sketching the scene or the families walking past with happy dogs at their heels. No one can say that I may not be here in spirit or make me pay a day-use fee somewhere south at Strawberry Hill or Neptune. No, I may park my van in front and wander down the access path past the blackberry bushes and turn into the great primeval bowl of greenery that borders our former beach. In those days now gone I could step onto the land and know that it was ours and that I was home, house or no house.

Land means so much to me because in Washington my house is only a boat resting on the sea. Land is the final end of all wealth as it is also the final end of our mortal bodies. If we are dust after all it should not be too much to ask that we own a little dust to which we may return. I wish that my father had seen it this way. But perhaps all is for the best. After all so many are dead now and already the earth is turning and the shadow of night is as inevitable as the tides in this my favorite place.

We are all of us moving out to sea, not just the environs of Otter Rock and Beverly Beach. I love the ocean perhaps for this fact more than anything else: that in the face of the infinite and even knowing that it will remain unchanged long after my fragile life is no more than the empty limpet shells that wash up with the agates and sea-wrack upon the sands below me, I may stand here and gaze upon it all, alive as only it is alive, immortal and as only it is immortal. I feel my pulse as equal to its own. Are not my tides as majestic in their way? After all I know it as it can never know me. My conscious life though passing is at least equal to its vast somnolent being.

So it is that I am Lord or Lady of my minor manor when I take a geographic and go down to the Oregon Coast. I can slip in among the locals who seem in their quiet way as permanent as the sea itself. I like going to a place up the coast a few miles and seeing smiles and hearing, "Hi, you are back." Human contact counts also. But even that comfort has changed. Local ownership passes and various well-heeled syndicates buy up what remains. But I can still remember all the years gone by when I would sit by the fire as the sun declined over the marshy bay to the north with a stack of old books from my favorite used book store. I would dream then of one day writing like Thoreau or Henry James, Jack London or Herman Melville, and that somewhere someone would enter the sounding shell of my brain and listen to the sad still music that resides there...

***

As I said above those visions are no more. A life of discontent I has met one more disenchantment. I have let go of what the ocean once meant for me: eternal youth, hope, continuity, and even perhaps personal significance. I find that as I grow older, I am being pushed away from all the things that I have ever loved or believed in. My sole fear though was to perish without leaving a record of a passage made, a voyage completed. I do not know what lies ahead for me now, perhaps to seek out a deeper anonymity wherein I can deny all that I have ever been and spend my last years trying to forget what has been my life. Is a late maturity worth the price of all that has gone before? I hope that I am not bitterer than the times demand. Philosophers are not always filled with the laughter of Democritus or the placid confidence of Socrates. I agree with Heraclitus that all is change, but I am not happy that it is so.

The Universal Donor and Receiver:
The Bi-sexual Transsexual

So as a coda to this section I find myself asking, "Who am I sexually after all?" It is like projecting various hypothetical scenarios into an unlived past. Sex, the gateway to vulnerability; sex the bait that leads to hell. It is difficult to know with as little overt genital experience as I have had what might have been. Instead I have usually substituted the affections of the heart alone without sex, a choice that few heterosexual persons must ever make. For someone as complex as I am I need someone who has been there, one who has lived along the same dreary night edges of the world that I have known inside myself. A caretaker type might once have done me good and made my life easier to bear, but I prefer to be the universal healer and to find my own healing in the process. But turn-about is alright and for the first time I am at a stage where I might be humble enough to accept it.

I have lived my life as a Catholic though in self-imposed exile, so sex with anyone was out of the question without assuming, as its necessary prerequisites: marriage, monogamy, and heterosexuality. In addition many in the Church see post-op transsexuals and perhaps pre-ops as well as presumptively incapable of meeting the essential duties of a heterosexual marriage (for various reasons) so even marriage at least in the Church, which for me is all that counts, is problematic.

The marriage contract requires as its definitive seal the ability to engage in "the marital act," not of course with the new genitalia but only with the original equipment (at least once) in order to consummate the marriage. Morality measured in centimeters. I once read a book by one expert on Catholic medical ethics who speculated how many centimeters of penetration were sufficient to consummate the marriage. The devil, as they say, is in the details. In any case marriage with a male was out for me because one's former assigned sex is held to be permanent and unchangeable.

Transsexuals of the Male-to-Female variety like me often still prefer women as partners anyway, not only because we love them and find them sexy, but because they are also our best friends and natural peer group as well. It isn't that we don't like male attention, anything that confirms our female identity is thrilling to us, but for me unless they are gay in sensibility and drag-queen in appearance they were for me what most heterosexual men are ... boring! I am not into "rough-trade."

If there is anything specific to Transsexual sexuality as such it may be that we reserve part of our sexuality to simply trying to be the best and most complete women that hormones and/or surgery can make us. If this seems like an obsession then perhaps it is. We aren't fetishists though, unless one's entire body and mind can be a fetish. I think I can sum it all up by saying that we want it all and if that isn't a definition of a woman then I don't know what is!

It is not that I have ever been proud of erections as I suppose most men are. To me male erections were simply an involuntary and tell-tale sign of sexual interest that could not be acted on and the thought of which let alone its discovery was embarrassing and humiliating to me. Control of all things was meant to be my mantra. The male sex and its intense drives were always alien therefore to my sense of self. Far from feeling empowered by orgasm I felt a fear that in feeling and being exposed by enjoyment I would be inevitably betrayed and diminished, compromised in my iron control of my own desires, revealed as needy and requiring another human being in my life.

Strangely, I do not feel that female sexuality or its exercise would be similarly compromising, but then perhaps that is because I am in many ways a woman. Sexual shame appears to be confined in me to a male identity, to simply being another lustful male, feared by society, and opposed by countless obstacles to the acceptable use and enjoyment of sexual fulfillment. I know that for most women this shame at being male must seem contrary to the enjoyment of my supposed "male privilege," but I for one never experienced this as anything but a condemnation and as an exercise in pretence.

Nor have I allowed myself experiences with a male, the prerequuisite to which would be not only a functional vagina to match my inner imagery but also the ability to forget the long years of suppression of precisely those desires. Besides, I would need to be proud of abandoning forever the quest for normal male experience, engaged with a woman who was not only loved but seen as my opposite rather than the object of my secret envy for simply being what I felt that I always wished myself to be. I have never negotiated this passage without which I am always aware that some significant element of my humanity is missing.

So what does that make me? Am I gay, straight, lesbian, or none of the above? I only know that I am me and for significant portions of my life even that has been uncertain, thus at least one of my sources of discontent, perhaps a very important one. Is there ever a cause of action for those of us whose sexuality like mine was shattered at the very dawn of life by the maledictions drawn from the catacombs of the collective guilt of the human race? Or did I need that protection after all, with a heart as frail as mine?

Still Seeking Solace

Autobiographies are always premature because there is still some measure of unlived life ahead where possibility still beckons. A reversal is always possible. In fact the real hope of redemption is that even the most contrary of lives may be reevaluated as a person's strength wanes and the stillness of death freezes cell by cell into the immobility of death. Perhaps my present discontent is some measure of the sense that I have that whatever I have presently assembled is incomplete and inadequate to fulfill even my poor idea of happiness.

The thing about life is that you eventually run out of time to define yourself. If you want to conceive of me think of me then like some primordial seabed. Layer upon layer of life has been deposited so that whatever I might have been as a transsexual is buried in all of the years when I tried so hard to be male. What flowers bloom in my autumnal soil? Would a late in life vagina,

235

now that it is more generally affordable through insurance, be for me anything more then a relic of what I might have been; gender reassignment really only matters to me when it would open a door to a life. It matters most of course when the overture of our lives is still playing. But I am approaching that time of life where everyone is waiting for the fat lady to sing and the curtain to come down, so isn't it a little late to risk any more surgeries or to refine flesh by any lifts and tucks?

Of course I could do what old ladies have always done, forget the flesh and blind any audience that may remain with expensive furs and jewelry. Old ladies must make it on attitude and colorful reminiscences. I don't want to face old age with an empty checkbook and a pretty face and submit to the unrelenting biological gaze of men who are programmed to seek out nubile forms because they guarantee healthy offspring.

Of course I could still always claim, "I am, big; it's the movies that got small;" but then I 'm not really a star except perhaps upon my own little stage. If women come up to me and say, "Honey, you are wearing too much lip-liner," I can still say to them in reply, "But Darling, I paint for the back rows, those little people out there in the dark." But the theater of our lives is only booked through 70 or 80 seasons and the house is only really packed for a woman that is until she is about fifty ... if she's lucky. But why do we think that women must retain their youth when men are balding and looking more pregnant with every year of advancing age; maybe because it is so hard to give up being a Goddess. For a short time, thanks to cosmetics and silicone and clothes, clothes, clothes, oh and shoes, we can be.

Malls abound with goddesses who walk from Forever 21 to Victoria's Secret and back. Every town in America has its cat walk, which if it is not Milan, is at least Dallas or Amarillo. Even here there is change. In fact pregnant is the new thin. Women are coming back to themselves as women and it's about time. Power is the ultimate aphrodisiac only if you are a man. Women have always been more rooted in the ultimate realities of life and death, which exist outside the artificial lighting of the corporate boardroom. So I suppose, if I am really a woman, that I should not be appalled by time; but I am. I keep on wanting to eat yesterday's bread rather than the stale loaf that is offered to me by whatever improvements I have still to make to be more "real" as a woman.

I have to emerge once in a while from beneath a sea of cosmetics and face the mirror with only my naked facial skin. I joke around of course and tell my friends that when it really gets bad I will skip cream foundation and move on to Home Depot for plumbing filler and spackle. Fortunately, I possess enough lip fullness to last and won't have to go in for plumping agents that make your lips look like they are waiting for a hotdog bun. I can draw on my eyes and hide them behind lashes and I have already learned to contour my contour with three shades of blush. I still love hair, especially if it looks like it is all straight and blond and windblown and an imaginary Scavulo is standing in front of me with a camera clicking away. I wear boat-shoes when I want comfort but I can still run a mile in heels since I started wearing them at six years of age. It's too bad that furs are passé because old ladies used to have cachet if they could sport a bevy of little fox heads and paws around their necks. When nature failed them there was always adornment and artifice. It's hard to face old age with nothing more then clogs and granola.

But I'm not finished yet of course. No star ever is and I am still carrying about with me my early role models and trying to find an echo of Kim Novak or Marilyn in voice or gesture. Maybe age is the great unifier where the great beauties finally lose their edge and have to come down into the sawdust of the everyday circus of life. We all grow more democratic as we age. But I suppose I will still be looking for miracles bestowed at the edge of a surgeon's knife in future years. I will still page through books looking for techniques of preserving youth that fall just short of the means adopted by Countess Elizabeth Bathory's desperate practice of blood in a bathtub.

As it is I already hear the curtain call, but am I still determined to face the years ahead with grace before I finally acquiesce to time's winged chariot drawing near and embrace the deserts of vast eternity. I still enjoy reading and watching people and imagining my own unlived life by hearing their stories. I see the fresh young faces of people that have not been exiled from all humanity by being transsexual, by being denied their very being from their earliest memories.

Even our sexuality is denied us as the next section of this book will show. Along with gays and lesbians we are defined as having an innate disposition to commit acts that are "inherently disordered." It is a tough definition with which to begin, or even to end a life for that matter, but for many years it was all I had. I have struggled along to maintain an alliance with this very institution that has traditionally so readily condemned me and others like me, an institution that though its assigns all other human ills to living in a fallen world demands that where sex is concerned that human beings live like disembodied spirits. Its leadership is consists of and its moral teachings have been defined by enforced celibates who police the sexual lives of others with an aura of their own relative immunity. Celibacy is the source of their unique vocation and at least as regards the priesthood includes the power to hear and forgive by proxy the delinquencies of others. This may have inevitably bred both an overemphasis upon the mystique of sexuality and a fear of the consequences of sexual expression. Other cultures have not surrounded sexuality with so many prohibitions or encumbered its exercise with so much shame and guilt. The real scandal of the sex abuse by priests was they had for so long been assumed to be sexless, part of a rare and sanctified order of semi-celestial beings, rather than mere flesh and blood like the rest of us. We appear to demand that at least some human beings shall be immune to the human condition and thus capable of loving us in all of our shamed inadequacies.

Many supposed men of God have imagined that only an unaccountable but fortunate mercy keeps God from simply wiping out all of creation by shifting his attention away and leaving is in an eclipse of the divine regard without which we would cease to be. So much of Christian theology leaves one with the impression that God just doesn't really like us. Severed in Eden we are as males and as females fundamentally incomplete. But transsexuals are twice removed: we desire another to fill that other half of ourselves and we desire as well that the half that we only appear to possess be other than it is because we cannot use it as a base from which to search for that other who will make us whole by loving us. Transsexuals such as I are trapped in a confused set of feelings and convictions the vocabulary and syntax of which are even now being defined by psychologists, surgeons, and on occasion recently even by ourselves after the many false starts and clumsy efforts of the last sixty years, the years that have largely spanned my life's course.

This account of my impressions is too short to be an autobiography, too summary and selective. I cannot speak for others and do not desire here to be any sort of role model. I would rather serve as simply an example of the conflicting and abortive attempts at finding a sense of unity that still eludes me and may forever do so. I do not know what the future course of my life may entail or whether as I hinted above it is too late to imagine and too painful to pursue any life solution but that which alone my years in the Catholic Church seems to afford me now – to simply endure my present divided state in patience as only one of the many ills to which we human beings are subject on this side of the grave.

Whether this recommended approach to life for what at this period of history at least are termed transsexual persons is the way that transsexuals should pursue as the best path and shortest way to the peace of a good conscience is not for me to decide for others. I do hope that any renunciations that I have endured or feel in the future compelled to make will be pleasing to God and therefore that I may be assured of finding salvation at last rather than wasting my last years in a vain search for an elusive sense of univocal contentment in my own skin.

As I get older I find that I am increasingly weary of the general prevalence of the struggle to find exterior validation for who I am as a person. The Catholic faith (and Christianity in all those outlying districts occupied by the various groups that have pealed away over the years since Jesus Christ first founded His Church and prayed that they would remain one even as He was one with His Father) seeks God as our final end. This means we are part of each other and destined to a unity with the One Divine Source and Origin of all things. There seems to be little room in this conception of life for the exhausting struggle for personal acclaim and separation that consumes our days and nights. Love and forgiveness should, it seems to me, so encompass us that egoism in both nations and persons should be extinguished.

This is a lot for a self-styled out and proud "Trannie-Goddess" to admit. The search for a better way of life, beyond the discontents that I have known, now consumes me. Already I am evolving another book, one far wiser than this one, to describe that less trivial pursuit. I see family and the wider sympathies of various communities as the obverse of the rabid self-interest that severs love between persons and nations. What this means is that I hope that this book is already a retrospective on a way of life that is well-nigh exhausted. I hope for better things to come because sifting through the trivia of my days and nights I find only straw. Thomas Aquinas also felt this essential lack when he reviewed even his masterful synthesis of theology and metaphysics from the mystical perspective of the light of God's grace as revealed to him in prayer.

The catacombs are the best testimony to the brevity of human life and a fleeting happiness here, even if attained, is all too little for the hunger of the human spirit. There must be something more that will heal all wounds and make good all losses so that as the mystic, Julian of Norwich, said, "All will be very well." I believe in life and in the cooperation of the sexes to achieve it and to preserve and nurture it. Like the poet Shelley I have here tried to scatter my words, ashes and sparks, to kindle a fire if not of recognition than of sympathy. My hope is that what I have kindled may be contained by more wisdom than my rebellious spirit has been willing to countenance. Like most romantics, who are poets at heart, I enjoy my own lyrics, which should show how much self-will in me needs to be purged into a purer stream of that loss of self-regard that alone seems to make for happiness and joy.

With this final caution as you reflect back upon all that you have read here, it is time to make an end at last to this section, for in many words there is much weariness of spirit. My concluding es-

says will now leave most of my personal past behind and attempt
to assess the present situation of transsexuals and to give at least
some sense, some premonitory vision, of what the near future
may bring for us all.

The Concluding Essays

(Andante con Pomposo)

Preliminary Note

The topics of the essays below trace their origin to the realization that transsexualism is by its very nature political and implicates anyone touched by it in a daily struggle of conflicting loyalties to those larger entities to which transsexual people may belong such as our family, church, employer, and community. My own struggles in this area as shown in the occasional essays below may therefore serve a paradigmatic role of what this struggle may entail, even for those who do not share my own particular beliefs and conflicts.

The conflicts that have already been explored in this book only grow in complexity and the anguish that this may entail when religious questions are stirred into the brew. It is little understood by most people that, for Catholics at least, morality is not an empirical discipline where rules are built up based upon inductive reasoning from lived experience. Catholics receive our moral norms pre-digested as it were and from an authoritative and hierarchical structure. This structure has its own historically molded internal jurisprudence and it is only in light of these interpretive rubrics that individuals are allowed the freedom to reach their own conclusions based upon their own individual life experiences. In our fluid, transient, and politicized world few people understand the pressures that this can bring to bear on someone who feels personally at variance with the stated mandates of the Roman Catholic Church.

I would also like to point out that as with much of this book I am not unbiased or unemotional in dealing with issues that have caused me much pain over the years and I am only too aware that not every transsexual person has had the advantages of my education and of my training in the law. This training and my own interior predispositions make me both adversarial and confrontational at times and at the same time give me the ability to argue both sides of any case with equal vigor. Particularly in the essays below these personal traits of mine will be evident. These essays are polemical in intent and as such should be understood as less statements of fact than an effort to draw attention from various persons within the Church to what I feel are fundamental needs of the GLBT community that must be pastorally addressed at a much deeper level than has been our experience to date.

I want to state clearly that I am resentful for much of what I have observed through the years of the ways that pastoral care has neglected or simply failed to notice the special challenges of being gay, lesbian, or transsexual. At the same time I wish to make it abundantly clear that I do believe in the right and the mission of the Roman Catholic Church to teach authoritatively and correctly, the Church that was instituted by Jesus Christ and commissioned by Him to spread the truth of the gospel throughout the world. It would therefore be a misuse of this book and contrary to my intentions in writing it at all to use anything that I may say in my book to support an individual in turning aside from the sure and precious anchor and support of the Roman Catholic community or to abandon the possibility of reaching an agreement with the Church through pastoral dialogue and prayer. I would rather have foregone writing the book at all than to turn people aside from what I firmly believe to be the firmest and most sure path leading to our eternal peace and salvation and the beneficent purpose of God for all souls. If I have learned anything at all from being transsexual it is that this life is limited in the bliss that it may bestow and I have no illusions that simply changing one's sexual presentation or body is the path to an easy Valhalla.

I have named this book "Transsexualism and its Discontents" for a reason. Life makes difficult demands of us all and transsexuals appear to me to have known as much of life's frustrations and cruelties as any group of people one might choose to consider. I desire then to instill hope but not to presume what measures any individual transsexual

243

may choose to adopt to deal with this issue in his or her life. Above all I have tried to convey something of my own experience as a transsexual, of one with a tough hide and a prickly hedgehog-type of mind and personality. I adhere as a writer to the fundamental adage practiced by members of the medical profession: above all else to do no harm. But, it is often hard to act affirmatively in this world and to avoid all harms that may flow from the act of publishing a book. I have taken the chance of writing this book in a spontaneous fashion, which is typical of the genre of the informal essay since it was first practiced by Michel de Montaigne. If it is read in this fashion then any harm that it may do will be diminished and it may be of some use to others so that overall it is better that it exist and be read by diverse audiences than that I had simply held my peace or written this book in another way. In any case this is my hope for the book.

Before I Begin…

It may seem obvious to Americans who have memorialized these sentiments in The Declaration of Independence that even governments are subservient to the people and that the people have a right to pursue happiness that such a natural right is beyond dispute. When there is added to this assurance in this age of human history the extraordinary aids that modern technology offers, at least to those who can afford its gifts, it is little wonder that any limitations imposed by moral strictures, traditions, or hierarchies are seen as vast impositions on the individual whereas formerly these were life's great givens, the background against which all human actions were based. Even today most people on this planet live lives of massive constraint as regards what is possible for the individual to expect from life let alone to actually achieve.

To take an example, within a decade of my birth (and I am still alive and even without mummification still well preserved) the world engaged in the greatest single blood-letting in history in the two great wars of the 20th century. Most people are unaware though of the extent of the loss of life from the great Chinese famines under Chairman Mao which occurred during my childhood years when the Second World War had ended. Many millions were prevented by an early death from achieving happiness or even living out their natural span of years. Even at this hour over a billion people live on less than two dollars per day. It must at least be noted here that the assumption that even the most ordinary means to happiness will be readily available to anyone is a great assumption indeed.

In light of the scarcity and pain that has traditionally been most characteristic of the human condition it has been natural for religious strictures to exist among humankind without drawing excessive notice. These same rules and inhibitions today though (at least in modern technological western societies) appear as a vast imposition and as unjustifiable, whereas formerly these same rules seemed if anything to increase human happiness by setting limits to human folly and to excessive human ambitions to attain excessive pleasure and longevity. I mention this because it is important to understand the background of Church teachings before daring to criticize them. In a world where women workers in textile sweat shops seeking to unionize once sang, "Give us bread … but give us roses," it may seem the height of extravagance to speak here of such innovations as facial feminization surgery, breast implants, and other alterations that were formerly only the province of the ultra-wealthy and of movie stars now being extended to ameliorate the unhappiness of transsexuals. The baseline of human happiness seems to be going up all of the time and conditions that formerly simply needed to be endured are now presumed to have a generally available solution the benefits of which can be claimed by right as a necessary prerequisite to the attainment of happiness.

What is this ever elusive right to happiness? Does Gender Dysphoria have a presumptive cure by restoring a supposedly natural condition of "gender euphoria?" Gender and sexual limits were formerly viewed as the given background of life just as gravity is. The great question to be answered by transsexuals then is: however much we desire it, do we have a right to alter one of the great determinants of human destiny by changing our apparent sex? I will try to answer this question here.

We know that the nature is careless as to the fate of the individual. However sanguine or despairing we may be as regards the survival of our planet and of the human species we must at least admit that various illnesses and accidents can prevent the living out of any individual human plan or destiny. It can only make it easier therefore if we assume that some measure of suffering is innate to the human condition. It has been the province of religion to help us to endure the inevitable by showing us that suffering can have meaning. To remove religious strictures from human decisions may at first seem to promise freedom and open new horizons for us, but it may be as well to reflect that anything achieved comes at a price.

A moment of reflection may reveal that for the male-to-female transsexual the newly assigned gender may bring burdens for which she is unprepared due to a lifetime of living in the status and to some extent the enjoyment of the way of life and societal forms that have been assigned to the male sex in which she was raised. But be that as it may, it has been the Church's traditional position (largely dictated by a belief that providence plays some role at least in gender assignment) that from this stability of gender flow many goods for the individual, the mate, the family, and the vast external society against which private lives are lived out. It is therefore in the view of many a premature and puerile act of temerity to presume that there is no wisdom or purpose in Church teaching as regards human sexuality and it should be the burden of those who advocate extraordinary remedies to justify them by absolute necessity before adopting what may be irrevocable changes in the human body made under the assumption that happiness is sure to follow through these interventions.

If on the other hand gender were a mere social construct, then the entire purpose of gender transition would be pointless. If there is no destination to a journey, then the journey would be needless. Most people would admit that our bodily givens of gender traits constitute a discrete language of self-definition and separate social and sexual possibilities. The body is not infinitely malleable, even by hormonal means and surgical interventions. Even in those few fortunate instances where complete assimilation to the gender-of-identification is achieved there still remain

246

the memory and associations let alone the relationships acquired in one's former life in the gender assigned at birth. It trivializes the often agonizing process of the transsexual search for gender peace and harmony to say that the whole thing doesn't really matter because the sexes are in more ways then one functionally equivalent.

If this were so then why not simply stay where one is? But – and this is the point – gender and external sexual embodiment matters so deeply to all people that alteration becomes a responsibility not to be entered upon absent the most grave reasons and only after exhausting all less invasive and strenuous means to re-define one of the most pervasive elements that constitute any individual's mode of humanity. It is here that the general reticence of the Church to bow to the conviction of people who identify as transsexual should become members, at least in a phenotypical sense, of the opposite sex should be considered and evaluated for any inherent prudence and wisdom that may reside in that perhaps at first disappointing position.

With this preliminary qualification I submit the following essays to the debate on transsexualism. They are not objective and may be in some cases ill-considered or take contradictory positions, but they stand as written and may be valuable as showing the state of mind of one who has "been there" at ground zero of the debate over the transgender and gay movements.

First Principle and Foundation

St. Ignatius of Loyola in his famous manual of "The Spiritual Exercises" makes no bones about declaring from the outset his view of life as an unconditional pilgrimage towards God. For those who are lost in confusion about what course their life should take Ignatius provides an immediate and absolute criterion, a moral North Star for perplexed mariners on rough moral seas. He explains that the human race was created to manifest the glory of God which it does by first discerning the manifest will of God and then by seeking to conform our every action to that of the divine will. Since God by definition can only will the general good of all things and since providence harmonizes all individual goods to advance the goodness of all of creation, there can be no real conflict between the individual good and his or her proper place in God's collective plan for all people. Any apparent conflict in our natures and desires then is a residuum of original sin which may be remedied by a strict process of constant weeding out of evil tendencies and a corresponding choice to embrace the good.

A program of daily examen is recommended to aid us in attuning our every action to the advancement of the Kingdom of God on earth to the greater glory of God. There is no mention in this view of the role of individual earthly happiness, freedom from internal stress, or any of the other absolutes that a worldly point of view substitutes for the eternal destiny of each person as willed by God. I mention this view of the goal for an active Christian life because St. Ignatius simply followed to its end the logical consequence of possessing an active Christian faith.

I cannot but contrast this ready acceptance of the demands of the cross with the efforts of many Christian sects today which speak of a new gospel of fun, pleasure, and prosperity as the proper ends of human life. The best and most productive periods of Christian growth have always coincided with periods of trial and persecution. A faith without demands is soon dismissed as irrelevant by its bored practitioners. There is a direct relationship between the decline in fast and abstinence days which mandated self-control and sacrifice as identifying elements of Catholic observance and the falling away of church attendance.

Religion requires rites, ceremony, and sacrifice in order to nurture faith. A church which is entirely compatible with today's consumerist ethic that emphasizes above all else individual self-determination and definition of "what is true for me" will have no positive message, no substance to help those seeking meaning and purpose in their lives when inevitable tragedy strikes.

Taking the above into consideration seems essential to me in approaching the transsexual dilemma. I have always believed that gender matters. Indeed I think that most transsexuals are gender essentialists. Of what use would transition be if gender made no difference in how we behaved or were treated? If each gender was identical, then the entire concept of "trans" would disappear. There is no Odyssey if there is no Ithaca! It is the quest for wholeness and authenticity that motivates the entire transsexual life course.

The question to be answered then is whether this quest is compatible with Catholic doctrine so that transition in fact increases the total good of the person and liberates him or her to find after transition in a cross-gendered role a fuller platform from which to interact with the world.

I have wrestled my entire life with this question so much so in fact that I could not write a book on transsexualism with the usual bland assurance that says in effect, "Come on in, the water's fine." I think that candidates for extensive body alterations should face a high burden of proof before proceeding. But I also believe that society should not be the goal-tenders. Various psychiatrists and others by acting as gender toll-booth attendants simply add to the costs of transition (and profit thereby) and these often unnecessary costs must be paid for by transsexuals. I think that the question of transition must remain with the person who must bear the costs of a faulty choice, the transsexual herself.

I do not desire to be a wet blanket or add to the depression and anguish of people who are considering a gender reconfiguration, but I do believe that in the face of the continuing breakdown of sex distinctions and the politicization of primary avenues of human identity and expression that certain cautions before proceeding are in order. Gender is simply too important to be treated as trivial. Being transsexual is a central facet in a human life. Entire spectra of human relationships and experience are altered by our sexual and gender identity. To pretend otherwise is to betray often vulnerable individuals to facing alone a world that does not conform to the easy deconstructions of current gender theory. The full truth only becomes manifest when one leaves the classroom for the streets. It is then that the artificial and temporary support of the gender theorists and clinicians falls away and the new woman (whether constructed or not) must face the world and its prejudices and presumptions alone.

What about Miracles?

I also believe that anyone who is trying to devise a general anthropology to explain the purpose and ends of human life needs to consider the possibility that something has been overlooked. Our society tends to believe that human happiness is an attainable end for our efforts and that our lives can make sense, at least for certain fortunate ones, by seeking happiness in this life alone. But this assumption is not in accord with most religious traditions nor is it a fair estimate of the life experience of most people throughout history.

Mortality in childhood still cuts short the course of countless lives. The extension of the human life-span has meanwhile condemned western cultures to face the issues raised when far more people are living into their eighties and nineties than ever before. Even these people are finally forced to endure the brutal fact of the inevitable failure of the human body due to sheer material obsolescence and genetic entropy and fragmentation. Is it any wonder then that many people feel that transsexuals are asking too much when we desire to escape from one of nature's great and determinate limits, the possession of a sexed body that is presumed to mirror the soul and the psychological predispositions of each person?

The result is that many people first approach transsexuals by urging us to be reconciled to our fate and these have devised therapies to do this by seeking to adjust the mind to accept the body's facticity. The question that I would pose to them is whether these efforts are not a sort of inner violence done to the integrity of the person that is far more brutal, radical, and uncharitable than what are now called the various sex-change procedures, or in a more gentle terminology, gender-reassignment. It is my hope that as time goes by more people will realize that transsexualism is more than a misdirected cultural anomaly or a weird shared delusion being spread by excess media coverage and an overly liberal and Godless society. But at the same time I am also aware that my faith counsels me to not expect closure from the point of view provided by this life alone.

Certain figures like the French Priest of the town of Ars St. John Vianney and St. John Bosco manifest that our world is permeated by a supernatural dimension that can on occasion bend nature and its laws in quite powerful and mysterious ways by the sheer grace and power of God. An unbiased investigation will reveal that our comfortable reductionism of all reality to bland and inhumane scientism is as much a faith as it is an exercise of scientific method. Just as I believe in the existence in the saints of supernatural virtues I have no doubt that a demonic realm also exists, one that manifests itself in more than the usual evils of child abuse, murders, terrorism, and wars. The specific realm of the demonic is fortunately seldom encountered without first being clothed in ordinary selfishness or human mental and moral imbalances. It is seldom encountered unmasked. The demonic takes as its specific goal the total degradation of our human nature and any manifestation of the holy. Only the highest in humankind is worth this more specific attention of the lowest elements of fallen creation. We are therefore most of us fortunate in our mediocrity. All of which is to say that I believe in the supernatural order of God and the angels, fallen and otherwise. At the same time I do not think that we should depend upon the miraculous as a matter of course to alter transsexualism any more than we should depend upon it to extinguish any other human ailment by direct means.

Transsexuals report a depth and extent of lifelong anguish and dysfunction shared by few other diagnosed conditions physical or mental. It is therefore within the mandate of charity to make every effort to not deprecate or minimize their sufferings and convictions by suggesting facile solutions. But I would also counsel transsexuals to ask themselves if there is any measure of reconciliation that they may have overlooked that might make it possible to seek and find some way to avoid the painful and difficult transition experience with its often imperfect results. Desperation often yields a desire to attain the alleviation of pain only by acquiring still greater pain. Patience and growth require time so as to avoid mistakes that may be irreparable. To provide time and comfort to desperate people rather than the curt dismissal of their witness of their experience seems the best gift that those who do not experience intense gender conflict can bestow on those of us who do.

Incommensurable Values

We often resolve value disputes by seeking some higher order value that will resolve the conflict by favoring one position over the other one, but a point will sooner or later be reached where further appeal is impossible because the two values in dispute each claim a sort of absoluteness that cannot be subsumed into anything higher or more general. These are called incommensurable values, the values that divide our ultimate loyalties and our selves with them. To go in one direction is to abandon the other contenders. Our own age tends to resolve these disputes by simply presuming that there is no final ground of being. Instead we exist among temporary templates for experience, some with more appeal in certain areas than others, but none deserving of the absolute affirmation that faith demands of us. We have learned to make room for each other in a pluralistic world. We accept the uniqueness of subjective experience and are willing to make room for divergences of opinion and loyalty by virtue of civility and good manners or just to keep the peace.

When Pope Benedict XVI surrendered the office of the Papacy he broke a long period of history since a reigning Pontiff had resigned his office. By retaining the title of Pope Emeritus former Cardinal Joseph Ratzinger created in some quarters what might be called a state of functional nostalgia. Some were even so bold as to suggest that the new Pope Francis was somehow only a sort of quasi-Pope. His efforts at reform could thereby be framed as a brief hiatus from strict orthodoxy and be corrected after what might be a short Pontificate. Meanwhile many Vatican bureaucrats shifted uneasily in their usual orbits and various Bishops muttered disgruntled comments that would have been considered impertinent or even irreligious had the tide been setting in their direction rather than ebbing.

They lamented among other things that a Third World Pope was in office. They had loved Pope John Paul II for his condemnation of communism but here was a Pope who dared to criticize capitalism as being flawed also when seen from the higher perspective of Christian morality. The easy alliance of many Church prelates with the wealthy and respectable was suddenly looked upon with askance and the street people, the broken and the morally maimed, were seen as less of a problem than many Bishops had assumed they were. Maybe condom use for instance as an issue was not as demanding as institutionalized militarism and global warming in the scale of human evils. Maybe there was a natural law that was being violated in destroying the planet that had somehow slipped through the cracks. Accustomed as many Bishops were to bask in the comforts of their office this new Pope was an embarrassment and an inconvenience, entirely too much like Jesus in the Sermon on the Mount as recorded in the Beatitudes.

This functional nostalgia was brought home in an article that I read yesterday that the former Pope Benedict now retired had given an interview in which he lamented that since the Second Vatican Council the Church has admitted the possibility that those of other faiths who are not baptized do not necessarily end up in hell. The former Pope, now no longer in a position to exercise the special prerogatives of his former office, concluded that this doctrinal loophole was somehow undercutting Catholic missionary vigor by leading to an implicit universalism and also weakening the importance to our salvation of leading a good Christian life.

As a merely practical statement he is probably correct. Fear has always been an effective motivator for human compliance. What his statement did not reflect however was a sense that the former viewpoint may have had as much to do with cultural imperialism as with theology. No one seemed to have been upset in past ages that this view seemed to make God into an ogre. The attitude that the heathens were always a Godless lot so why shouldn't they be damned was probably as natural to a 15th century Spaniard as multi-cultural attitudes are to us today. But should we see this change in our assumptions as a crisis as though to practice the faith from enlightened love and a desire to perfect our human nature will never measure up to the sprightly vigor that was once induced by sheer terror. Is Baptism somehow less valued among the faithful because its meaning is seen as less formal and more dependent upon its signifying power to the community as distributed over a life of constantly renewed commitment? Was there never a chance given by God in past eras to those men and women of goodwill living beyond the confines of Judeo-European influence to attain salvation, people who might only in death meet their savior? Couldn't the Holy Spirit set the final parameters of sacramental efficacy rather than abandon the effort while millions were lost only because a ship bearing a missionary did not get to them in time?

Even today the Christian message is more likely to be lost as much by such apparently partisan statements as it ever was by the existence of geographical barriers. The real universalism is that of the Christ as He appears in the ardent Epistles of Saint Paul. Will Jesus as the beginning and the end of all things be frustrated by mere historical contingencies? This is the hope that makes the mandate to share the sacraments more an upwelling from the fullness of the divine life within us than a presumptuous sense that we are saved and they are not. If the Christian life needs a constant kick from behind to motivate us then we have yet to attain to the love of God.

Ritual Purity

It is hard for most people at this present time to understand what holiness and purity might mean and why the Catholic Church still talks about chastity, solidarity with the poor, the value of human life, world unity, and hope for the end of wars in spite of the witness of history to repeated human failure in each of these areas. Today personal authenticity seems to demand the unveiling of our darkest and most secret desires so that we can each claim as in the great poem by Ernest Dowson to have been faithful to Cynara but only in our fashion.

We collectively worship at the shrines of various fleshly goddesses, the various embodiments as icons of Venus. We see these women in magazines at the checkout stands in grocery stores and in the tabloids as not immune from cellulite and wrinkles when they are caught without make-up or air brushing on some beach in the Bahamas by the ever vigilant paparazzi. The secular is everywhere. Where would we be if some institutions did not remain to ask higher things of us and not be like those therapists that try to assume a constantly affirming stance to their patients no matter how evil or immature they may be behaving at great cost to themselves and to others?

Ideals after all must still be preserved somewhere and by someone. Without an occasional rumble of thunder would any of us ever look up from our vain pursuits and regard the sky, our best approach to the transcendent order that underlies all things? If human beings are to simply copulate at will with no guidance from what the Church calls natural law in the sense meant by Aristotle and Aquinas would not a terrible boredom soon ensue?

Still, between the banality of sex in the secular world and the rigid insistence upon strict standards of sexual purity in religious teaching we also have the spectacle of what people actually do, how they in fact live their lives. The Church of course does not consult the Kinsey Report prior to pronouncing what God expects of human beings, but to conclude that this most volatile area of human passions is in reality a moral mine-field rather than to treat it with the humor of Chaucer or Shakespeare seems to betoken an unrealistic structural approach to human life that is quite frankly inhuman. If sex can be used to dehumanize and to degrade other people, it may also be possible to use abstinence and fear of sex in a way that is equally damaging to others and to ourselves. Personalities can become far more twisted it seems to me by envy, resentment, and pride through seeming to triumph over their bodies than when we pay at least marginal tribute to those parts of our humanity that are part of our animal heritage.

Various moral hysterias have done far greater evil in this world than that done by the most licentious of libertines. Holiness will always be difficult for most human beings to comprehend. The prudent man or woman is content to find even marginal decency in most human beings. Imagining countless human beings floating about in a sea of fire because of a spasm in the loins does more to bring contempt upon divine justice than it does to inspire the higher values within us that may be achieved by fidelity and sacrifice in marriage.

The real failing where sex is concerned is the damage to our need to be loved and not abandoned by our intimate partner. Sex entails an implicit promise to remain and to nurture each other. For this reason casual sex seems to me to be a contradiction in terms. Sex is never casual to human feelings. But to focus moral concern upon the pleasure as dirty or illicit rather than to the broken promise aspect of misuse of the sexual faculty is to appear prudish rather than prudent. This is my problem with much that has passed for Catholic moral teaching in the area of human sexuality. It is a position easily stated but inadequately explained and thus does not tend to be persuasive. Moral edicts invite rebellion whereas if they are approached in humility as a universal dilemma imposed by our common nature then no one is offended without cause by unchastity and no one is exalted beyond our shared station as human beings through inordinate pride in resisting elicit sexual expression or proclivities. To have seen much of life is to forgive much in this area. Our greater sins are easier to overlook as we gather stones to punish those who are not rich enough, powerful enough, imaginative enough, or cruel enough to entertain the greater sins of pride, blasphemy, and idolatry.

"Break, Break, Break on Thy Cold Grey Stones Oh Sea"

The title of this essay, a lamentation of sorts, is drawn from a poem by the great poet Alfred Lord Tennyson, captures the theme of all too many of my days and nights. There is a razor-sharp edge of pain and desolation that goes with loss and with grief that shakes the margins of the soul and that makes even night with its promise of sleep a fitful friend. To never have been at home in one's own flesh or to have felt that automatic congruity between impulse and acceptable action that goes with a secure sense of gender, one that is mirrored back at one by our surroundings, is to be thrown back as a refuge upon a vicarious existence. I have within myself the capacity to be dissolved at times into various personae and to love in such a fashion that part of me is forever held hostage. I am always engaged in volunteering to "go over the top" into that wasteland where shell craters gather autumn rains and where the corpses of the brave battles of yesterday lie on their backs gazing sightlessly at the broken sky.

I understand all too well the poetry of Francis Thompson, of Ernest Dowson, and of Gerard Manley Hopkins. There is an edge to events that is often insupportable and an insight into abysses that should remain un-discerned. For instance, if the iceberg had been a mile to leeward the Titanic would have arrived in port to applause and renown rather than being an early warning of what would soon engulf the nations of Europe, all because a disgruntled Serbian was standing by a stalled motorcade in Sarajevo when the heir to the thrown of Austria-Hungary passed by. Thomas Hardy was right: all too often happiness seems to be based upon mere chance and a perverse one at that. We mourn longest for people whom we should never have met while all unglimpsed we have passed unnoticed those who might have rewarded our devotion with fidelity. The struggle of life will always have premature victims. It is sad but true that not all of us appear able to make it across this vast plain that is beset by predators of various sorts. Addictions winnow the herd and everywhere opportunities are wasted among nations and individuals that might have led to happiness. Perhaps happiness, because it tends to dull us to the risks it imposes to the attainment of virtue, is the greatest deceit of all. Undeserved suffering serves to awaken compassion within us and to remind us of our temporary sojourn on this unlikely region of Earth, one that is so inimical to our desire for peace and justice.

I feel that I have spent a good part of my life walking along the naked shingles of Matthew Arnold's "Dover Beach" while across the waters of circumstance lay a garden party in Deauville to which I was not invited. Only now and again have I been able to embody beneath paint and synthetic fiber a vision of the self that I imagined would draw love to me, imagining that attraction could through the alchemy of desire be sublimated into the precious metal of unconditional regard. Perhaps I have overestimated beauty and grace and what they may instill in others.

Seeking rescue for myself I have often played the rescuer and all the while after swimming outward through the breakers have discovered that it has been too late and I myself too far from land to make it back to shore again. I feel in consequence that I have lived many lives and that each of my lives has been a successive incarnation, each as inadequate as its predecessor has been.

Desolation Blues

I do not know if there is such a thing as transsexual culture in the way that there is a gay and lesbian culture but this book may describe what one might look like. If transsexuals are a separate tribe or anthropological category then it seems about time that some of us as underrepresented voices spoke about how the world looks to us. We may possess capacities that are not generally shared and may function as the type of numinous beings that some cultures believe that we are. We are after all so seldom consulted before significant actions are taken by world leaders. I would be happy to share my cell phone number and take conference calls from Vladimir Putin and Barack Obama, "Well guys, it's like this…"

As an oracle in the Temple of Diana I might after all have something useful to say. A little political attention would be flattering if nothing else since I have been long neglected in corporate counsels and international tribunals, my unerring judgments notwithstanding. One of my guiding principles is to take care of the big issues first, like creating a world without the various horrible things like the avoidable deaths of children, nuclear arms, regional wars, ideological intransigence, and general egotism (with the exception of me). I am not egotistical because of course I really am the Trannie-Goddess, she who must be obeyed. I have been waiting for years to wake up in a world that is worthy of being lived in by human beings and since I'm getting older I am now getting impatient.

I have thought a great deal about my early days and the edge of loneliness and terror that faced me each day. I spoke to the world from an abyss of alienation that only the sexually conflicted may know. In the past I erected a base of sheer will to confront the world. I endowed nature with a personality to speak to me when no one else would. There is a still sad music that only poetry can capture and that trans-people sing in silence to comfort our broken hearts. Some of us fracture into pieces as we assemble various separate personae to face the world. "Who do I need me to be today?"

I survived by diffusion. I absorbed various roles and learned to hide in plain sight. As I get older though I am getting more demanding and less tolerant of errant idiocy and there seems more of it to put up with all the time. As the years allotted to me grow shorter I realize how far I am from assembling my experience into a form that will possess harmony. Instead I have succeeded only in painting here a study in contrasts. Let the web of my life be woven tightly but still possess some flexibility. May I have a gentle touch but a mind of steel!

Success

The era in which I was raised went from expecting an immanent take-over by the communists or a thermonuclear war to an era of naïve idealism in the sixties and political disillusionment in the seventies, but what never changes in America has been the desire for success, socially and economically, for our children. When I graduated from high school I knew that what I most despised was the moderate success represented by possessing a house in suburbia. My ideals were formed and conditioned by my reading of Victorian novels. Nothing less than becoming a member of the landed gentry would do for me. I had not yet discovered the joys of P.G. Wodehouse so I was utterly without a sense of humor as applied to my pretentions. This was the male side of my character. Meanwhile the female persona that I harbored within me (one even more naïve) wished for a body and face that could grace a Vogue cover. She dreamed of walking her Afghan or Borzoi and eating lunches at terraced cafes in Paris while wearing designer hats and being scouted by various film directors who might whisk me off to Cannes, to Capri, or perhaps to Biarritz or Deauville for a weekend while remaining chaste of course because my unassailable virginity was part of my charm and had already made me a legend among the discriminating nobility who pursued me through the various social seasons in the various capitals of Europe. How often had I not stood upon the Bridge of Sighs in Venice while engaged in re-reading a letter from some Duke or Baronet only to let it fall unanswered into the turgid waters below?

Meanwhile back on planet earth I was simply one of each year's graduates poured forth with neither skills nor expertise and with the added burden of having lived all of my life in a world of fantasy tinged by a vague familial sense that I would find some way to grasp the ring that Americans term "Success." Of course as a Catholic I knew that anyone who dies without having perished in a state of mortal sin is a success at least insofar as having reached the grim shores of purgatory. These souls were bound to make it to heaven eventually. Only Protestants were sufficiently presumptuous to claim that they were definitively saved without labor. The Calvinists of course would still have to wait to see if they were indeed among the elect or had been already assigned irrevocably to hell while they still slumbered as innocent babes in their mother's arms due to the divine foreknowledge and omnipotent will of all events.

Later I read lots of F. Scott Fitzgerald, Thomas Wolfe, and Ernest Hemingway about what success in America really meant and of how elusive it was for anyone who was not named Gatsby. What no one advised me though was that success could be purchased by changing my sex. The transsexual lot was a poor one of rejection and exile unless you were taken up by Salvador Dali or were one of the denizens of Andy Warhol's Factory. To be a transsexual then was to be a statistic in some psychological study and it is only marginally better today for most transmen and transwomen. What I needed above all else all along was a guardian or mentor who would listen to me and gently unveil my illusions while showing me a way into what passes for real life. This wise guide might have pointed out to me that success was a relative term and that I was not in debt to the vague expectations of the past or present generations of my family. A little more reading of Henry James or Edith Wharton might have disillusioned me as to the real prerogatives of wealth which all too often meant bondage to a way of life that was rigid and stultifying so that it often served to crush the spirits of those who were born to opulence and elegance.

If I were speaking to a young person today I would advise them to stay away from universities, pick up a valuable skill early, to start working and to save their money. I would advise them to avoid hasty marriages and not to conceive children while they remained children themselves. I would advise that no irrevocable decisions or commitments be made until age thirty. Until then I believe most people are in various degrees certifiable as a danger to themselves and to others. That I have made it through life as well as I have is a testimony to a Guardian Angel that should be given a long sabbatical if I ever make it to heaven.

The waning of life's powers is often the closest that we come to virtue. Saints should either die very young or very old and if old dedicated to a life of penance and atonement. I am fortunate in never having had much power or authority over other's lives, but even I may have left my own trail of havoc simply by being me. I like to think that I have bred a spirit of tolerance in those who have watched me waltz through life, but I am not in control of the responses elicited in them, only the confusion I may have sown. Above all else I have left much undone that less pretentious folk seem to have managed with grace if not with ease while for me everything has been a vast prolegomenon to that era when I imagined that I could dictate to the world my conclusions about life and fate. All in all I should have done better to have sat beneath a fir tree in China and have drunk tea or wine with Li Po or Tu Fu, to leave a few lines quoted by my friends, and vanished as most of us do into a blessed obscurity rather than to have dreamed such elaborate scenarios of Success.

Her Tuna Comes from Thailand

When I was young I knew where everything came from: brisling sardines came from Norway not Poland and tuna came from the United States along with cars and almost everything else. Seafood came from U.S. ports and everything was wild-caught. Shrimp came from the gulf coast not India and firecrackers came only from Dutch Macau. Fishy meant vaguely suspicious not the drag equivalent of feminine perfection as in "You are really serving up fish girl!" And tuna from Thailand would not be a quaint way of saying, "She went to Thailand for her surgery."

It is amazing how fast the world has changed about us and how little resistance we have collectively mounted to those changes as a culture. The future shocks are now so continual that they are not even shocking. What is shocking is to recall how recent everything seems to be. But then to recall means to remember and that means you have to be old enough to have been there. It is hard for me to realize that the Bill Clinton presidency is to the young of today what that of Herbert Hoover was to us.

My generation thought that we possessed youth as a permanent possession as though we had a tag on everything with a date on it from the sixties. I suppose that the surviving French citizens who were young in 1789 must have felt the same way well into the first half of the 19th century. As we age the option of making a sort of eternal return to our past so as to begin again becomes first remote and then impossible. We are what we have made of ourselves through the fleeting years. But what if in our own eyes that just isn't enough? We want more perhaps than what is humanly possible, to be a sexual universal.

It seems to me that to undertake a late in life gender transition has this great difficulty: it appears to be an effort to remake what has already been. The Greeks advised us against stretching the boundaries of human nature too far lest we bring the Furies down upon us. Harmony requires adaptation from our desires. There may be a direct proportion to the violence to our humanly integral boundaries including from a surgeon's knife and the degree of our hubris. Harmony seems to demand relinquishment more than it does the ardent pursuit of the ever elusive and illusory ideal.

It is this reflection that gives me pause in my advocacy of what I have myself sought to embody over the years as recorded here. I do not wish to be set down as a traitor to the cause but neither will I accept a party-line to curtail my doubts. I am more uneasy each day as I watch a few individuals suddenly vaunted into the public eye as normative for our community. I fear the damage that is being done. The mere notoriety of our issues does not mean that we are meeting or going to be received with more compassion and enlightenment from the non-transgender masses. I fear that a storm is coming, a back-lash that will color the remainder of my days as an aging transsexual. I still feel alone in the pursuit of my own authenticity.

The rewards of simply becoming diminish for me daily until I feel that I cannot find any period of my life to provide adequate grounding for one final attempt to take the hill and place my unique flag of authenticity there to wave proudly from the summit. Caught between the prospect of more of the same and the impossibility to transform a past that has already been I have written this book to record my condition and to trace its antecedents to their source.

Good Breeding

It might be thought that as a transsexual person I would be able to rejoice in the progress that has been made by male to female transsexuals when they take their place in the gallery of glitz and bling encrusted icons that can arouse the male gaze and capture the envy of other women but to suppose so would be wrong. I have come to believe that the female form is in fact treated similarly by Islamic culture and by our own post-modern media culture. If Islam conveys fear of female sexual power by wrapping women up in cloth, our own society achieves the same thing by stripping women down into parts and displaying all until the female body becomes a cold exercise in geometry.

The initiation rites have moved a long way from the upper class debutante and the more plebian rites of various high-school proms. This general objectification and even industrialization of femininity has made it relatively easy to create the living dolls that so many of us long to be if only to avoid being "clocked" as possessors of unfortunate male indicia to remind us from whence our journey commenced. When we are not objects of fear and derision, we are reduced to being products of sophisticated gender technology, marble-like sculptures in silicon and lace. Beneath much of the anger that pervades this book I often detect a hunger to escape all categories and even identity itself so as to avoid becoming generic.

My shame triggers are as exquisitely sensitive as a seismograph when it comes to moral or physical compromise. My loyalties have always been to the I.W.W. activists and others like them. I tend to despise the managerial class and the comfortable corn-fed Republican types that talk about independence as they shop at the big box grocery stores for high fat burgers and bratwurst on Independence Day. But I am not pleased either when I go to Gay Freedom Day or Gay Pride Parades and watch the same groups march by that I saw thirty years ago. Much has changed, but resentment, cynicism, and violence continue to be directed at us, particularly if we are young.

I have lived my life along the parameters of disillusionment in government, in commerce, in the operations of high finance, and in law. Each of these can make me cringe in shame. But add to this that my childhood dreams of familial advancement have witnessed the diffusion of resources and my romantic dreams that we were all secretly of the aristocracy and that someday a landed estate would make our lives stable for years to come as we escaped forever from the tacky and imitation world of housing developments and various suburban nightmares that have made the east coast of America one continuous highway of strip malls and neon have come to naught.

America has a remarkable ability to confine intellectuals to late-night television where their antics can amuse viewers like so many dancing bears. Even universities are now infused by a commercial spirit. Students are solicited by various credit card companies, clothing manufacturers, and by various businesses located in proximity to or even on the campus. This recruitment to 21st century consumer capitalism makes people mere cells in a process that originates in Chinese goods and ends in various garage sales and storage units designated to hold all the junk that we have accumulated. So it is that I look upon the 21st century's relative acceptance of transsexualism and the market access to the LGBT community not as acceptance but as exploitation of our former pioneer status as individualists and even outlaws.

From whence is good breeding derived? Just a few days ago at this writing a horse called American Pharaoh broke what has been a thirty-seven year drought to win the Triple Crown. The excitement that comes from witnessing nobility or excellence is the exact opposite of the engineered experiences of theme parks, the predictable uniformity of many best-sellers on the racks in grocery stores, and the general leveling out of public consciousness in today's world. Even politically correct speech manages to strive towards politeness by denying the less savory but all too real aspects that define the group in question.

If I have one underlying central trait it is the desire to escape easy assignment to a functional class apart from my own inner sense of self. Contradiction is my semaphore to the world and the signal that I send is, as Whitman said, "my barbaric yawp." I am stubborn to a fault and as tenacious as a terrier once I get my teeth into something. It makes going to the Sacrament of Reconciliation difficult because I am likely to deconstruct the categories in the very process of admitting my offenses. I tend to see things at multiple levels and skip as swiftly between topics as a flat stone over a pond on a summer day. This is natural to me, but since this book is personal, accuracy and truth demand my unvarying adherence to this habit of mind, which in any case has grown to be innate within me.

If I seem unable to make up my mind in this book about being transsexual it is because I tend to see things as always in suspense, as a tension between opposites. Dialectic is as natural to me as tying my shoes. But I will attempt to summarize my point here: good breeding means the search for excellence. It means feeling the wind in your mane while hearing the hoofs that are behind you flying along the track then opening a lead of three or four lengths and bringing it home to the finish line.

Maybe it is an illusion but the world of my youth seemed so much cleaner and more ordered to me than the world that I now inhabit. People seemed to have dignity and to possess a sense of belonging that has been fragmented as my life has progressed. People used to make an effort at least towards morality and respectability. The Churches were filled on the Sundays of my childhood. People dressed well. Ladies wore hats and even veils and the Buick-and-Cadillac-filled parking lots seemed to speak of gentility that no modern spectacle of BMW or Nissan imports can equal. Americans relied on each other more for company rather than rushing off to some anonymous big box store for cheaper priced goods rung up my underpaid sales clerks only to fill storage units in a few years or be sold at garage sales. Who wants someone else's junk?

No one is standing in line though to compete with transsexuals for our unique experience of being alienated even in our own skins. We walk around with invisible scuba tanks strapped to our backs with just enough air to get us through one more day. Some like me make a slow burning anger and bitter scorn take the place of sorrow. It isn't my most likeable trait. Even today I don't as much wish to be female as I wish to dissolve into some vast neutrality where questions of identity can remain trivial and where only vast events and mass issues implicating cause and effect matter. But I know that to deny humanity in oneself is simultaneously to deny it to other people as well. No group explicitly dedicated to human improvement exists that does not bear in its train a string of perhaps unintended but still real atrocities exercised against those who fail to remain true believers in the program. I think that early on I recognized this and became enamored of outcasts even while desiring acceptance under any terms that I could negotiate with a non-accepting society.

The mark of the aristocrat as opposed to the outcast is the degree of eccentricity and individuality that can be exercised while not forfeiting invitations to extended family social gatherings. This is why I have always loved what I call "interesting biographies." Every great writer should have his "Sturm und Drang" period. Decadence becomes merely squalor though when no great art results from the bouts of drinking absinthe and the periodic visits to the demimonde of Soho, Montmartre, or Morocco.

Of course the real masters are those who can view the disorder of existence from the Apollonian heights of reason or have managed to create new forms like James Joyce out of the "dear dirty Dublin" of our existence. In the debate as to whether it is better to repent than to regret, whether to yield or to rage against the dying of the light, I tend lately to adopt a resignation like Faulkner and to trail my flags in the dust.

I have always preferred Bloomsbury to the Berlin of the twenties. I do not doubt that the human race needs limits to avoid destroying ourselves and others. Without standards we will all soon drown in a universal permissiveness. Savagery is only kept at bay by various structures and even by various classes that prevent us from becoming an undifferentiated mob voting for the political party that can convince us that it can better produce prosperity out of debt. America today seems caught in a vast moral Ponzi scheme while sailing blithely onwards towards ruin. For this reason I do not think it amiss to sound a little bit stuffy, prissy, and dowager-like here as I lament the past and fear for the future for my nation and for myself. It is more than my own image in the glass that is fading.

I look in vain for that thrill that used to awaken such hope in me that this was to be the year when everything would finally come together. Now I am content if no favorite stores close or friends move to New Mexico. I crave at times the long nights of winter because it is easier to sleep without being awoken by the impetuous sun kicking me forth into a new day. I miss the sad love songs of the seventies and eighties that channeled my desire for the ripened fruit of love when its costs were less apparent. To sit before a computer and soar over the earth to Siberia, Mongolia, or even Tristan de Cunha is to see that the earth looks much like parts of America that I have already visited, whereas when I was a child the mere vacant lot next door seemed to possess infinite promises for exploration.

One looks in vain today for sagas of family life by Galsworthy or for the light at the end of Daisy's dock as Gatsby once did. What has taken their place is a series of tabloids recording who is being treated for drug dependency, who has just concluded a bi-sexual fling, and which screen-goddess of yesterday was caught on a beach in France with visible cellulite on their thighs.

The Mini-Skirted Girls of 1968

When I was in high school it was assumed that my generation was somehow engaged in some sort of vast collective enlightenment experience, as though world peace could be purchased by simply reaching out your hand with what was then called "flower power." Greed and war were about to be buried forever in some sort of tsunami of love in a world lit up by the plasma of lava lamps while skinny sirens with large black eyes, perpetually open in a state of wonderment, looked on and applied white ice-pink lipstick to their lips. But by 1968 the country was beginning to realize that the war of liberation in Viet Nam was spinning out of control, new cultural movements and artistic forms were springing up like magic mushrooms, and posters with long-haired youth and bright pastels were suddenly everywhere. I think of 1968 now as the pivot year for our nation and the generation that came of age at that time as being just what we thought we were – a pivotal generation. As usual our various dreams and visions did not lead to the promised utopia though. Instead the days when we could all just be happy together and go surfing, the days when it had all only just begun are walled up in the morgue of the once modern 20th century.

You know that you are old when what you once looked at as the perpetually and immortally new becomes only a stale residue of nostalgia. The thing is that age for me just does not compute. It is not that I am a practitioner of positive thinking, no – I am just engaged in deep and entrenched denial. Life has always appeared too small for me. My plan was to read about five thousand biographies and then chart a perfect life-course filled with adventure, romance and of course social service so that when I left this earth at last the world would in truth be new and I would leave behind me a vast repository of valuable memorabilia for future scholars to ponder. All of this would be combined with breaking out of my shy male chrysalis at last so that I would be transformed into one of the girls of 1968 who seemed to have blossomed overnight into idols with all of life's delights before them. Dawn seemed to me then to be a perpetual state of being so that what I was asking from myself and from the world was only in tune with the spirit of the times in which I lived my youth.

How strange it is now to see that beneath the veneer of perpetual youth and unending promise of those days, now so long ago, there was always the same framework of humanity so that when the burnished shine wears through it reveals the structural antecedents of all human lives. Yet still for me to enter the past is to imagine that in some sacred reserve the bodies that were once ours still exist and all that has happened for good or ill in our lives reposes forever beyond that mist of illusion that alone allows us to face what life will inevitably bring.

At graduations in America various yearbooks capture and record a last legacy of innocence in the faces that have yet to encounter whatever trials await them in the troubling years to come. Only in retrospect is it possible to discern behind the faces some ironic turn in a smile or some inner pain or disillusionment at dawn that will soon be manifest in adult life and lead them to take one door rather than another along the dark corridors of the future. If what we shall become is a product of decisions confronting opportunities, there is still the presence of an underlying bias that is already present based upon who we imagine ourselves to be as we graduate and feel that the world is about to be opened before us. Neither beauty nor early promise is a guarantee of who will be among the survivors who will remain fifty years in the future to gather to review and to display who they have become in that vast interim that feels so short in its passing. What strange turns and challenges each life must face were hidden in that vast inventory of days and nights that then lay ahead.

As the self-sustaining rehearsal of the closed-society of high school or college is taken on the road to play in various venues all manner of fates may be encountered. The sheer number of separate lives tends to overwhelm us and our sense of individual worth to be diminished as our collective sense of who we were even as a class is itself diminished. History records the fate of eras rather than that of populations. We are identified by those vast swaths of the grim reaper that kills thousands rather than by our individual deaths. It is strange after a period of long separation to think that during each day of our lives our former friends and associates were also pursuing some unique version of their own vision of human happiness. Few will leave a record of their lives or impose upon others as I have done here an account of where they have been and why. The transgender journey is notable merely because of its rarity, but it does open a door to communication about the general losses and triumphs that we each must encounter in our own ways. This is the reason why this book exists.

Reunion Season

To one who has always been looking for that perfect place, that correct sex role, and that perfect articulation of experience, towards the goal that writers strive to achieve, the idea of closure is anathema to me. (Now there's a sentence for you!) It might be thought that in the era of compression of meaning that we inhabit writers such as I am would cease reading Marcel Proust and Henry James for stylistic models. But I love elliptical discourse and tangential references. If the reader has indulged this proclivity of mine thus far, a little more will do no harm. The personal essay relies upon the particular incident to illumine general meaning.

So yesterday I spent swimming in the waters along a lovely inlet in the southern reaches of Puget Sound. The wind was coming in bearing that salt-tang that is the essence of freshness. Madrona trees and all manner of rich undergrowth lined the shores and a long dock with a single boat completed a scene that was as lovely as might be found anywhere on earth. I had spent the morning engaging in a long deferred task of sorting papers and mail that I had disposed of in two great boxes in a closet aboard my boat. While I am not a hoarder, I am at least a deferrer of tasks that require a decision that I am not yet ready to make. I am always foreseeing some marginal use in various articles or communications from family or friends, so I let nothing go until it dissolves into moldy parchments of no possible use to anyone but me. What might be called "the detritus of a life" is unique to every person. In my own case besides papers and more papers it is books of all sorts, half-used lipsticks by the score, and various manifestos and speeches to address injustices and to fight back against incursions of various sorts. There is a tidal drift in more than yesterday's swimming that can carry anyone away but particularly one who despises organizational conformities and boards of directors. I always seem to outlast them but I bear the scars of battle.

The problem is that I am getting weary of conflicts lately and the bravado of a Ulysses is ebbing within me so that I am less likely to relish conflict or to dream of those further shores where adventure beckons. The urge to summation is upon me, an urge that is perhaps natural to a lawyer to rest one's case at last and to hope for a favorable verdict. This long preamble of course merely brings me to the subject of this particular essay – reunions.

It is a peculiarity of American culture that it thrives upon bringing together, presumably for comparison, lives that have diverged since high school or college. Armed with photographs of grandchildren, houses, or vacations and attempting to hide the scars left by various plastic surgeons, former students gather to see who is still alive, who looks better, and who might just have had a happy and successful life. If the people attending these affairs were truly friends of course, then the reunion would be unnecessary. If nothing else, years of exchanging Christmas cards would have kept them informed of the major events in each other's lives. The real function of reunions then is to observe the workings of time in the ones who were comparative strangers while in school together so as to see how one has been doing. After a certain time has passed since graduation, it is the equivalent of walking through a museum or a gambol through a sort of premature cemetery. My recent paper sorting has convinced me that a disinterested scholar would conclude the following of my own life:

✓ That my father was my most faithful correspondent and that we talked a great deal about various asset classes and political matters

✓ That I have received tons of solicitations to apply for various credit cards, under the assumption that I would live to pay my debts, and similar solicitations that I should apply for life-insurance, should I die young, so that my life would at least amount to something of use to someone

✓ That I have the habit of saving every sign of love directed my way in the form of various Christmas and Birthday Cards kept by me as talismans to ward off the uncertainty that my life mattered at all

✓ That I retain few personal mementos with the exception of various rocks that I have picked up along beaches through the years as though I were planning on opening the business of a rock and gravel quarry when sufficient rocks had been accumulated

✓ That I have retained various plans for vacation houses that were never built on land that my extended family no longer owns

✓ That I have maps and charts and reminders of many journeys and voyages taken

✓ That I retain various obscure auto parts, fittings, and hardware in case I should ever need them

✓ And finally that there is evidence that my life has been spent in far too much struggle and unhappiness with most of it caused by my very best efforts to find happiness after all

So what this means is I might just as well have let someone else plan my life as to have done it myself. This is just what the vow of obedience assumes had I remained in the Jesuit Order, that God and discernment would have provided a more secure beacon for my life. I have remained just as poor and about half as chaste as if I had become a priest instead of becoming a transsexual vagabond who has never stopped trying to be male while flushing estradiol through my liver like a sieve to become a convincing female. Somewhere surely there is an English country cottage in Yorkshire or Cornwall with geraniums in the window tended by a faithful spouse while I spend my mornings writing before taking my constitutional with a brace of devoted spaniels at my side. I could walk the moors deep in philosophic meditation and be welcomed home at tea time by my devoted wife who would of course think of nothing better than to sit by my side in the evening and hear me inveigh on one of my current enthusiasms or subjects of political indignation. She would be indulgent if I buried myself at times in books or went off to the local pub or golf course and assure me that I am still the same gallant lad who once made a name for himself when he was a young candidate in parliament, one whom the prime minister is still happy to call his friend.

Give me a life like that and I would be happy to go to reunions in the states if only to see how the colonials are doing. Or I could just go anyway and tell the truth of what my life has been and of the price that has been exacted for being transsexual in the Jurassic era in which I have lived. Maybe I could show them this book and say, "Here just read it for yourselves and don't forget the essay about reunions." Or is my real life still before me? Where does one look for redemption in one's own eyes if not in God's? God seems at times far more indulgent of our follies than we are. The thing that seems clearer to me every day is that I share that sense of time's loss that Proust recorded in his great masterpiece and that I understand the tender irony with which he regarded the human experience as it is lived in any era of history. Sooner or later we come round upon our own tracks in the forest of existence and wonder that we have been walking in circles all the time.

The Suffering Sweepstakes

Psychologists call it having a punitive superego, one that demands suffering as the price of authenticity. One of the unfortunate aspects of transgender politics has become that many assume that to be considered a real member of our community requires a display of wounds. Psychic scar tissue confers status; this inversion of the usual invitation to display good fortune rather than misfortune shows just how deeply many transsexuals have been wounded. Bonding to pain is the last resort of the helpless. Transsexuals have been tutored to assume that one of our rites of passage demands the surgical shedding of blood like some unending menstruation. This all began during that era when sex-change was almost without exception a mere matter of genital reconstruction as though the capacity to be penetrated was the very definition of woman. The blood, risk, and expense were the final test of our sincerity. Similarly manhood was reduced to possession of a penis. The threat posed by men disappears with the flesh. This preoccupation on body-parts betrays the holistic body and indicates a shallow reductionism when it is made a matter of social acceptance even among our own ranks. To say to another transsexual, "You have not suffered enough to speak for us," is to deny the ability to learn from the pain of others and to forge links of solidarity from a less compromised life history. We cannot afford to attack each other. It pleases bigots and fools to see us engaged in catfights. Anyone not against us is a potential ally. Those of us early ones were not so persnickety. We took aid wherever we found it and were grateful. We learned not to throw away free gifts. I remind the community of this as we seek to fine-tune our transgender discourse so that no one is ever offended. You know when a revolution has failed when it can afford to start in with purges from among the party of the faithful.

The Glamour of Evil

The search for faith has preoccupied me as much as my search for gender-congruity. Throughout this book and the many moods that have prevailed within me during its composition I have kept looking for final answers, not ones necessarily applicable to others, but one even adequate to myself. Along the way I may not have revealed that my true passion is history. It is not a pleasant pursuit. The record of the ages is a sad and sorry one of missed chances and of squandered opportunities to find peace, justice, and happiness. Even the desire to find goodness can betray one to feelings of pride when we believe that we have attained to it. It is no longer a surprise to me then that the highest of the angels is said to be the very prince of the devils. The ways of despair and of renunciation may at times appear to be upon parallel tracks. Both yield a desire to escape from the nightmare of identity if that identity is not grounded in God. Despair may be defined as renunciation from which hope has been subtracted. Healthy renunciation in turn is the response of one who has carefully examined the alternatives to God that are presented like some vast parade of insubstantial delights that collectively may be called the glamour of evil. Evil is the insubstantial rot at the core of the apple in Eden, a vast emptiness of unfilled promises.

As far s history is concerned, to pretend that we live in a rational world that pursues the goods of progress and enlightenment is be blind to the record of past follies and to anticipate a new golden era while ignoring past eras where various cultures have prematurely announced that era's arrival. The only alternative to ceaseless lamentation in the face of our actual history would appear to be a desperate adherence to order, submission, and petition. In the realm of theology these are called dogma, contrition and penance, and finally prayer. Each of these is easily lost. It takes constant discipline and vigilance to achieve them. The last steps on the way to Calvary are the hardest. Perhaps it is for this reason that Jesus assured the women of Jerusalem and those of the final era of time that we should weep not for Him but for ourselves. We are all in the place of those women today as we watch as the planet warms and life is compromised.

As this book is being written a sense of drought appears to afflict the earth. A short examination of the earth from space on the internet will show the spreading blight of urbanization, of the green yielding to the grey. Pope Francis to his credit has called attention to this phenomenon as a moral issue facing us all. There is a deeper drought though, one of the spirit, one that recalls the atmosphere in the grim novels of Franz Kafka, Graham Greene, or Albert Camus. The sensitive spirits always mirror historical realities before the events arise that serve to confirm prior intuitions. The post-modern era has been awaiting a new infusion of life and vigor for a very long time. Science can only measure and as a result has not provided this infusion of meaning. The spread of uniformity and convenience has only brought an excess of lotteries, casinos, designer foods, and culture as a theme park attraction to replace the former elephants and trapeze artists.

To anyone who observes these phenomena of our present world it is understandable finally why the exiled Jewish people could not sing the songs of Zion in the foreign land of their Babylonian captivity. But what if the whole earth is held captive so that Zion itself is symbolized simply by a series of walled compounds in Palestine? Where then shall we turn? It is in times like these that I desire renunciation. I would gladly purge my memory of every poor choice that I have ever made in my life, most of them in ardent pursuit of youth, happiness, and sustained well-being. My only comfort at times is that malice falls behind us if we continue to intend the good and to know that we cannot produce it nor sustain it without grace.

When a Catholic dies the priest blesses the coffin at the funeral mass and honors the residual flesh by incense to imply our collective trust that the soul's ultimate fate rests in the mercy of God and that final penitence and persistence will attain to heaven. The rest is only the quiet sound at noon of insects in the summer grass at the cemetery and the fading memories of the ones who will soon follow.

Unless … and upon that great "unless" everything depends as two thousand years of Christian history has believed, that a tomb in ancient Judea was found empty on the third day.

Poets' Journeys

My readers may or may not recall this reference to the grim poem by Robert Browning in the title, "Childe Roland to the Dark Tower Came," but be that as it may this is how I feel at times lately, just like a post-modern version of Childe Roland. In my younger days I was engaged in doing battle for gender fluidity and acceptance. I despised those who called into question the issue of gender passage from male to female who claimed that by transitioning we were traitors to the cause. But, I am growing weary of causes and crusades. I am weary alike of irate evangelicals, stodgy Catholic prelates, self-serving politicians with an anti-gay axe to grind, and of bright young things using the temporary intersection of the sexes at adolescence to transition and assume that they will be young forever.

No one likes a bitter transsexual, but I understand that even this term is growing old and tattered with overuse. The Trans-people of today demand nothing less than full manhood or womanhood even as these categories themselves are being called into question. As definitions slide into one another words lose their meaning and discreteness. It takes an enumeration of passing qualifiers to say what anything is and even that present consensus may soon transform and be unrecognizable.

The will is becoming more sovereign with each day and the realm of the given proportionately diminished. It is the purpose of this late essay then to inquire whether the quest begun so long ago with Loomings is not ending as Childe Roland's did with a darkening plain and a squat tower reared up against the shadows of the coming night falling all too swiftly all around us. The knight no sooner announces his arrival than he realizes that all that remains to him is to say that he has come to that which he imagined at last only to find no gathering crowds to witness the placing of his pennant upon the Dark Tower. The bestowal of tolerance for transsexuals is increasingly not real acceptance but only the grim realization of the gender pilgrim that no one really cares about anything in our world of isolated perceptions. When everything is subjective all meaning perishes. Definitions require opposition and progress requires sacrifice; this has always been the way of the world.

Secrets and Sacrifices

The lives that we live are only partially our own. We enter upon a stage where the play has already been partially written and we must fit our way into the ongoing action as best we may. Ancestral guilt and curses may taint our natal blood. The change in a mother's countenance is immediately read and recorded by the child as a judgment upon its tiny life. We are born seeking the smiles of confirmation that we matter to someone. Our very survival depends upon that approval.

As time passes we begin to notice that we are often seen through a clouded lens by other people. "If they only knew my heart," we say to ourselves, "Then they would know how I suffer and how much I am trying to reach out to find them."

The years fall and drift about us and only the novelists seem to understand our human struggle. A few sympathize when our hearts are broken but they cannot know how various losses trigger old memories within us. They do not feel the glass shards shifting just beneath our skin.

We were told to keep our secrets and many that are not ours at all. Some of us were set aside before birth as sacrificial victims on the pyre of a family's pride. These become a symbol and are only given the meaning that is appropriate to symbols, linkages without substance or individuality. We miss each other through the indirection of time. "I waited for you," we say, "But you never heard me calling. You never believed that I could love so much."

Somewhere beneath a pine tree a sage is writing a haiku with a stiff and aged brush that will not be read by any eyes but his own.

Who can count the number of the voiceless dead? History like a whirlwind sweeps all things before it.

Who will record our passing? The urns smoke and the rain drops sift down out of grey skies onto the sodden mosses. A fountain made of lava rock spills our tears in a Japanese garden. Beneath a willow a single girl kneels at the riverside with her hair cast forward over her weeping eyes.

Secrets can only be spoken in the dark. Most of them are never told. We were taken by surprise and did not see the robber when he stole into the sanctuary and took the fire. The shrine is empty now. The sacrifice smokes on the naked alter and the worshipers have all fled.

The Problem of Proportionate Concern

By my phrase "proportionate concern" I mean putting nuclear disarmament, the international unrest centered on the Ukraine, and the growth of shanty towns like donuts around cities like Manila, Mumbai, and Cairo on a similar level to the panic over same-sex marriage. There can be no doubt that the vessel of the world is presently moving out into unfathomed waters. As this chapter is being written the Northwest where I live has been undergoing record high temperatures and last week the Supreme Court extended the benefits of marriage to same-sex couples to join countries like Spain and Ireland, Catholic countries both that have already recognized it. Even the White House was il-luminated last week with rainbow colored spot-lights while the ghosts of certain past Presidents turned over in their graves.

Over the weekend I also heard of the death from AIDS of a friend that I had known in the seventh grade when we both attended a small California country grammar school. Over the weekend various Gay Freedom Day parades celebrated politi-cal victories that had once seemed impossible in the dark era of President Reagan and conservative domination when Christian broadcasting stations could lambast us at will and when only bars and bathhouses could proclaim that the GLBT community even existed. I grew up in the era of tarnished drag artistes and darkened movie theaters on 42d street in New York. There were few examples to be imitated of a successful or healthy gay or transgender lifestyle then and marriage was a refuge not to be thought of by the gay clones of San Francisco and West Hollywood. To the dismay of conservatives the closets that had once contained our lives were not only open but have since morphed into vast reception rooms serving appetizers to all comers. We are not only "not in Kansas anymore" we are evidently plunged into a veritable mid-summer night's dream.

When I was debating against various bigots the cause of a civil rights ordinance in Tacoma to protect our community our position, which went down twice to defeat, these present changes would have appeared absolutely astonishing. Discrimination was everywhere and the doors of even ordinary opportunities appeared to be forever closed to us. I decided after those days of disillusionment to leave my former career and to fly beneath the radar by moving out onto the sea. Now just over twenty years since those local struggles our dreams of recognition and respect all seem to be coming true. I no longer need the "trannie-curse" to repay the business owners who used to tell me that I would not be served because they were a "family friendly establishment." The days when I was told by security representatives at malls that cross-dressing was grounds for being barred entry under threat of prosecution for criminal trespass may seem so archaic as not to be unbelievable now but I assure you that this was how it once was for us. I recall my indignation and humiliation from that period and the scars will remain with me forever. Even today national civil rights will need to follow marriage rights and legally married gay couples may still find that no one needs to rent housing to them in many states.

If I seem dubious of progress in this section of my book it is because many of the gifts of this period are coming too late to change what has been the course of my life. The only horizon that I see before me is the one that my faith tells me will demand that I abjure what I am increasingly too weary to even pursue, a continued cross-gendered existence with the belated freedom to explore not only sexuality but intimacy. For this reason I have dusted off my old aspirations and left the parade just as it has finally turned down into the dimly lit streets where I once sought solace in my cross-gendered youth. Rather than join the cotillion of blue-haired old ladies I am debating a long delayed menopause for my non-existent uterus.

As what may be called a "post-sexual" I may just be able to speak as an oracle in what time remains to me or just perhaps catch something of the fleeting hetero-normative era that is passing away and let someone else bear the inevitable burdens of being a female in America. If I make this concession though I exact as my price the privilege of turning an accusing finger against that very hetero-normative existence that has failed in so many ways to deserve the protections that conservatives still demand as their exclusive right, the right to religious freedom.

The failures of the American family are not due to the assaults or undermining influence of the LGBT community. That failure is instead a product of the loss of shared belief in a human life as opposed to our becoming mere adjuncts to corporate commercialism. Wage disparity and male defection leaves many women to raise children alone. The family mythology that is preserved in Catholic and Fundamentalist Christian rhetoric is honeycombed with vast swaths of brutality and abuse. The reality of life in American families is seldom aired fully anywhere but before private psychotherapists.

Only when proportionate concern is spent addressing social realities over sentimental images will it be possible to see whether the family is in truth the bulwark of the social order that it is supposed to be. You see I do agree with the conservative bishops who proclaim their call for true solidarity between the sexes and for children to possess the right to have homes based upon the procreative aspect that unites the sexes in intercourse. What I find troubling is the concentration upon a complementarity that is all too often a wall of incomprehension as men and women reach across the gender habits and modes of thought that currently divide us. Having walked the proverbial mile in someone else's high-heels I can bear witness that being a trans-woman or any kind of woman for that matter, "just "ain't no crystal stair."

Ideals are admirable but until translated into practical charity they will always come up short and be unpersuasive. I want my

Church to connect all the dots and to see where we are moving on this planet that begins to resemble a knee with a scab on it. We live on a big version of Noah's ark and we are moving out into uncharted waters. I hope that no sour and disgruntled Republican candidate will use our present victories to usher in a backlash in he is elected to the Presidency or that various individual members of the LGBT community will pay the price for our collective victories by being injured in the attacks upon us that have never ceased to be an adolescent rite of passage for insecure males.

In the future will the Laura's, the Millie's, the Samantha's, or the Gladys's, all the television housewives of my youth, soon be sharing recipes for jelled salads or sitting together at PTA meetings with their gay and lesbian married neighbors? Will the drag queens still ride around on the anniversary of Stonewall each June or will our new rights finally render these icons just too retro? I wonder whether in a post-gender world genital reassignment will be the moral equivalent of a tonsillectomy. Who can say what this "brave new world" will be like for people like me, the few trannie-goddesses who care to write their memoirs only to find that we are the human equivalent of a stack of old 45's sung by fifties artists asking "Where the boys are?" Your guess is as good as mine, but for various zealots who feel that we all stand on the eve of destruction I answer, "Oh Mary, please girl! Don't be so dramatic; there are other issues you know."

The vast poker game of the stock market that floats on a sea of derivatives may collapse. North Korea may finally push the envelope of its hateful rhetoric too far. India and Pakistan or maybe India and China may finally decide by force of arms which nation should dominate Central Asia. Or maybe the earth will finally just dry up like a bottle of perfume left open and without its stopper. Somewhere there is maybe a little manikin cultivating his Hitler-style mustache and working up his speech that we have all been betrayed by judicial activists and that it is time for the people to shake off the "stab in the back" and restore the old order when we all knew what to do with "people like those."

The Art of Interpreting Texts

I believe that in the pragmatic order of a diverse society that more problems are raised than solved by using supposedly authoritative texts to resolve the problems raised. The concept of authoritative texts is not a popular one at the present time, although this concept is the darling of the conservative mind because it presumes that a static vision of science or of government is valid for all time. This is not a new issue in our history. The primary objection to the biological doctrine of evolution in the 19th century was that it blurred what were presumed to be intact species, each created separately and irrevocably and transferred to safety by means of the seemingly infinitely capacious confines of Noah's Ark.

This literalistic view of nature was not only static and confined but it was one that made few allowances for human intervention in its operations. Divine causality was presumed to govern not simply the origins of all things but also to govern their most minute daily operations with the sole exception of the human will, which after Original Sin experienced the possibility of opposing the will of God rather than simply ratifying the pre-existing will that manifested the Divine intention for all things in natural law. The question of free will was a paradox that made many theologians uncomfortable. If God was all powerful then perhaps even grace must operate, not to undergird human freedom, but to coerce it through predestination. If all of creation was altered by human choice then Original Sin may have decreed the form and character of physics as well as the inner dispositions of human our nature.

Since time is required for deliberation and decision it might even be maintained that the very existence of the space-time continuum was a direct result of the decision of our primal parents to unilaterally change their nature from radical innocence to experience with all of its concomitant burdens of sin, shame, and guilt. Theological truths are of their nature mysterious and must be clothed in metaphor in order to be even partially understood. The question that arises though is how authoritative texts are to be interpreted so as not to confuse metaphor with a direct description of mundane detail or adopting an instrumentalist vision to support current assumptions or conditions that could not have been discerned by the original readers of the text.

This leads to the further question of authorial intent. If the author is presumed to have acted under divine inspiration does this divine power choose words that are self-adapting to new requirements or must they be understood as to some degree limited by the age in which they were first written and the social conditions that were present at that time? Even when all of this has been taken into consideration the weight of meaning conveyed must at times strain the adequacy of words simply considered as words and not as precise mathematical symbols. To assume that textual readings are simple and self-evident is to ignore these potential problems in interpretation.

For this reason it requires some final arbiter to render an authoritative interpretation of texts. Problems arise though when such texts are read to support an agenda of presently existing power structures anxious about the solidity of their institutional role as opposed to asking critical questions about the transferability of meaning over time or as applied to radically different social conditions. To assume that every age hears and comprehends metaphor in the same way is more indicative of presumption or of a biased reading than it is of an accurate reading of the original text.

In the wake of the recent Supreme Court decision recognizing same-sex marriage a friend who is unacquainted as are most Americans with the complexities of Constitutional adjudication assured me that what we were observing was the prospect of a government that is out of control. Many people like him feel that the Constitution is some sort of bulwark made of self-evident propositions rather than what it really is, an aspirational structural document from the 18th century that is inadequate to anticipate let alone to decide most contemporary Constitutional problems. Constitutional Law then is in its own way analogous to statutory laws passed by Congress being a manifestation of intent to be filled in later in the light of experience rather than being made up by some distant concatenation or reverberation of something enunciated once and for all at the Constitutional Convention or to be found in "The Federalist Papers" by Madison, Jay, and Hamilton.

My friend then went on to ask that I answer yes or no to the following question: Is it the business of the courts to enforce the Constitution as written or to further the interests of the people. I answered that he had posed a false dichotomy, but in any case it was not the business of the courts to do either. It is not the business of the Courts to enforce the Constitution as written because ever since the case of Marbury v. Madison it is the courts that must decide what the Constitution means. Interpretation is by its nature legislative to some degree. It is also not the business of the courts to discern the will of the people because that will is not monolithic or discoverable even by due diligence. What this means is that absent a revolution we must live with the decisions of the courts unless they are overturned in due course by other judges.

In our scheme of ordered liberty the test of Constitutional rights must pass what is called strict scrutiny whenever a fundamental liberty interest is at stake. Absent a compelling governmental interest the private liberty interest will prevail whenever what is termed a fundamental right is at stake for a discrete and insular minority that can be identified. If a marriage is considered to be a fundamental civil right then it has passed the strictest of scrutiny tests and the states are bound to enforce this determination. This is enforcement of the Constitution, at least according to the judges in the majority opinion, and that is sufficient to settle the matter. This is what institutional due process is all about and to presume some other arrangement is to revive a confederation of independent states in the place of the existing federal republic of the United States of America.

The phrase, "In God We Trust" may decorate our currency but has no Constitutional standing in our arrangement of the separation of Church and State. Pious gestures aside, we are a secular government that is as uninformed by charity as it is by faith and hope. It is obvious then that the term, "marriage," which has been purloined from its origins in theology when used by the government is without the content that is presumed to follow automatically from its use by Christians.

The further questions of procreation, legitimacy, and of child custody associated with marriage are thus severable from the question of the civil status of the partners to a marriage. In a world where substantial numbers of children are being raised by single parents or by foster parents the model of the nuclear heterosexual family is already so severely compromised that a general overhaul of divorce or of child-birth outside of marriage should precede any concern about gay or lesbian couples adopting children. The abuse statistics and numbers of homeless children would indicate that children need anyone who is responsible and willing to undertake their care and maintenance. Until these problems are resolved the current indignation at same-sex marriage is misplaced or at least should be postponed subsequent to the real problems surrounding marriage that already exist in our society.

Then there are the Biblical texts that are used to make of marriage a univocal institution as though God was a writer for television family dramas from the great age of American television. I am sure that the royal families of Europe viewed marriage quite differently from Ozzie and Harriet," from "My Three Sons," from "The Brady Bunch," and from "The Partridge Family."

This version of the American family has not been a univocal creation sustained in daily practice or even reflected back to us by our media for many years. We look in vain through the precepts of ancient Canaan for how to raise teenagers who are now armed with cell phones and online social media accounts. Only the Amish seem to follow a way of life that preserves some of the actuality of what the various institutes proclaim and conservatives celebrate as "family values." Texts cannot solve complex social problems nor can they answer the practical questions posed without being first further dissected to decide what is at stake and what remedies are available.

Umbrella terms are useless except as window dressing. This is why both celebration and outrage are equally misplaced in the light of many recent cases decided by our highest court. I would dismiss all such questions for lack of subject matter jurisdiction and defer them to the marriage chapels in Las Vegas which seem to reflect the state of the art of marriage in modern America.

I do not wish to abandon ideals but to pretend that they are already present among us and were overturned by same-sex marriage is an absurd pretense. If anything same-sex marriage may awaken heterosexuals to the value of an institution that their behavior has held up to ridicule and contempt for many years.

Family Values

Much of the outrage expressed against the LGBT community stems from the belief that our existence serves to undermine what are called "family values." Of course the values that are celebrated cannot be applied to all existing families in America today or even most. This will become clear if we simply list some of those values:

- ✓ Monogamous
- ✓ Heterosexual
- ✓ Neither party has been divorced
- ✓ A single shared domicile for spouses
- ✓ Children not being raised by a single parent
- ✓ No unmarried partners
- ✓ No single parent adoption or foster care
- ✓ Each partner can serve as a proper heterosexual and cis-sexual model for the psychological modeling of the children
- ✓ Their relationship of the spouses will usually be patri-centered
- ✓ Children are to be formed to mirror parental standards and beliefs no matter how bizarre or insular they may be
- ✓ The family unit will emphasize the common American values of independence, material acquisition, and patriotic militarism
- ✓ Father's primary role is that of provider
- ✓ Woman's primary status is derived from her role as a mother
- ✓ Each family unit should manifest independent economic sufficiency without any form of state aid
- ✓ Each family is an independent value center with its own secrets, traditions, and right to control its children

286

✓ Children have no independent rights of self-determination if in conflict with family values

I could go on with my list but it will be evident immediately that many of these values will be unapologetically included in most lists of family values. The point is that this model is far from being universally found in contemporary America. How then will the real needs of actual family units be met if it is assumed that this monolithic model still prevails? But the greater issue is whether the traditional family unit manifests the model for psychological health that it is presumed to do. Any sociological text will demonstrate how often the American home is one that is beset by child abuse, alcoholism, incest, and spousal quarrels and brutality. Most of these conditions thrive in precisely the private and secretive world of the patriarchal family unit. Many people spend years in psychotherapy simply trying to undo the damage that was inflicted upon them as children by this traditional structure of American life.

Even a short walk through the plays of Shakespeare will reveal the true dynamics that emerge from family life from Romeo and Juliette to King Lear. Even the phrase, "family law," will reveal that the existence of family is often a failing proposition; one that is often marred by the presence of jealousy, envy, violence, and twisted self-images supported by the shaming and guilt of parents and other authority figures. Only stir some toxic religious doctrines into this bubbling brew of dissention and add a couple of firearms for good measure and there you have it, conservative American family values. Compared to this mess the real question is why members of the LGBT community, many of them refugees from just such families, would want to be tainted by ever forming families of their own.

Any empirical study will be of far more value to clarify the true nature of these sub-clinical entities, American families, than the sentimental images so often held up by various religious leaders who use the family values stick simply to beat-up other people. I have yet to hear of a conservative candidate for office who is in favor of school lunches for poor children, aid for dependent children, or a living wage for single Mom's. I am confident that when the true extent of child abuse in this country is finally revealed that the "spare the rod spoil the child" tyranny will finally be revealed in all of its malice. Until then all we need to do is to listen to the street kids who have been driven out of their Christian homes, ones that were evidently too pure to contain them.

My problem with "family values" is that in most cases they have nothing to do with family or values. Instead they represent a shared ideology of abuse and subjugation of the weak by the strong. Proof of this assertion is not difficult to find. The political parties and the candidates with a conservative agenda usually advocate the following policies:

- ✓ A strong posture of defense thus demonstrating the basic paranoid stance of those who feel that their collective power might be compromised by revolt at the periphery by those nations and peoples who are subject to their control;

- ✓ A commitment to fertility and the right to impregnate that is divorced from a consideration of the social costs that go along with children, their education, and the biological issues of most concern to women;

- ✓ There is a direct proportion between the distance from the actual demands of raising a family and the degree of sentimental rhetoric that is used to describe procreation and family relationships;

- ✓ The ethos of independence decries aid to struggling families even as it advocates various tax breaks, subsidies, and outright bailouts for banks, investment bankers, and corporate industries;

- ✓ The preoccupation with power usually also includes a fetish for gun possession in spite of the almost continuous witness of school shootings, road-rage killings, mass-murders by various psychopaths, and mistaken shootings in homes;

- ✓ Service in the military is similarly exalted no matter how our troops are actually used, for instance to police the borders of the American Empire and punish unruly nations that object to the global assertion of American cultural and economic power;

- ✓ Sex role indoctrination and territorial imperatives are reinforced by a sports ethos in high school and colleges (this reaches an apotheosis in the virtual hysteria surrounding such absurd national pastimes as the celebration of Super-bowl Sunday as a sort of national holiday, a virtual orgy of advertising, eating, and the usual sexual display provided by the half-time show;

✓ A tendency to distort the actual costs to the nation of prior "conservative" administrations (such as: no-bid contracts for military hardware/Iran-Contra/no weapons of mass-destruction found in Iraq/ etc.).

What all of these have in common is a bizarre phallic centered mentality that masquerades as care for all of the members of a family unit whether in the immediate domicile or in the nation as a whole rather than celebrating the preservation of vested (male) wealth and power. It is not too much to say that America manifests a national psychosis regarding male virility from a terror of (gasp!) erectile dysfunction to the results that would follow if we ever closed our national off-shore prison facilities or gave prisoners of war a fair trial.

The relevance of this latest diatribe to transsexuals is this: to change sex, particularly in a male to female direction cuts at the base of the phallic tree and thus awakens a sexual terror in a system that is based on seeing women as stimuli to male fantasies of sexual climax, power, and pride.

We are the canaries in the coal mine. When we drop from our perch you can be sure that something noxious and deadly is present in the atmosphere of America.

Exile

Most us remember as a wound occasions where we lost what had been precious relationships with friends or family because they would not accept us as transsexual. We were treated as bearers of some strange communicable disease; we were not who they thought we had always been because we had been trained all of our lives not to let them see us. We were condemned as duplicitous at precisely the moment when we dared to be honest with them.

This is something that young transsexuals may not believe, surrounded as they are by at least some protective legislation. The word for us is now ubiquitous in public discourse. People expect that they might run into us somewhere sometime. We are no longer visitors from some distant planet.

What do the words of exile sound like?

289

- ✓ You are a stranger to us now.
- ✓ We feel we don't know you now.
- ✓ You are no longer part of our family.
- ✓ You need to repent and ask God for forgiveness.
- ✓ You will make an ugly woman.
- ✓ No one will ever love you.
- ✓ What are those things? Are you wearing a bra?
- ✓ You'll catch AIDS.
- ✓ Don't let the children to know.
- ✓ Those clothes are women's clothes not yours.
- ✓ I can tell that you have been wearing make-up.
- ✓ You aren't welcome at Christmas unless you come as your old self.
- ✓ Don't bring your lover.
- ✓ You look like that lady in the Robin Williams movie.
- ✓ No one will hire you.
- ✓ People will never understand.
- ✓ Why don't you just do it behind closed doors?
- ✓ I can't believe you want to be a damn woman!
- ✓ Men have it made, what are you thinking of?
- ✓ But you always used to be so manly.
- ✓ I want a divorce; you are disgusting.
- ✓ You are denied custody.
- ✓ We don't interview people like you. We owe it to our customers to keep this place a family-friendly place.
- ✓ The doctor doesn't treat transsexuals.

It is comments like these that have driven so many of us away, often forever. Along with the usual street abuse that most people will never know these comments made to transsexuals have made many of us strangers in our own homes and regional locales. We woke up one day without a gender passport. We were aliens that no wall could keep out because we are everywhere. We know that now. We didn't know that then.

Transaction Costs

One of the primary schools of modern jurisprudence is the discipline of law and economics. A common point of discussion in the pursuit of a unified theory of law within that approach is to examine the concept of transaction costs. These costs are those imposed in order to reach alternative agreements or to alter a present condition of affairs through unilateral action. Another way of saying this is that any action creates repercussions and these repercussions may be quantified and compared with those generated by alternate courses of conduct in order to evaluate their efficiency and their respective contribution to an overall policy of increasing the general good of society as measured by wealth.

One of the weaknesses of this approach to the laws is its failure to take into account what may be termed "incommensurable values." These values are the ones that moralists call normative values, in other words values that should be considered to have general validity for all human beings.

Normative values cannot be reduced to a mere pragmatic calculus let alone reduced to market value in a monetized system. So when it comes to evaluating incommensurables it becomes necessary to find some other criterion for choice between various alternatives. One of the primary sources of normative values today is a belief in personal authenticity – to live one's individual truth. There is a remarkable trust from this point of view in subjective feelings and impulses as the ground of truth as opposed to the consensus of the collective experience of past ages or an outside authoritative source.

This is why dialogue on these issues is often impossible. There is simply no way of bridging an abyss that is determined, not by the issues in dispute, but by the very categories of evidence that are deemed admissible and persuasive in order to resolve them. This in turn reduces communication to being merely the equivalent of noise because it becomes impossible to discern patterns without at least some preexisting parameters in order to structure the debate and to find common ground. The end result of this is that everything is reduced to polls and democracy becomes more than just a form of government, it becomes its own metaphysic.

This mode of ungrounded thought is not confined though to our modern relativists, it is as likely to emerge even among those who rely upon a position supposedly grounded in an absolute and authoritative text or a personal commission to enforce norms or at least to announce them. If the former error is that of a radical subjectivism, the error of the latter (and it is at least an error in persuasive strategy) is that of presuming that universals are easily discernable in human affairs. To make of the common good a procrustean bed rather than to ask why diversity exists is to fail in inquiry and compassion. Many of the terms that have appeared in the debate over homosexuality and transsexualism are terms of abuse rather than of an invitation to discover value in what are presumed to be completely natural and innate characteristics of all human beings. This closed approach precludes all direct understanding or even analogy between the opposing views existing today on human sexuality.

The very essence of an act of de-humanization of the other is to so polarize human experience that faults become categorical and not a mere matter of degree. If it is essential to reduce variance to the completely alien in order to win an argument, then it would appear that some lingering doubt remains as to the possible validity of the opposing position. Emotional rhetoric arouses the suspicion that either logic is lacking or that one's base is more insecure than one will readily admit. To assume that the common good is so fragile that to admit exceptions can cause it to collapse is either to presume an inability of the masses to defend their own interests or that values are opaque and undiscoverable.

The result is that if neither an examination of transaction costs nor the relativism implied in a state of sustained and co-existing but opposed and incommensurable values can provide a point of unity, then the world of discourse will be reduced to nothing more than a condition of a mutual stand-off characterized by bitterness and mistrust – hardly an optimal outcome.

I do not have the answer to this current social tendency to silence an opponent by ridicule and refusal to dialogue. I can only attempt to clarify the situation for others to resolve as best they may by bridging these insuperable ideological gaps that carry their own rather high transaction costs.

Small-Craft Warnings

As this book draws to its close and my final essays flicker out like so many votive candles before the shrine of my hopes and aspirations I wish to address those who are still looking for a harbor. When storm winds threaten the wise mariner either seeks a snug berth or gives the land a wide margin and heaves to until the storm passes. If seeking harbor the rule is to keep red buoys to the starboard side of the vessel, "red right returning." To avoid running aground on a lee shore, vessels still at sea must give the land a large margin of seaway to allow for the drift of wind and current. To be transgendered is to exist at sea beset by all manner of forces that stress and try our emotional stays and halyards. In my youth I kept most of my inner secrets well battened down and out of sight. Later on I took my chances and ran with the storm under light canvas taking my chances that I would come through alright. I took chances, most of us do, but I kept afloat and corrected course to pursue my old compass headings when I could.

Yet if my life was lonely and painful, it might have been far worse. I am still looking about though for a better narrative than the one I have reported here. I am often tempted to bring the helm hard over and to come about and seek harbor by returning to the silence of an anonymous male presence in the world. I see my body now as no longer the trim and ready vessel that it once was, but as one that must simply convey me on like those outmoded clipper ships that survived by carrying grain or coal in their holds rather than silk and spices. As the female body leaves aside the years of fertility and fashion the questions of the basis of self-worth arise again. Where do we locate the self in our own and other's eyes? Do we begin to separate our essential being from the body as we age? As the balance of time switches from the future to the past our dreams become not prospects but retrospectives. I am often ashamed of my own unhappiness because I would wish to be able to present a story without insult or indignity. I desire this so that no other transsexual will need to have her doubts confirmed by my witness to the reef-strewn coasts that I have known.

Just how imperative is the transgender drive or condition? I know its strength, not only from my own life, but from the witness of others as well. Cis-gendered people cannot imagine the anguish of Gender Dysphoria; they must simply take our experience as witness. I do not wish to encourage or discourage others in the course of considering transition but simply to tell my tale and move on. As for those who know comfort in their assigned sex, let them not condemn but rather pray to whatever gods may be for those in peril on the sea.

All Hallows Eve

Nothing can be more insulting to a transgender person than to imply that what they are manifesting is only a masquerade. A little reflection though will reveal that much of what we term personality is an effort to coordinate elements that are profoundly at variance with each other. The mere existence of Multiple Personality Disorder shows that vast chasms can exist between various aspects of affect and functioning within a single human body over time. Much of what we do is role playing as we attempt to integrate ourselves into various social groups. Even in the ancient dramas of Greece and of Japan it was customary for the players to wear masks. The freedom to escape from our customary norms is felt by those who celebrate various Carnival festivals.

This universal tendency to vacillation and change through occasion or circumstance may indicate that transsexualism is merely a desperate effort to preserve the personality from dissolution by undertaking the desperate gamble of gender transition when the role expectations of the assigned gender appear impossible to assimilate. If there is the slightest possibility that this is so then gender reassignment becomes a sort of high-tech psychic defense mechanism for those personalities threatened with dissolution. Just how in tune we all are with our fate is always in question. Can a gender role be maintained by anyone without outward social support? The march of the generations appears to cease as it encounters Gender Dysphoria and the various procedures undertaken to transition. These render the transsexual sterile and at the very least, genitally challenged.

I address these issues in the context of Halloween because All Hallows Eve is the one universally celebrated festival that loosens social bonds in America and allows the upwelling of forces that recall what is usually repressed. On this one day each year many gender variant people traditionally found their only outlet for what was held in chains and silence throughout the rest of the year. As a child Halloween meant so much to me that its shadow was cast across my succeeding days and nights. Now at my age when all shadows grow longer and the pale sun illumines paler prospects of futurity I find myself wondering whether the day following All Hallows Eve is not the real feast of my aspirations. Sex and procreation cease to be the role expected of one in later life in spite of the preposterous ads to cure erectile dysfunction as though our society profits in some way by having a great number of erect members in those already knocking upon the doors of eternity. Many men apparently hope to enjoy a few last quick ones before stepping into the vessel moored by the River Styx and setting sail for the underworld. Meanwhile the exaggerated and plastic versions of women that appear in media everywhere may torture adolescents sufficiently without arousing sexual desire when it should be gradually mellowing into wisdom and surrender to the grave.

Death is the one unnamed blasphemy. It stalks among us unseen because its prelude of old age cannot be acknowledged without shame. Thus this short essay is placed before you to ask whether it is proper or salutary to assume a body whose promising contours cannot be validated by procreation and reinforced by all of those social norms that make it possible to support an identity. Without support, community, and daily reinforcement any identity, however visually convincing, must always exist over an abyss of doubt as to whether the transaction was valid that allows a male body to assume that of a female.

Negotiation of stigmatized behaviors cannot rely indefinitely upon legal mandates to survive nor can individuals swim forever against an opposing tide. Caught in this dilemma I have spent my life. This book has recorded some of the price exacted in being a transsexual. It is a price that like many mortgages has still left much of the principal unpaid as I enter my final decades of life. Without daily reinforcement in a gender role over many years a sense of inner masquerade becomes inevitable. To maintain an identity by sheer effort and a repeated declaration of rights becomes presumptuous and arbitrary and therefore the denial of our status becomes equally arbitrary and presumptuous. The result is a shouting match waged across a shifting border.

This is the condition of the gender discourses of today. Transsexuals are caught in the middle of a cultural divide and we pay a heavy price in personal anguish by being so situated. I do not possess the short answer to this dilemma. Instead, my desire here is to bring out the dimensions of the conflict and the costs imposed as is appropriate for one trained to adopt a jurisprudential view on various phenomena. To occupy a middle-ground is sometimes the only way to view the extremes without being too distant from one or the other and losing sight of the full circumference manifested by the various points of departure. Method must precede content in any inquiry and in the case of a breakdown of formerly mutually exclusive categories such as gender that form the basis for so much else in social life this is even more essential. The essays in this book are therefore partial articulations rather than a finished synthesis. To repeat this point often has seemed to me essential to the understanding of what I am doing in this book.

The central problem that I have grappled with here is a personal struggle, but it is also a significant struggle of the age in which we live. Male and female are not mere designations of a personal body style; they are the iconic and polar extremities that set up a human psychic gravitational field. By dividing various traits between the sexes and by inhabiting bodies that are adapted to procreation and the nurturing of our young we find ourselves as embodied beings and have some idea of the tasks of human psycho-social maturation. Deprived of these indicia of where we stand in life and where our primary relationships reside we are reduced to being independent units where anything is at least theoretically possible but unfortunately no longer practically possible. For a thing to be practically possible for a human being it must be contained in some way and know various limitations. The human spirit must meet resistance if it is to have points of orientation around which decisions can be made and commitments may be reached. An unconstrained human spirit would soon disintegrate because all options would be equal and no human spirit could tolerate that degree of universality. In an effort to be all things we simply exhaust ourselves.

There must be an orientating field against which we can measure our progress and find our place. If instead we must begin at scratch and in a sense self-conceive our identity, then there is no outside witness or point of origin around which we can assemble the various traits that are personal to us, even if arbitrary and based only upon chance. Freedom cannot be absolutely unconditioned. If gender identity is merely a matter of declaration followed by political recognition then it no longer represents a central and fundamental polarity around which an identity can be formed.

Human life craves a basis outside of our desires and imaginations as a given. If we are responsible for everything, then we are finally responsible for nothing. This is so because with no exterior criteria to measure our actions against, without a pre-existing standard, then everything becomes irretrievably subjective and only force can compel recognition by other subjectivities. If the personal is always political, then it is not even personal. To be authentically a person we require others to both resist and to confirm us and that they cannot do this if we presume to possess an unlimited ability to choose that must be validated by others simply because we choose it and not because it is right. Without an appeal to an objective and discrete order to validate us all we can do is make a blind appeal and hope for an affirmative response.

This is the reason that transsexualism cannot remain political. Rather, it must be validated by sources of evidence: physical, genetic, anthropological, and psychological. Even then, sexual alterations will remain the rare procedures that they are. To choose a course that does the least damage to the individual in order to ensure psychic and social wholeness appears both prudent and moral under the principal of the totality while to those who do not feel the anguish of Gender Dysphoria the issues raised by transsexualism should simply be taken in stride in a spirit of compassion. This approach does honor to the objective order while still allowing for variance in an imperfect world.

Opinion Poll

The year 2015 may go down in history as the "Year of the Trans-sexual," the year when transgender became a mainstream phenomenon. It was the year when we emerged from the status of being rare birds on the verge of extinction and suddenly appeared to be everywhere all at once. We were on magazine covers. We were cheerleaders. We wanted the right to use restrooms without courting the prospect of assault from some panic-stricken male in a men's room should we enter in panty-hose and heels. Unfortunately we got sandwiched in between the hysteria that followed the Supreme Court decision ratifying and even demanding nation-wide compliance with same-sex marriage and the unyielding resistance posed by the deep underlying bigotry and hatred of those Christians who would like to return us all to the condition of early nomadic Judaism as represented in the priestly codifications of Leviticus and Deuteronomy.

It was also the year when Pope Francis proclaimed a Jubilee Year of Mercy and called for a Church that is more sensitive at all levels to the needs of the poor and the outcasts. This attitude of outreach was not embraced in various Protestant circles. This was also the year when various advocates for religious freedom were explaining how calling for the death penalty for gay people was pleasing to God. This concept of using religion as a sword rather than a shield in order to oppress others and to deny them equality and the freedom of their own conscience never seems to penetrate through the skull to the grey matter of those who love to posture and preen themselves as attacked simply because their victims finally have a recourse in law from discrimination. "Serve thou no pizza to faggots lest thy house shall fall down and thou be ruined utterly!" Oh really?

Yes, 2015 was a mixed year for us. It was the year when our President mentioned the need to secure basic recognition and rights for transgender people in his State of the Union Speech, but it was also a year when many advocated that America should become a theocracy the better to wage interminable wars against infidels and purge America of sexual diversity by means of stoning if possible. Various Presidential candidates thought nothing of courting the votes of people who if they were quoting the Koran rather than the Bible would be called terrorists and be given a one-way ticket to Guantanamo.

The hatred that I once knew (and had thought to have left behind me) in the 1980's when I first lived openly as a transsexual showed that it was alive and well and that American ugliness and its simmering brutality were ready to burst forth like a flood if the laws would only allow. The sexual panic of the American male appeared to be boundless when confronted with anything that would appear to challenge his presumed ability and right to have sex any time he wishes with absolute assurance that even if drunk he would not have to look twice as a precautionary measure to be sure that his target had two X-chromosomes. The same contempt that allows men to see women as bitches motivates hatred towards male-to-female transsexuals as well. To say that it is an unreasoned and instinctual response is to belie the fact that it is rooted in a sense of male entitlement that when politicized and militarized explains much of our current American foreign policy. Any reasoned response that appears to challenge our fragile collective identity as "God-fearing Americans" elicits the predicted response: "Kill them all."

Even cis-women occasionally contribute to this malice, on occasion by implying that womanhood is a pay-as-you-go status that demands menstruation for authenticity. "You can't be a woman until you have suffered enough." Sex differences finally emerge as a power-struggle through delineation of gender limits, a sort of border dispute transferred from the deserts of Arizona to the genital region. "No sexual illegals wanted!" posted on bathroom doors. All of which is to show that our discontents are still alive and well and that my journey might just as well have occurred when it did as in these "more permissive times." Obscurity had its advantages. Blessed was the subterranean existence of those who stood alone in lipstick and heels without the current media acclaim that may vanish with yesterday's fashions. We at least had our edginess and our outlaw status to raise a protective coat of spines along our backs when we were confronted. We were the porcupine-girls with quick tongues, defiance, and boundless contempt for anyone denying our status as out-and-proud. We accepted exile as the price for existing at all and learned to adapt to our loneliness. It gave us a language and a street vernacular appropriate for facing abuse head-on. It is a useful skill and one that has not been entirely superseded by our apparent political and social gains. I say apparent because without that built-in guard to danger that early transsexuals like me still possess as a sort of post-traumatic legacy, people can assume that they are at fault when abuse emerges out of a clear sky and like a thunderbolt lands on their heads.

I am as outraged now as I was then when I read in the comments beneath articles on the web that people like me deserve to die. Just imagine an equal degree of hatred dished out to someone whose actions are equally personal and private and essential to their identity and sense of self. Must the sky fall if the uniform of our sexuality leaves a brass-button without polish or if we forget to salute a fellow "penis-bearer" with a properly disinterested, "Hey Dude what's happening?" Is maleness really so precariously balanced on its fragile platform of antiquated "privilege to penetrate" that transsexuals are such a threat that they must be feared and loathed? How many of us have to die before an entire society asks these questions and makes room for everyone at the table of life?

This abuse would be bad enough to tolerate if it was not reinforced by the recent rhetoric surrounding religious freedom. Most of the calls for religious freedom come from various Christian denominations that presume that religious freedom entails an unqualified right to refuse service to anyone who does not mirror their own religious convictions. Building upon the notion that there exists some sort of seamless web between Christianity and America because a few groups of dissenters from the established Church of England, self-styled Puritans, were found sufficiently obnoxious in England that they were forced to seek refuge on a new continent where they promptly began slaying the Pequod Indians. These modern inquisitors feel entitled to ignore the laws of our secular republic with impunity. They presume that they are somehow advancing the cause of evil by providing normal services in their various businesses for people with whom they disagree.

Carried to extremes a gasoline station operator could refuse to sell gasoline to someone on the way to some clandestine rendezvous under the presumption that to help someone travel is to materially assist evil. Bakers of wedding cakes feel equally entitled to refuse service to lesbian couples, a problem that could be alleviated by a sign with a disclaimer that says that every cake is gender neutral and any modifications done after it leaves the bakery are the entire responsibility of the purchasers and that no guarantee for a particular use accompanies said cake. If gay or lesbian couples sought to elude this boycott of the bakers by opening their own baking cooperative then various suppliers of flour and eggs could refuse to sell to them because some of the resulting batter might be made into cakes which would be used at weddings of same-sex couples. By building a wall of similar non-service to GLBT people in all walks of life the hope is that their lives would be constrained and made sufficiently intolerable that they would repent or at least functionally disappear.

Taking their tutelage from the Nuremberg Laws that were used so effectively against the Jewish people in the 1930's, various movements are afoot to enshrine their prejudices in legal terms. By taking untenable legal positions and then meeting the consequences of that choice various persons are becoming the poster faces for this absurd movement. It is not uncommon for the persecutor to claim to be the victim and before long every such group will boast its own Horst Wessel Anthem.

As usual the candidates from the fanatical wings of the Republican Party appear at various functions that defend the death penalty for those whom they term sodomites. American aggression against the Islamic heretics is demanded and brutal parenting practices such as "conversion therapy" are defended. When a social order desires to advance a sensible pluralism and by this means to ensure domestic tranquility these very groups demand a right to break the law because they construe religious freedom as entailing more than the rights to believe and worship as they choose. They demand as well the right to use religious freedom not as a shield of privacy but as a sword to advance some particular crusade, in this case against those who refuse to enforce Levite justice. Woe to those who eat pork chops or who do not wash their hands to the elbow before they eat!

Assuming as they do that the long awaited "Rapture" is about to occur and licking their lips at the prospect of Armageddon they show remarkably little compassion as they whittle away at the budgets for domestic programs of health and education. They love guns and weapons of mass destruction though as long as they can pick their targets. No demands for increased military spending are tabled because of our national debt but school lunches for ghetto children are another thing - no money for schools but plenty for guns and prisons. The viciousness and brutality of the hand of God, as they mistakenly conceive it to operate, is everywhere apparent in their teachings and policies. As the rest of the civilized world stands appalled before America's neo-Calvinists, GLBT people are serving as a test-case for just how far a combination of American arrogance and imperial corporate aggression will be allowed to proceed at home and on the world stage. The one thing that Putin's Russia and America shared prior to the Obama Presidency was the persecution of GLBT people. As the dread year of 2016 approaches and the primaries decide which conservative candidate will slither his way onto the ballot the question must arise, "How safe are we from those who believe that even God demands our extinction?"

Executioners

Most transsexuals eventually will find their way to support groups to confirm what has heretofore seemed to be a unique and anomalous experience of gender exile. I can still recall the early support group meetings that took place on Pike and Broadway in Seattle. The rain would be beating along the pavement and the traffic lights would make rainbow patterns along the wet streets.

I would climb the stairs and meet others like myself. Where else could I go? Imagine having a support group meeting to simply exist where the only bond is not of shared interests or of social class but of simply claiming your gender. That's like having a support group for people with noses. What can be more basic than gender and its expression? Who should care if someone is wearing a skirt and heels? Unless that person is disqualified for some reason: too big, too old, too anything - oh, too male! Then panic sets in for some people and they go out hunting and another transgender person dies and joins the ranks of her dead sisters/brothers/human beings. Dead because someone thinks that they have no right to cross gender barriers because if they do the sky will fall and the pillars of the universe will be shaken. MALE AND FEMALE CREATED HE THEM!

BAM, just like that!

The result of such rigid gender strictures is women in burquas in Afghanistan who are denied an education and another dead transsexual on the streets of New York City. Some zealot in Arizona will be reduced to hysteria and pace back and forth like a tiger proclaiming, "No homos here!" Various bathroom brigades will erect gender "Berlin Walls" to keep the transsexuals out. Presidential candidates will posture and preen as saviors of America by implying that two lesbian ladies who have lived together for twenty years pose a threat to the baking industry if they tell the world who they are and how they have chosen to live their love and their lives. To recognize what they proclaim does not invalidate heterosexuals who proclaim a more exclusive definition based upon religious revelation and tradition. If it is so firmly established in practice and proclivity then the exceptions will not displace or engulf the more usual practice of heterosexual marriage as conservatives seem to fear. Same-sex marriage may however awaken heterosexuals to the desuetude of the institution of marriage in general in the face of the frequency of divorce and the damage that divorce does to children. It will be interesting to see if gay and lesbian unions prove to be more enduring.

For every bloody minded executioner there are hundreds of people whose attitudes to transgender people promise the executioners immunity from public outrage and encourage their acts. There is little real difference between calling an integral aspect of a person's life "intrinsically disordered" and calling them a faggot. During World War Two many Danish people chose to wear the yellow Star of David insignia to show the Nazi invaders that people are people. Something like that response should arise whenever hatred is manifested as it is towards transgender people.

A show of solidarity could end violence against trans-people and let those who claim a religious freedom to deny ordinary resources to others know that bigotry and discrimination are always wrong when applied because of a status or trait that is essentially personal and harmless to others. Who we are is our own business. It will take effort to eradicate the vicious training that so often accompanies a Christian upbringing in America. It may even take a few trials for violations under the U.S. Patriot Act as terrorists for those who advocate killing LGBTQ people to make it clear that Christian terrorism and Islamic terrorism have common roots in ignorance and intolerance. The abandonment of LGBTQ youth by their families needs to be condemned rather than subtly endorsed by the various non-profits that claim to care for the family unit while in reality preserving the very units that are so often guilty of child-abuse and mental cruelty to lesbian, gay, and transgender children.

To unmask the forces that produce the end result of so many dead GLBT people is the first and essential step to saving these innocent lives. A short review of the websites that post the details of their deaths on the Transgender Day of Remembrance will reveal the extent of the malice towards us that every transgender person can confirm from her/his own experience. This must be seen as it is and reforms must be made in the laws to ensure our safety from both threats and the defamation that precedes them. Until then the chant of shame, shame, shame should echo throughout the land.

The history of Europe is largely the story of various religious enclaves in conflict. Ethnicity and religion often go together and the memory of past atrocities does the rest to keep this trend alive. When they came to America our ancestors hoped to break this vicious cycle. The makers of the Constitution knew that to extirpate religion was impossible not only practically but as a violation of human liberty. Instead, a carefully mapped zone of neutrality was established. The government would not choose among religions through the establishment clause nor prevent its normal exercises of worship, catechetic instruction, and missionary efforts. Certain communities like the Amish might even choose a degree of isolation from the mainstream of society with impunity. What was not allowed however was to use religious belief to presume to structure the entire society according to its normative ideas and interpretations. This practice would divide the union and we are in prospect of doing precisely that at the present hour. The present religious freedom bills are focused on one particular area, that of sexuality. It is of interest to me that no similar bills arose to prevent recent trends in American policies such as torturing prisoners of war, targeted killings of American citizens, and capital punishment.

The complexity of our society cannot accommodate all manifestations of private conscience and continue to function. We do not get to choose the nature of the imperfect world that we inhabit. We may seek to advance morality through criticism of certain features of contemporary life but we may not selectively tailor the republic to embody our own convictions at other's expense. Religion by its very nature is oriented to an unseen world of transcendent concepts: sin and atonement, the influence of grace upon our souls, and a future state of existence. These are not within the ambit of the government or the laws to advance or to retard. A policy of careful neutrality will best preserve for religion its prerogatives without plunging our society into dissolution and chaos as various groups vie with each other for supremacy. Tennessee has just confirmed its rebel legacy by passing a religious freedom bill. The following months will provide a certain Litmus Test for an understanding of basic civics and the law in the provinces. The more conservative members of society at least share this with Putin and Russia, the importance of stopping the trend of recognition of GLBT rights. No one is denying religious groups the right to believe, to teach, and to persuade others of the correctness and righteousness of their views. Our country accepted from the beginning the power of principle and debate over exclusion and force to protect the rights of all of the people by protecting even those who might disagree with the majority and to act in a contrary manner if their acts do not injure others directly. The current zealots must bear the burden of proof to advocate a different approach.

The Day of the Malibu Barbies

Since 1952 Americans have known about transsexuals. Ever since George Jorgensen returned from Denmark as Christine and said with dignity, "It is nice of you for coming but it's really too much." Ever since then we have waited to go mainstream and it looks like in the past two years we have finally done so. The Berlin walls that have surrounded us are coming down one by one. School districts have stopped turning a blind eye to the silent terrorism of the bullying of LGBT youth and other likely victims of the High School practices of forcible gendering so that non-conforming youth can fit comfortably into our own culture of sexual samurai warfare between the so-called hot-girls and the studs.

Still there are signs present of a backlash as well. In a recent speech a Republican Presidential candidate suggested that an enlightened bathroom policy would invite adolescent males to opt for being transgender simply to attain a peak at the girl's facilities. Besides being completely ignorant of the life-long struggle of transsexuals (which in a Presidential candidate is bad enough) this shows the quiet predatory assumption that goes with our sense of what being male is in this society. It is the same mindset that refers to women in boot-camp derogatively as "Little Suzie's." This so-called normality of American gender politics that soothes male insecurities by adopting an assumption that males are all rape-prone is as degrading for males as is the assumption that no woman could successfully resist any attempt. As long as sexuality is used to preserve power structures in America it will be hard to accept that gender transition is really possible. Instead it will be presumed that being transsexual must of its nature include a life-long sentence to misery, alienation, social rejection, and economic marginalization. Fortunately the days when people from red states could oppose civil rights and cloak prejudice in religion or in presumptions that their own narrow life-experience is in fact universal are coming to a swift end. The America that they represent is the world of lynching, the KKK, the opposition to unions, child-labor, the Wounded Knee massacre, skin-heads, neo-Nazis, and the other unsavory elements of our gradual progression out of savagery.

It is hard not to feel a subtle envy for those trans-persons who will not come from the era of the trannie-goddesses who with the drag queens took it to the streets before mainstream acceptance was any sort of possibility. But the battle is not over. It may take a few celebrity trans-folk to get us into the mainstream of visually conscious and beauty obsessed fashion icons. This status will never be the norm for us but that it is possible at all should dispose once and for all with the image of transsexuals as "men in dresses."

My hope though is that when the glitterati and the paparazzi parade passes by that the everyday transwomen and transmen who live all over America will find a little more understanding and support to live our simple, decent, and dignified lives without the brutal experiences that are recounted in this book and without the facile religious condemnation that digs in the ruins of the Dead Sea for the infamous Cities of the Plain in order to characterize us. We have an extensive list of those who manifest the spirit of the Sanhedrin of today while engaged in name-calling, using phrases like, "Worse than Pagans" or "a tragedy for humanity." But we represent a significant group of the population in all nations and cultures and whether attacked by the new African nationalism or the old American tent-preachers we will always be here, there, and everywhere because we are human and deserving of love, respect, and a chance to live our lives without harassment, threats, and psychological violence. History will judge whose sin was the greater, if sin is even the appropriate category to apply to simply being – those who looked to ideas divorced from experience or those who realized that experience carries with it its own truth.

It is time to listen at last to our witnesses whether they are driving an old Plymouth or a new Mercedes or BMW. But I hope that the fortunate ones of us will not forget those of us who take their lives in their hands as they wait at bus stops to do a midnight-shift at a convenience store. May those who can afford all that medical science can provide to erase what testosterone has wrought so that they can pass in their preferred gender not forget the many transsexuals who don't pass, but must still go out daringly each day to face the world alone!

I hope that the young will not forget those of us who could only face the rigors of transition when their children were raised and that the older ones will not forget that the only gift that many transwomen will experience from their youth is to be the bait for those who want them for sexual services.

If anything can divide our community it may be by putting us in different social classes. America has always thrived on classism. If there is a true and lasting legacy of Stonewall I hope that it will include equality and solidarity among us, at least insofar as our common identity and validity as transsexual is concerned. These are characteristics that mainstream society still lacks. I would hope also that we would not be tempted to quantify our bodies as in – she has the best damn body that she can afford – state of the art, right off the assembly line.

As our daily lives become more media saturated, more artificial, more translated through a few spokespeople, and more handed to us all wrapped up and defined rather than emerging as our authentic search for an identity that is neither fixated nor so fluid as to respond to every fad, each transsexual will need to resist our friends as well as our foes simply in order to retain our freedom to be. Not everyone will opt for synthesized beauty simply because we expect women to manifest eye allure. Not everyone will have bottom surgery simply to pass bathroom checks.

Did we struggle for so long simply so a few of us can climb the last few yards to victory and claim it as their personal possession with residuals and endorsements? Does making every stereotype ever held about us a highway to success advance our cause? Since when did the trivial become a virtue?

Great Expectations

The class system of America is all the crueler because it is enacted against a democratic background that is presumed to deplore invidious distinctions and to provide economic opportunity for all. The statistics show that male-to-female transsexuals fall into several very disheartening categories that when combined serve to confirm that the discontents described in this book are still operative. Unfortunately the increased transgender visibility of 2014-2016 is as likely to fan the flames of hatred as it is to breed general understanding for our plight. From now on it will be harder to present ourselves as people with a rare but private anomaly; now each of us will have to carry the burden of the fear that we are the spearhead of the general meltdown of gender distinctions and that we are massing out there somewhere for an assault on the nation's sex-segregated bathrooms - today a bathroom in Houston; tomorrow the world!

As resistance mounts at our perceived strength and numbers we are almost reaching the point where we are a campaign issue, daintily tripping along with ISIS and affordable healthcare as threats to the nation's security. An article posted in today's news said that M to F transsexuals are fifty times as likely as a member of the general population to acquire infection with HIV. This is largely due to the discrimination our community faces in jobs and housing and the fact that many younger transsexuals seek out a livelihood through undertaking sex-work to survive. As long as sexual attractiveness provides the most reliable indicia of authenticity as a woman transsexuals will be pushed towards seeking internal confirmation and outer acceptance by using their new-found sexuality and seeking out various forms of male patronage to get what they want and need. The numbers of tran-swomen murder victims is also up in a year that might have gone down as the one where we finally arrived at the point where we might be treated with some degree of dignity and respect.

What this means is that the temptation to retreat into obscurity or a stealth existence has never been greater. There is a law of diminishing returns as one grows older. Openness and authenticity mean more when they can yield rewards. The long journey of transition entails so many hidden costs that can rear up to entrap and isolate us from our full measure of life that even the most proud and politicized of us may become weary of a struggle that must be taken up each day just to receive the basic recognition and affirmation necessary to the ordinary usages of life. We are in many ways still treated as aliens, stripped of all former categories and identities once we cross the gender barrier. Pursued by the Republican version of the Taliban we transsexuals often live in fear, hounded by mistrust and undeserved obloquy.

This is why I caution those whose innocence may not be proof against the insults, the neglect, and the condemnation of others that they may have to face that they retain as much as they can of their old life even as they transition. Sometimes strategic retreat is necessary. The legacy of Stonewall was one of youthful defiance when the entire nation was questioning many of its old assumptions. Today our multicultural world seems one of liberalism and generosity but I suggest that as economic competition increases it will be economics that will dictate outcomes. Our current position is new and highly tenuous. If the economy should plunge again into recession or worse there will be a search for scapegoats and we are tailor-made for the role. Our expectations are as likely to be reversed as they are to be confirmed as the election year of 2016 nears.

Regardless of the outcome of the election we still have a long way to go to achieve medical parity for the health issues that are particular to us. There is little consistency in how various social agencies perceive us. Until our civil rights are universally recognized and consistent many of us will continue to have to seek individual solutions and to fight lonely battles simply to go about our all too ordinary lives. Our allies are growing but many people are still willing to sacrifice us to preserve the monolith of sex differentiation. Nothing is as brutal and implacable as long held convictions when they are in the course of being revealed as premature or fallacious. Care is warranted when dealing with hysteria and religious pride. The spirit of the inquisition is still with us – alive and thriving in America. Will the people who so easily turn away from the appeals of the deserving poor by seeking to reverse the recent gains in health care grant us sanctuary when we seek to adapt our bodies to the inner imperative of our natures?

As long as we are perceived to be following a self-indulgent whim in seeking to be sexually-reassigned and to follow our inner conviction of gender membership it will be easy to assign us to the status of being mere artifacts and not real people at all. Recognition and validation are more than simply a matter of consent to share what is termed a delusion. Transsexual identities are not merely assumed at will as many people suppose. Even the term transition is perhaps a misnomer for what is really involved in changing sex - it is not a matter of making a sudden discovery or taking a radically new course. Transsexual people usually report a very early onset of their cross-gender feelings and aspirations followed by many years of repression, depression, and alienation as they make every effort to accommodate themselves to living in a sex/gender role that is opposite to the one that they feel best prepared to assume, if they are allowed to do so without courting rejection, ridicule, and violence. Transition must be seen then as a sort of reparative therapy to learn what was not learned because forbidden while ceasing to carry about the burden of an assumed identity, one that has been adopted simply to comply with the presumptions of a strictly binary and mutually exclusive concept of gender and sex roles.

This is not an easy process. One does not traverse years of developmental gaps overnight and without mourning, regrets, and much soul-searching. But to add to the anguish and difficulty of this probing of the self at a level that is so deep and fundamental by trivializing the process or treating with contempt those who feel driven to enter upon this process is an example of the worst sort of human callousness and lack of empathy. I am astonished at the comments that appear on the internet beneath virtually any item dealing with the topic of transgender issues and appalled by those who preen themselves as good Christians or as being somehow more virtuous because they are not transgender themselves. That such fundamental ignorance masquerades as knowledge about the challenges facing transsexuals by implying that a mental illness explains it all is presumptuous and inaccurate.

The truth is that the stresses of inner conflict and outer cruelty have left their marks upon transgender people. Transition should be conceived then as a remedial process and like most remedies these are bound to show a less perfect fit than would be the case if no injury had ever existed to be remedied. To reduce transsexual procedures to mere technological interventions and to set a standard of technical excellence achieved as the measure of a successful transition is therefore a great mistake. It merely serves to re-inflict past injuries to compare transsexuals along a scale of attractiveness or "readability." However pleased our community may be when we can boast that certain of our number are functionally undetectable to the casual gaze or meet our conventional standards for youth and beauty, this "success" should not determine the basic validation and respect granted to a person as a human right or influence our response to each transsexual due to her simply because she exists. That women are forced to carry about a battery of sexual significations that have nothing to do with their individuality is oppressive to trans-women and cis-gender women alike, even if not always equal in type or degree. This legacy of the harem and of screen sirens damages us all and reduces womanhood to simply one other item to be acquired and consumed as the following essay will explain.

Sex-change: Acquisition or Recognition?

The year of 2015 was one of mixed blessings for the transgender community. The problem was that suddenly average Americans were hit in the face with the concept that sex-change had become a commodity rather than a designation for what had formerly been seen as a mental illness. By assuming that one is transsexual simply by virtue of our declaration that we are rather than by being diagnosed with a mental illness by a "qualified professional" it suddenly seemed as though transsexualism was simply the fad of the moment and that we would soon be popping up everywhere like dandelions. If only deprivation of sex-change procedures and the resultant Gender Dysphoria appears in the DSM in the future, then the real problem becomes that gender re-construction technology is still a luxury item for most people. As the new state of the art was displayed on television and magazine covers and as schools began making allowances for transgender students nationwide all the old barriers seemed about to fall. This public offering hit the newsstands before we were ready with assurances to allay panic. The changes in the laws had heretofore been quiet and incremental and hence sensitive to our condition of pain, exile, and discrimination as well as our small actual numbers. The recent panic in Houston is the result of assuming that transsexuals are the new pink and that just everyone may soon jump on the bandwagon to claim their fifteen minutes of fame by transitioning. If before we spoke of gender transition as a quiet, private, and therapeutic action now the public viewed gender change as an acquisition rather than as therapy. Suddenly sex change was not the realization of a pre-existing cross-sexed identity but the bodily equivalent of buying and driving a Lamborghini.

To average street trannies this new image was as appalling as it was untrue. The new bar of non-readability was set so high that few of us can reach it. Until insurance rules make surgery more affordable and universal for transsexuals the newly evident class-gap will pose an even more impermeable barrier to those seeking public acceptance. Attractiveness is now expected of us all, even as we proudly display our superstars. Maybe this is how cis-women have always felt at the prospect of beauty pageants and center-folds. But in any case it hurts that what should have been our best year was one in which the murder rate of transsexuals doubled and even cosmopolitan Houston locked its bathroom doors against us and told us to get lost because gender, unlike class or citizenship, is assigned, permanent, and inalienable. From this ill-informed and biased point of view that had perhaps always been present like a latent infection pre-operative trans-persons are suddenly seen as the genital equivalent of smugglers and a penis is viewed as contraband in the sacred region of restrooms and other locales designated as "gender-exclusive spaces." The current restroom and locker-room hysteria that has caused Houston to rescind protections for GLBT persons is directed at the male organ as the offending member. This remarkable resurgence of phallic consciousness is analogous to the lingam figures that adorn various shrines in India. Must the penis be sheathed like a sword lest it run amuck, the latest in the invasions of our homeland security? The whole thing is just too ridiculous!

To be consistent jurisdictions that favor laws to foment such blatant discrimination should mark the doors with a big "yuck sign" and a T with a line through it to warn away trans-persons. The absurdity of asking female-to-male transsexuals to go trooping back into the ladies room with facial hair and lowered voices is of course never addressed. Instead these statutes are leveled at pre-operative male-to-female transsexuals as though every penis was some sort of improvised explosive device that might explode out from cover at any moment once the threshold of a restroom has been crossed. No advocates for these bathroom protection laws has pointed out that transsexuals usually make every effort to fit in and avoid excess scrutiny so this image of willful exhibitionism is a cruel calumny. We are the ones being beaten up and killed, so why should we be asked to go into the men's room in lipstick and heels because all other avenues have been foreclosed to us. Of course the real message to us is, "Just die and go away." Discrimination always carries the message of extinction. There is an inherent progress from exclusion to elimination and that is all too evident here. As a community we are making our final bid for universal recognition along with our gay and lesbian brothers and sisters. The closet door has closed behind us; there is no way left for us now but to go forward and demand recognition, everywhere.

New Packaging

In the year 2016 big changes are in the air for transsexuals. As the transsexual condition is repackaged from being considered as a mental illness or as an indicator of a mental illness where the desire to change sex is only a symptom of an underlying lack of identity adaptation to perceived the biological programming of assigned sex we in the transgender community will need to search for new analogies and metaphors in order to ally ourselves with concepts that are sympathetically viewed by the public.

314

In the past, prior to 1966 and Harry Benjamin, our condition did not even have a name. Instead we were viewed as having an unstable and unrealistic delusion that we belonged to the other sex. This suggested a diagnosis of what was then called border-line schizophrenia. We were unhappy with our condition in the genetically assigned sex so other theorists thought that we might have Manic Depressive Psychosis, what today is called Bipolar Disorder or Major Affective Disorder.

But those days are largely in the past. Now we are moving towards what our sheer numbers at about 1% of the population would indicate: that we are just another normal human variation along with race, ethnicity, body-type or shape, and blood type. The problem then becomes less one for the medical community but rather one of the search for legal recognition and protection from persecution by the laws or by private discrimination. The idea here is that if the desire to change sex or to embody our conviction that we already are members of the desired sex inside is morally neutral then the various physical interventions from hormones to surgery are justified to allay our emotional distress and there should be no social price exacted from us for transitioning. This trend leaves several questions unanswered however.

First is the question of just how far medicine should supplement what the body can provide from within itself out of its own resources. There is no question that we use countless drugs from aspirin to hormone supplements at menopause to alleviate and make more tolerable various human ailments or transitions. We use beta-blockers for heart arrhythmias, insulin for diabetes, and drugs to even treat the supposed illness of male erectile dysfunction. One person's concept of ailment or illness may vary from what another will accept as valid. The balance will usually be weighed in favor of making human lives easier to bear unless some other contraindication is present. Unhappiness and melancholia are no longer viewed as natural to the human condition to be born with simple fortitude and resignation if something that is not unduly harmful or arbitrary may address what is causing the complaint.

How is this parameter of justifiable intervention to be weighed when applied to transsexuals? Is transition worth the risks of hormone therapy (infertility, lessening of erectile capacity, or a possibility of blood-clots)? Is the surgical procedure of genital alteration the destruction of healthy tissue or a reconfiguring of it to provide a more functional totality for the person in light of their desired body-image and sexual orientation? What are the limits of human freedom and of the social acceptance of individual human choices?

Another question is whether social change should be guided and formalized by legal pressures until what was once considered to be an astronomically rare anomaly becomes part of accepted everyday culture and experience in schools, businesses, and in private life. The current "culture wars" have focused undue attention upon us as the supposed vanguard of anti-Christian decadence and degeneration, a term left over from the 1890's. By becoming the fulcrum for the unhinged anxieties of the present hour we are likely to be increasingly victimized on the streets by various zealots. This is precisely what many older transsexuals feared. We preferred to rely on a private medical legitimacy within established norms followed by the gradual one-on-one acceptance of our local communities. We did what most minorities initially do in order to survive: we don't unnecessarily antagonize those who still have power over us.

But events are moving too quickly now to be contained, so even those of us who might have hitherto counseled prudence and patience can not avoid the necessity to place our shoulders to the wheel and push. It's now or never. Fail now and we enter a new dark age, one all too familiar to those of us who came up in the pre-internet age. The blending of ideas and images across cultures means that we all are wearing international velvets and lace. Even Iran deals with its transsexuals by supplying surgery rather than stoning. You really know a Christian conservative when they can even outdo the Taliban in their maledictions towards us.

No insularity remains in our world; we are all going global and even bakeries cannot hope to stem the tide. For the first time the recognition of national civil rights seems not far away for us. It would be too ridiculous to let us marry only to be fired from our jobs and kicked out of our housing for being who we are. Legitimacy is finally achieved when private justice cannot claim sanction under claims of religious freedom as in, "I don't like you because I don't think God likes you; so no cake or cookies for you."

As our small community of individuals emerges from the weight of social anxiety and religious panic that has so often made our lives even more painful than they needed to be maybe the first real human to human dialog will finally take place on the essential questions of our common humanity and our search for self-acceptance, spiritual peace, and dignity.

Entitlements

Maybe the whole question of being transgender comes down to a question of entitlement. Those people who oppose gender transition are committed to the idea that it is usurpation for someone to adapt the bodily indicia or form that signifies the other sex. There is no mix and match option to sexuality from this point of view. Gender is held to be destiny. In law it is customary to grant various forms of property entitlements from a revocable license to various estates depending upon diverse human needs. By segmenting and isolating sex from a mere trait to an essential destiny it becomes customary and indeed essential to make the personality fit the form or template of each sex at all costs. To those who oppose our freedoms no command not to fold, staple, or mutilate matters where irrevocable destiny is in play and if it hurts us then that's just too bad.

When I hear people talk like this I always want to ask them where their compassion has been misplaced. But then I run up against the further assertion that compassion is misplaced when we are talking about sinning. Life is supposed to be hard. God's judgments are harsh and inscrutable. Spare the rod and spoil the child. Suddenly I realize that there is a reason why child abuse has been ignored for so long and why the very idea of self-determination is so threatening to the type of mind that stems from a distorted sense of religion. The streets of America are thronged with kids kicked out or forced out of their homes by self-righteous parents who would rather that their kids were killed or raped than to "condone such behavior in my house."

Even those without religion though can still be made uneasy by gender variability. I believe that this is because it opens up a range of relations and options that are decried not because they are inconceivable but because they are well within the range of behavior proper to our species. Heterosexuality is not normative by nature but is the product of severe enforcement of prohibitions as to what one may permissibly feel. Repression works best when it preempts even the suggestion of an alternative set of perceptions. The enforcement must come from within. By turning the mind against itself and using shame and its more specific manifestation as guilt it is possible to build the confines of what is held to be possible within the mind itself.

If anyone would know just how much effort it takes to retain the current system of gender role differentiation all that is necessary is to observe the violence and ridicule that attends the persons who dare to question gender norms. Every other imperative of civility is vanquished and suspended in the face of sexual or gender rebellion. No primitive tribe is more irrational and fearful of taboo actions than we are when we are confronted with transsexuals. The numbers of our dead prove this every year and few take note and draw the necessary conclusions. Until these barriers are broken down by individuals who will smudge the margins by taking on the task of making gender injustice manifest in all its forms it will seem permissible to ask that people be used as sacrifices to perpetuate the adamantine distinctions between the sexes that we enshrine and uphold by our violence and our scorn.

Gender oppression is real but more real still is the way that we leverage sexual differences to achieve various distortions in our common human nature. One does not need to be Jean-Jacques Rousseau to believe that children who are not overpowered by adult violence might reveal that human nature is less fallen than we believe it to be. If allowed to spontaneously develop our sense of ourselves we might all be far less "gendered" than we imagine. This "wait and see attitude" may show us just how wrong we have been to presume that we know all about human nature when all we really know is how people act when forced to use power and force to achieve predetermined ideological ends. What does the female genital mutilation practiced in Africa reveal for instance about male sexual anxiety in a post-colonial world? Is it surprising then that African Bishops will ally themselves with absurd sentences for homosexual conduct seen as some sort of cultural threat imported from Europe? The current LGBT movement is not waiting for clarity to emerge in the debate about human nature before declaring what we are and what types of intimate bonds we may form. Is this an example of sheer willfulness or simply the determination not to sacrifice our one unique life to the slow glacial creep of history? "They are not long the days of wine and roses," as the poet Ernest Dowson has told us. Time's winged chariot soon closes the doors to the opportunities that youth alone can embrace. To enter the age of memories and regrets is to realize all that was lost to us before it could even be defined.

There was no vocabulary for transgender experience in my youth. I only knew that I felt from the beginning some form of lonely sexual exile and that even to mention it was to enter upon forbidden ground. Even now I look at men and women differently, perplexed and yet insightful in a way that most non-transsexual people are not. I feel at times as though I have left gender behind me to inhabit a sort of generic and undifferentiated humanity, timeless and observing, as though I had passed into the literature that was my substitute for living. I find my thoughts in the process of writing them down. Not accustomed to speak my mind under the stimulus of the moment it requires the written word to tell me what to think in due season. Even then I am aware that I live in a world of definitions that even my legal training does not allow me to dispute because they are authoritative in a way that the truths of personality as I experience them are not. The power of general jurisdiction is not entrusted to us even over the form that our bodies shall take. No fee simple absolute is bestowed on us but only a life estate and even that is defeasible or subject to restrictive covenants with religion and society.

My fractured and chameleon nature has been evolved over the course of a long guerilla war waged against the usurping powers determined to reach inside and adjust me. Have I been wrong all along? Is anyone raised as male able to bear gracefully the burdens of the feminine world? All the charm and magic seem to vanish as the biology of womanhood becomes more familiar with acquaintance. Womanhood is encased in symbol and the décor that we assume simply goes with being a woman. What secrets dwell within that elaborate façade that society has created and celebrated in pageant and parade? Had my wishes been granted early might I have sought escape rather than to follow the inscrutable course of the feminine Nile to its source? Was it rather manhood that because portrayed as so functional and prosaic became prematurely diminished in my eyes? Is each sex a mystery to the other because it has not been de-mythologized? What wizard manipulates various levers behind the curtain that we are so fascinated and appalled in turn by each other? Only add love and jealousy to the mix and see where we are – Romeo lies dead of poison and a happy dagger rests beneath the breast of Juliette.

Entitlement or choice, freedom or destiny, we dance about each other in a cosmic masque while some few seek transmutation rather than bonding only to find that incompleteness still seeks another to be whole. Love mocks us with disillusion and all the while time hurtles us on into that realm of old- age where we become as strangers even to ourselves. Where has fled the glory and the dream? No naiad bathing in a stream but a beldame hoping that she will not be read by any gang of callous adolescents of either gender who may strip her bare with a glance and a word.

It is questions like these that explain why I am a Janis figure today able to see in two directions at once and as often deploring both those who condemn us without empathy and also to warn those who may be lured to their destruction as they seek the Happy Isles of gender-congruity that there are breakers ahead. This political profile is meant to show the costs of what should have been ground for experimentation and exploration in a less gender-weighted continuum of human experience. But that was not to be, at least not in my life. The result is these reflections which may have pleased no one because they are meant to be both impassioned and dispassionate in turns as becomes a goddess of stone whose words must always be taken as tentative, Sybil-like, and inconclusive. After all an oracle is meant to suggest rather than to confirm to truth of what she utters – her meaning is wrought more often than it is found by the devotee who comes to her seeking wisdom.

Danish Girls then and Now

Recently I sat in the local art movie theater to watch "The Danish Girl," the most recent entry in the list of movies dealing with transsexuals. The theater was built in the 1930's and reflected the same mood as this movie about Lili Elbe, the first recorded person to attempt conversion from male to female. Both of the major characters in the film are artists. Is it surprising then that the transsexual body is portrayed as merely another artistic creation? What begins as a mere experiment in acting as a surrogate female model soon grows into an obsession on the part of the husband to become a woman. The alternate persona of Lili appears to grow from a transient seed planted by accident and her possession of the formerly sexually aggressive husband is portrayed as something like a state of obsession that skirts the borders of Multiple Personality Disorder. As drama the movie succeeds but its message leaves a sense of ambiguity that can only serve to muddy the transgender waters at a time of particular political significance for our community.

I do not wish to be unfair. Perhaps no attempt however sensitive in its efforts to depict us can fail to injure us when so much ignorance about transsexualism abounds. The death of the main character is an example. By leaving so many unanswered questions this film (in most aspects quite sensitive) can arm the determined opposition to transgender recognition and rights that has surfaced again and is currently engaged in wrapping its constrictive coils about our recent progressive gains in order to strangle them. The film ends with a vampire pale Lili finally finding maternal acceptance in a dream, but was it worth it? Pity soon yields to regret – we must save these poor deluded creatures from themselves.

The sympathy of the audience to the plight of Lili is compromised at various points throughout the film. Newly liberated Lili starts to explore her long suppressed sexuality with men while her spouse begins to realize that the Lili artifact has caused her formerly devoted husband to become a weepy outcast pursued by various doctors who alternately want to commit her as insane or to operate on her and score a medical first, the transformation of man into woman. The ideological problem that I am having with the production is that the politicians and the general public will be confirmed in many of their convictions and misapprehensions with regard to people who experience profound gender discomfort – that the whole thing is a meretricious act of surgical hubris and people insane enough to ask for these ministrations.

The failure of the genital surgery and the subsequent death of Lili are not redeemed by being placed against a closing background of David Lean style panoramas of Danish sea and mountain, beauties that in any case poor dead Lili will never see again. The audience is left with the impression that it all just wasn't worth it. Her motivations for transformation appear to be hysterical and unbalanced and whatever sympathy she evokes is vitiated by the fact that her apparent "obsession" leads to the break-up of her marriage and finally to her death. This sort of thing does not advance transgender acceptance and comprehension by the general public. If anything it arms those who wish to use reparative therapy to save us from ourselves and to supposedly protect the sacred precincts of women's restrooms from invasion by various penis-wielding mental cases.

Anything that reinforces an image of insanity undermines our dignity and credibility as a community. A little foresight and imagination will swiftly resolve the matter of restrooms so that no one is embarrassed or needlessly exposed. Sexual predators will not gather like sharks, put a ribbon in their hair, add a little mascara, and claim to be transsexuals. Is it really a safer and less disruptive alternative to send people who really may be attacked into male restrooms in their dresses and heels? The message to the transgender community is to just die or disappear, precisely the message given to the early victims of AIDS. We have all been over this ground before. It is still considered permissible to ask routinely if a transgender person is a pre-op or a post-op with regard to her genitalia. This reinstates the focal definition of gender, males as penis bearers. Curb the rebellious organ and make the world safe for democracy! Already certain representatives from the agrarian hinterlands of Washington State are opposing the trend in schools and recreation to protect transgender youth from bullying, harassment, and suicide by finally being treated as members of the sex that they are trying to embody at great personal cost and risk.

Will we never cease being menaced by people who are unwilling to spend an afternoon on the internet to learn something about transsexual and inter-sex conditions? It is these nabobs who lament, "Where, oh where, did those glorious gender divisions of 1950's America go? Sure wish Ike was back! Remember to duck and cover!"

To an aging member of our community it is just too disgusting to watch various self-styled members of the political Sanhedrin as they conduct their little mini-inquisitions while transgender kids are still killing themselves. This feeling is more than just discontent, I am angry. Christine Jorgensen came home from Denmark in 1952, a new and successful Danish girl. We should all have adjusted by now to welcome her sisters and leave poor Lili Elbe to rest along with all the other early transsexuals and those who flocked to the institute run by Magnus Hirschfeld for relief before it was shut down by the Nazis as an example of the decadent trends of Weimar Germany that Hitler and his minions would stamp out in Dachau and Mauthausen. Will liberation never come when our community has paid such a price decade after decade? Will we ever get beyond medical definitions of who we are?

I hate to say it but our very success cases are trotted out to prove that we are artifacts after all and not people. When we are portrayed as viable candidates to be cover girls we are to that extent seen as rare and beautiful icons, bearers of various sexual indicia, well-wrought figures on a Grecian urn locked into a timeless world of the eternal pursuit of an authenticity that only a well-wielded scalpel can grant to us. Even then someone can look behind the curtain of what they claim is our presumptuous claim and tell us, "You will never be a real woman." Fortunately it is not for them to say.

Doing the Time Warp

As the terminology of cross-gender identification has changed and moved from being a medical category of human experience to one that is far more political the experts have stepped aside and deferred to self-identification which has to some extent taken their place. Just as the internet has opened new realms of choice and self-direction the new gender politics is opening new options for the treatment of gender issues. Genital reassignment is no longer the gold standard for recognition in the new gender role. Indeed, the human body is assuming a new plasticity in which definitions and mandates are seen as increasingly irrelevant except as options. Less can be presumed each day about us and the letters behind LGBT increase with every year. As networks expand and our presence in cyberspace increases our existence is becoming more a body of data as opposed to one of flesh and blood. The human mind may someday become a mere puppet-master to manipulate various idealized images of our projected selves as embodied in various holograms. If that is to be the future then the old days of unmediated flesh may seem to be unimaginably primitive and sex-change surgery will be as antiquated then as cave paintings are now.

As our animal nature is extended through various tools and the information media provides data and new modes of relating and of gathering information our individuality is being extended. Identities may give way to various gaming postures and strategies and our devices will become like new sensory modes all feeding into a new central processing unit: THE SELF (selected, elevated, liberated, frontier) EXPERIENCE. Perhaps the current fascination with zombies is our collective intuition that the body is becoming a phantasm when set against the far more real world of permanently encoded data in computers with their promise of immortality and endless growth. Perhaps the experience of the whole human race will someday be reduced to an algorithm and be beamed out into deep space from the last remnants of a dying planet, "If anyone is receiving this … data stream to follow."

I say all of this because certain signs are everywhere that what is fanciful is becoming just one more menu choice in a world of apps. The motto of the day seems to be this: as to what is optional nothing is written with finality. Whole libraries can now be contained on gigabyte devices. Books are mere streams of data that can fit in a purse or pocket and are as perishable as a command from a delete key. We are more disposable than our devices. Only a succession of pulses keeps the body alive with its coughing, sneezes, tears, and laughter. Meanwhile at our sides are various terminals and security systems that guard our essential data: our I.D., net worth, social presence, and domicile in cyberspace. As time goes on it will be increasingly difficult to define what is irreducible and given in our natures as human beings. Maybe we should make the effort to communicate with our fellow primates before they all die off. They may remind us of our animal nature.

Human to gorilla: What do you think about all day while munching your vegetarian-diet in the jungle?

Gorilla to human: We think, "What's the matter with you guys?"

Human to Orangutan: And what do you think about all day?

Orangutan to human: We don't think much, but we do worry a lot. Just look at our faces.

What all this means is that this book may sooner rather than later be just one more artifact in a changing world, but by then I will be gone and be just one more grinning skull asking the same eternal question as all of the dead of the past ages, "What's next?" So it is that I read the writings of Sir Thomas Browne and meditate often on death. I seek that same summary certitude that he possessed one of grim acceptance yet one still charged with hope. Though it will not be long until I join the others in the long defile of time and like them have my light in ashes it will still matter that I once had a voice and a mind that questioned many things in the course of my leasehold on human existence.

Gender Ecology

On December 21, 2012 Pope Benedict XVI Included in his Christmas address to the Vatican Curia some comments in relation to gender change and choice. These comments sought to draw a parallel between concern for the natural world as expressed by ecologists and a concern for the natural order of human creation and in particular for gender and sex roles within a familial and social context. The Pope was in essence saying that sex roles are assigned by nature and that marriage, the integrity of the family unit as the basis of all social stability, and the proper raising of children demands that sex and gender be viewed as assigned by God. There is a human ecology just as there is an environmental ecology and that to imply that these are amenable to the human will or changeable is a dangerous interference with the wisdom of God as manifested in the created order. The Pope went on to imply that children have an essential human right to be raised in a nuclear family manifesting gender difference by having a mother and a father and that these roles may not be assumed by single-sex partners in contrast to the clear diversity of a male father and a female mother present in heterosexual families.

As dismaying to the GLBT community as these comments were, the headlines were somewhat excessive in their criticism of the Pope. This was no bigoted statement but one that the Pope assumed that no one could responsibly oppose since it squares with the general experience of most of humanity. The problem was his assumption of an order that nature does not invariably follow. The assumption of a clear and distinct sexual order is precisely that, an assumption based on a generalization drawn from the experience of the majority. As such the comments simply beg the very question at issue and in doing so assume that GLBT people oppose a univocal order found present in all human beings. A short discourse on the variety of intersex conditions disposes in short order of the chromosomal argument and once the existence of intersex conditions is admitted the orders of male and female are simply no longer distinct and mutually exclusive categories. These exceptions in nature further open up the question whether our innate sense of ourselves is constrained by phenotypical gender. What is done to address the situation of those on the sex or gender periphery need not affect those whose experiences are more typical. It is similarly not necessary to constrain and conform GLBT people to a heterosexual norm for fear that these exceptional cases will somehow invalidate or violate the usual order if that natural order is not invariable in nature itself.

The charism of his office does not extend to everything that the Pope may say with an implication of equal authority. Popes are not guaranteed socio-political, philosophical, or scientific infallibility by virtue of their holy office. This is particularly so on the peripheral application of general principles. The problem seems to lie in an equation of transsexualism, homosexuality, and marriage on a single plane seen as threats to the sacramental order and the integrity of human nature as such. The effort of the pope to assume that a single monolithic unity unites all of these complex issues considered individually and as a whole as contrary to the will of God fails to address what is at stake in each. Once it is assumed that all of these manifest a willful and united opposition to God and nature then no deeper discussion of the questions needs to be considered. Instead it is assumed that ready condemnation may be obtained simply by appealing to those people who do not (as GLBT people do) feel these issues to be personal, insistent, and essential to their identity and human affections. To interiorize these comments without further reflection as to their merit would be as damaging as to use them to hammer members of the GLBT community as humanly non-ecological and a threat to the divine order.

Pope Benedict was on stronger ground by pointing out that these are not trivial issues and that one's sense of oneself as male or female is not simply one option among many. To assume that there is such a thing as mere undifferentiated human flesh and that we may mold our identities and our fundamental attractions at will would be conceded by most reasonable people to be a reckless assertion. Rather, GLBT people identify as such because that identification is perceived as stating something essential and unchangeable about their inner sense of themselves and their humanity.

Upon reflection then there is an underlying agreement between the Pope and those who were appalled or dismayed at his statements in his Christmas address. The comments were not a gratuitous and off the cuff insult to a beleaguered people but a guarantee that the issues at stake are worthy of a higher level of scrutiny than either a bigoted religiosity or a facile acceptance affords them. Nothing could be more disrespectful to transsexuals than to say that the massive efforts that transsexuals make to attain inner congruity is the equivalent of a mere hobby or affectation. Much is at stake here and at least the Pope realizes this. It may have been a timely reminder then that complete gender fluidity is in contrast to human experience. For the rest, a more probing look may disclose where Pope Benedict may have begged the questions at issue so that others may value his intentions yet disagree with his assessments and on a respectful basis. Not everyone who seeks gender reassignment is free of impulsiveness or temerity in doing so. But there are cases that lie within the gamut of intersex or transsexual conditions that appear to admit of no other remedy than surgical intervention in order to help these persons achieve the fullness of their individuality and humanity. The need for careful inquiry and much consideration of the irrevocable consequences should govern all requests for gender change. Values are often worth considering rather than rushing into a polarized and oppositional posture whenever criticism is encountered.

Secular vs. Sacred

Part of the legacy of science in the last hundred years has been to call into question the way that we envisage nature. From a belief in substances science has come to perceive fields of interaction as the primary basis of physical reality. We know things by their effects in processes of interaction. There is even a belief in what is called anti-matter which, should it come into contact with matter as we know it would annihilate both in an explosion of pure energy. Then there is this whole question of elementary particles/waves/strings that make up the universe of matter as we know it. Matter and energy appear to be two separate aspects of a common underlying reality. Various high-speed and even mass-less particles such as neutrinos speed about and go through solid substances as though they were only clouds. But none of these radical revisions have changed the way that we view the natural laws of human affectivity. Males and females are considered to be discrete entities and not a spectrum of genders. Such is the concept of complementarity that governs the natural law basis for the Church's teaching on the inherent and intrinsic disorder of same-sex sexual relations. Combined with this is the belief that sexuality has a final end in procreation and perhaps would not exist if it was not ordained to precisely this end. To sever pleasure from cellular exchange is looked upon as impermissibly hedonistic and due to its innate sterility a blasphemous misuse of a function that cannot be subsumed into other channels. The redundancy of the human sexual drive is reduced to a disorder between the senses and the will called concupiscence. It is assumed that the imbalance between desire and restraint should always be decided, as nature is held to demand, towards a conservation of response, which is termed the virtue of chastity, not consented to as a voluntary and salutary sacrifice but as a permanent and obligatory disposition which if not attained is sinful.

For this reason it is irrelevant how many people may be attracted to same-sex partners or may secure some degree of tension reduction by aut0-erotic acts. The human sexual instinct according to official teaching simply must be contained, restrained, and channeled towards the meeting of a vagina and a penis so that at male climax (which alone is necessary for procreation) no artificial barrier will prevent the cellular meeting of egg and sperm. Even if an egg is not present, the sperm may be at least take comfort in swimming about in a familiar sea. No exceptions are allowed to this inevitable biological result. The sheer superabundance of human fertility and expression are again irrelevant because sexuality itself is seen as disordered. The word for this disorder is as mentioned above, concupiscence. The default position of human sexuality is thus sin. Marriage is not the rule but the exception. It elevates and in fact licenses (and exclusively at that) the measured expression of what otherwise must be contained. The emission of sperm under the wrong conditions is seen as the moral equivalent of shaking a flask of nitroglycerin. Moralists have been less concerned with whatever the oscillating excitation might be that females may sexually experience, perhaps because in past ages female responsiveness was generally ignored. Reduced to a mere culture medium for the life provided by the male her moral stature was of less import. From this perspective the female orgasm must appear as one of nature's strange excesses like the pit in an avocado or the luxuriance of an orchid.

Now add to this natural law conception of human sexuality the maledictions of the priestly caste of Judea as recorded in Leviticus and Deuteronomy and it is easily understandable why Catholic prelates are unwilling to take an alternate few to that of summary condemnation of same-sex relations even within a committed relationship. They explain that this sort of thing is intrinsically disordered and can in no event be approved. It will not do to prevaricate or to look behind the cultural usages of Judea immersed in a welter or contending tribes and peoples in ancient Canaan. The strictures of the Old Testament in this regard are presumed to be for always and to be universally binding. To doubt this is to be in error and in need of correction by a re-affirmation of the same thing said over and over again with various degrees to umbrage and distaste that the issue has even been raised. It will not do to speak of marriage equality because there can be no question of even qualifying for marriage absent the required divergence of the sexes. This means that any advocacy of equality and talk of the civil-rights of same-sex "couples" is functionally meaningless in a rational moral universe as it is conceived by traditional Catholic teaching. Only by stating the case this plainly can we understand the scope of the abyss that opens up when "alternative sexual discourses" begin to question Catholic teaching.

The severity applied to sexual questions is unparalleled. "No parvity of matter" was the phrase used in moral theology to express the idea that violations of the Sixth Commandment always involve "objectively serious matter." Violations in this area thus always raise the possibility of mortal sin and eternal punishment in hell. This was the specter that haunted my own adolescence and has not left me to this day. This is the background against which the Irish people have always evaluated their own experience of sexuality. This may explain why the clergy abuse scandal has left such a feeling of bitterness in so many people who had come in practice to look to the celibate clergy to manifest personally a uniform chastity, the same standard that was demanded from the laity. From the shock of clergy abuse and the complicity of the Bishops in keeping these matters secret many have yet to recover. The recent vote for same-sex marriage in Ireland may be understood in the context of this breakdown in the trust that the laity traditionally maintained towards the clergy. The abuse scandal is not determinative of the electoral outcome but it may at least have been a contributory cause.

It may seem strange to the modern liberal mind that what may look like an organization that people embrace voluntarily could ever exercise this kind of control over its members. The terror purveyed by the Church though has always been quite real. Nothing is more terrifying than a threat that cannot be verified or refuted. The severity and certainty that has always characterized the tone of the Church in discussing sex has made its threats credible. Since hell is an either/or it is also not remediable based on later insights or regrets. How was I not to take this diagnosis of the human condition as dispositive? There simply was no escape from the Church.

I had no more confidence in the secular world as a member of the post-war generation. I was raised in a world that told children what was expected of them; to appeal a decision was pointless when all of the jurisdictions that I encountered shared a common point of view. Even today it will not do to speak of a separation of Church and state. Secularism is as incomprehensible to Christianity as it is to Islam. The crowned heads of Europe were supposed to be servants of God and subject to the authority of the Chair of Peter. This explains the mistrust of democracy in the Papal documents of the 19th century. Democracy merely means the right to choose your abuser.

Nor did science provide a sanctuary for me; human nature is not to be consulted in matters of morality because it is the business of religion to alter human nature and to prepare us for the life that might have been our destiny without Original Sin. The moral perfectibility of humankind does not look to our desires to embody norms but rather to the demands of the moral law. Life is a struggle to embody these values as best we can. The goal for the Catholic is final perseverance in this quest as opposed to the facile certainty of the heretical Protestants that they are "saved." If this seems brutal it is no more so than the brutal nature of life and death; these refuse to bow to our desire that there be an easier way to account for our fallen world and to manage to find purpose and salvation.

In contrast to the prevailing ambiance of my youth there is the present secular view that now predominates even in many Catholic countries. Words like sacrifice, atonement, and penance have been divorced today from the very real content that they once had with the result that a vote for same-sex marriage may appear to many voters to raise no real moral issue at all but only to expose an antiquated prejudice and to replace it by tolerance and recognition. This is seen as less of a revolution than just a matter of good manners when approached from a secular perspective. The result is fission between two antithetical views of human life, human nature, and what ethical norms should prevail. To be caught between such divergent positions as I am may explain the anguish that has accompanied the writing of this book.

Moral Protocols

I give this essay the title of "moral protocols" because they represent alternatives to the usual way of dealing with transsexuals and gay people. The usual course for transsexuals is to aid them to transition to the sex role that they feel best able to embrace in order to live a full life. This sex role includes sexual as well as social elements. For transsexuals who will be transitioning from male to female their treatment may include hormonal sterilization, castration, and vaginoplasty.

These procedures raise moral concerns in several areas:

1. The loss of the ability to procreate children;

2. The question of whether a valid marriage may be contracted (if with a female person it may no longer be possible to con-

summate the marriage and if with a male person the new vagina may not be admitted as presumptive moral evidence of the new female moral stratus);

3. The question will also be raised as to whether sex change procedures do a sort of violence to the human body without adequate reason and thus show disrespect to the Creator and the dignity of the human being.

It has been the teaching to date of the Church that only one model exists for human sexuality: one that is heterosexually normative and that assumes a non-problematic binary sexual identity and attraction or affectivity for all persons. All expressions of human sexuality are confined to validly married couples and even within marriage sexuality is presumed to require sexual intercourse in which sperm is deposited within a vagina in order to conform to the Church's interpretation of the natural law. No artificial barrier to conception may be used. These strictures are meant to protect what is termed "the integrity or finality of the act," which in turn is meant to assure that human sexuality should mirror the firm belief that only a complete and mutual life-long commitment of the partners is truly human and holy. Anything less is not only wrong but an example of what the Church terms "grave matter," in other words mortally sinful, which if not repented before divine judgment is rendered could send a soul to hell for eternity.

By stating this position blankly and coldly it will immediately be evident that most of what actually occurs among most human beings in contemporary western culture is in direct variance with what the Church demands in furthering its assigned mission of bearing an adequate witness to the revealed will of God. The compromises with actual human imperfection evident elsewhere in its moral demands are not evident here. The Church accepts that Catholics may in good conscience serve in a military establishment that may order them to kill without asking difficult moral questions. The Church has accepted the final triumph of democratic governments and many other positions that were once condemned in the Syllabus of Errors of Pope Pius IX. But the Church has not accepted a broader reading of human sexuality on issues such as masturbation, homosexuality, and gender identity.

One major Catholic apostolate has been to reconcile homosexual Catholics to a practice of life-long sexual abstinence by comparing their desires to that of an alcoholic desire for alcohol through using a twelve step approach to attaining life-long chastity and abstinence. This approach does not recognize that a homosexual identity may be a source of even a valid cultural witness to humanity since it is held that nothing positive or creative may proceed from what is assessed along the single parameter of homosexual desire as manifesting an example of a disordered inclination to sin. This approach sets the homosexual at war with what he feels to be an integral part of himself or herself and goes further still to enlist the person as a willing ally in the suppression of his or her sexuality by implying that anything less is an affront to chastity, a chastity that for homosexuals is an absolute command to abstain from sex for life whereas in most areas of human life no similar stringent perfection is demanded as a prerequisite to our salvation. There is no demand for instance that we attain justice by achieving an absolute equality in the share of material goods.

To say that this position that homosexual persons must take towards themselves is an occasion for profound moral distress to LGBT people is the very least that can be said. My question is how any human being can ask this of another, not as an exercise of heroic virtue, but as the bottom line where failure means damnation unless repented before death. I agree that we should all aspire to sainthood, but I can think of no other area of human life where the Church is as insistent upon perfection for all persons, in all places, and in all conditions. Would anyone, for instance, be able in good conscience to work for any of today's modern business corporations knowing that many such business entities pursue evil ends or at least fail to manifest perfect charity?

The sexual mandates of the Church are imposed on individuals with a rigor that is visible nowhere else. These mandates have never been practiced in all of human history. Chastity has never been an absolute or widely practiced virtue nor has nature cooperated in making this possible by following the example of most animal species, which only come into heat seasonally. The best that can be attained by most people is to achieve a degree of relative temperance in their use of their sexual faculty. To ask more of human nature is to create a situation where in practice there is often an inevitability of a revolving door of sexual sin and partial repentance for the majority of modern men and women. Does "the natural law" really demand so much? Even if a greater chastity could be achieved through strenuous efforts would the results not so distort human nature that a greater set of personality imbalances might be almost certain to occur?

I have no answer to these questions beyond a sense of personal dismay. This entire pass/fail mentality as applied to sex alone with this degree of rigor seems to suppose a perfect intentionality in the one area of life that most ties us to the primal in our animal nature. Medicine, psychology, history, and anthropology are seen from this point of view as irrelevant at least when applied to human sexuality and affective pairing.

Why is this? Is it not far more likely that we are in the presence of an institutional imperative based upon faulty cultural assumptions rather than a true and adequate moral teaching? Far greater evils continue unabated while this area of life monopolizes the attentions of moralists. Does Divine Mercy never manifest itself by some adjustment to fallen human nature, particularly considering that many people often live their lives with only minimal outward signs of possessing a spiritual nature at all? By choosing to begin here where our animal nature is most resistant hasn't the Church missed an opportunity to address far greater evils where pure rationality and control are more likely to prevail and where the failure to achieve perfection is far more costly in human life and social welfare? Does the Creator of the universe and of its laws set us so at odds with ourselves so that we possess all of the earth in imperfect rule but must treat our genitals as some sort of nuclear reactor core to be contained behind walls of lead lest they lead to an explosion that will leave the soul in ruins?

Yet for all of what I have just said I do not embrace the contrary views that we should couple at will or abandon the virtues that

335

a marital exclusivity demands of us. We should try to advance in moral perfection. The costs of promiscuity are everywhere seen in broken hearts, sexually transmitted diseases, uncared for children, abortion on demand, and a general co-opting of the sexual function for commercial purposes and even for human sex-trafficking and slavery. The witness of the Church to chastity must not be lightly set aside. What is advisable however is a realistic appraisal that while not compromising the ideal might still recognize and give some moral weight to what we are currently learning about human sexuality, a set of data that previous generations did not possess and that even had it been available would probably have been evaluated and judged according to the pre-existing norms of the foregone conclusions of Jewish laws as represented in the Old Testament. An ethics that assumes an unwarranted rigidity of Divine Revelation manifests the danger of literalism in Biblical interpretation that is decried in many other areas in the present light of hermeneutics and Scriptural studies.

But even having said this, I wish to emphasize that this book and this essay in particular are not meant to be seen as conclusive. The suggestions that I appear to advocate here should be read and understood by my readers as the moral equivalent of a legal petition for review by an appellate court. Lawyers are particularly sensitive to procedural irregularities and the function of an appellate court is to review the trial transcript and to consider the relevant law before deciding to affirm or overrule a decision of the trial court and any prior appeal.

I suggest that a similar procedure might be undertaken here by Church authorities who alone have the duty and commission from God to pronounce and decide these matters that are now so debated in all quarters and then to apply their conclusions in a pastoral context to guide and comfort individual souls. The task of clarification need not imply insubordination or contempt for what we have traditionally received. Morality is never an empirical discipline but experience does have some indicative value as evidence of theological overreaching.

Catholic Jurisprudence

I cannot conclude this book without a few comments regarding what might be called the jurisprudential basis for Catholic dogma. The doctrinal definitions in the Catholic Church are derived from two sources. The first is called the Ordinary Magisterium. This might be summarized by the phrase, "what has been taught always and everywhere." In other words this source of dogma deals with a question of faith or morals where the answer has been so long standing that to doubt it now would be to reverse a trend of thought the truth of which is guaranteed by its longevity and by its universal acceptance by both the bishops and the body of the faithful. The best evidence that something is within the Ordinary Magisterium is for this to be expressed in a dogmatic document from a Church Council.

The second source of infallible teaching is what is called the Extraordinary Magisterium. This power is reserved to the Pope. It refers to a solemn pronouncement by the Pope addressed ex cathedra to the entire Catholic Church and phrased with clear language that indicates beyond any doubt that the statement in question is a solemn definition that cannot be reformed at a later date or by any later pronouncement. Such statements are de fide, "of the faith" and are to be held as such by all of the faithful. These statements are extremely rare and deal more with questions of the mysteries of the faith than they do with any particular moral position. This means that a Catholic should approach dogma with a clear understanding of the delicate balance and the wide spectrum that exists in Church documents. This provides a gradient for official Church teachings in the degree of assent that is required.

Catholics should at all times accept statements made in Papal Encyclicals and other Vatican documents with respect and deference but the final acceptance of absolute faith is reserved for statements that either sum up a teaching that is within the ambit of the Ordinary Magisterium or has been proclaimed as de fide by an exercise of the Extraordinary Magisterium when the Pope speaks ex cathedra.

Now then what does this mean to persons who are of other religions or who even if nominally Christian are non-Catholic or even to many average Catholics who are not particularly sophisticated on the nature of various official pronouncements from the leadership of the Church? We live in a world that assumes that democracy and the right to exercise even uninformed personal opinion makes all truths relative or at least arguable. The very concept of moral absolutes makes little sense in our current politically correct world. The strength and endurance of the institution of Roman Catholicism is due however to the firm view and unity in holding the proposition that such absolute truths do in fact exist. When seen in this light the distinction that I have attempted to make between the Church as a socially conditioned and historical entity and as a divinely instituted organization must always have as its backdrop the firm belief that the Holy Spirit protects the Church from manifest error in certain essential matters. Any doubts that I may have raised here are meant to be confined to that arena where individual questioning is still permissible to a Catholic person without endangering the loss of her faith and should only be accepted as such. When I exceed those bounds my affirmations, no matter how strongly phrased, should be held in a state of suspension while seeking further clarification rather than a blithe acceptance by my readers.

One of the greatest challenges in writing this book for me has been to balance my desire to present a fairly uncensored and authentic narrative of what I have been able to observe of the transsexual quest and the sufferings of transgender people while at the same time seeking to not lose sight of the fact that to many people the transsexual journey is itself an ill-conceived and immoral choice. One of the biggest problems in reporting any experience that others do not share is to find metaphors that can convey personal experience in terms that by analogy can be grasped by others who do not share that experience. This process of writing entails a degree of advocacy that may compromise other more essential values.

I am aware that from the Catholic point of view and the restrictions that it imposes I may have taken certain liberties here in the effort to spare transsexuals from rejection, hatred, and discrimination by those who are biased against us and unwilling to endeavor to enter sympathetically into our inmost feelings. I am also aware that for many people the teachings of the Roman Catholic Church are not received as authoritative and binding. The linguistic style that is used in many Church documents appears as both arbitrary and authoritarian. Faith makes certain demands upon credulity that exceed proof. The hidden dimension of faith is trust and the common identity that finds that we are all indeed of one body in Christ as St. Paul has said.

My book then is both a transsexual book and one that is conditioned by my prior loyalty to the larger body of which I am only a part. It may be startling but is nevertheless true that among my own contradictions is a rampant individualism combined with a deep desire to belong to something greater than myself. If I had no belief in God and an eternal destiny I would be left with only this tale of my life that has been presented here, and quite frankly it is not enough. Even had I succeeded in being the diva of my dreams these memoirs and essays should be read as partial and spontaneous utterances rather than firm conclusions. To seek a final meaning in life I should hope that I might desire to have achieved something more than a series of colorful and extravagant adventures.

As my allowance of time remaining is diminished I will no doubt abandon the futile quest to retain youth and beauty and seek out one of the shadowed cathedrals the majesty of which still beckons us to recall a world where humankind once knew its place in this vast universe and where even the most insignificant and despised of us could know that we are loved and that each of us plays a small but essential part in the dance of the universe, one that has been created by God. This could be the greatest period for missionary activity that the world has ever known. The sheer numbers of people, all alive at once, surpass all prior history in the opportunity presented for the human race to resolve our differences. I hope that this book may be a tiny part of this essential dialogue of human experience. Extremes may cancel out and the median may prevail. Of course final truths are not usually attainable by mere statistical means, but to ignore minority testimony, even if it is biased to a degree, seldom leads to truth.

Catholic Morality and Transsexualism

The following essay represents my sense of the way that the division of the sexes may be approached from a meditation on the Holy Trinity. Catholic moral teaching is founded on the belief that all human beings are destined by their creator to ultimately share in the very life of the Trinity through what has been termed the Beatific Vision. The split nature of humankind into male and female has been designed by the Creator so that both men and women will feel deeply within themselves a need for another to complete them and in whom they may contemplate what they themselves are not. Human perfection is not meant to be realized within one sex alone or in one individual. We achieve the fully human only by giving ourselves in love to another and in being for that other what he or she is not. From this need within us arises the requirement of the differentiation of the sexes. Difference makes it possible to form complementary relationships which only add to the stability of the bonds formed. The individual person cannot from within his or her own personality generate the beloved. Only God can do this and has done so in the case of the Second Person of the Blessed Trinity who is of one substance with God the Father and yet has become man in the mystery of the Incarnation of Jesus Christ.

In taking human nature Jesus subjected His own divine nature to the same radical incompleteness that comes with being a human. We are confined in our humanity to being members of either one sex or the other. It was not that Jesus could not have been born as a woman instead of a man but that to be human at all was to be one or the other. Granted the patriarchal world-view of the Jews at the time of the mission of Jesus, it would have been even more likely to fail to be heard had Jesus been born as a woman instead of as a man. Sex is only metaphorically predicated of God.

God is spoken of as Father, not because the first person of the Divine Trinity is male (for to do so would make each member of the Godhead in the image of mere physical creation) as a practical concession to a patriarchal culture. God is completely one in each of the three persons of the Blessed Trinity. The Trinity in other words is not a parceling out of the nature of God (as in three equal slices of one pie). God's nature is so complete that each member of the Trinity knows the fullness of divinity within itself.

The relations of the Trinity are not imposed from without by some sort of necessity so as to counteract a divine narcissism but are acts of freedom and choice at a level that we cannot comprehend. For this reason divine love within the Trinity has no element of self-interest or egoism. Each Person of the Trinity is fully God and has no need as such for anything to complete that perfection. Perfect freedom creates and manifests perfect love.

No human being may ape this inner perfection which belongs to God alone. For this reason the transition element in a transsexual is quite real. It is not as though a transsexual can both retain a prior gender and now acquire a new one as well so that he or she completes humanity in the circle of his or her own singular being. One cannot have intercourse with oneself. Instead, transsexuals experience within themselves an inner gender incongruity. As they transition they leave something behind, not all of themselves, but they do in actualizing the gender to which they feel that they belong sacrifice many of the prerogatives and gender insignia of their former state of life. Since they exchange one sort of human incompleteness for another, there is no net metaphysical gain in being. Transsexuals must adapt to the same need for another that faces all human beings through chastity broadly defined as the proper use of sexuality.

Chastity is not the direct equivalent of temperance, although temperance does enter into the use of the sexual faculty. Chastity is in the final analysis the virtue that allows us to contemplate the human in one other human being who by being attached to us allows us to love the human in one other with a perfect contemplation of love (proportionate of course to a fellow creature). When returned in kind the result is a bond that is the closest human equivalent of the love that exists within the Trinity. This is the Sacrament of Marriage.

Out of this metaphysic of the human person the teaching of the Church approaches the question of gay, lesbian, and transsexual love. The traditional teaching has regarded the sexes as mutually exclusive and at times more as contradictories than as complements of each other. As we have come to see how large the intermediate zone is between the sexes, we may be in the process of discovering that, although biology makes certain demands of us as sexual beings, biology itself has its intermediate and for that reason indeterminate area. Human freedom and morality must always adjust itself to a world of what has been termed "physical evil" which flows from the fallen nature of the world that we must live in and in which we must work out our salvation.

What makes perfect moral sense from the perspective of a non-fallen world may not make sense in a world that now shows significant limitations. This raises the question whether what the Church currently views as natural law as regards sex is an indication of the will of God or whether it is instead modulated by the existence of physical evil. If sex is treated as a mere accidental rather than the essence of each human being that imposes an immutable discreteness upon individuals, then a new evaluation of the morality of sex-change may become possible. If the function of sexual difference is not to make us first of all "sexually identified souls" but instead merely to enhance the bodily gift that we may give to each other, then that gift may still be present by analogy in same-sex love, a love that still sees the other as other and not as a mere mirrored image of oneself. This posits a primal respect of persons as being the essence of love. We must allow the other to remain other even while loving him or her.

Chastity that is merely formal (from this point-of-view) is not chastity at all but simple lack of moral imagination. Many supposedly valid marriages in the past have failed in principle to live up to this dimension of gift of the self. Many heterosexual marriages have manifested a dynamic where the wife simply disappeared after marriage and was absorbed into the ego of her husband. So common was this dynamic that it appeared to escape notice and condemnation by the Church preoccupied as it was by looking first at the mere outside sufficiency of the form of the sacrament while failing to inquire as to the actual working out of the marriage vows. Many marriages have been de facto dead-letters as relationships yet were presumed as valid through adherence to mere formalities.

We turn now to what factors indicate that love might be present and that some degree of actual complementarity might be found even within a union of same-sexed partners. If it is true that in heaven people are not in a condition to marry or to be given in marriage might this not an indication that the souls in heaven are essentially genderless or at least trans-gender? This argument is not conclusive of course but it indicates at least that in the presence of God in heaven united within the Mystical Body of Christ the Church all souls are though discrete still so unified with others that any marriage bond would be superfluous. The special grace of marriage would thus appear to expire upon the death of one or both spouses. For this reason a widow or widower may marry again even on earth without committing an injustice towards his or her former spouse.

Perfect chastity as an anticipation of the Beatific Vision attains its end by seeing and respecting each human being in the relation of his or her final end, that of resting in Christ and hence in God. It is this chastity which forbids indiscriminate coupling. Perfect love is not expressed exclusively in human beings by sexual love but in our capacity to seek God through one unique other until death, an arrangement best suited to our present capacities as fallen creatures. This is impossible without the aid of grace. The sacramental grace of Marriage is required in order to sustain us in this exclusive relationship which would be attenuated by human weakness and selfishness if we could switch partners at will. Can these goals find a place in same-sex unions?

Same-sex unions have been traditionally viewed as lacking two essential elements: 1. Lack of sexual complementarity; 2. the inability of a same-sex union to procreate or even to symbolize fertility. Same-sex coital relations are void ab initio. It has been held that the objective order as well as the symbols of marriage and the goods that they are meant to symbolize cannot be present where two such fatal defects are present. It has therefore been held that gay, lesbian, or transsexual persons must exist (unlike their heterosexual fellow humans) within a mandate that (even in this fallen world) they must live in life-long celibacy with no possibility of even a less-than-perfect union. This seemed the only solution that would sustain the essential definitional structure of marriage.

The question that I would raise at this point is whether there is a fundamental shortsightedness and lack of charity in leaping from the need to sustain the holiness of marriage, its objective goodness, and its indissolubility (except through the death of the spouse), the natural need to provide stability for children, and other essential elements by denying similar consolation and fulfillment in any aspect to gay and lesbian sexual relations? Could we not in good conscience allow for a parallel relationship between persons who for whatever reason, physical or psychological, cannot enter into a traditional heterosexual union?

In all other areas of human life we accept less than perfect charity. Though we are asked to give away all of our possessions to the poor and to come follow Christ, we recognize that those who are not up to this degree of sacrifice are not per se seen as being in mortal sin and ineligible, without prior repentance, for salvation. Yet we insist that gay, lesbian, and transsexual persons must sustain definitional structures that they as human exceptions have neither the wish nor the ability to abrogate. This heroic sacrifice appears to be required merely to benefit the heterosexual and cis-gender majority by partially de-humanizing and de-legitimizing the options available to GLBT persons. May not GLBT persons attain from within the limitations that they encounter in their own sexual natures some partial measure at least of human love and fulfillment?

To place the heavy burden of life-long involuntary celibacy upon them and to presume that each and every one of them will be given the grace to live a life of contemplation sufficient to deny the ordinary sexual comforts of our human nature seems to me to be callous, shortsighted, and presumptuous. A little inquiry and imagination will show that gay, lesbian, transsexual, and intersex persons do not owe their limitations to mere willful conduct but rather sustain them as a result of what may be seen as analogous to any other physical or mental limitation that we find in other conditions that limit the full expression of our humanity but do not require such a qualitative difference in expression.

To its credit the Church has come to recognize the malice of discrimination. Not all human ills are signs of sin or moral culpability. The Church does not wish to mirror the Pharisees who asked of the blind man in John's Gospel, "Who sinned, this man or his parents that he should have been born blind?" Similarly I would argue that human limits such as involuntary orientation to a same-sex attraction or gender incongruity should not be morally dispositive as regards the morality of a permanent sexual union between two committed persons. The Church has not been willing to see the merits of this suggestion.

Though the fullness of Sacramental Grace is necessary to sustain heterosexual marriages and procreation, might not GLBT persons still find in what remains to them some solace and comfort in another type of life-long, one-to-another relationship. If so then Marriage might be seen as analogous to the Sacrament of the Sick, which is not today bestowed only upon the dying in their extremity but may be invoked whenever the need for this particular sacramental grace is needed.

Similarly transsexuals might be allowed to assume the gender to which they feel that they belong without forfeiting, as is now the case, the ability to marry which is imposed as a necessary cost exacted by their physical transition. I suggest that male-to-female transsexuals should not be denied marriage on the mere grounds of their sterility any more than a woman who has undergone a hysterectomy be denied marriage. Nor should the inability to consummate a marriage through lack of a penis mandate that female-to-male transsexuals be denied marriage either. The goods to be attained by sexual expression may be better preserved by seeing an essential chastity to be present even in a same-sex or what appears to be a same-sex union. From this point-of-view, to demand that sexual contact must achieve all of its aims in human life before having any value at all sufficient to be both honored and preserved is to ask too much of human nature. Without being viewed as disordered and sinful, persons of the GLBT community may finally find full acceptance and contribute in their own way to the community of the faithful. The grace of the sacrament of marriage should then be allowed to in a manner of speaking seek its own level depending upon the needs and sexual condition of the persons involved. The maintenance of our present discrete definitional system is creating a terrible condition of anomie within many persons in our society and breeding a hatred and contempt for them in heterosexual persons who do not share their particular limitations. It would appear then to be the more moral choice to take a closer look at our understanding of the Sacrament of Marriage rather than to summarily conclude that our present distinctions, which may have been the result of cultural limitations and not of the final natural order of things, have dictated the approach hitherto taken to same-sex unions, to gender change, and to the latitude allowed to all people to explore and express our sexual nature.

Even having suggested this possible avenue to reform I believe that the other side should be considered as well. The teaching role of the bishops according to the Documents of the Second Vatican Council includes the duty to bear witness to the larger civil society and to seek to conform it to the revealed will of God. For this reason the bishops have no choice but to speak out on issues that are primary to the functioning of the moral order in societal forms and structures. This way of looking at the world is less fundamentalist than it is fundamental. By this I mean that the Catholic world view looks to natural law as indicative of the residual goodness of God's initial plan for creation compromised by Original Sin. To this way of looking at things grace when operative can aid people to live saintly lives that parallel God's initial will for all human beings, lives that will culminate in eternal life. In contrast to this our modern view is that the natural order is a mere mindless substratum that can be modified to fulfill human will and desires through technical progress. The natural order is seen as good but not necessarily morally good. We look only to ourselves to define the goals of human happiness. God is seen as a convenient myth that can be traced to those periods of human history characterized by relative human powerlessness. By placating the gods pre-technological man could achieve his ends by motivating celestial beings to aid mankind or at least not to oppose our best efforts to build a better world for ourselves.

The function of women in this natural order was held to provide what she alone could achieve: to give birth to a new human life.

From the male point of view women were both of infinite value but were simultaneously a humiliating link to the limits imposed by nature to human will. This in turn bred in male consciousness both a fear and hatred for women which is manifest in many Biblical prohibitions regarding the uncleanness of women post menstruation and even of the uncleanness of men after a nocturnal emission. Gradually theology managed to come to terms with sexuality by seeing it as part of a divine harmony (an attitude that the I Ching of the Chinese recognized swiftly and without the intermediate stage of dread of the feminine principle). On the other hand the followers of Islam still have a terror and contempt for women.

If the division of the sexes in not a mere accident of nature in order to create genetic diversity but is in fact a primal statement of God's will that the human dyad be similar but not identical to the community of Divine Persons in the Trinity, then the profound opposition of the Church to same-sex marriage can be seen as essential and required. To an extent though, this view begs the question because homosexual relations are not a direct analogue to heterosexual relations. Instead, they are an assertion of choice rather than of biological necessity. They parallel human technology which holds that human life in pursuit of its goals is not bound to the natural order. We need not await a future and eternal life to attain our desired earthly goals. For this reason homosexual conduct appears to be transgressive and promethean in its very nature. As such it appears to be a rebellion or at least an assertion that human life must look to its own resources if humans are to find a temporal version of happiness.

As regards monogamy the human family is not given by nature but is merely one of the many political forms though which men have dominated nature, in this case nature is represented by women. By refusing to reduce women in their individuality to a mere procreative force, gay men have been seen as natural allies to feminists and lesbians. These examples of "the new women," freed of the necessary burden of procreation, have welcomed the GLBT critique of normative heterosexuality and monogamy. By viewing heterosexual men as essentially sexual colonizers of the bodies of women rather than as possessing within their own bodies a unique and essential spark of life with which to engender human life, feminism has taken the position of essentially going on strike until its demands for sexual equality are met. These demands center upon control of the use of female bodies by men. Heterosexuality is portrayed as just another form of animal husbandry. In this struggle gay and lesbian conduct has been seen as a way of achieving sexual fulfillment without subjecting one sex to the will of the other. If sexuality as procreative is not a good in itself but is rather the field of a political battle whereby one sex is necessarily co-opted by the other, then heterosexuality is presumptively the field of sexual assault and the heterosexual family is not seen as a loving community but as a residual form of dominant patriarchy.

For this reason Church's teaching has been seen as itself a mere reflection of the male need to dominate and subdue women through the threat of moral condemnation and punishment in order to get them to submit to overweening male desire. The history of the Church has no doubt paralleled the desire of European males to colonize and to exploit native peoples by treating them as women with a mixture of patronizing solicitude and enslavement. For this reason the sentimental and symbolic view of marriage and complementarity that the bishops propose is seen by those who look to the actual relations of the sexes throughout history as being purely mythological and sentimental.

Feminism in contrast to theology is based on a sense of radical praxis. The advent of the feminist movement was meant to achieve an end beyond mere freedom, just as gay liberation was similarly motivated to end the genocidal impulses represented by Jewish thought which mandated that sexually active gay men were to be put to death. In this view Judeo-Christian teachings on sexuality appear as violent and exploitive by nature so that what is called natural law is in fact profoundly political in nature and favors heterosexual male dominance over women and gay men. What could manifest this better than St. Paul's injunction that wives be submissive to their husbands? The real opposition to birth control is therefore not seen by feminists as stemming from a desire to maintain the integrity of the marital act, but to keep women bonded to men through childbirth. The phrase, "the integrity of the act" only reminds women that they are part of nature like the soil or like the sunlight. A woman's humanity is only secondary to her sexual function. Woman in heterosexual culture only exists fully in the dyad of marriage when she is united with a man and not as an individual.

Even if most people will reject the implications of this radical view, women do disproportionately bear the costs of procreation. If this is doubted one needs only to look to the practical order of the day to day world and see how many men simply walk away from their children while few women do so. To this unequal and deplorable discrepancy the Church can only advise women to submit one more time and trust their husbands. While to homosexuals of either sex the Church advises them to adapt a life devoid of sexual intimacy and conversion and repentance for any past offenses followed by mandatory celibacy for life so that "the natural order" may be preserved.

Is the natural order ever viewed as so precious in other areas of life? Was not calling it sacramental and binding a mere convenience for males who wished for a regularly accessible sexual partner? Much suffering and inequality hides beneath this talk of complementarity which all too often was that of the master and the slave. The anguish of Catholic married women is a story that needs to be finally told. Until it is told, the static and idealized image of marriage that is held up by the bishops will fail to convince anyone but themselves.

Framing the issue usually determines the outcome. This is a truism in legal advocacy. The current battle being waged over the question of gay marriage is a case in point. Last Sunday among the prayers in my parish at the offertory was the prayer that our state legislators would see their duty and "uphold the sanctity of marriage." The implication of course is that any recognition of a permanent bond between two gay people or two lesbian people must not be called a marriage because such a union is not sanctified. The public cannot deny that such relationships exist but they must be kept to a status that in no way manifests the dignity of a heterosexual marriage. By controlling the definition it is possible to use such words as "sanctity" which calls to mind

God's blessing of the union of the two persons involved. Since homosexuality is still considered to be a sin or in the more carefully phrased language of recent Church statements, "a grave disorder" and inclination to sin, gay marriage becomes in the eyes of many an ongoing blasphemy. Is it any wonder then that gay people who have lived their entire lives under just such a stigma see actual marriage as the prize of the legitimacy that they have long sought? The long struggle for their civil rights will not be complete for the GLBT community as long as they are deprived from the only lasting relationship between two people that forms the basis of a loving and affirming union, even of a family. GLBT people are deprived of everything that family means by being defined as permanently single and insofar as they are such, they are without support or membership in the larger social fabric. As necessarily single individuals they remain dead limbs upon the tree of their families of origin. All of this is due to the idea that love between same-sexed individuals is by nature sterile.

Yet marriage is also a matter of bonding so that society still sees heterosexual marriages as valid even if the couple is beyond the childbearing years or if one or the other partner is sterile. The implication is that the other differing mental and physical characteristics of same-sex couples are inadequate to even simulate and symbolize a fruitful union. Gay or lesbian love is sterile ab initio and as such must fail to provide the foundation to qualify for marriage. It is no illusion though that behind all of this talk of natural law there remains the maledictions of Leviticus and Deuteronomy towards GLBT people.

As long as members of our community are defined as manifesting an "objective disorder" in our very being, we will never arrive as being considered to be full members of the human family except by adopting this same jaundiced view of ourselves. Self condemnation in one's inmost being is then the prerequisite for social acceptance and full sacramental presence in the Church for GLBT persons. To put it bluntly, in this view a gay or lesbian union or even one between a postoperative transsexual and a member of the sex assigned to her at birth is viewed as unsanctified and in some way lessening to the value of marriage per se. In other words every heterosexual marriage is somehow less holy because now that same recognition has been extended to relationships that are deemed as sinful in their very nature.

This means of course that such relationships not only cannot produce children but are de facto an unhealthy environment in which to raise children, not because they do not manifest fidelity and love, but rather because they are an ongoing offense against God and the entire human order through lack of gender complementarity. Is it any wonder then that GLBT people see in the institution of civil marriage their final escape route from lives spent as victims of seemingly justifiable hatred, condemnation, exile, and violence towards us? Unless all human rights are bestowed, particularly this most fundamental right, all other rights become mere honoraria bestowed by upon us by generous heterosexuals and therefore revocable at will. In the end people are either considered to be fully human or they are not.

Adjusting to the Supreme Court Decision on Same-sex Marriage

The age of the temporal hegemony of Catholic Bishops ended with the feudal order that once sustained it. It may be sad but is nevertheless true that the Bishops and the Church as a whole is now perceived in our global and secularized society as only one more poor voice in the clamor of opinions. That voice must now speak in the tone of persuasion more than of command.

In contrast to the Church the civil order exists to keep peace among various absolutist claims to speak with the authority of God. As such it may not choose between various views nor may it use the doctrines of any particular religion as the basis for its substantive or procedural legal rules, rights, and processes. The role of the Church vis-a-vis the civil order is to bear witness and to act as a missionary voice. There are no Papal States here, no Prince Bishops, and no anointed kings who may put armies into the field to compel Christian allegiance. There are no Crusaders to regain the Holy Land or expel the Moors or the Albigensian heretics. Even the synods of the Bishops are unfortunately for most Catholics perceived as distant events of no greater interest then meetings of similar boards of directors of large, anonymous, corporate bodies since few ever read the outcomes of these meetings.

The result is that Bishops live in an illusory world that their command and control station has any real penetration and effect among the parishioners who may smile and laugh at their jokes on the few occasions when the parish may actually receive a visit from a Bishop for a Sunday sermon or to celebrate Confirmation. For the rest, the average Catholic has no real relation to the distant bureaucracy of the Church even when the "local ordinary" speaks out.

Even the awesome apparatus of Canon Law is only of concern to Catholics when seeking annulments. The praying of the Divine Office has fallen into neglect and has no longer the power of Gregorian chant even in the monasteries to accompany it. Even Sunday mass attendance as a minimal exercise of religious duty has come to be seen as an optional event and the Sacrament of Reconciliation is regarded by many, incorrectly I might add, as little more than a legacy of fear from the oppressive Catholic childhoods of those born before Vatican Two.

In the light of all this it might be expected that the Bishops would tend first to their own house before venturing forth into the civil arena, one over which they have no special jurisdiction beyond the right to bear witness to the differences that exist between the secular world and the ideal world of a universal Christian praxis. When the Bishops attempt to tell the civil authorities the scope of their ability to define purely civil marriages they imply that the State must uphold the Sacramental view of marriage including, inter alia, that the very existence of divorce on demand is invalid from a sacramental perspective.

The sacramental view of marriage was abrogated long ago in the civic arena (or did the bishops not take sufficient note of this). Civil marriage no longer has any real relation to anything beyond tax breaks, community property rules, and other contract-like rights and privileges. It is legal and pragmatic in intent and whatever moral legitimacy it may bestow on same-sex couples is one that they claim as civil citizens and not before the throne of God. This is precisely the time to make this distinction clear rather than to seek to use civil power to mandate an understanding of marriage that is no longer shared by a considerable proportion of the population. The Church only grows in power when it admits openly that it is a contrarian voice in a secular world. By its nature it is a voice calling in the desert; to act as a comfortable ally of the government in most other areas while raising their common voice as bishops on same-sex marriage and in such a strident manner serves to hide the many areas where U.S. policies are profoundly unchristian while receiving less emphatic protest. Is the best use of what may be limited ammunition? The public is easily bored by hyperbole. Particularly in the sexual arena the bishops are perceived as living in a glass house after the sex-abuse scandal. It may be time to deal with other pressing issues first and regain a little credibility among the masses. This has been the emphasis of the new Pope and he has paid a price for it. Several bishops, who seem more concerned with their august position and prerogatives than they are with collegial unity, see the present Pope Francis as an intruder, a poacher on a well-stocked spiritual estate, and have not forsworn comments designed to sow the seeds of schism. To seek out the lost sheep always takes more effort than simply proclaiming them to be sinners.

To appear less personally sour and disgruntled and instead to manifest that they are sincerely curious about the spiritual dry-rot that is pervasively invading our lives as Catholics would be a vast improvement. Reform must be comprehensive to be believable. Less umbrage and more mea culpa in high quarters would be more likely to encourage the rank and file Catholics. It is all too easy to lose a generation. To effectively capture hearts and minds can never be merely a matter of making routine pronouncements assuming that they will be heard and obeyed.

Let us now look here at some of the empirical realities involved in the same-sex marriage debate. There are many people of all sexual orientations who prefer to live a libertine existence of unprincipled serial coupling. For years it was common to view gay men in particular as manifesting an inordinate appetite for compulsive sex with strangers. In order to come out as gay it was presumed that gay people constituted a sort of unbridled sexual tribe whose primary bond was indiscriminate bathhouse sex. Gay life was seen even by gay men themselves as a sort of unending sexual carnival! Many gay men came to entertain this view of their own nature in precisely this way so that a gay culture of sorts could spring up, one that led finally to the massive deaths from AIDS of an entire generation.

Nothing would have been more surprising to the early advocates of unlimited sexual freedom than that marriage would be seen as the final prize for the GLBT community. Who would have thought then beneath the flashing disco lights that the real gay pioneers were the sedate and elderly queens of the forties and fifties who only hoped to be able to walk hand in hand through a park without being mugged by the young crusaders with baseball bats? But so it now is. Gone are the days of Fire Island meat racks, of Dan White and his "Twinkie Defense" for murdering Harvey Milk and George Moscone. The former invisible people are now seen as part of the great "us" of America.

Except for one last bastion that always served to remind us that gays and lesbians were not really fully human after all. Homosexuals must not marry! They must remain celibate for life as nature's chosen eunuchs. A lesbian mother in other words was a better mother as a single person than if she had a permanent partner of the same sex whom she loved and who shared her entire life including the sexual aspect. Yet such "families" do exist. Well then our societal task is to make clear that both they and the children they are raising should be in no illusion as to the lack of holiness or acceptableness before God and man of their supposed union. Sin is occurring in that house so that the entire household in a sense exists under a ban, the ban of no legal marriage!

How else, reason the appointed representatives of God, will the human race continue if same sex unions are recognized? Once recognize gay marriage and everyone will just turn gay or at least feel okay about it which is no way to motivate them to condemn their feelings! GLBT marriage will, some fear, import a principle of sterility into marriage itself so that what began with artificial birth control has now come to this final pass: that the differences between men and women are not a matter of substance any more but of mere trivial detail. If it becomes irrelevant which sex you marry or whether your children come from test tubes or intercourse then where does the human act of sexual union in marriage remain? Is everything that we may do permitted to us? When does the human become inhuman?

Some of these concerns are worth our earnest consideration. In any case this is what is really at stake for believers in the same-sex marriage debate, the fear that we are in the process of desiring to create ourselves in our own image and according to our own dictates. Can human cloning be far behind? How then are we to balance these points of view as a society?

In order to answer this we have to ask ourselves if the human order exists primarily in nature as given or in our own freedom. If Adam and Eve chose to be like God knowing good and evil, then they must decide what is good and what is evil and take responsibility for the consequences at least in the practical order. We do not habitually ask if our business structures and our entire way of life militarily and economically is Christian.

There is no doubt that we are already violating natural law in other arenas of the positive law in America. The Supreme Court of the United States for instance recently decided that corporations are persons with all of the rights of free speech and even religious identity implied by human personhood. Presumably among those rights of persons is the right to marriage so that mergers of companies are no longer a business affair but should presumably be celebrated with flowers and rice with tin cans rattling behind. Meanwhile the Supreme Court adamantly refuses to see human fetuses as persons but views them as mere lumps of non-differentiated fetal flesh and marketable flesh at that. I suggest that gay or lesbian marriage, even if viewed as contradicting the natural order and distorting human nature, is far closer to the authentically human than what the law is already manifesting in judicial opinions that have not provoked similar outrage from religious leaders. I would further suggest that we will not find the answer to the question of the legitimacy of gay marriage in nature but in our own sense of compassion, a compassion lacking in many contemporary diatribes against the GLBT community.

It seems strange to me that the same nation that has no trouble swallowing the idea that corporations are persons or that "illegal combatants" may be held in custody indefinitely without trial and tortured at will or that fish genes can be spliced into our morning corn flakes is disturbed by two brides marrying in a civil ceremony.

The above sentiments are not to be taken as a definitive moral position on the question of gay or lesbian marriage. This provisional venture into permanence of communities that formerly had the advantage of sexual fluidity may come as a social shock to all parties. Marriage has long imposed as many restrictions as delights and with it has come a set of middle-class and property imperatives that may seem alien to lives formerly centered upon the gay urban experience of gay bars and the Fire Island ethos. But then today's GLBT community may be as distant from the days and nights of the disco seventies and eighties as it is from the days of Oscar Wilde and Walt Whitman.

If marriage is to be more than just another symbol of contemporary acceptance or indifference it will have to become fully integrated into gay culture and expectations. Only then will it be seen if marriage within the GLBT community is a fully compatible act as citizens, one that the GLBT community does not wish to use to de-sanctify marriage but to honor it and to share it as fulfilling a need of all human beings to find another person with whom to share a life.

Even then religion may properly choose to withhold approval of what are viewed as unholy unions and it is their right to do so. It may help though for those who believe that God's plan for marriage is one man and one woman until death to realize that the laws of the civil order in America do not embrace any particular religious dogma. The civil order does not exist to fulfill all of the needs for law and governance in any society. It is rather a compromise between recalcitrant human nature and the ideal social order set forth by God. The steps to an ideal marital appropriateness and fidelity may need to adapt to the limitations of the existing sexual order.

GLBT people after all do exist and in vast numbers. The question for governing bodies and for the wider electorate then becomes whether within the life experiences of these people, marriage may yield a more socially responsible and integrated outcome for society as a whole than by the present practice of seeing all marriage-like relations within the GLBT community as only meretricious relationships unworthy of any blessing or official secular recognition.

I suggest that pragmatically it may even be salutary at the present time for heterosexual couples to witness the permanence and devotion that is present in many gay and lesbian couples, a fidelity that sometimes exceeds their own heterosexual fidelity when half of all heterosexual marriages break-up in spite of the unifying motivation and reason to stay together that the presence of children provides.

Only with experience after its institution will it be possible to see whether the recognition of gay marriage reduces respect for the very institution of marriage itself as is so often asserted by opponents to its recognition or whether gay and lesbian unions may serve as a new source of stability among gay and lesbian people and a witness of fidelity to the general society. It is possible that social recognition of gay and lesbian unions will lessen the stigma and isolation of gay and lesbian youth, will end their persecution and bullying in our schools, and finally end the practice so prevalent in supposedly Christian families of throwing their children out of the home to swell the population of homeless street children as an example of "tough-love" to cure them of their wicked ways.

It was once thought that to give up burning heretics in Germany would invite complacency on the essential definitions of faith. Even in this country Rhode Island was founded largely to absorb religious dissidents from Massachusetts. Many states are currently engaged in considering the passing of various religious freedom acts. These are virtual acts of secession insofar as they manifest disobedience to a standing decision of the Supreme Court on a question that the majority of judges viewed as involving a question of fundamental liberty. These decisions are not easy to overrule even if the composition of the court changes in the future.

Rather than advocating a return to a theocratic America that has not existed since colonial days a more sophisticated response is called for here. The various Churches should admit their powerlessness to determine national policy in a secular republic. This should not be as difficult as it seems to be or is portrayed as being since in most areas where moral questions are raised the Churches have already acquiesced to the policies of American empire building and militarism and to the power of transnational global corporations in the private sector to govern people's lives by their internal policies. If the same-sex marriage issue reminds people of how distant our world is in most respects from the pilgrim's vision of a Christian society it will have rendered some social good to the republic. The history of theocracy in this country is not a pleasant one. The Pequod Indians were the first Americans introduced to the benefits of theocratic rule. If marriage is indeed the foundation of even civil society then GLBT people would like at last to form personally part of that foundation.

Endgame

During my time of living on the water I have seen many supposedly apocalyptic moments come and go. I have survived Y2K, the Recession of 2008 that has only been temporarily deferred in its economic malignancy like a cancer in recession, and the successive reigns of any number of port commissioners who have made the renting of a hole in the water as complex and oppressive as they can make it. When I moved out onto the water I was seeking a last frontier of freedom. The liberty I thought to find by embracing an unconventional and even desperate mechanism to simplify my existence did not go unnoticed by the forces that insist upon drawing us all into the mortgage-debt-and-regulation world that surrounds us. Only a virtual presence in cyberspace appears for the present to be really free and even there we are assaulted by unsought news items and by various commercial appeals.

The life of rebellion is being gradually reabsorbed into the new life forms of networks. Human life is menaced everywhere. The news speaks of desperate refugees who are seeking asylum and a homeland where some security and order may prevail. I am beginning to see that I am less at the end of an old age than I am already in condition of being swamped by a new one in the 21st century that is now well underway. The pressure of the rising generations is beginning to be felt as they appear in endless succession like waves a mile offshore that grow in height as they approach the shore.

What will not change must perish. Longing for a fantasized life based upon a supposition of eternal youth is folly because memories and the loyalties that memories breed cannot be avoided. As we age the ghosts of our past multiply until they are everywhere around us and the twilight sun however prolonged in delay must finally approach the horizon. A grizzled November light now appears to me to pervade everything. Cherished notions are superseded and the presumptions of yesterday bear the fruit of their miscalculations as we age. The chances to renew and to replenish our exhausted resources are pillaged by time and T.S. Eliot's doorman holds our coat and snickers.

It is at times like these that an underlying essence and identity become valuable simply because these cannot be changed. Transition of any sort seems to imply vulnerability as the separate cells divide. Which cell contains the original protoplasm? As the one gender recedes does a new self arise that will be impervious to this transitory flesh, itself changing under the relentless scalpel of time? Have we transsexuals been attempting to hit a moving target all along and just missed achieving our aim?

Our aim was true but alas the target has been elusive. What woman is has been so corseted and coerced by commercial images that even the coveted double-X folk appear unsure of it themselves. To be an air-brushed trollop is the tropism of the day as long as the pretence of freshness will support suggestive winks and grimaces. Images reflect, embody, and reflect in endless succession at grocery store and make-up counter. So many promises with so little fulfillment make one hunger for the honesty of the maternity ward and the plus-sized stores where the women with tired-feet and longing eyes leave the mall-bunnies to scamper about and pose. The ship to a glorious and pampered existence has long since sailed for me and I will soon be more likely to hear someone say, "Move it granny!" as to hear, "May I help you Madame."

Men have it no better though as twilight nears. Perhaps the loss of power is bitterer than the loss of pulchritude because it is slower to decay. Women at least have each other to help them bewail a woman's lot in life while men must often mourn alone. Maybe that is why barstools are so often warmed by single men afraid to look up from their beer into each other's eyes and see the loneliness and despair written there.

When I moved out onto the water I sought freedom and signif-icance. I found a little of both and was comfortable for a time. I slowed the course of inevitable demise by grasping at an elusive vision. As a gesture it may have been valuable, but such defiance is doomed to fail. My life has been a combination of gestures and a search for the ultimate signifiers of an elusive truth. I do not know what to conclude. Is transsexualism only one more desper-ate gamble to find authenticity? If so it is likely to end as all such bold experiments usually do in a confusion of rival definitions. How finally does one become real in a world where reality itself becomes a mere construct and a shifting one at that? Are gen-itals the ultimate signifier or is beauty in the desired sex role or should mere declaration backed up by law suffice? Convention confers validations that rebellion cannot provide.

Did I live in the best of times after all for a transsexual sim-ply by coveting that ultimate privacy conferred by rejection and alienation? By being a community of one, by believing that I was right because of my own inner imperatives, and meanwhile brooding over my discontents while awaiting vindication I pro-cured my own victory. Has it finally come at last? If so then why am I so skeptical at our common progress? I find myself won-dering whether human life is marred in some essential way when the sexes part company. The discordant notes of heterosexuality may be part of the synapse of humanity as we reach across to each other to find wonder in one who possesses what we do not. Is not anything else a short circuit that reaches its end too soon? Are we not made to take a circuitous course in order to embrace our own limits by leaning on another and to endure our bodies by knowing that another finds attractive in us what we ourselves may disparage or even despise?

As I watch the generations engendered by loins not my own I feel that I have failed to stake a claim on the future through leaving progeny. Surely history would not be so oppressive to me if my loyalty had already shifted to lives that will exceed that poor span allotted to my one single life. As I grow older I tend to forget as much as I remember so that the days that are not freighted with unusual events soon merge into one grey mass of uniformity. Where is that freshness of apprehension or anticipation that I could carry the course of my life in directions chosen by me rather than playing catch up to the new applications of a smart phone as the world is reinvented daily about me?

I have scarcely done justice to the dreams of yesterday before they have been supplanted by some new trend that reveals them in all their vanity and transience. Recently, my evaluations of my life in a transsexual body begin to seem like one of those facades on a movie set that may appear to be three-dimensional but are finally revealed as having no depth. One enters a door only to find that it opens onto the empty grass-strewn stage-lot behind. Without social support and integration it is not possible to maintain a gender identity.

The full price exacted from us by the rejection that transsexuals experience is more than the loss of our political rights; it is moral and emotional exile from the human race. The price exacted of us cannot be made good at once by a belated ordinance, the damage has already been done and it has been paid for in lost time, in absent memories, in caresses foregone, and in that lack of witnesses to our unique history that celibacy has imposed upon many of us. We need children to refract the dying light of our setting sun and turn it to gold. What appear to be arbitrary religious commands may entail a subtle and accurate reading of what is entailed in our nature as human beings. The price of being exceptions must often be born alone. For this and the many other reasons explored in this book I counsel compassion from others and understanding for whatever causes some of us to exist on the outer perimeters of sexual experience and to covet what we do not find confirmed in our own development within a human body.

As we digitalize more and more of human experience so that we live out of direct proximity to others and mediate our experience through machines, the distinctively human and animal dimensions of our lives become more precious. The drama of the body becomes more than merely one other discourse let alone something to be condemned out of bland moral condemnations derived out of context and applied to maim and reject us. Both sides to the debate over transgender rights fail to address the full human dimension of all human variations in experience and to say with Whitman, "Nothing is alien to me for I am part of mankind."

What can be said for religion? To revisit the role of grace and nature is to encounter again the perils of Jansenism; we must presume a degree of latitude in divine judgment that is all too often obviated and dismissed by the human desire for moral certainty. We all too often use a majoritarian calculus to dismiss the witness of the individual. To do so it seems to me is to fail in the deeper dimensions of charity. It is a facile essentialism that can read into perennial human nature the priestly redactions of the Pentateuch addressed to the understanding of a monolithic Jewish audience with cultural needs that we do not share today. The final parameters of revelation would appear to be less certain than what persons who will not tolerate wider interpretive and hermeneutic norms for Scripture are willing to entertain.

Woe to you Lawyers

Yet even saying the above, my doubts remain. The essays that have been included in this book were not written sequentially. The divergences in tone and in the conclusions that I have provisionally reached in them are meant to mirror the anxious search of the author as she has grappled with these issues rather than merely the presentation of an orderly exposition of her finished views. After all much is at stake in these questions. Religion is not merely a cultural construct to be viewed as just one more loyalty among others. Theology and science share the desire to pursue ultimate truths. To this extent these domains are not political in the sense that many other disciplines are.

As a point of contrast, law and jurisprudence are not oriented to the true but rather to what is practical and capable of attainment. Law is an applied science, scientific in its use of induction and deduction, but always tempered by the need to seek a harmony among diverging interests. In this sense the law is always political. Transsexualism is as well. Transsexuals cannot escape the necessity of elbowing their way into various categories in their search for inclusion.

It is impossible to discuss the recent same-sex marriage issue without admitting that more than mere nomenclature is involved. General recognition of same-sex partners to a marriage and the availability of gender-change technology cannot but blur what we mean in our attributions of sexual and gender characteristics. This is bound to cause repercussions. Whole behavioral languages and long established cultural expectations cannot be changed in an instant. There is bound to be resistance but even more threatening is what might be called various emergent phenomena that such a vast and systemic change involving how we structure our personalities and relate to each other will entail.

As a believing Catholic when I find myself arguing as I have done here for positions that favor the LGBT community at the expense of strict orthodoxy this is being done because the opposition is usually so callous and obnoxious that I am disinclined to do otherwise than to support "my people." This is the legacy of my being a part of the Stonewall era of LGBT awareness. We resisted then because our very lives were at stake. Often exiled from our families as we were our only fallback position was to be found in our unity as members of various interlocked communities of exclusion from straight society. There was no fraternizing with the enemy. Religion was used to define us as evil, as threats to decency, as deviant. These memories have left many of us angry and bitter and many of us have had to face a lonely death without the comforts of the Church, feeling that to repent was to deny everything that we had ever suffered at the hands of supposedly decent people whose primary virtue was simply being heterosexual and cis-gendered.

Exile breeds alienation. We were entitled to the same mercy as those who condemned us. Our experience of "family unity" and "family values" left us cynical when the various virtues of male/female sex roles were described for us. We resented male power because those of us who were male-to-female transsexuals found males to have been our bullies and assailants from youth to maturity. They were usually also the ones that killed us in reprisal for having had sexual relations with us. Meanwhile we had transitioned and knew firsthand the real lack of innocence in the female population and the closeness to biology that is entailed by being the bearers of human young. Many of us disparagingly called heterosexuals "breeders" as though simply adding to the human race was to spread some kind of disease. We had often come to despair of family life as just one more big lie, part of American propaganda and a legacy of another era.

Camp sensibility involved ridiculing norms as essentially hypocritical and self-serving. We idolized bitchy women because we envied their power and admired their willingness to be as nasty as we felt them to really be. In all of this there was, at least among the drag queens, a barely suppressed horror at the processes of menstruation, conception, and birth. Whereas the transsexuals among us desired genital surgery, the drag queens held vaginas in horror and repulsion. It was as though women were some sort of pestilential infestation of gay male space. Even drag queens felt somewhat contaminated by their feminine inclinations and constantly reminded each other that "being fishy" was alright but it was all really just drag and not real. Transsexuals were, from this perspective, just trannie-bitches after all and as such not quite right in the head. Street culture is often impoverished, brutalized, and defensive and it was this culture that I came to know as an exile from my suburban youth in squeaky-clean white America. So it was that the study of law came easy to me because it presumed that conflict and self-interest were ubiquitous and that anything could be questioned by the zealous advocate.

What was this but high-class street culture with a British lip-gloss? Lawyer culture combines high-sounding aspirations with massive mistrust of human nature. What is termed "family law" is really the law that deals with various forms of familial fragmentation. So it was that when the same-sex marriage issue was raised it all seemed to me to be much ado about nothing. I shared the view of Dr. Samuel Johnson who stated that marriage was the triumph of hope over experience. Men and women simply did not belong together I had come to feel.

I had come unfortunately to entertain the view that human relations would always remain materially flawed and that marriage was simply the prototype of failed humanity in a vicious and take-no-prisoners world. At least in a same-sex marriage the biggest issues would be who would gain custody of the apartment and the dog or cat. Who cared about marriage anyway since so many people of all sexual orientations just lived-together without wedlock? So what if gay or lesbian couples got married instead of just being domestic partners? This would help transsexuals too; we could marry anybody or just stay married to our old spouse post-transition.

I still believed that marriage was a sacrament of the Church but I had long since despaired that the civil order had anything to do with morality at all. The function of the law was to enable human options, to explore political freedoms not to restrict them. In a world of red and blue states, multi-cultural and relativistic, there simply was no general practical normative morality other than to just leave each other alone. It was the function of law to keep the peace and preserve freedom. After that it was all about power exerted and the ability to resist its use – basically the law of the jungle. Happiness and harmony, let alone anything higher, were just not part of a legal outlook on life. These were relegated to being social exceptions in a brutal and predatory world and nowhere were these vicious relations more to be expected than among religious people, the very people who wanted to kill us and send us all to hell, the ones who supported gun rights, wars, and torture in places like Guantanamo and the various dark sites overseas.

Through all of this I tried to keep my faith in the Church intact and to reserve my resentment for the fundamentalists. At times I have even felt sympathetic to Islam because the evangelicals hated the followers of Mohammed and no Muslim had ever shouted faggot at me or salivated at the thought that those who had died of AIDS were to be found in "the lake of fire."

It is this history of my opinions ones that have been derived from sad experience that should be born in mind by my readers as they peruse much that has been written here. I recall what happiness once felt like and of how clean and beckoning the future once looked for me in my youth. I used to be afraid of being naïve; now I wonder if my desire to escape disillusionment by courting disillusion wasn't a great mistake. The poet W.B. Yeats once said that in the coming age everywhere the ceremony of innocence would be drowned. When I first read these words I did so with sorrow and regret; only later did I realize that they had become the lens through which I had gradually come to view all things.

A Summation of the Case

Lawyers at closing argument attempt to reduce the case in question to a demonstrable central core that will induce the finder-of-fact to render a favorable verdict. The Catholic Church does something similar but not identical when it issues summary statements such as that issued in 2003 dealing with same-sex marriage. That document in essence concludes that marriage is defined by natural law, by Divine decree, and by the common experience of the human race as demanding that marriage be confined to persons of divergent sex (male and female). The Church states that any attempt to extend "marriage" by what it terms "a false analogy" to same-sex couples is to elevate a moral disorder into a socially sanctioned and approved institution.

This in turn will have two disastrous consequences: first it will increase the likelihood that same-sex relations will occur and that what should be seen as individual acts of aberration will be transformed into a permanent disposition to commit such acts; second it will undermine and blur the distinction between the sexes which is an absolute prerequisite for a fully human use of the sexual faculty by at least potentially creating new life through "sexual complementarity" and by nurturing the institution of the family that will bring that new life to maturity and in doing so sustain the human race.

It is further stated that the common good is the proper end of all laws that are grounded in objective truth. This means that same-sex unions are invalid per se and that any attempt to recognize or sanction them is both beyond the power of the laws and is in addition a betrayal of the duty of the lawmaker to advance the public good of promoting good and avoiding evil. Lastly, it is stated that children have a natural law right to be raised in a family with two parents of different sex and that to deprive them of this right by recognizing same-sex unions as analogous to families is to undermine the social order and to fail to meet the legitimate needs of the child.

Although unstated in the document in question there is a necessary corollary that to change one's sexual identity signifiers is in essence to speak in a foreign tongue and to beckon where refusal is the only option. To make oneself attractive as a female when one has been formed by nature to inhabit a male body is to invite what can neither be assented to in good conscience nor acquiesced in by any male who responds to the outer assumption of a female aspect manifested by one who is irretrievably male. Similarly, the female-to-male transsexual is impliedly offering wares that he is not licensed to convey by nature. Although celibacy may prevent any actual conclusion of the sexual transaction it cannot prevent the existence of a contradiction in terms of the gender presentation. As such to be transsexual is frustrating for all parties; it is a fruitless endeavor and to that extent an objective moral evil in its own right, an overreaching of technology into the human realm as limited by natural law.

In our present world of "narratives" and "discourses," of "textual rules of interpretation and hermeneutics," this type of document does not tend to be well-received. If nothing else it seems to be an unpardonable intrusion upon the right of the individual to self-determine the course of his/her life and of the democratic nation-state to allow for our self-will within the pragmatic search for social order and tolerance. But there it is. To be a Catholic is to be willing submit to the discipline of faith as taught by the authoritative voice of the teaching Magisterium of the Bishops in communion with the Pope. As such a Catholic cannot dissent in good conscience but must in the final analysis consent and act in accordance with that consent to advance the good and to minimize any evils that will ensue from positions that have been defined as false in the world that we currently inhabit.

What this means for me personally is that in order to publish this book in good conscience I must conclude that on balance an airing of my own doubts and emotions and the partial unveiling of the course of my life will on balance do more good than evil and serve the end of explaining the many discontents that attend the transsexual condition the better to breed sympathy for those who struggle with these issues while in no way condoning or advancing homosexual relations or attempts to rationalize the potentially self-destructive effects of gender altering procedures in opposition to Church teaching. This has not been an easy task for me and even now I doubt whether I have succeeded. As an attorney I was trained to believe that the shortest path to reconciliation is to fully air grievances. In any case I must state clearly here that I consent to be bound by the teachings of the Church as stated above. This is an inner precondition for my act in publishing this book at all. My readers must bear this in mind as they read this book and reach their own positions as to its contents.

Though I have struggled with many aspects of Church teaching in my life and as expressed in some of these essays and at times been dismayed at the stern and inflexible tone that pervades many official Church documents on morality, I possess a hierarchy of commitments and as long as the Church retains its place in my loyalty I cannot in conscience oppose its teachings formally but must rather seek to reconcile the experience of a chaotic world with a view of truth that is not the fruit of public opinion, sample polls, or even current mores. I therefore desire that this essay be incorporated by reference as an addendum to any essay that has been included in this volume in order to balance my dissent with submission when a higher duty demands it.

Where does this leave persons like me who feel similarly sexually stranded? What is to become of those who have felt strong urges to adapt to or to embody femaleness in order to confirm our identities, ones that do not conform to what nature has apparently so indelibly inscribed? This book was written to express how problematic it has been for me to be a male with a female overleaf or a female with a male overleaf. This involuntary disposition alters and distorts every dimension of our lives as transsexuals. My desire in writing this book has been to find in doing so some degree of personal stability and to create an outside manifestation for my conflicting views the better to understand them myself, but simultaneously to retain my own peace of mind by not, for all of my gifts of persuasion, leading anyone astray.

I have endeavored above all to reveal and to unmask the latent complacency that mistakes being fortunate in one's own gender congruity as a cis-sexual for being virtuous. There is plenty of ground in human nature for accusations all around by those who prefer to take an adversarial stance towards others. God meanwhile seems to exercise a preferential option for mercy prior to imposing justice. True virtue seems always able to shift for itself with its clear eyes and its firm voice. I doubt that the world has ever been made better by exercising moral umbrage at the faults of others or by inquisitions directed outwards rather than by humbling ourselves and seeking to bear the condemnation that others may deserve but that we are willing to bear for them instead. This seems the way of love and the better path to embrace in all things while leaving the rest to God.

In our age of sound-bites and polarized opinion in virtually every arena the search for certainty or at least for a way to subdue our opponents has never been greater. Political conflict has become a way of life. At the same time we are making some progress in civility and in refraining from killing our opponents as in the mass slaughters of the 20th century. I would like to point out that only in Euclidean Geometry can it be asserted that parallel lines never meet. Today in many instances there is a sense that we live in a spherical realm wherein any line that is extended far enough will end up joining its point of origin eventually. Once we have traveled about the sphere of our limited experience that encases us often enough new insights will sooner or later emerge.

Unity is menaced though by premature dislocations. Never has humankind proposed vaster schemes to break down all of the old categories and never have those categories threatened with greater urgency to coalesce back into the place from whence they came. Human origins are lost in the manifold myths of various cultures and the future seemingly without a goal. Definitions tend to melt and collapse in upon each other like the walls of a ruined abbey. Before long everything becomes a mere mode of operation or a discourse among discourses. What I am today may be something else tomorrow. Once dispose of an infinite and transcendent source as both the origin and the goal of human life and everything tends to become self-defining yet simultaneously self-defeating. My solution is to show both sides of the equation by outlining opposing positions. What I am proposing is that it is precisely books such as this one that attempt to do the impossible by reconciling extremes in lived experience that cultural healing may occur. It is worth taking the chance.

The summit of all of my discontents is the recognition that in many ways I am a shattered person today, one who is so divergent in my feelings and aspirations toward gender questions that virtually nothing that I can ever say on this subject is without so many massive qualifications and codicils that its final meaning may not be deciphered. Part of having lived what I call "a derivative existence" is that my personal borders have been crossed and violated repeatedly until my sole abiding emotion is one of terminal disgust at the entire human condition. The current national media involvement in what had heretofore been only our small and uniquely perplexing and troublesome condition as transsexuals is not good news for the transgender community.

I do not enjoy being castigated by various Catholic bishops and protestant evangelicals as though whatever questions we may pose as cultural revenants is a vast threat to the social order or a major dislocating force to the divine plan. When various people of religion appear to take greater note of the threat to morals that is supposedly posed by accepting trans-children who identify as female into the girl scouts than they do of the future famines that may result from global warming or the present state of a nuclear armed world I am astonished and embarrassed for them. But I am no less pleased to see transsexuals becoming the new template for our cultural obsession with female beauty. Legitimacy has never been so reducible to the amount and type of surgical intervention that any given transsexual can afford than in these past two years. The result has been a backlash against precisely those transsexuals who fail to meet this new gold-standard of femininity – the so-called men in dresses.

The murder rate of transsexual victims is up and I believe this is because various malcontents are looking for us. There is a price for drawing the ire of people through greater media exposure who might otherwise have ignored us. The condition of women of all types is not enviable. A little time spent on the internet will reveal the global condition of women: female circumcision also termed female genital mutilation, child-brides, honor killings, and the multiple media means of exploiting the human body as an artifact are appalling and raise more questions than anyone seems to be answering. Sexuality seems to be what I would call a disproportionate problematic for all cultures perhaps because it is overlaid with power and status questions. By reducing half of the human race to a mere commodity status various markets emerge, from fashion modeling and reality TV shows at the high end to prostitution on the low end, but always along the parameter of embodiment as woman or as a man.

The difference in sex stereotyping is that woman is viewed as an analogous life form rather than as strictly human. Her humanity is viewed as an overlay to her primary status, one that is never severable from her sexuality. An entire spectrum of considerations is applied to her daily freedom to act as she wishes without triggering various meanings that have nothing to do with her as an individual but only with her generic status as a woman. She will be parsed, refined, categorized, rated, contained, and curtailed by a final report that will factor into consideration her youth, her beauty, child-bearing capacity, and how readily she may be confined to whatever religious/cultural norms are prevalent in her environment so as to reach some sort of nominal market value that will be used to assign her an overall place in society.

By thus making of woman something that is at once more and less than human the male world is similarly distorted. Expectations and presumptions of what a male should feel and manifest in order to avoid drifting too near to the feminine are every bit as strenuously enforced if not more rigid than the standards that are applied to women. All of these considerations make the transsexual life-course doubly stressful simply because to the essentialist mind transition is not possible. This means that transsexuals are viewed all too often as either counterfeit members of the reassigned sex or even if viewed as legitimate as flawed simply by making the choice to transition at all. This is particularly true for transsexuals who are transitioning out of a male identity towards one that is female.

Who would ever covet joining the ranks of the oppressed and marginalized? A review of the beauties of yesteryear will reveal how swiftly nature withdraws the superabundance of its graces to a young woman. How uneven and cruel is a gift that descends unasked for and is withdrawn all too soon and without any cause other than time's passing! The cultural ignorance regarding the human price exacted by our various certainties appears to be universal. As an example of the sources of these emotions and the effect that they produce within me I will simply highlight some recent news items and attempt to show that they manifest a common pattern.

There is much evidence that a major economic collapse or dislocation lies ahead for our consumer culture and our debt-based nation. Quite frankly, I am afraid that the resultant decline in our collective standard of living will set us at each other's throats. A recent study found that Wyoming leads the nation in registered firearms followed by the District of Columbia as measured by number of firearms per every thousand citizens. Virginia, Maryland, and Pennsylvania were also high on the list all of them regions surrounding or within the nation's capital. That Arkansas, Alabama, Idaho, and other conservative states are also placed high on the list should surprise no one of course. What displeased me most was that many of the accompanying pictures showed parents teaching their children to love guns. As a transgender person, part of a community that has known its share of violence, this mythos of America that couples guns, "family values," hatred for GLBT people, so-called "religious freedom" legislation (that really merely provides a license to discriminate in providing basic services), and the peculiar brand of religiosity that runs rampant in America, all collectively appall me to the extent that I simply cannot read the news without becoming depressed.

In many respects my mind and heart are as delicate and subject to harm as a Swiss timepiece. Throw grit in the gears and see what happens! Not the least part of this grit lately is the omnipresence of the female body in various media. It may seem the height of contradiction for a transsexual to claim that the female body can awaken a sense of horror and loathing in me. There seems to be something predatory in the urge to procreate that recalls all of the maledictions regarding the will made by the philosopher Arthur Schopenhauer. Recently I read that one of the functions of the female orgasm is to engulf sperm through the means of rhythmic cervical contractions. As an evolutionary adaptation this may make sense but the image implies a sort of amoebic reactivity of the genitalia that seems scarcely human. The function of the male as a mere adjunct to the procreative imperative is often far more reductive than that assigned to the female, but both sexes alike suffer from this primal exposure as being needy and incomplete and subject to sexual shaming.

It seems the height of temerity to deplore human sexuality and relationships until it is recalled that we step all over each other in our struggle to survive and to prosper. What are our dreams but fantasies of an ever-elusive integrity and fulfillment? The adage to do no harm seems best fulfilled to me by not imposing oneself upon others in any way. To speak at all is to interrupt and impose upon the basal hum of vast collectives our one unicellular presence. Nor does this process cease with our own deaths. We leave our offspring maimed by our own inherited conflicts. Each generation leaves behind its sad contribution to the waste and residue of events. Youth is burdened by debts not of their making. The vast grist-mill of insult and reaction feeds the wars and tills the fields with corpses. Perpetual regret should be the anthem of our age. The ashes from bombed Hiroshima are still falling all about us. They were falling before I was ever born.

Seen from this perspective the transsexual solution might be seen as a way of short-circuiting the sexual impulse by seeking an intermediate zone between the sexes to inhabit so as to oppose the march of the organic. Similarly, the rejection of family role playing is an ideal solution for someone who finds the demanding social back-drop of heterosexual expectations to lead to that very American mythos described above: one that is violent, property-based, and sustained by the primal command to be fruitful and multiply. The jaundiced view of human life was once more common in ages past that hoped less of futurity because the prospect of death was always near. To honor life once it is conceived is not to deny that the importunities of sex often drag us about like a chained beast. The family is as often as not a source of ills as a remedy for them. As we think to have mastered human life by technical means we have lost a proper sense of the tragic and the unseemly in human affairs.

Everywhere we are assaulted by gendered and sexual images. Even the recent panoply of transgender images in the media seems to partake of this same reductive carnality; beauty as iconography. Human sexuality rather than being tender and open to wider expressions of cultural life seems to me to be nothing more than an imposed burden that is personally distasteful and ecologically unsound. As a result I find that my early affection for the grim and stark images found in the poetry of Robinson Jeffers reveals a profoundly deep thread in my own nature. I would far rather distance myself from the present struggles that I see everywhere manifest than to endure them.

I believe that the damage done to me sexually is now well-nigh irreparable. I desire at times through a sense of pride alone to exceed the demands of chastity that my religion espouses and proclaims. I have passed over into an anger and bitterness toward sex itself. My abiding attitude is one that despises and rejects any sort of desire within me for intimacy: male or female, gay or straight. Sex and the relationships that it engenders have always seemed to me to be a trap for the unwary and a diminishment to

374

human freedom. As my stake in the future is not to be represented by posterity any lamentation that I may make is motivated only by sorrow that history is taking the course that it seems to be taking. That course is as momentous as the possibility of nuclear war and as trivial as today's politics and entertainment.

The fact that various "bathroom bills" are sprouting up in many states like mushrooms merely adds to my current disgust. The presence of transsexualism in public discourse is massively out of proportion to our numbers or the threat that we supposedly pose, as though Islamic terrorism and transsexualism were the real causes of the endemic hysteria present in this election year of 2016. It cannot be otherwise than alarming to see the signs of the times that are so clearly present in our national angst. I realize that to personalize history might be taken as the first sign of megalomania but the tremors of various social earthquakes are often first felt by the poets and artists among us and those who exist in a delicately poised personal balance. Proximity can be anguishing to one like me who seeks to elude all categories. I can find comfort neither in the past of my childhood in another America nor in the supposed progress that waves before my kind the chimera of acceptance. I feel that we transsexuals are merely totem animals, a current fad that will soon pass.

Our old opponents exist just beyond the circle of firelight with grim and glittering eyes ready to pounce. America has yet to be really civilized and the various world fundamentalisms are weighed with a heavy hand against us as well. Domestically we have not proceeded as far as we think from the days of the Salem witch trials. We are still a Puritan-ridden nation for all of our promiscuous proclivities. The comedy of our electoral pretensions is based as much upon a comparative theatrics of our national myths and delusions as it is a time for a substantive exploration of national policy alternatives. This realization only augments my sense of weariness and disgust. I would like to run somewhere to find a better time or civilization on our ever-crowding planet, but where, when, and how is this to be done?

The world seems to me increasingly to resemble an ever-expanding strip-mall. I am afraid that the culture of the globalized world resembles nothing more than the burned-out residue of the rich panoply of the formerly insular and discrete human communities that are required for any human culture to form. It takes borders and limits in order to frame excellence through concentration and containment. A culture of mere mercantile exchange and a science of various quarks, strange or not, do not give the human spirit sufficient grounding.

A true empiricism must be more than mathematic in nature; it must involve our human senses exercised in a human manner. We are more than mere appendages to various devices, surgical or media-related. But we seem to be drowning in various data streams ... as the knowable increases its significance and our own diminishes. It may be that my current state of being in reaction against what any retrospect of my life reveals is the product of what psychologists term a reaction formation, a psychological defense that is mobilized to shore up the walls of identity by proclaiming the opposite of what I really believe.

The uneasy alliance between the transsexual adolescent within me and the male adult role that I was raised to adopt and master may be breaking down as the time and prospect to attain comfort in either role diminish. My various mythologies of a unified self are breaking down around me and within me. My feelings are a sort of global nausea and alienation with all that surrounds us in this present era.

This gradual but insistent breaking down of concepts and images may be best summed up by a poem written by John Clare, who was one of the minor English Romantic Poets. I think that my present quiet sorrow and desperation is akin to the feelings that he has expressed so well:

I Am
by John Clare
an 18th century English romantic poet

I AM: yet what I am none cares or knows,
My friends forsake me like a memory lost;
I am the self-consumer of my woes,
They rise and vanish in oblivious host,
Like shades in love and death's oblivion lost;
And yet I am, and live with shadows tost

Into the nothingness of scorn and noise,
Into the living sea of waking dreams,
Where there is neither sense of life nor joys,
But the vast shipwreck of my life's esteems;
And even the dearest—that I loved the best—
Are strange—nay, rather stranger than the rest.

I long for scenes where man has never trod;
A place where woman never smiled or wept;
There to abide with my Creator, God,
And sleep as I in childhood sweetly slept:
Untroubling and untroubled where I lie;
The grass below—above the vaulted sky.

A Handful of Sand

In law it is called having a vested interest, one that is not contingent upon the happening of some condition precedent. We all assume that we have a part in time, that our lives have vested and we would consider it an injustice for someone to say to us that what we really possess is more like a leasehold interest rather than a fee simple absolute. Behind us unobserved the tides of reproduction have created a current of new experience that with each year flows higher about our feet.

One day we look up and realize that the waters have been rising for some time and that what we presumed to be our own eternal youth was a delusion that we stand exposed upon a sandy promontory, one that has been cut off from the mainland. It is then that we realize that we are being pushed backwards towards those waters of the past that have consumed countless generations before us. The face that we see each day in the mirror would once have been a stranger's face to us just as we do not recognize ourselves now in the callow and untried visage of our old yearbook photographs.

As our mind grows in subtlety and resource with age our bodies begin to fail us. Some of those whom we once knew have already born their unique witness to existence and passed on. Far from being examples of some premature tragedy their deaths meet the actuarial expectations on a chart in some dusty life-insurance office. The parade of hopeful youthful countenances is in fact as unending as the tidal flow on the beach that I am recalling as I write these words.

I can see the promontory in my mind and hear the windy beating of the late afternoon surf. The sun is falling swiftly and I can feel that strange pull that evening light always seems to impose upon me when I am there. In the past I would feel within me a fire, one akin to that lemon-colored sun resting on the horizon, and feel a confidence in all the dawns that still awaited me. I would count over the inventory of my future years and skip away to a beach fire along the shore, a beacon brave against the winds of night. Today I am not so sure. A fashionable poetic angst has yielded to a sense of the fragmentary and the incomplete.

Yet I am one of the lucky ones. I was born in a country with at least a veneer of culture and civilization and to a generation that sparkled under Technicolor dreams. I have had the leisure to record both events and my reflections upon them. Still there is a deep sadness within me. So it is that I bend forward in my mind and reach out my hand. Here before me is this record of my past like sand without an hourglass to contain it. Even the land where I stand now may retreat again beneath sea from whence it arose.

Suddenly my life that once seemed so infinite is dwarfed into the size of one of these minuscule grains of sand now falling from my fingers until my hand is empty. This flesh of mine is naked to the night and the wind and salt spray that comes on with the swift summer darkness. Words that once seemed so immortal become finally like the brave assault of waves upon these headland cliffs. Ideas and controversies seem suspended as they always are over the vast unanswered question of eternity and whether I shall play a part within it. It is at times like these that I long for a home that I have never found and a personal cohesion that was always just beyond my reach. As the sun nears the horizon I think of how this scene has always been my symbol for human existence and recall that I have always been fighting against this very tide. My voice is not so different after all from that of all who have preceded me and from all who will follow.

But the virtues of impersonality may be overrated. It is something after all to be just one more frail pulse along the coast this night. I take my life and cradle it to my breast and thank God to have been alive and for the privilege to take my chances on being reconstituted in some form that will still preserve some memory of me when the final and most real dawn breaks upon the earth. Until then I am working at being able to surrender my place gracefully at this moveable feast of a world (as Hemingway said of his sojourn in Paris).

My long acquaintance with the words of the poets will ease the final passage and my own words left behind will bear some witness that when I join the tiny creatures at my feet that there was really more to me after all than a mere handful of sand.

Did you ask if there was a time
when I was not discontented?

The short answer is no. I began life with a presumption that the ideal was attainable. Even now I have a bias towards the classics. I believe that a human and dignified life should be and can be pursued. Yet I realize that the tragic and the squalid are human constants and may serve as a salutary corrective to human pride, but there are also those blessed moments of exaltation when human beings shine out in beauty or in glory. Even my transsexualism was based upon the sense that the female form at its best is a wonder of design and realization. In comparison the male form is rather like a high-rise with steel beams rusting in the rain before completion. I have been happiest when I thought that I looked lovely as a girl. But I have also been happy when feeling noble or strong as when riding a motorcycle on a summer day through Oregon or skiing and feeling the water carved by the ski. I like shaking a fist at my fears or seeing form emerge in a composition. But even above all forms of realized happiness was my sense of hope that I could influence events in a positive direction – to do the good.

The good, the true, the beautiful - are these not the ends in some shape or form for all human activities insofar as we are in fact human and not mere animals? If I have a quarrel with the present times it is because they read like a novel by Theodore Dreiser – long, boring, and about tacky people. Too much direct lighting always shows the flaws. What do you do when everything leaves you feeling vaguely ashamed and in need of a long bath? Maybe if I just go away for awhile everything will just sort itself out.

So dreaming of contentment I have nevertheless ended up discontented. Well, I would remind you that I am of the generation of the sixties that sought to revalue the values of their elders, the generation that was later forged in the crucible of the duplicity and squalor of our involvement in Viet Nam. I have spent much time in pursuit of excellence and elegance in the arts and in the intricacy of legal study. I have loved travel and a natural existence close to the elemental facts of life. I have valued personal love as well, but only found it in a passing glimpse here and there.

Like Blanche Du Bois I have depended much upon the kindness of strangers. Perhaps they see in me alternately a person of great strength and glaring weaknesses. I am not soon forgotten by anyone who knows me but maybe that is because it is hard to forget a royal pain in the ass. I tend to ask for what I want and usually get the goddess treatment that I demand or manage to cajole out of others. I am withal a gentle despot and generally well intentioned. Yet I have imposed this book upon my readers. Do I ask too much?

The arrogance of composition always demands at least some confidence that others will find something of value in our individual experience. Discontents though always seem to savor too much of self-indulgence. Simply to be alive demands some gratitude. The discontents of being transsexual may have as much to do with my general personality as with the condition of transsexualism itself. Who can say what a typical transsexual is like? I may just be the exception that proves the rule. You decide.

Of Bells, Books, and Candles

Who does not dream of magic powers when more usual remedies for discontents are not at hand? During the years when I was being bullied I imagined that a few deftly cast spells might come in handy. Siren beauty for instance might have protected me from playground scorn. To flash a jeweled navel or white teeth revealed behind a coy and knowing smile is to know power.

Of course I didn't set out to become a real-life witch and I'm not really one now. My brief flirtation with naturalistic religion was simply the result of a desire to escape the historical legacy that most revealed religions tend to drag along behind them as part of the burden of history. There is always something appealing about simply celebrating the eternal renewal of the seasons and thinking positive thoughts and calling them spells. It is also rather nice to be personally vaguely spooky and mysterious and to practice a woman-centered cult. Animism may be primitive but it does take respect for life and nature further than religions that despise our present life and hold out the hope of something better at the price of disparaging what we currently know and are. There is also something neatly individual about a religion that lets each practitioner assemble her own collection of sacred objects and to weave about them her own web so as to provide comfort and support. But since the real function of religion is universal communion and a bridge across our own mortality I still remain a Roman Catholic and always shall so remain.

My brief flirtation with the cult of Diana drew a careful line between art and artifice and an actual creed. What I really wanted from "the craft" was to become like Kim Novak in "Bell Book, and Candle," or at least to resemble her longtime fan, Candy Darling. When the series, "Bewitched," was on the air I used to dream about being able to merely twitch my nose like Elizabeth Montgomery in order to get what I wanted. My first official act of course would be to find someone more exciting to be married to than the stodgy Darin Stevens and my second would have been to change Larry Tate into a toad, along with many of the bullies I encountered at school. There is nothing sexier than a pretty witch. She has the two forms of magic that every woman wants, her looks and the omni-competence of magic. People are both drawn to her and just a little afraid.

Good! A witch has behind her more than her Grimiore of course. She is part of the tides of the sea and the moon that causes them. Her breasts are the twin orbs that govern the earth. Her secret fertility is that of the world. Is it strange then that I wanted part of this, beginning with the secret budding forth of a body that could read my heart's desire? Now that I am leaving behind my years of being a glamour girl and am more likely to metamorphose into Margaret Hamilton than Kim Novak I am looking in vain for that magic secret of sustaining youth and though I am not Maleficent I am not Sleeping Beauty either. So it is that I long to merge with something greater than myself and to set aside the long and vain struggle for identity.

There are times lately when I long for a generic sense of the human where the sexes can communicate without roles or the barriers imposed by having a body. I find in the written word that very universal that was my comfort in my youth when I could escape into a book and forget for a time my own existence. Perhaps I was on to something then which may help me deal with my aging transsexual body. The worst part of aging for those of us who seem still stranded and dealing with adolescent or young adult issues late into middle-age is that as the available time ahead grows shorter it becomes impossible to assemble a viable life history. Where for me are the marriage and the children? Where the career? Where the life of fulfilled and gender-congruent sexual experience? Many of us emerge at last with an intact body only to find that much of the parade of life has already passed us by. It is at times when I feel this most acutely that I imagine myself as one of the sacred ones, one of the fair-folk, a belated pixie casting my spells on young and old alike, so that like Elwin Dodd in Mary Chase's wonderful play, "Harvey," people see me coming and smile because I'm something special, neither pooka nor witch, but still something special in this dull and dreary world.

For a life like mine
some further assembly may be required

It is my private belief that cross-gender identification is not a univocal phenomenon but rather a spectrum. For early onset cross-gender identification there is probably a clear physical cause in brain morphology or the ability of genes to be activated by the sex hormones. For late in life transitions on the other hand I believe that certain learning factors and traumas may play a role in alienating the person from their assigned gender and making gender-transition a preferred path to adapt to life. I believe that many members of the transgender community may suffer from Borderline Personality Disorder but whether this underlying syndrome is a cause or an effect of the frustration of their gender conflicts I cannot say. What I can say though is that any BPD symptoms must be addressed at some point in the transition process if their gender-transition is to be successful.

A human body is not a mere accoutrement of our humanity but an integral constituent of our being-in-the-world. It would trivialize our quest to attain personal unity to pretend that the sexes are completely interchangeable socially or physically. Our animal roots are not mere functions of politics or of culture; the gender-identity that we feel within us transcends our unique personalities and invite us to play our part in life's succession and to find in another what we do not possess in ourselves alone. Family, community, and other affinity groups are more than mere matters of declaration. They must resonate at a level that is rooted in our animal nature.

Mere willfulness cannot determine those semi-instinctual aspects of our nature that need no laws to compel or laws to forbid. Our intellects do not make us immune from the emotions or the passions that play no small part in our total humanity. It is an impermissible reduction of our dignity to ignore the debt we owe to past generations and culture and the link that we are to the future of the human race. LGBT people prior to the recent legal recognition of same-sex marriage have been largely self-defining and have existed primarily as members of a tribe most visibly represented in various urban ghettos. It may be that this period in our history or herstory is now coming to an end. Going with the mainstream now may entail an encounter with the limits of all humanly imposed definitions. To enter into the common march of humanity by marrying may be to encounter as many limitations as liberations. From the hot New York summer of 1969 at Stonewall to the Supreme Court decision of the summer of 2015 has been a long journey in terms of our experience but a short one in time. In less than half a century a diverse group of people drawn from every sector of society has broadened the realm of human experience and redefined their status from one of moral condemnation and criminalization to one of Constitutional protection.

Even the demographics of religion no longer line up staunchly behind traditional Church teaching. This divergence creates crises of loyalty and problems in catechesis that the Bishops of the Church must now resolve or at least address in more than the summary fashion that has been the preferred mode of that discourse in the past. Various new stress points are emerging at the same time that the present rainbow consensus has made much of the prior oppression that has been mentioned in this book and gained as a result public sympathy and support.

Still, many adamantly deplore the present trend. Category crises occur when institutional understandings diverge from praxis or when long latent conflicts emerge into the open. The testimony of time is that no idea is ever submerged. Certain issues persist in the human debate as to our nature and destiny. This book is by its very nature an exercise in indeterminacy. Philosophy grants a continued license of debate to opposing positions so that truth may hopefully emerge more clearly out of the conflict. Combativeness is an occupational hazard of philosophers and lawyers. It becomes a habit of mind for those who wander onto a ground littered with the past errors that collectively define the borders of what is true and lasting.

If my readers will bear this in mind they will withhold premature assent to anything that I have said in this book. I assure them that it has been more troubling for me to write than it may ever be to be read. The time has come to leave you now with this convoluted testimony to my transsexual life, one that may be more personal than it is representative. It may represent a period more than a group and perhaps not even that but only my sole and solitary life. Turn about and turn about, which face do I show to the world?

So here I am for better or for worse (hopefully better). I am still looking for a way back onto the great interstate highway of life after spending most of my days and nights bouncing along the rutted blue highways that take transsexuals to strange and out of the way destinations. I think often of what heroism or sainthood would look like when our vanity and our ego needs would just melt away and the joys and sorrows of all people could substitute for my own lonely search for happiness. Maybe all of the distinctions that we make between persons are like the thin membranes that separate the cells within the human body. We are all of us really all connected and part of a larger destiny than anything that we may ever imagine.

I often wonder about these times that we are living through today. Can so much opposition between mutually exclusive positions not eventually cause what such hatred has so often caused before in history, some dreadful bloodbath of the nations, some meltdown made possible by the constantly opposing rhetoric of each mini-community seeking vainly for some elusive absolute?

It is at such times that the marginal ones must play their unique role, those who keep unquiet slumbers in the dead of night. These know what it is like to feel the cold, biting like foxes at their ankles. They have walked the lonely boulevards and seen yesterday's notices tacked up on telephone poles or in the windows of abandoned buildings. These disconsolate ones know what only poetry and sad songs can ever convey. Maybe they keep an old Vogue cover of the model Gia Carangi as a token of a bygone era and wonder why beauty alone is so often not enough to yield happiness to its possessor. They remember how still the room is after someone dies. Blunted lipsticks must often tell the story of a life. That was the year when I bought the shade called Saturday Night Red. History is just facts; it is poetry that really tells our stories. Nobody can really sum us up, only ourselves by confessing, not just the bad but the good things that may have been so long forgotten.

Where are the feelings that surface only for a moment and are gone? How do we bring back who we once were and find again what we might have been but for our mistakes? What is the function of the individual when so much is collective? Fragments, fragments... But these alone are life solid, discrete, and personal. The world has suffered too long from grand gestures and big plans. I have great hopes now for insignificance because it asks so little and therefore is open to surprises. Whenever I think of God I wonder whether in the light of the certainty of those who claim to know His mind He is not really saying, "That's not what I meant at all. Just care for each other. Seek a common ground."

Are transsexuals a part of the connective tissue that reminds us all that even our most fundamental differences are not as great as we assume they are? What do people finally see when they look at us? Are we only a screen for the projections of what they feel as men and as women about themselves? Are we some sort of universal human solvent that dissolves and merges into form the ragged edges of human incompleteness? Are we a clear epoxy-resin to glue the sexes together into a single body? Are we creatures of industrial realism or only a single universal type of the androgynous figure that I once saw reclining in the Louvre in Paris?

Has this book been a contribution as intended towards a unified field theory of human sexuality or has it finally been only the fragments of a broken mirror? I could keep writing on and on and even then I might find that the circle that seems so complete only joins its point of origin in the doubtful child who I once was (and perhaps still am) to this present me. Is a book only complete when someone says, "Stop, it's there; you might say it differently or find a new constellation of meanings but you have to finally steer one final course because time is passing swiftly and there are other books to write."

Oh for a text that would allow itself to be re-written as new insights come but like an old LP album it holds only yesterday's songs and to even play them now is to hear all of the scratches of my repeated plays through the years. So I place in your hands this improvised sketch of my thoughts and my life and what is was like for a transsexual before the advent of hormone blockers and before the coming of our fragmentary civil rights. It was a time when talk-show hosts specialized in using transsexual targets to boost their television ratings, when transsexuals showed up regularly portrayed as hookers on police-themed television shows, and when besides these sensational venues few people wondered about the everyday lives of the transsexuals who lived among them.

Even today we are not beyond the occasional media feeding frenzies staged at our expense. There must certainly be conditions that are more disruptive of society than merely feeling conflicted about our gender, conditions that cause real harm and manifest real malice. Why then are we still burdened by such irate condemnations as though transsexualism posed a general threat to an already unstable social order rather than being a source of unparalleled personal trauma and unhappiness?

I have written here of the times when I lived my life as a transsexual, the only life that I will ever have. It was a time when it cost me more to be transsexual than I probably will ever earn. It was a bitter time but also one lived among extraordinary people, many of whom are now dead. I got to witness history as the human race labored to define its fundamentals in what has proved to be all too often uncaring ways. I made it through while many others didn't. I am a surviving transsexual but one who is still uncompleted as most of us human beings are. We try to excavate and sculpt a self from the quarry of possibilities and decisions that we encounter daily.

I am always curious about what the next page of life will reveal and I am still pursuing the grand synthesis whatever that may be. I'm not sure when I will finally arrive at a complete sense of self. Maybe those outside of us that simply see us as shadows dimming the light of their own self-concern have it right. We transsexuals are like ghosts haunting our own bodies, the very bodies that we know are transit zones for energy exchange the very substance of which is always altering. What do we have that is permanent? What after all is the remainder in the crucible of experience when we are reduced to the elemental us?

I do not think that transsexuals are the aliens that we are so often made out to be. Our quest is akin to text that goes off the page, just drag the cursor down and we find that the text is still there. So is that what gender reassignment is, the equivalent of cut and paste? Or are we like the paper dolls that existed when I was a child with primitive male and female templates and with everything else as just accessories? Those who deny our reality go rushing about with cotton mouth-swabs looking for our DNA or they strip-search us and look for our genitals. Some size us up and if they find us sexually attractive enough they are willing to grant us a free-pass for the day to enter the human amusement park. To still others each of us was imprinted at birth by an indelible designation and a little tag: THIS IS A MALE; REMOVAL OF THIS TAG IS AN OFFENSE PUNISHABLE BY LAW! By what source or sanction without our prior consent is this conformity so enforceable? Perhaps we are all punished by many of the discontents that I have tried to include in this book and many more that I haven't thought about or included here. There are if nothing else the interiorized ideals of maleness or of femaleness that we see, not only present within ourselves, but working in the other lives that surround us. Age leaves a vast residue like debris from a withdrawing glacier behind us.

How do we escape this personal history and construct or have constructed a body that will pass muster in this world? The tides of my life are already flowing swiftly out to sea and the magazines with their various sculpted testimony to female beauty and fertility both beckon and accuse male-to-female transsexuals by denying us admittance except on the terms of the post-menopausal lassitude and invisibility that is a common experience for aging women in our society. Even technical means of stripping away the testimony of time cannot restore a history that never was. Transsexuals must face metaphysical dilemmas that no mere therapist or surgeon may ever bridge. Who are we? What are we? How much affirmation can suffice to convince us that all has gone well in our transition and that we have finally arrived to stand proudly and justifiably waiting for our pedicure or salon styling with the other women?

The legacy of female disappointment is legion. Our materialistic society has its own versions of the expectation that the wife will immolate herself upon her husband's funeral pyre. Woman as commodity or as Sex Goddess is still functionalized and her parts are turned into the iconography of various bulges and curves, mere exercises in the geometry of fertility, the illusion of youth, and the promise of infinite golden tomorrows.

If I had to write an autobiography there are lots of things that I would rather have discussed than Transsexualism. I would have liked to speak about literature, art, music, or nature all of which I love or about why for all of the adamantine grittiness of its history I still feel such a sense of peace when I sit in the local parish church at night before the candles that never seem to go out before the figure of the Virgin Mary. The flickering red altar-candle reminds me that God is there. Perhaps if I had simply allowed life to have its way with me my body would have fulfilled its function and spread one more circle of life in the expanding rings of history. I know that a time is coming when I will be dispersed to the winds.

No visitor to the catacombs will ask why beneath this smiling skull and ribcage there are two little silicone pillows with the manufacturer's emblem still legible. They will lay me out in black silk dress like Mortisha Addams or worse some young guy at a mortuary will see me smeared and half put together and ask, "What should I do with this one?" Will some part of me be peering over his shoulder, "Dummy, I look awful in orange! I'm a winter! I need a deep red with blue undertones and you drew my brows on wrong!" But then again maybe I won't care all that much. I sometimes wonder why it was all such a big deal.

Why pay such a high price that the story of our struggle can fill a book like this one, let alone make me one in the company of all the other transsexuals whose stories will never be told? I like to think that transsexuals act as moral prisms: we separate and divide other persons by how they treat us. The very extremity of response forces other people to show how they will behave by the ultra-violet light that we shine upon them. I have seen many supposedly good Christian people show a dark violence and many a pagan show compassion. I have also seen many liberals discover a conservative side when they encounter us that they never knew they possessed. I guess we are what intellectuals call "a problematic category of human beings."

We used to be less visible than we now are, suffering in silence and keeping our secrets to ourselves. Some on the various chatboards would say to us, "Yeah, shut up already! When will you deviants stop asking for special rights and just be who you are supposed to be and love whom you are supposed to love? Join the rest of us. Just stop! Get a clue! Look between your legs; there's your answer!" As if none of us ever tried to do follow that advice, often over most of the course of our lives.

I don't think it should ever be the first option to launch ourselves into orbit where like human satellites many of us orbit round and round wondering when we will ever lose enough momentum to re-enter the common atmosphere and maybe explode into flames if we try. Too many have done so. From this day forward may no transsexual ever die again by her own hand or by violence committed against her! Never forget, we are valuable, we are precious, and we have a witness to bear to others about what it means to be human. I made it through and so can you. Hang in there! Be careful, patient, and wise.

The usual transsexual story is by now a familiar one to me. After reading as many memoirs and psychological studies as I have done through the years in search of a personal direction the themes of rejection, inner conflict, and broken relationships can become very old. I don't know if a new day is dawning for us or whether the current thaw that we seem to be experiencing is a false spring. I do know that the pain that I and others have known is greater than what most people can imagine and that there is a great waste involved in complacency and the rejection of any human being. I can also say that I have always been looking backward to find a golden era when I knew how to heal the two sides of my being into one and have never found it.

The result has been an uneasy coalition within me of the male and the female with now one and now the other claiming precedence. My life has been one of many discontents but hours of hope and joy as well. The pain has given this book its title and the confusion and conflict that still persists its theme. The result is not meant to cause anyone to reach simple conclusions. I agree with Mark Twain in Huckleberry Finn that those seeking for an underlying moral to the story should be shot. Life is too confusing to provide most people with easy answers. Maybe simply this recognition will do much to help people to live with themselves whether they are gay or straight and whatever their gender may be. In closing I wish everyone God's blessings on their journey back to Him. I like to think that what we have gone through is of some use or will be someday.

So now as diva-like as Evita I bid you all adieu and as a self-styled glamour girl, having finally had my close-up, I may withdraw now behind the footlights and let the curtain ... fall.

The End

A Brief Afterword

Legacies

To write an autobiography without the precondition of possessing antecedent fame may savor of an inordinate sense of one's own personal worth. Why should anyone care what my particular profile is, political or otherwise? Or is it as an archetype that I would have my readers view my own experience and reflections? But what authority have I that my experience is normative for other transsexuals, particularly when I have proceeded to qualify its witness with as many conditionals and cautions as I have done here? But then every autobiography is by its very nature unique because only one author is entitled to write it. He or she who is privileged to live out the full span of allotted human life will at some point begin to notice that the tide has imperceptibly turned. The species has extracted all that it may from the individual and his continued existence only serves to perpetuate past follies. The old may be free from the swift presumptions of youth but they are burdened by far too many memories to easily entertain new possibilities. The neutral byways are simply too worn by repeated journeys down the same paths to reach the same conclusions. Gradually the dead begin to outnumber the living in one's bank of personal acquaintance. The seamless faces of the young become a reproach to one that bears witness to every emotion that one has ever entertained. Forgetfulness and oversight become a source of daily frustration. Last efforts to assemble a fortunate and felicitous life are met with the shrinking reservoir of time and the vastness of the desert to be irrigated.

In spite if this inevitability though we all desire to leave some legacy, something to say: that though we may no longer be present as active agencies in history we have altered in some manner the resistless onrush of events. The more particular and singular our contribution is the greater it will seem. For this reason artists, because they are more individual in their witness, are least replaceable. A scientist leaves little of himself in the truths he may discover and describe; but a poet, a musician, a painter, and perhaps even a philosopher is so closely identified with his creation that he becomes immortal.

Of course words are frail things after all and styles change. Perhaps if our present trend toward the triumph of the image and the "special effect" and the spread of a new and fashionable illiteracy replaces the written word then even this consolation to the poor writer will vanish. Recent years have witnessed the mass closing of independent bookstores and the advent of mass bestsellers that eclipse all variety in discourse. A mass real-politic in America, one that must eventually look askance at the slim topic of transsexualism, let alone the recriminations and regrets of one individual transsexual, may doom books like this one to a quick obscurity; perhaps though it may ride the crest of the current wave of interest in this topic before falling into the trough of neglect that follows all social trends. The reduction of active readers of course counsels a sound-bite approach to everything, one that is absent from the complex dialectic of a book such as this one.

I spoke to a publisher recently who patiently tried to tell me that the secret to success for a writer is general approachability. He left this term rather ill-defined at the time but I knew instantly that he was speaking of that personal mass-appeal that refuses to change the reader by confirming his already existing prejudices and preferences. This of course is not why I use my allotment of diminishing hours to turn out manuscripts in a last effort to leave a legacy. The writers whom I most esteem are precisely those who make extraordinary demands upon the reader in order to make them see in a new way – James Joyce, Virginia Woolf, Marcel Proust, Henry James, Robert Musil, Herman Broch, Thomas Mann, and the creators of the new experimental novel forms. These artists present the world re-created by assembling words in new ways. On Amazon the book reviews of many of even these masters are decidedly mixed. Many agree with my friend that approachability is the key to sales, wealth, and acclaim and that thus the legacy will be greater, at least when reckoned in monetary terms.

The cost factor is decisive in many areas of human life, more so today than ever. Vast sums for instance are wagered on films that will be scarcely recalled in three years, huge military cost-over-runs beset all nations while children, our only hope as a species, still starve and die. The human race may only just now be emerging out of savagery. If we are still here in five hundred years and anything green is still growing then we will have emerged into the full light of the human.

Sterile positivism and Hegelian idealism have alike failed to deliver the human race to a general ethic of insight and compassion and the religions of the world have done little better. While in the secular realm it has remained to the artists even more than to the scientists to preserve what has been best in human life. We stopped having much faith in scientists after the Trinity Test of the first atomic weapon in New Mexico in 1945.

Artists as a rule do little harm although some philosophers can be problematic, if anyone believes them and takes them seriously. It has even been advocated that the best legacy is to keep silent and let the world simply find its own way. This has been a temptation that has often appealed to me if for no other reason than that writing is difficult and publishers chary of making an effort to produce books that are not "approachable."

This unapproachable quality may take many forms. Today the most common source is simply the pursuit of excellence, a quality that is always self-defining for anyone who aspires to develop an individual voice. Of course to write like others is by its very nature an exercise in redundancy and in a busy world to simply repeat a message that has already been delivered is both boring and impertinent.

So where does this leave us? Only with the two alternatives that have beset every author since Genesis was first penned – to write or to keep silent. You the reader may yet prefer that I had chosen the latter, but if you are reading these words then this book may have pleased you or at least have led you to this point when it must trail off into other efforts.

No book is ever really concluded because if nothing else a re-reading of it is possible. Human life is not amenable to this power. It is finally what it has been and thus every autobiography must stand on the witness of what is has been said. It is not subject to reformation; it is forever what it is and in this aspect alone it is akin to the immortal.